Generic Programming and the STL

Addison-Wesley Professional Computing Series

Brian W. Kernighan, Consulting Editor

Ken Arnold/John Peyton, *A C User's Guide to ANSI C*

Matthew H. Austern, *Generic Programming and the STL: Using and Extending the C++ Standard Template Library*

David R. Butenhof, *Programming with POSIX® Threads*

Brent Callaghan, *NFS Illustrated*

Tom Cargill, *C++ Programming Style*

William R. Cheswick/Steven M. Bellovin, *Firewalls and Internet Security: Repelling the Wily Hacker*

David A. Curry, *UNIX® System Security: A Guide for Users and System Administrators*

Erich Gamma/Richard Helm/Ralph Johnson/John Vlissides, *Design Patterns: Elements of Reusable Object-Oriented Software*

Erich Gamma/Richard Helm/Ralph Johnson/John Vlissides, *Design Patterns CD: Elements of Reusable Object-Oriented Software*

Peter Haggar, *Practical Java™ Programming Language Guide*

David R. Hanson, *C Interfaces and Implementations: Techniques for Creating Reusable Software*

Mark Harrison/Michael McLennan, *Effective Tcl/Tk Programming: Writing Better Programs with Tcl and Tk*

Michi Henning/Steve Vinoski, *Advanced CORBA® Programming with C++*

Brian W. Kernighan/Rob Pike, *The Practice of Programming*

S. Keshav, *An Engineering Approach to Computer Networking: ATM Networks, the Internet, and the Telephone Network*

John Lakos, *Large-Scale C++ Software Design*

Scott Meyers, *Effective C++ CD: 85 Specific Ways to Improve Your Programs and Designs*

Scott Meyers, *Effective C++, Second Edition: 50 Specific Ways to Improve Your Programs and Designs*

Scott Meyers, *More Effective C++: 35 New Ways to Improve Your Programs and Designs*

Robert B. Murray, *C++ Strategies and Tactics*

David R. Musser/Gillmer J. Derge/Atul Saini, *STL Tutorial and Reference Guide, Second Edition: C++ Programming with the Standard Template Library*

John K. Ousterhout, *Tcl and the Tk Toolkit*

Craig Partridge, *Gigabit Networking*

J. Stephen Pendergrast Jr., *Desktop KornShell Graphical Programming*

Radia Perlman, *Interconnections, Second Edition: Bridges, Routers, Switches, and Internetworking Protocols*

David M. Piscitello/A. Lyman Chapin, *Open Systems Networking: TCP/IP and OSI*

Stephen A. Rago, *UNIX® System V Network Programming*

Curt Schimmel, *UNIX® Systems for Modern Architectures: Symmetric Multiprocessing and Caching for Kernel Programmers*

W. Richard Stevens, *Advanced Programming in the UNIX® Environment*

W. Richard Stevens, *TCP/IP Illustrated, Volume 1: The Protocols*

W. Richard Stevens, *TCP/IP Illustrated, Volume 3: TCP for Transactions, HTTP, NNTP, and the UNIX® Domain Protocols*

Gary R. Wright/W. Richard Stevens, *TCP/IP Illustrated, Volume 2: The Implementation*

Please see our web site (http://www.awl.com/cseng/series/professionalcomputing) for more information on these ti

Generic Programming and the STL

Using and Extending the C++ Standard Template Library

Matthew H. Austern

ADDISON–WESLEY

Boston • San Francisco • New York • Toronto • Montreal
London • Munich • Paris • Madrid
Capetown • Sydney • Tokyo • Singapore • Mexico City

Many of the designations used by manufacturers and sellers to distinguish their products are claimed as trademarks. Where those designations appear in this book, and we were aware of a trademark claim, the designations have been printed in initial capital letters or in all capitals.

The author and publisher have taken care in the preparation of this book, but make no expressed or implied warranty of any kind and assume no responsibility for errors or omissions. No liability is assumed for incidental or consequential damages in connection with or arising out of the use of the information or programs contained herein.

The publisher offers discounts on this book when ordered in quantity for special sales. For more information, please contact:

Pearson Education Corporate Sales Division
One Lake Street
Upper Saddle River, NJ 07458
(800) 382-3419
corpsales@pearsontechgroup.com

Visit AW on the Web: www.awl.com/cseng/

Library of Congress Cataloging-in-Publication Data

Austern, Matthew H.
    Generic programming and the STL: using and extending the C++
Standard Template Library / Matthew H. Austern.
        p.   cm.–(Addison-Wesley professional computing series)
    Includes bibliographical references and index.
    ISBN 0-201-30956-4
    1. C++ (Computer program language) 2. Standard Template Library.
    I. Title.   II. Series.
QA76.73.C153A97   1998
005.13'3–dc21   98-29950
                                                              CIP

Text printed on recycled and acid-free paper.
ISBN 0201309564
7 8 9 101112 VB   03 02 01 00
7th Printing   February 2001

To my parents, Norman and Wilma Austern

Contents

Part III Reference Manual: Algorithms and Classes   173

Preface

This is not a book about object-oriented programming.

You may think that's odd. You probably found this book in the C++ section of the bookstore, after all, and you've probably heard people use *object oriented* and *C++* synonymously, but that isn't the only way to use the C++ language. C++ supports several fundamentally different paradigms, the newest and least familiar of which is generic programming.

Like most new ideas, generic programming actually has a long history. Some of the early research papers on generic programming are nearly 25 years old, and the first experimental generic libraries were written not in C++ but in Ada [MS89a, MS89b] and Scheme [KMS88]. Yet generic programming is new enough that no textbooks on the subject exist.

The first example of generic programming to become important outside of research groups was the STL, the C++ Standard Template Library. The Standard Template Library, designed by Alexander Stepanov (then of Hewlett-Packard Laboratories) and Meng Lee, was accepted in 1994 as part of the C++ standard library. The freely available "HP implementation" [SL95], which served as a demonstration of the STL's capabilities, was released the same year.

When the Standard Template Library first became part of the C++ standard, the C++ community immediately recognized it as a library of high-quality and efficient container classes. It is always easiest to see what is familiar, and every C++ programmer is familiar with container classes. Every nontrivial program requires some way of managing a collection of objects, and every C++ programmer has written a class that implements strings or vectors or lists.

Container class libraries have been available since the earliest days of C++, and when "template" classes (parameterized types) were added to the language, one of their first uses—indeed, one of the main reasons that templates were introduced—was parameterized container classes. Many different vendors, including Borland, Microsoft, Rogue Wave, and IBM, wrote their own libraries that included Array<T> or its equivalent.

The fact that container classes are so familiar made the STL seem at first to be nothing more than yet another container class library. This familiarity diverted attention from the ways in which the STL was unique.

The STL is a large and extensible body of efficient, generic, and interoperable software components. It includes many of the basic algorithms and data structures of computer science, and it is written so that algorithms and data structures are decoupled from each other. Rather than a container class library, it is more accurate to think of the STL as a library of generic algorithms; containers exist so that the algorithms have something to operate on.

You can use the existing STL algorithms in your programs, just as you can use the existing STL containers. For example, you can use the generic STL sort as you would use the function qsort from the standard C library (although sort is simpler, more flexible, safer, and more efficient). Several books, including David Musser and Atul Saini's *STL Tutorial and Reference Guide* [MS96] and Mark Nelson's *C++ Programmer's Guide to the Standard Template Library* [Nel95], explain how to use the STL in such a way.

Even this much is useful. It is always better to reuse code than to rewrite it, and you can reuse the existing STL algorithms in your own programs. This is still, however, only one aspect of the STL. The STL was designed to be extensible; that is, it was designed so that, just as the different STL components are interoperable with each other, they are also interoperable with components you write yourself. Using the STL effectively means extending it.

Generic Programming

The STL is not just a collection of useful components. Its other aspect, which is less widely recognized and understood, is that it is a formal hierarchy of abstract requirements that describe software components. The reason that the STL's components are interoperable and extensible, and the reason that you can add new algorithms and new containers and can be confident that the new pieces and the old can be used together, is that all STL components are written to conform to precisely specified requirements.

Most of the important advances in computer science have been the discoveries of new kinds of abstractions. One crucial abstraction supported by all contemporary computer languages is the subroutine (a.k.a. the procedure or function—different languages use different terminology). Another abstraction supported by C++ is that of abstract data typing. In C++, it is possible to define a new data type together with that type's basic operations.

The combination of code and data forms an abstract data type, one that is always manipulated through a well-defined interface. Subroutines are an important abstraction because using a subroutine doesn't require that you depend on (or even necessarily know) its exact implementation; similarly, you can use an abstract data type—you can manipulate and even create values—without depending on the actual representation of the data. Only the interface is important.

C++ also supports object-oriented programming [Boo94, Mey97], which involves hierarchies of polymorphic data types related by inheritance. Object-oriented programming has one more layer of indirection than abstract data typing, thus it achieves one more step in abstraction. In some circumstances you can refer to a value and manipulate it without needing to specify its exact type. You can write a single function that will operate on a number of types within an inheritance hierarchy.

Generic programming, too, means identifying a new kind of abstraction. The central abstraction of generic programming is less tangible than earlier abstractions like the subroutine or the class or the module. It is a *set of requirements* on data types. This is a difficult abstraction to grasp because it isn't tied to a specific C++ language feature. There is no keyword in C++ (or, for that matter, in any contemporary computer language) for declaring a set of abstract requirements.

What generic programming provides in return for understanding an abstraction that at first seems frustratingly nebulous is an unprecedented level of flexibility. Just as important, it achieves abstraction without loss of efficiency. Generic programming, unlike object-oriented programming, does not require you to call functions through extra levels of indirection; it allows you to write a fully general and reusable algorithm that is just as efficient as an algorithm handcrafted for a specific data type.

A generic algorithm is written by abstracting algorithms on specific types and specific data structures so that they apply to arguments whose types are as general as possible. This means that a generic algorithm actually has two parts: the actual instructions that describe the steps of the algorithm and the set of requirements that specify precisely which properties its argument types must satisfy.

The central innovation of the STL is the recognition that these type requirements can be specified and systematized. That is, it is possible to define a set of abstract *concepts* and to say that a type conforms to one of those concepts if it satisfies a certain set of requirements. These concepts are important because most of the assumptions that algorithms make about their types can be expressed both in terms of conformance to concepts and in terms of the relationships between different concepts. Additionally, these concepts form a well-defined hierarchy, one reminiscent of inheritance in traditional object-oriented programming but purely abstract.

This hierarchy of concepts is the conceptual structure of the STL. It is the most important part of the STL, and it is what makes reuse and interoperability possible. The conceptual structure would be important purely as a formal taxonomy of software components, even without its embodiment in code. The STL does include concrete data structures, such as `pair` and `list`, but to use those data structure effectively you must understand the conceptual structure they are built upon.

Defining abstract concepts and writing algorithms and data structures in terms of abstract concepts is the essence of generic programming.

How to Read This Book

This book describes the Standard Template Library as a library of abstract concepts. It defines the fundamental concepts and abstractions of the STL and shows what it means for a type to model one of those concepts or for an algorithm to be written in terms of a concept's interface. It discusses the classes and algorithms that are part of the basic STL, and it explains how you can write your own STL-compliant classes and algorithms and when you might want to do so. Finally, it includes a complete reference manual of all of the STL's concepts, classes, and algorithms.

Everyone should read Part I, which introduces the main ideas of the STL and of generic programming. It shows how to use and write a generic algorithm, and it explains what it means for an algorithm to be generic. Genericity has implications that go far beyond the ability to operate on multiple data types.

Exploring the idea of a generic algorithm leads naturally to the central ideas of *concepts, modeling,* and *refinement,* ideas that are as basic to generic programming as polymorphism and inheritance are to object-oriented programming. Generic algorithms on one-dimensional ranges, meanwhile, lead to the fundamental concepts of the STL: iterators, containers, and function objects.

Part I introduces the notation and the typographical conventions that are used throughout the remainder of the book: the terminology of modeling and refinement, the asymmetrical notation for ranges, and the special typeface for concept names.

The STL defines many concepts, some of which differ from each other only in technical details. Part I is an overview, and it discusses the broad outlines of STL concepts. Part II is a detailed reference manual that contains a precise definition of each STL concept. You may not wish to read Part II all the way through and, instead, may find it more useful to look up a particular concept only when you need to refer to its definition. (You should refer to Part II whenever you write a new type that conforms to an STL concept.)

Part III is also a reference manual. It documents the STL's predefined algorithms and classes. It relies heavily on the concept definitions of Part II. All STL algorithms and almost all concrete types are templates, and every template parameter can be characterized as the model of some concept. The definitions in Part III are cross-referenced to the appropriate sections of Part II.

In an ideal world, the book would end with Part III. Unfortunately, reality demands one more section, an appendix that discusses portability concerns. When the STL was first released, portability was not an issue because only one implementation existed. That is no longer the case, and whenever more than one implementation of any language or library exists, anyone who cares about portability must be aware of the differences between them.

The old HP implementation is still available by anonymous FTP from butler. hpl.hp.com, but it is no longer being maintained. A newer free implementation, from Silicon Graphics Computer Systems (SGI) is available at http://www.sgi.com/ Technology/STL, and a port of the SGI STL to a variety of compilers, maintained by Boris Fomitchev, is available at http://www.metabyte.com/~fbp/stl. Finally, there are several different commercial STL implementations.

If you are writing real programs, it isn't enough to understand the theoretical design of the library; you also have to understand how the various STL implementations and the various C++ compilers differ. These unglamorous but necessary details are the subject of Appendix A.

Who Should Read This Book

While this book is largely about algorithms written in C++, it is neither an introductory textbook on algorithms nor a C++ tutorial. It does explain some of the unfamiliar aspects of both subjects. In particular, since the STL uses templates in ways that are uncommon in other sorts of C++ programs, it discusses some advanced techniques of programming with templates. This should not be your first C++ book, nor should it be your first exposure to an analysis of algorithms. You should know how to write basic C++ programs, and you should know the meaning of notation like $\mathcal{O}(N)$.

Two of the standard references on algorithms and data structures are Donald Knuth's *The Art of Computer Programming* [Knu97, Knu98a, Knu98b], and *Introduction to Algorithms*, by Cormen, Leiserson, and Rivest [CLR90]. Two of the best introductory C++ books are *The C++ Programming Language*, by Bjarne Stroustrup [Str97], and *A C++ Primer*, by Stanley Lippman and Josée Lajoie [LL98].

How This Book Came About

I joined the compiler group at Silicon Graphics Computer Systems (SGI) in 1996. Alex Stepanov had left HP to join SGI several months before. At the time, SGI's C++ compiler did not include an implementation of the Standard Template Library. Using the original HP implementation as our source base, Alex, Hans Boehm, and I wrote the version of the STL that was shipped with release 7.1 (and subsequent releases) of SGI's MIPSpro compiler.

The SGI Standard Template Library [Aus97] included many new and extended features, such as efficient and thread-safe memory allocation, hash tables, and algorithmic improvements. If these enhancements had remained proprietary, they would have been of no value to SGI's customers, so the SGI STL was made freely available to the public. It is distributed on the World Wide Web, along with its documentation, at http://www.sgi.com/Technology/STL.

The documentation, a set of Web pages, treats the STL's conceptual structure as central. It describes the abstract concepts that comprise the structure, and it documents the STL's algorithms and data structures in terms of the abstract concepts. We received many requests for an expanded form of the documentation, and this book is a response to those requests. The reference sections of this book, Parts II and III, are an outgrowth of the SGI STL Web pages.

The Web pages were written for and are copyrighted by SGI. I am using them with the kind permission of my management.

Acknowledgments

First and foremost, this book could not possibly have existed without the work of Alex Stepanov. Alex was involved with this book at every stage: he brought me to SGI, he taught me almost everything I know about generic programming, he participated in the development of the SGI STL and the SGI STL Web pages, and he encouraged me to turn the Web pages into a book. I am grateful to Alex for all of his help and encouragement.

I also wish to thank Bjarne Stroustrup and Andy Koenig for helping me to understand C++ and Dave Musser for his numerous contributions (some of which can be found in the bibliography) to generic programming, to the STL, and to this book. Dave used an early version of the SGI STL Web pages as part of his course material, and the Web pages were greatly improved through his and his students' comments.

Similarly, this book was greatly improved through the comments of reviewers, including Tom Becker, Steve Clamage, Jay Gischer, Brian Kernighan, Jak Kirman, Andy Koenig, Angelika Langer, Dave Musser, Sibylle Schupp, and Alex Stepanov, who read early versions. This book is more focused than it would have been without them, and it contains far fewer errors. Any mistakes that remain are my own.

Several mistakes in the first, second, and third printings of this book have now been corrected, and I wish to thank Sam Bradsher, Bruce Eckel, Guy Gascoigne, Ed James-Beckham, Jon Jagger, Nate Lewis, CH Lin, Shawn D. Pautz, John Potter, George Reilly, Manos Renieris, Peter Roth, Dieter Rothmeier, Andreas Scherer, and Jürgen Zeller, for bringing these errors to my attention.

I am also indebted to the staff at Addison-Wesley, including John Fuller, Mike Hendrickson, Marina Lang, and Genevieve Rajewski, for guiding me through the writing process, and to Karen Tongish for her careful copyediting.

Finally, I am grateful to my fiancée, Janet Lafler, for her love and support and for her patience during the many evenings and weekends that I spent writing.

Our cats, Randy and Oliver, tried to help by walking over my keyboard, but in the end I deleted most of their contributions.

Part I

Introduction to Generic Programming

Chapter 1

A Tour of the STL

Computer programming is largely a matter of algorithms and data structures. What-ever type of programs you write, one thing that every program has to do is organize and manipulate some kind of data.

Instead of writing the same algorithm over and over again whenever you need it in a slightly different context, the C++ Standard Template Library (STL) lets you reuse existing algorithms. STL algorithms are generic—they aren't tied to any particular data structure or object type—but they are also as efficient as if you had written them specifically for the task at hand. The STL is even extensible. STL components interoperate with components that you write, just as they interoperate with each other.

1.1 A Simple Example

The best way to see how this works is to look at a simple program that uses a few pieces of the STL. As an example, consider a simplified version of the UNIX sort utility, a program that reads lines of text from the standard input stream and writes them, sorted, to the standard output stream.

This task has three parts: read text from the standard input, breaking it into separate lines; sort the lines; and write each line to the standard output. Each part is a standard algorithm and, using the STL, putting them together is extremely simple:

```
int main() {
  vector<string> V;
  string tmp;

  while (getline(cin, tmp))
    V.push_back(tmp);

  sort(V.begin(), V.end());
  copy(V.begin(), V.end(), ostream_iterator<string>(cout, "\n"));
}
```

We create an empty `vector` (the simplest and the most useful STL container class),
add one line at a time, sort the `vector`, and then copy its contents to the standard
output. By default, `sort` arranges its arguments in ascending order, but all you have
to do is write:

```
sort(V.begin(), V.end(), greater<string>());
```

and it will sort the lines in descending order instead.

The last line of this program is particularly interesting. The STL algorithm that it
uses, copy, is the same one that you would use to copy elements from one array to
another. Its arguments—like the arguments of all STL algorithms—are *iterators*, and
an iterator can be anything ranging from an ordinary C pointer to, as in this case,
a wrapper for an output stream. You can use copy to copy elements from anything
that looks like a source to anything that looks like a destination (in Chapter 2 we'll
make this more precise), so, naturally, you can use it for output.

You can also use copy for input, provided you have the right kind of iterator. You
need one that returns one line at a time from an input stream. There isn't such an
iterator in the STL, but it's easy to write one, and once you've written it you can use
it not only with copy but with many other STL algorithms:

```
class line_iterator
{
  istream* in;
  string line;
  bool is_valid;
  void read() {
    if (*in)
      getline(*in, line);
    is_valid = (*in) ? true : false;
  }

public:
  typedef input_iterator_tag iterator_category;
  typedef string value_type;
  typedef ptrdiff_t difference_type;
  typedef const string* pointer;
  typedef const string& reference;

  line_iterator() : in(&cin), is_valid(false) {}
  line_iterator(istream& s) : in(&s) { read(); }
  reference operator*() const { return line; }
  pointer operator->() const { return &line; }
  line_iterator operator++() {
    read();
    return *this;
  }
  line_iterator operator++(int)  {
    line_iterator tmp = *this;
    read();
    return tmp;
  }
```

```
    bool operator==(const line_iterator& i) const {
      return (in == i.in && is_valid == i.is_valid) ||
             (is_valid == false && i.is_valid == false);
    }

    bool operator!=(const line_iterator& i) const {
      return !(*this == i);
    }
  };
```

Don't worry if you don't yet understand why everything in the line_iterator class
is there; parts of it are only necessary for technical reasons. (The full set of requirements is provided in Section 7.2.) Once we have this class, our sorting program becomes even simpler. We can do away with the input loop and create a vector directly
from a range of iterators:

```
  int main() {
    line_iterator iter(cin);
    line_iterator end_of_file;
    vector<string> V(iter, end_of_file);
    sort(V.begin(), V.end());
    copy(V.begin(), V.end(), ostream_iterator<string>(cout, "\n"));
  }
```

An Alternate Method

This is an attractively simple way of reading and sorting lines, but is it the best way?
Probably not. The problem is that sorting a range of objects means performing a great
many assignments. Since string is a large and complicated data structure, assigning
one string to another is likely to be fairly slow. What we really ought to be doing is
sorting pointers to lines, not the lines themselves. (Your implementation might use
special tricks to speed up string assignment, but then, it might not. In any case, it's
best not to rely too much on special-case details.)

   If your program uses a great many strings, it's often best not to use a string class
at all. It's often more efficient to combine all of the strings into a single "string table"
and to point into that table whenever you need to refer to a particular string.

   This technique is a little more complicated than simply using a vector<string>,
but the STL can still accommodate it perfectly well. Instead of a single vector to store
the strings, we now need two: one for the string table itself and one for pointers into
the string table. We first build the string table and then the vector of lines. Because
of the way that most STL algorithms work, it is convenient to represent each line as
a *pair* of iterators into the string table, one pointing to the first character of the line
and one pointing just beyond the last character.

   Since we're representing a line as a pair of iterators, we now have to tell sort how
to compare two such elements—using the < operator to compare them no longer
works. There's nothing difficult about that, though. We've already seen that there's a
version of sort that takes an extra argument, precisely because it's often necessary to

compare elements in some special way. What we have to do is to write a comparison *function object* that will get passed to sort. While we're at it, we can also write another function object to help with output:

```
struct strtab_cmp
{
  typedef vector<char>::iterator strtab_iterator;

  bool operator()(const pair<strtab_iterator, strtab_iterator>& x,
                  const pair<strtab_iterator, strtab_iterator>& y) const {
    return lexicographical_compare(x.first, x.second, y.first, y.second);
  }
};

struct strtab_print
{
  ostream& out;
  strtab_print(ostream& os) : out(os) {}

  typedef vector<char>::iterator strtab_iterator;
  void operator()(const pair<strtab_iterator, strtab_iterator>& s) const {
    copy(s.first, s.second, ostream_iterator<char>(out));
  }
};

int main()
{
  vector<char> strtab;          // Create the string table.
  char c;
  while (cin.get(c)) {
    strtab.push_back(c);
  }
                                // Parse the string table into lines.
  typedef vector<char>::iterator strtab_iterator;
  vector<pair<strtab_iterator, strtab_iterator> > lines;
  strtab_iterator start = strtab.begin();
  while (start != strtab.end()) {
    strtab_iterator next = find(start, strtab.end(), '\n');
    if (next != strtab.end())
      ++next;
    lines.push_back(make_pair(start, next));
    start = next;
  }

                              // Sort the vector of lines.
  sort(lines.begin(), lines.end(), strtab_cmp());

                              // Write the lines to standard output.
  for_each(lines.begin(), lines.end(), strtab_print(cout));
}
```

1.2 Summary

Even with two simple examples, we've illustrated the broad outlines of the STL. It contains generic *algorithms*, like sort, find, and lexicographical_compare; *iterators*, like istream_iterator and ostream_iterator; *containers*, like vector; and *function objects*, like less and greater.

These examples also illustrate some of the most important aspects of using the STL:

- *To use the STL is to extend it.* In both of these examples we ended up writing our own STL components: a new iterator for the first and two new function objects for the second. (We could have carried this even further: instead of writing a loop to parse the string table into lines, we could have written a general parsing iterator.)

- *The STL algorithms are decoupled from the containers.* Adding an algorithm doesn't require you to rewrite any containers, and you can mix and match the containers and algorithms as you please. Given N different algorithms and M different container classes, you don't have the burden of dealing with $N \times M$ separate implementations.

- *The STL is extensible and customizable without inheritance.* New iterators, like line_iterator, and new function objects, like strtab_cmp, don't have to inherit from any special base class. They need only satisfy an abstract set of requirements. You aren't burdened by the overhead or the implementation details of inheritance when you extend the STL, and you don't have to contend with a "fragile base class."

- *Abstraction need not mean inefficiency.* Generic algorithms, like sort and copy, and generic containers, like vector, are as efficient as if they had been hand-crafted for one specific data type.

The STL provides a new way to think about programming, one in which algorithms and abstract sets of requirements are central. These abstract requirements are the basis of the STL and of this book.

Chapter 2

Algorithms and Ranges

I cheated a bit in Chapter 1. I showed how easy it was to extend the STL, to write parts that interoperate with existing STL components. It is easy—but only if you know which requirements you have to satisfy. It's useless to know that STL algorithms are defined in terms of iterators unless you know what an iterator is.

This chapter introduces the important idea of algorithms that operate on a linear *range* of elements: a one-dimensional collection where there is a first element and a last element, where each element (except the last one) has a successor, and where, by stepping through the list from successor to successor, you can get all the way from the beginning to the end. These algorithms are the core of the STL.

Closely related to algorithms on ranges is the family of *iterator* concepts, which are also introduced in this chapter. Iterators are the most important innovation in the STL, and they are what makes it possible to decouple algorithms from the data structures they operate on. The other parts of the STL—function objects (Chapter 4) and containers (Chapter 5)—are best understood in terms of algorithms and iterators.

This chapter discusses the ideas behind algorithms and iterators, and it uses those ideas to illustrate *concepts*, *modeling*, and *refinement*. You should read this chapter even if you are already familiar with iterators and generic algorithms, because it introduces the notation that is used throughout the rest of the book.

While this chapter introduces algorithms and iterators, the detailed documentation is deferred to the reference section of the book. Iterator concepts are documented in Chapter 7, and STL algorithms are covered in Chapters 11-13.

2.1   Linear Search

One of the most basic algorithms is *linear search* (or *sequential search*, to use Knuth's terminology [Knu98b]): finding a particular value in a linear collection of elements. If the elements were sorted or organized in some other special way, we could use more sophisticated and specialized algorithms. Linear search is the most general search algorithm, and it makes the fewest assumptions about the data structure that it searches.

2.1.1   Linear Search in C

Before seeing how to write linear search as a generic algorithm, let's look at a specific and familiar example: the function `strchr` from the standard C library. Its signature is

```
char* strchr(char* s, int c);
```
and it searches for an instance of the character c in the string s. Here is one plausible implementation:

```
char* strchr(char* s, int c)
{
    while (*s != '\0' && *s != c)
        ++s;
    return *s == c ? s : (char*) 0;
}
```

The general idea of linear search is simple: finding where a particular value appears in a linear sequence of elements by stepping through the sequence from beginning to end testing each element in turn. If the current element is equal to the specified value, the algorithm returns the current element's position in the sequence. If not, it advances to the next element. If there is no next element (that is, if we have reached the end of the sequence), it returns some indication of failure.

Any implementation of linear search has to answer the following questions.

- How do we specify which sequence we're searching through?

- How do we represent a position within the sequence? (We have to know that so we can represent the "current element" and so we can return a position when the search succeeds.)

- How do we advance to the next element?

- How do we know when we have reached the end of the sequence?

- What value do we return as an indication of failure?

Since `strchr` is written in C, the sequence we search through is a string: a null-terminated array of characters. We specify the string by passing a pointer to its first element to `strchr`, and `strchr` knows when it has reached the end of the string because the last element is a null character. Naturally, a position within the string is also represented by a pointer; we return a pointer to the first element that is equal to c or a null pointer if there is no such element.

This function is useful, of course, but it isn't as general as it might be. Part of the problem is that it can only be used to search for a char in an array of chars (as opposed, say, to searching for an unsigned char or a wchar_t). Another problem, unrelated to the type signature, is that the interface restricts `strchr` to a search through one specific kind of data structure.

The problem is that `strchr` demands that its argument be a pointer to a null-terminated array of characters—and that's not as general as it might seem. Strings in

C are often represented as null-terminated arrays, but even in C other representations are equally important. For example, how do you represent a substring? A substring of a null-terminated array is not itself a null-terminated array, so it must be represented some other way.

There are two obvious ways to modify strchr's interface. One is to provide an integer count: Search through the first n characters of the array beginning at s. A different choice, providing a pointer to the end of the array we're searching through, turns out to be more convenient. This is the form we will use for find1, a generalization of strchr.

There are several reasons why a pointer to the end of the sequence is more convenient than an integer count. First, that's how we would probably implement the search anyway; incrementing a pointer is easier than maintaining a separate count. Second, it's more consistent. The beginning and end of the sequence are represented the same way, as is the return value. This makes it easier to use the result of one search operation as an input to the next. Third, and most important, it will turn out to be necessary later in this chapter when we generalize find1 still further.

```
char* find1(char* first, char* last, int c)
{
   while (first != last && *first != c)
     ++first;
   return first;
}
```

This implementation of find1 uses the common C idiom of looping though an array by using a pointer *beyond* the end of the array as the termination condition. The loop in find1 terminates as soon as first is equal to last, and last itself is never dereferenced. That is, find1 searches the elements pointed to by every pointer from first up to *but not including* last.

To search through an entire array of characters, for example, you would write:

```
char A[N];
...
char* result = find1(A, A + N, c);
if (result == A + N) {
  // The search failed.
}
else {
  // The search succeeded.
}
```

We are using the pointer A + N to represent the end of the array, but A + N doesn't point to any of the array's elements—the array's elements are A[0] through A[N-1]. By the time we reach A + N we have already passed through every element in A, and we may terminate the loop.

This raises an important technical point. In general, C is rather picky about operations on pointers. You may not perform the comparison p < q, for example, unless p and q point into the same array. Similarly, you may not perform pointer arithmetic on invalid pointers such as the null pointer. So why, in this example, are we using the seemingly invalid pointer A + N?

There is a special rule in C (C++ has the same special rule) that was introduced precisely so that code like find1 will work. Loops typically run from 0 through N−1, so "past-the-end" pointers like A + N are valid in C—but only for a few special purposes. Every array in C has one pointer past the end. You may not dereference that pointer, because it doesn't actually point to anything, and you may not increment it, because each array has only one past-the-end pointer, but you may use it for comparisons and for pointer arithmetic. (By contrast, arrays do not have "before-the-beginning" pointers; the expression A − 1 is not valid C. It might work sometimes, but it also might fail disastrously.)

C therefore has three different kinds of pointers: ordinary valid pointers, like &A[0], which you can dereference; invalid pointers, like NULL (*singular* pointers); and *past-the-end* pointers that you can't dereference but you can use in pointer arithmetic.

2.1.2 Ranges

In find1 we are searching through all of the pointers from first up to but not including last. This sort of interface appears so often in the STL that there is a special notation for it: the *range* [first,last) consists of the pointers from first up to but not including last. The notation comes from mathematics. It is written in this asymmetric form to emphasize the fact that [first,last) is a half-open interval that includes first but not last.

Sometimes the notation [first,last) refers to the pointers first,...,last − 1, and sometimes to the elements *first,...,*(last − 1). It is almost always obvious from context which one is meant, and we distinguish between the two meanings, on the rare occasions when it is necessary, with the phrases *range of pointers*[1] or *range of elements.*

A range [first,last) is *valid* if all of the pointers in [first,last) are dereferenceable and if last is *reachable* from first—that is, if, by incrementing first a finite number of times, you eventually arrive at last. So, for example, the range [A, A + N) is a valid range and so is the empty range [A, A). The range [A + N, A), however, is not: A + N comes after A, not before, so it makes no sense to talk about the elements from A + N to A.

Generally, ranges satisfy the following properties:

1. For any pointer p, the empty range [p, p) is a valid range.

2. If [first,last) is a valid and nonempty range, then [first + 1, last) is also a valid range.

3. If [first,last) is a valid range and if mid is any pointer such that mid is reachable from first and last is reachable from mid, then [first,mid) and [mid,last) are both valid ranges.

---

1. Soon to be generalized to *range of iterators*. The underlying idea is the same.

4. Conversely, if [first, mid) and [mid, last) are both valid ranges, then so is [first, last).

Why use such an odd, asymmetrical definition of ranges, one that includes one end of the range while excluding the other? What it really comes down to is convenience. The notation for half-open intervals may look unfamiliar at first, but it turns out to be easier, both for formulating definitions and for the more mundane purposes of writing and using algorithms, than the alternatives.

To some extent, we have already seen that in find1. The while loop in find1 is simple because last is not included in [first, last). Moreover, as Andrew Koenig points out [Koe89], asymmetric ranges help avoid "off-by-one" errors: the number of elements in [first, last) is last − first, just as you would expect. This is especially convenient in C and C++, where arrays start at zero instead of one: An array of N elements is described by the range [A, A + N), even though the last element in that array is actually A[N − 1]. Finally, defining a range as a half-open interval lets us represent empty ranges just as easily as nonempty ranges: [A, A) is an ordinary range (one that happens to contain no elements), so find1(A, A, c) is valid—as it should be.

Fundamentally, ranges are defined this way because if a range contains n elements, we need to be able to refer to $n + 1$ distinct positions, not just n. In find1, for example, we need some value that we can return as an indication of failure. Similarly, it's often important to refer not only to the existing elements in a range but to a location where a new element might be inserted. In a range of n elements, there are $n + 1$ such positions: the beginning, the end, and the $n − 1$ gaps between the elements that are already there.

2.1.3 Linear Search in C++

As we have defined it, find1 can only be used to search through an array of type char. But in C++, where we can use templates to parameterize a function's argument types, there is an obvious and straightforward generalization. We can use a function just like find1, but instead of pointers to char, it could take pointers to any type T. This hypothetical function, find2, could be declared as follows:

```
template <class T>
T* find2(T* first, T* last, T value);
```

The STL uses a slightly less obvious generalization. The STL linear search algorithm isn't find2, but find:

```
template <class Iterator, class T>
Iterator find(Iterator first, Iterator last, const T& value)
{
  while (first != last && *first != value)
    ++first;
  return first;
}
```

Why find, instead of the more obvious find2? What have we gained?

What we have gained is a function that is far more general than find2. While find2 requires its arguments first and last to be pointers, find makes no such restriction. It does use the syntax of pointer operations (operator∗ to obtain the value that first points to, operator++ to increment first, operator== to test whether first and last are equal), but that doesn't mean that Iterator has to be a pointer, it only means that Iterator must support a pointer-like interface. Like find1, find still performs a search through a range [first,last) and still assumes that that range satisfies all of the properties described in Section 2.1.2, but find no longer requires the elements in [first,last) to be the elements of an array.

With find, we now see the sort of algorithm that was promised at the beginning of this chapter: a generic algorithm that searches through any data structure that supports the notion of a one-dimensional sequence of elements. All we require is to be able to examine an element, go to the next element, and check to see if we have finished processing all of the elements—the basic operations without which it wouldn't make much sense to think of [first,last) as a linear range in the first place.

Search Through a Linked List

As an example of find's generality, we can use it to search for a value in a singly linked list. Arrays and linked lists provide different ways of organizing values into a sequence, but we can use find for both.

Almost every nontrivial C program contains a list of nodes chained together, each of which contains some data and a pointer to the next node. For examples:

```
struct int_node {
  int val;
  int_node* next;
};
```

The code for traversal looks something like this fragment:

```
int_node* p;
for (p = list_head; p != NULL; p = p->next)
  // Do something.
```

(This is a simplification, of course. In a real program a node would be a struct with multiple fields; a single integer isn't worth the trouble.)

One common operation on this kind of linked list is searching for a specific value—that is, performing linear search. Since a list of int_nodes is a linear sequence, we shouldn't have to write linear search again; we ought to be able to reuse find. How can we do that?

We can use find to search through a range [first,last). In all of our earlier examples first and last were pointers, but in this case that won't work. If first were a pointer to an int_node, then find would try to obtain the next element by performing the pointer operation ++first. That would be disastrous because this is a linked list, not an array. If p is a list_node, then the next node is supposed to be p->next, not p + 1.

The solution follows immediately from the problem: C++ allows operator overloading. If operator++ has the wrong behavior, we need to define it in such a way that find steps through the list correctly.

It isn't possible to redefine operator++ for arguments of type int_node*. C++ allows you to define the meaning of operator expressions, not to change the existing meaning. (Imagine what could happen if it were possible to change the meaning of operator+ so that "adding" two ints really meant subtracting them!) What we can do, though, is almost as straightforward. We can write a simple wrapper class that looks like an int_node* but defines operator++ more appropriately.

We can generalize this slightly, since int_node is hardly the only list node that has a next pointer. Instead of defining a wrapper class that works only with int_node, it's just as easy to define a template wrapper class that works with any type of list node that has a next pointer:

```
template <class Node>
struct node_wrap {
  Node* ptr;

  node_wrap(Node* p = 0) : ptr(p) {}

  Node& operator*() const { return *ptr; }
  Node* operator->() const { return ptr; }

  node_wrap& operator++() { ptr = ptr->next; return *this; }
  node_wrap operator++(int) { node_wrap tmp = *this; ++*this; return tmp; }

  bool operator==(const node_wrap& i) const { return ptr == i.ptr; }
  bool operator!=(const node_wrap& i) const { return ptr != i.ptr; }
};
```

Finally, just as a convenience, we can define an equality operator that lets us compare an int_node to an int:

```
bool operator==(const int_node& node, int n) {
  return node.val == n;
}
```

To search for an int_node with a specific value, we no longer have to write any loops. We can reuse find, and we can write the search as a single function call:

```
find(node_wrap<int_node>(list_head), node_wrap<int_node>(), val)
```

The second argument, node_wrap<int_node>(), uses node_wrap's default constructor. It creates a node_wrap that contains a null pointer. Since the last list node has a null next pointer, we are searching from list_head through the end of the list.

The wrapper node_wrap looks (and is) trivial, but it allows us to do something remarkable. The struct int_node makes no reference to generic algorithms; it might have been written years ago, before generic algorithms (or the C++ language) even existed. By using a tiny wrapper class we have achieved interoperability between an old data structure, the list of int_nodes, and a new generic algorithm, find. The node_wrap class serves as the intermediary between the two with no loss of efficiency. All of node_wrap's member functions are defined inline, so writing w++ for a node_wrap<int_node> should have exactly the same effect as writing p = p->next for an int_node*.

Note that node_wrap follows the properties of ordinary C pointers very closely. It provides the basic pointer operations of dereference (operator*), member access (operator->), and both preincrement and postincrement. The version of operator++ that takes no arguments is preincrement, and the version that takes a single argument of type int is postincrement.

2.2   Concepts and Modeling

Just how general is find? Or, to put it differently, what requirements does find impose on its template arguments?

We could make a list of the assumptions that find makes about its template argument Iterator: You can use operator* to dereference an Iterator, you can use operator++ to move to the next Iterator, and so on.

But find was deliberately written to be as general as possible. The assumptions it makes about its arguments are always true for any range. This set of requirements, then, is applicable well beyond find: It applies to any algorithm that operates on a range.

The set of requirements is important enough to have a name of its own: find's template parameter is an *iterator*. Iterators are a fundamental part of the Standard Template Library.

Requirements and Concepts

It is a truism that problems in computer science can often be solved by adding a level of indirection. In this case, we solve our problem by adding a level of indirection to find's requirements. The most important requirement is that Iterator must be an Input Iterator.

This special typeface indicates that Input Iterator is a *concept*. Throughout this book, the names of concepts are always written like this. A concept describes a set of requirements on a type, and when a specific type satisfies all of those requirements, we say that it is a *model* of that concept. For example, char* and node_wrap are models of Input Iterator.

We use the special typeface to remind ourselves that a concept is not the name of a class, a variable, or even a template parameter; it is not anything, in fact, that can appear directly in a C++ program. However, concepts are extremely important in every C++ program that uses the methodology of generic programming.

As an example, consider the difference between the template parameter Iterator and the concept Input Iterator. Iterator is a formal template parameter. Syntactically, within the C++ language, it appears as a type, and for any particular instance of the function template find, the template parameter Iterator stands for some particular type. The concept Input Iterator does not stand for any one type. Instead, it stands for a list of *requirements* that a type must satisfy.

It is possible to imagine a language where you could declare concepts directly. You could declare a list of requirements, give it a name, and then, just as you can declare a variable to be of some specific type, you could declare that a type or a formal template parameter is a model of some specific concept. That hypothetical language isn't C++, though. In C++ there is no way to declare that a template parameter must be a model of a specific concept. We have given find's template parameter the name Iterator, but a C++ compiler has no way to associate that name with the concept Input Iterator because concepts are not part of the C++ language.

What Is a Concept?

If a concept isn't a class, a function, or a template, then what precisely is it? There are three ways to understand what a concept is, which seem very different at first but which turn out to be equivalent. All three approaches are useful for understanding some aspects of generic programming.

First, a concept can be thought of as a list of type requirements. If a type T is a model of a concept C, then T satisfies all of C's requirements. Describing the properties that a type must have is almost always the easiest way to specify a concept.

Second, a concept can be thought of as a set of types. The concept Input Iterator, for example, consists of the types char*, int*, node_wrap, and so on. If a type T is a model of a concept C, this definition says that T belongs to the set of types that C represents. The way we can see that this definition is equivalent to the previous one is to consider the set of all types that satisfy a list of requirements. This definition involves the set itself and the preceding definition involves the requirements that define that set, but these are just two different ways of looking at the same thing.

Third, a concept can be thought of as a list of valid programs. By this definition, the significance of a concept such as Input Iterator is that it is used in find and many other algorithms. The concept itself consists of the properties that the type Iterator has in common in all of those algorithms. This definition may seem much more abstract than the other two, but it is important because in a sense it is actually the most practical of the three approaches. It is how new concepts are discovered. Concepts are discovered and described not by writing down some list of requirements *ex nihilo* but by defining specific algorithms and studying how the formal template parameters are used in those algorithms. We discovered Input Iterator by studying find, and all of the other concepts in this book are similarly motivated by algorithms.

Formal specification systems such as Larch [GHG93] and Tecton [KM92, KMS82] define concepts in terms of mathematical logic. Tecton, for example, defines a concept as "a set of many-sorted algebras." This book does not use formal logic.

Concept Requirements

What does a concept's set of requirements look like? We can't very well say that the requirements are a list of member functions. We certainly want to say that char* is a model of Input Iterator, but char* has no member functions. Anyway, that's not how function templates work. You may call find with arguments of any type Iterator provided that, once you substitute Iterator every place in find where Iterator appears, the resulting function makes sense.

What it comes down to is that the requirements are a set of *valid expressions*. We require, for example, that if Iterator is a model of Input Iterator and i is an object of type Iterator, then *i is a valid expression.

Even such a simple requirement already involves two different types: Iterator (the model of Input Iterator) and the type that you get when you write *i. This is quite typical. In the most general case, a concept C includes a list of valid expressions each of which involves a type T that models C *as well as some other types that are associated with* T. Often, the details of that association are among the concept's most important requirements.

Basic Concepts

Some operations are so fundamental that almost every reasonable type provides them. In generic programming, these operations correspond to a few very general concepts, ones that are so general and so fundamental that most STL algorithms rely on them. Indeed, they apply to more than just the STL; these concepts are fundamental to any generic library.

One of those basic concepts is Assignable. A type X is a model of Assignable if it is possible to copy values of type X and assign new values to objects of type X. This isn't quite as trivial as it seems, because all of the different forms of assignment and copying have to be consistent with each other. For an Assignable type, for example, you can rely on the property that x will have the same value if you write

    X x(y)

as it would if you had written

    x = y

or

    tmp = y, x = tmp

Similarly, you can assume that assigning a new value to x won't have the side effect of changing the value of some other variable y. It isn't enough to have a copy constructor and an assignment operator. They must also be consistent with each other and with the fundamental properties of the C object model.

The other basic concepts are Default Constructible, Equality Comparable, and LessThan Comparable.

Just as a type that is a model of Assignable has a copy constructor, a type that is a model of Default Constructible is one that has a default constructor: a constructor that takes no arguments.[2] That is, a type T is Default Constructible if it is possible to

---

2. In C++, if you don't declare a class to have any constructors, then that class has an implicit default constructor.

create an object of type T by writing

    `T()`

and to declare a variable of type T by writing

    `T t;`

All of C++'s built-in types, such as `int` and `void*`, are Default Constructible.

The concepts Equality Comparable and LessThan Comparable deal with comparisons involving two objects. Specifically, T is a model of Equality Comparable if it is possible to compare two objects of type T for equality by using the expression

    `x == y`

or

    `x != y`

Similarly, T is a model of LessThan Comparable if it is possible to test whether one object of type T is less than or greater than the other, using the expression

    `x < y`

or

    `x > y`

A *regular type* is one that is a model of Assignable, Default Constructible, Equality Comparable and one in which these expressions interact in the expected way. For a regular type, for example, you may assume that if you assign x to y, `x == y` is true.

Most of the basic C++ types are regular types (`int` is a model of all of the concepts from this section), and so are almost all of the types defined in the STL.

2.3 Iterators

Iterators are a generalization of pointers; they are objects that point to other objects. They are important for generic algorithms like `find`, because they can be used to iterate over a range of objects. If an iterator points to some object in a range of objects and the iterator is incremented, then it will point to the next object in that range.

The reason iterators are important to generic programming is that they are an interface between algorithms and data structures. If an algorithm like `find` takes iterators as arguments, then it can operate on many different data structures, even structures as different from each other as linked lists and C arrays. We merely require that it be possible to access all of the data structure's elements by traversing them in some linear ordering.

Given the discussion in Section 2.2, it would seem that iterators should be defined as a concept and that pointers are a model of that concept. That's almost right, but not quite. Pointers in C++ have many different properties. The generic algorithm `find` relies on a very small subset of those properties. Other generic algorithms, though, rely on different subsets. In other words, there are several different ways of generalizing pointers, and each different way is a distinct concept. Iterators aren't a single concept but a family of five different concepts: Input Iterator, Output Iterator,

Forward Iterator, Bidirectional Iterator, and Random Access Iterator. (A sixth concept, Trivial Iterator, exists only to clarify the definitions of the other iterator concepts.)

2.3.1   Input Iterators

We were able to search through a linked list with find because find uses its template argument Iterator in only a stylized way. Iterator must be similar to a pointer type, but it does not have to support all of the operations that are defined for pointers. Iterator must be a model of Input Iterator, where, roughly speaking, an Input Iterator is a type that satisfies find's requirements. This isn't a circular definition—not quite!—because we are about to enumerate precisely what those requirements are. More to the point, it isn't a useless definition. Input Iterator is an important concept because many algorithms, not just find, have similar requirements.

Essentially, an Input Iterator is something that is enough like a pointer that it is meaningful to talk about a range of iterators [first, last):

- As with ordinary C pointers, there are three kinds of values: an input iterator can be *dereferenceable, past the end,* or *singular.* And as with pointers, [first, last) is a meaningful range only if first and last are both nonsingular.

- It is possible to compare two objects of type Iterator for equality. In find, after all, we compare two iterators for equality to test whether we have reached the end of the range.

- Input Iterators can be copied and assigned. In find, for example, you'll see that first and last are passed by value, which requires calling Iterator's copy constructor.

- We can dereference an object of type Iterator. That is, the expression *p is well defined. Every Input Iterator has an associated *value type,* which is the type of object that it points to. In the case of node_wrap<int_node>, for example, the value type is int_node. (Later in this chapter, we shall see that Input Iterator has other associated types as well.)

- We can increment an object of type Iterator. That is, the expressions ++p and p++ are well defined. As with ordinary C pointers, ++p means to increment p and return the new value while p++ means to increment p and return the old value.

The things that aren't on this list are just as important as the things that are.

- In find we *examine* the values in the range [first, last) without modifying them. An Input Iterator points to some object, but it doesn't necessarily provide any way to modify that object. You can dereference an Input Iterator, but cannot assign a new value through the result of that dereference operation: the expression *p = x is not necessarily valid. (For example, you can't change the value that a const int* points to.)

- An Input Iterator need only support a tiny subset of the operations that we're used to using from pointer arithmetic. An Input Iterator can be incremented but not necessarily decremented. (For example, node_wrap has no operator-- member function.) Similarly, expressions like p + 5 and p1 – p2 are not necessarily valid. The only form of iterator arithmetic that an Input Iterator need support is operator++.

- Just as Input Iterators support only a very limited form of arithmetic, they also support only a limited form of comparison. You can test whether two Input Iterators are equal, but you can't test whether one comes before the other. For example, p1 < p2 is a valid Boolean expression if p1 and p2 are pointers but not if p1 and p2 are general Input Iterators.

- Linear search is a "single pass" algorithm. It traverses the range [first,last) once and never attempts to read one of the values in that range more than once. This is the *only* correct way to use an Input Iterator. You may not traverse a range of Input Iterators more than once, and you may not use two iterators that point to different elements in a range of Input Iterators. Each range can support only a single active iterator at one time. For example, you can't write p1 = p2++ and then go on to use both p1 and p2. Similarly, if p == q, you cannot assume that ++p == ++q.

It is also important to remember what these restrictions mean. They are restrictions on *algorithms that use* Input Iterators, not on types that model the concept Input Iterator. For example, although the type double* is a model of Input Iterator, double* does support "multipass" algorithms. The Input Iterator requirements are a minimal set of functionality, but models of Input Iterator may (and usually do) go beyond that minimal set. However, an algorithm that works with Input Iterators must not assume anything beyond the minimal functionality guaranteed by the Input Iterator requirements.

These restrictions are very severe—particularly the one that an algorithm that uses Input Iterators must be "single pass"—and you may wonder how you can possibly be expected to implement every algorithm you write so as to comply with them. The answer is that you aren't expected to do anything of the sort!

Input Iterators are one of the two weakest iterator concepts, and many algorithms require different kinds of iterators. It comes as no surprise that many algorithms can't be written in terms of Input Iterators. What is surprising is that many algorithms can be. In addition to find (page 199) and related algorithms such as find_if (page 200), Input Iterators are used in such algorithms as equal (page 220), partial_sum (page 285), and even such complicated algorithms as random_sample (page 277) and set_intersection (page 327).

The name Input Iterator suggests the reason for this seemingly odd set of requirements. Using an Input Iterator is like reading input values from a terminal or reading data over a network connection. You can examine the current value, and you can request the next value, but once you request the next value the previous one is gone. If you want to be able to access previous values, you have to explicitly store them from the input stream yourself. The algorithms that you can write using an Input

Iterator, in other words, are much like the algorithms you can write when you work directly with values that you read from an input stream. In fact, if you use the STL's predefined Input Iterator class `istream_iterator` (page 354), you are simply reading values from an input stream.

2.3.2   Output Iterators

If Input Iterators are iterators that behave as though they are reading from an input stream, you might expect that there are other iterators that behave as though they are writing to an output stream. They are called Output Iterators.

Understanding a concept really means understanding the algorithms that use it. One example of an algorithm that needs to perform output is the simple operation of copying values from one range to another. The input range can consist of Input Iterators, but the output range can't. Input Iterators don't provide a means for changing the value that an iterator points to. By using Output Iterators, however, it is easy to implement an algorithm that sequentially copies a range:

```
template <class InputIterator, class OutputIterator>
OutputIterator copy(InputIterator first, InputIterator last,
                    OutputIterator result)
{
  for ( ; first != last; ++result, ++first)
    *result = *first;
  return result;
}
```

This is the STL's copy algorithm (page 233), and it uses the Input Iterator concept exactly as `find` does: It is a single pass algorithm, and it reads each Input Iterator only once before advancing to the next one.

The way that copy uses Output Iterator is very similar, allowing for the difference between input and output. We use Output Iterator to write a consecutive sequence of values. We write a value, increment the Output Iterator, and write the next value. We never write through the same iterator twice, we never back up to a previous output iterator, and we never skip an iterator. The output range is write-only just as the input range is read-only, and copy is a single-pass algorithm with respect to both output and input.

The Output Iterator requirements are similar to the Input Iterator requirements:

- As with Input Iterators, we can copy and assign Output Iterators.

- We can use an Output Iterator to write a value. That is, the expression *p = x is well defined.

- We can increment an output iterator. That is, the expressions ++p and p++ are well defined.

Output Iterators share many of the same restrictions as Input Iterators. An Output Iterator must support the ++ operator, but it need not support any of the other operations of pointer arithmetic. Similarly, all algorithms that use Output Iterators must, like copy, be single-pass algorithms, and, as with Input Iterators, you cannot have two different Output Iterators pointing to different places in a range at the same time. "The moving finger writes, and having writ, moves on."

Additionally, the Output Iterator concept has two other important restrictions. One is obvious: Just as Input Iterators are read-only, Output Iterators are write-only. So, for example, you can write *p = x, but you can't necessarily write x = *p. The other restriction is somewhat less obvious but is illustrated by copy.

In copy we have both an input range and an output range. Each of those ranges has a beginning and an end—a total, then, of four locations. However, there are only *three* iterators in copy's argument list: the input range [first,last) and the beginning of the output range, result. We can get away with this because copy has to write the same number of elements as it reads; the end of the output range is implicit.

Thus while copy has to perform the test first != last, it never performs any such test on result. Since copy, and algorithms like it, never need to compare one Output Iterator to another, the Output Iterator concept does not provide that capability. A "range" of Output Iterators is always specified by a single iterator and a count. In copy, for example, the output range is defined as the range that begins at result and that has the same number of elements as [first,last) does.

It's possible to write algorithms that obey all of the restrictions of the Output Iterator concept; copy is one such algorithm, and so are transform (page 240), merge (page 316), and many others. Is it necessary? Is there really any reason why you would ever want to use a write-only iterator that supports only single-pass algorithms?

The answer is yes. Output Iterators are in fact very common and very useful. One of the most important is insert_iterator (page 351), which, along with its relatives front_insert_iterator and back_insert_iterator, inserts values into a container. The simplest example of an Output Iterator, and one that illustrates many of the characteristics of the concept, is ostream_iterator (page 357).

The ostream_iterator class is the mirror image of istream_iterator, and it is an Output Iterator in the most straightforward sense. If p is an ostream_iterator, then *p = x performs formatted output of x onto an ostream. The definition of ostream_iterator is simple, but enlightening:

```
template <class T> class ostream_iterator {
private:
  ostream* os;
  const char* string;
public:
  ostream_iterator(ostream& s, const char* c = 0) : os(&s), string(c)  {}

  ostream_iterator(const ostream_iterator& i)
    : os(i.os), string(i.string) {}

  ostream_iterator& operator=(const ostream_iterator& i) {
    os = i.os;
    string = i.string;
    return *this;
  }
```

```
      ostream_iterator<T>& operator=(const T& value) {
        *os << value;
        if (string) *os << string;
        return *this;
      }

      ostream_iterator<T>& operator*() { return *this; }
      ostream_iterator<T>& operator++() { return *this; }
      ostream_iterator<T>& operator++(int) { return *this; }
    };
```

This class definition illustrates both of the unusual features of Output Iterators. It shows how it is possible to define a write-only iterator, and it also shows why an algorithm that uses Output Iterators must be a simple single-pass algorithm of the same form as copy. If you keep ostream_iterator in mind, the restrictions of Output Iterator no longer seem so arbitrary.

An ostream_iterator can only be used in a single-pass algorithm because the ostream_iterator class does not keep track of a particular position in an ostream; it performs output, and nothing more. You can't save an old position by copying an ostream_iterator, because every ostream_iterator that writes to the same ostream is identical. An algorithm like copy behaves as expected:

```
      copy(A, A+N, ostream_iterator<int>(cout, " "))
```

copies a sequence of integers to the standard output, but only algorithms of this form can use ostream_iterator.

We can also see both how and why ostream_iterator provides write-only access. Write-only access is necessary because of the semantics of the ostream class itself, and the easiest way to provide write-only access is with the usual C++ trick of defining a proxy class. We want the expression *p = x to perform some action, so we define *p to return a proxy object, where the proxy object has an appropriate operator= that performs that action. The only slightly unusual feature of ostream_iterator is that, in this case, the proxy class is ostream_iterator itself. We could have defined a separate class instead, but there is no reason to do that.

It might seem that we've gone to a great deal of trouble just to be able to write *p = x instead of os << x, but we really have gained something important. Generic programming relies on syntactic constraints. This uniform syntax makes it possible to use the same algorithm, copy, for every operation that involves writing values to any kind of output range. The copy algorithm can move elements from one array to another, insert elements into a container, or write elements to the standard output.

2.3.3   Forward Iterators

Many algorithms can be written solely in terms of Input Iterator and Output Iterator, but it should come as no surprise that many algorithms cannot:

- Input Iterators are read-only, and Output Iterators are write-only. That means that it's impossible to use those concepts for any algorithm that involves reading and modifying a range. You can write certain kinds of search algorithms in terms of Input Iterators, but you can't write a search and replace algorithm.

- Since algorithms on Input Iterators and Output Iterators can only be single pass, that immediately restricts us to algorithms whose complexity is linear in the number of elements in the range. But we know perfectly well that not all algorithms are linear. Most useful sorting algorithms, for example, are $\mathcal{O}(N \log N)$ or $\mathcal{O}(N^2)$.

- There can only be one active Input Iterator or Output Iterator on a range at any one time. That restricts us to algorithms that work with only a single element at a time. We can't write algorithms that depend on relationships between two or more different elements.

Algorithms that use Forward Iterators do not have these restrictions. Forward Iterator supports the same subset of pointer arithmetic that Input Iterator and Output Iterator do (you can write ++p, and not --p or p += 5), but it is much less restricted in other ways. A type that is a model of Forward Iterator is also a model of both Input Iterator and Output Iterator, thus making it possible to write algorithms that use the same range for both reading and updating. One such algorithm is replace, which searches for all instances of old_value and replaces them with new_value:

```
template <class ForwardIterator, class T>
void replace(ForwardIterator first, ForwardIterator last,
             const T& old_value, const T& new_value)
{
  for ( ; first != last; ++first)
    if (*first == old_value)
      *first = new_value;
}
```

Like the algorithms that use Input Iterators and Output Iterators, replace is a single-pass algorithm that works only with one element at a time. We need the stronger Forward Iterator concept because we are using the same iterator for both reading and writing. Forward Iterators also allow algorithms that use more general access patterns.

Consider, for example, a variation on linear search. Rather than searching for an element that has a particular value, instead we will search for two consecutive elements that have the same value:

```
template <class ForwardIterator>
ForwardIterator
adjacent_find(ForwardIterator first, ForwardIterator last)
{
  if (first == last)
    return last;
  ForwardIterator next = first;
  while(++next != last) {
    if (*first == *next)
      return first;
    first = next;
  }
  return last;
}
```

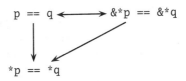

Figure 2.1:   Identities of iterator equality.

This algorithm is defined to use Forward Iterators: Even though adjacent_find is a read-only algorithm it can't be written in terms of Input Iterators, because each iteration of the loop compares two different values, *first and *next. An algorithm that used Input Iterators only would not be able to use more than one iterator in the same range.

What is important to realize is that Input Iterators and Output Iterators have very odd properties, and algorithms that use those concepts are restricted to one stylized form, one simple kind of loop. An algorithm that uses Forward Iterators, though, has no such restriction.

The fundamental difference is that Input Iterators and Output Iterators do not quite follow the ordinary C memory model, but Forward Iterators do. The linked list adaptor node_wrap from Section 2.1.3, for example, is a Forward Iterator. An object of type node_wrap points to one specific address, just like an ordinary pointer does.

If p and q are ordinary C pointers, then you can write the sequence of operations

```
p = q;
++q;
*p = x;
```

and you can expect that you have changed the value that p points to but not the value that q points to. This is a fundamental property of the C memory model: *Distinct pointers point to distinct memory locations.* If p and q are both dereferenceable pointers, then p == q if and only if *p and *q are the same object, and this can reasonably be taken as the definition of what it means for two pointers to be equal.

Forward Iterators obey that same identity. This identity is basic and important. Without it, we have no reason to expect that sort sorts or that reverse reverses. It is also a strong condition. To begin with, if two iterators p and q are equal, then *p == *q. But the condition is much stronger than that: p and q don't just point to the same value but to the same object. If you modify *p, you are also modifying *q. We can write this as &*p == &*q, since two objects *p and *q are the same if they have the same address.[3] Figure 2.1 illustrates these identities.

As with ordinary pointers, it can be taken as the definition of what it means for two iterators to be equal. (That's one of the reasons Output Iterators can't be

---

3. This isn't always quite right. Normally, *p is the object that the iterator p points to, so &*p is that object's address. Remember, though, that in C++ it's possible to overload the & operator. If & is overloaded, then &*p might mean something quite different. Most of the time, we can ignore that technicality.

compared for equality. If you can't examine the value that an iterator points to, then this definition isn't meaningful.)

Constant and Mutable Iterators

The algorithms `replace` and `adjacent_find` both use Forward Iterators, but there is an important way in which their use of Forward Iterators differs: `replace` modifies the values in the range [`first,last`), but `adjacent_find` does not. Not all algorithms that use Forward Iterators actually need to modify the values that the iterators point to.

A Forward Iterator may be *constant*, in which case it is possible to access the object it points to but not to assign a new value through it, or *mutable*, in which case it is possible to do both. So, for example, `int*` is a mutable Forward Iterator, as is `node_wrap<int_node>`. (It is also an Input Iterator, and also an Output Iterator.) By contrast, `const int*` is a constant Forward Iterator.

The term *constant iterator* is used consistently throughout this book, but it is slightly confusing: A constant iterator is not necessarily (not even usually) a const object. A constant iterator is one that cannot be used to modify the value that it points to, but the iterator object itself may or may not be const. So, for example, a `const int*` is a constant iterator, since it can't be used to modify the value that it points to, but an `int* const` is not. It is a const object, but it can be used to modify the value that it points to.

We could express the distinction between constant and mutable iterators by splitting Forward Iterator into two different concepts, but that would be an unnecessary complication.

2.3.4 Bidirectional Iterators

Like Forward Iterators, Bidirectional Iterators allow multipass algorithms. Also, like Forward Iterators, Bidirectional Iterators may be either constant or mutable.

As the name suggests Bidirectional Iterators support motion in both directions. A Bidirectional Iterator may be incremented to obtain the next element or decremented to obtain the preceding element. A Forward Iterator, by contrast, need only support forward motion. An iterator like `node_wrap` that traverses a singly linked list, for example, is a Forward Iterator, while an iterator that traverses a doubly linked list would be a Bidirectional Iterator.

The algorithms that use Bidirectional Iterators are ones that need to step through a range in reverse order, algorithms that, given an element, need to find the preceding element. For example, we have already seen the `copy` algorithm, which copies elements from one range to another. To copy the elements in reverse order, though, requires backwards traversal through one of the input and output ranges:

```
template <class BidirectionalIterator, class OutputIterator>
OutputIterator reverse_copy(BidirectionalIterator first,
                            BidirectionalIterator last,
                            OutputIterator result) {
    while (first != last) {
```

```
            --last;
            *result = *last;
            ++result;
        }
        return result;
    }
```

We don't need to traverse both the input and output ranges backwards, only one of them. We have chosen the input range, so that `reverse_copy` can have an interface very much like copy's. The input and output ranges are denoted by three iterators instead of four, and the output range consists of Output Iterators.

In `reverse_copy` we decrement `last`, instead of incrementing `first`. Bidirectional Iterator supports all of the operations of Forward Iterator, but it provides operator`--` as well as operator`++`. Note the way in which `reverse_copy` differs from copy: in `reverse_copy` we decrement `last` before dereferencing it. That may look a little odd, but in fact it makes perfect sense. It is necessary because the range [`first`,`last`) is asymmetrical, because `last` does not belong to that range but is instead the iterator just beyond the end. It is illegal to dereference a past-the-end iterator, but decrementing a past-the-end iterator is well defined.

2.3.5   Random Access Iterators

The last four iterator concepts each provide only a small subset of pointer arithmetic: Input Iterator, Output Iterator, and Forward Iterator define operator++ alone, and Bidirectional Iterator adds only operator--. The last of the STL's iterator concepts, Random Access Iterator, includes all of the remaining operations of pointer arithmetic: addition and subtraction (p + n and p - n), subscripting (p[n]), subtraction of one iterator from another (p1 - p2), and ordering (p1 < p2).

Random Access Iterators are important for algorithms like sort (page 292): sorting algorithms need to be able to compare and exchange elements that are widely separated from each other, not just adjacent elements.

At first it seems obvious that Random Access Iterators are necessary. You can write p + n if p is a pointer, so there certainly ought to be an iterator concept that does the same thing. After you think about it for a little while, though, you might wonder whether we really do need to define Random Access Iterator after all. Most of the Random Access Iterator operations can be defined in terms of operator++ and operator--. For example, we can (and the STL does) define a function advance so that advance(p,n) increments the Forward Iterator p as many times as necessary. Do we really get anything fundamentally new from these operations, then, or are they just syntactic sugar? And if they're nothing but syntactic sugar, why provide them for some iterators and not others?

The answer to that question depends on something we haven't yet considered: the *complexity* of algorithms. If p is a Forward Iterator, advance(p,n) repeatedly executes operator++. We can reasonably expect that advance(p, 500) will take roughly five times as long as advance(p, 100). In other words, advance is $\mathcal{O}(N)$.

But that's not how pointers work. If p is a pointer, then p + 1000000 is no slower than p + 1. In other words, pointer arithmetic is $\mathcal{O}(1)$. Accessing any element in an

array is just as fast as accessing any other, and algorithms that operate on arrays rely
on that fact. Quicksort, for example, is a fast sorting algorithm on arrays precisely
because it is possible to access an arbitrary array element in constant time. It would
make no sense at all to implement quicksort on a data structure like linked lists,
where the only way to get to an arbitrary element is to step through the list one
element at a time.

The true distinguishing characteristic of a Random Access Iterator is random
access to arbitrary elements in constant time. The notational differences between
Random Access Iterator and Bidirectional Iterators are a reflection of that fact.

2.4   Refinement

A Bidirectional Iterator is something that satisfies all of the requirements of a Forward Iterator and some other requirements besides; or, to look at it from the other
direction, any type that is a model of Bidirectional Iterator is also a model of Forward
Iterator.

The relationship between Bidirectional Iterator and Forward Iterator is common
enough, and important enough, to have a name: *refinement*. A concept C2 is a refinement of the concept C1 if C2 provides all of the functionality of C1 and possibly
additional functionality as well.

Modeling and refinement satisfy three crucial properties, all of which are easy to
verify by thinking about concepts as sets of types:

1. *Reflexivity.* Every concept C is a refinement of itself.

2. *Containment.* If a type X is a model of the concept C2 and if C2 is a refinement
   of the concept C1, then X is also a model of C1.

3. *Transitivity.* If C3 is a refinement of C2 and C2 is a refinement of C1, then C3
   is a refinement of C1.

The practical consequence of this is that if an algorithm requires its argument
to be of a type that models some concept C1, then you may always provide a type
that models a concept C2, provided that C2 is a refinement of C1—which is a fancy
way of saying something that you knew already. The algorithm find, for example,
requires its template argument to be an Input Iterator. But you already know that
you can pass pointers to find and that a pointer type is a model of Random Access
Iterator.

A type may be a model of more than one concept, and a concept may be a refinement of more than one other concept. Forward Iterator is a refinement of both Input
Iterator and Output Iterator. In general, a collection of concepts forms a complicated
hierarchy.[4]

---

4. Strictly speaking, it shouldn't be called a hierarchy, but a "directed acyclic graph." The use of the
   word *hierarchy* is traditional, even though it is technically incorrect.

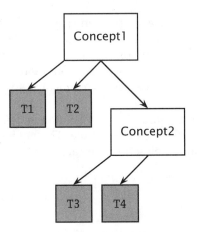

Figure 2.2:   An illustration of refinement and modeling.

Concepts and Inheritance

Modeling and refinement are both relationships between two different things. Modeling is a relationship between a type and a concept (a type T is a model of a concept C), and refinement is a relationship between two concepts (a concept C2 is a refinement of a concept C1).

Both of these are "is a" relationships, but every introductory C++ book describes another "is a" relationship: inheritance. It is often said that a class D should inherit from a class B if a D "is a" B. Does this mean that modeling and refinement are nothing but inheritance, that templates are unnecessary, and that we can emulate all of generic programming by means of inheritance and polymorphism?

The answer is no, and one moral of the story is that we should beware of vague phrases like "is a." Modeling, refinement, and inheritance are three distinct kinds of relationships, and it is impossible to emulate any one of those relationships in terms of either of the other two.

You can understand the difference formally by considering the definitions. Each of these relationships works on a different level. Inheritance is a relationship between two types, modeling is a relationship between a type and a set of types, and refinement is a relationship between two sets of types. If a class D inherits from a class B, then every object of type D is also an object of class B. By contrast, refinement is defined at the level of types rather than the level of objects. If a concept Concept2 is a refinement of a concept Concept1, then every type that is a model of Concept2 is also a model of Concept1.

This point is illustrated in Figure 2.2. Even though Concept2 is a refinement of Concept1, and even though T3 and T4 are models of Concept2, the types T3 and T4 aren't necessarily related in any special way to types T1 and T2, which are models of Concept1. There is no inheritance relationship, for example, between T4 and T1. What these four types share is purely an interface; they are not constrained by any irrelevant implementation details.

As an example, Random Access Iterator is a refinement of Input Iterator, and char* is a model of Random Access Iterator. But that can't possibly mean that char* inherits from every other type that is a model of Input Iterator!

Less formally, the easiest way to see that inheritance and modeling are unrelated is to try to implement modeling in terms of inheritance. It doesn't work. You could imagine representing a concept as an abstract base class, but it is impossible to express the necessary relationships. Consider, for example, writing Assignable as an abstract base class. You might begin with something like this:

```
class assignable_base {
public:
  virtual ~assignable_base() {}
  virtual assignable_base& operator=(const assignable_base&) = 0;
};
```

Right away, we're in trouble. A class that inherits from assignable_base doesn't automatically get the operations of a type that models Assignable. And polymorphism doesn't help; the type assignable_base itself doesn't provide those operations, either. If a generic function takes an argument of a type that models Assignable, then that function can assign to values of that type, create new variables of that type, and so on. A polymorphic function with an argument of type assignable_base* or assignable_base& can't do those things. If a polymorphic function takes two arguments of type assignable_base*, it can't even assume that the two are of the same type—and if they aren't of the same type, there surely is no reason to think that one can be assigned to the other. Assignable is useful as a concept, but it is useless as an abstract base class.

Concepts like Input Iterator, which involve more than one type, are an even worse problem. How can the notion of an iterator's value type be expressed in terms of inheritance and polymorphism? The types double* and node_wrap<int_node> are both models of Input Iterator, but the value type of one is double and the value type of the other is int_node. There's no useful sense in which they can be taken to be subclasses of the same abstract base class.

None of this is intended to deny the importance or usefulness of inheritance and polymorphism. It is simply necessary to recognize that inheritance and modeling are useful for different things. Inheritance, modeling, and refinement are completely separate relationships, and any methodology that tries to make do with only one of them is incomplete.

2.5 Summary

Section 2.3 began by defining iterators as a generalization of pointers, and we can finally see what that means. Pointers can be generalized in many different ways, depending on which properties we are abstracting. Iterators, accordingly, are not a single concept but a family of concepts related by refinement. This family is illustrated in Figure 2.3.

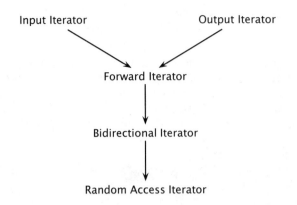

Figure 2.3:   The hierarchy of iterator concepts.

Input Iterator and Output Iterator are the most restricted concepts. One is read-only and the other is write-only; both support forward traversal through a range and allow simple single-pass algorithms. Forward Iterator also supports forward traversal through a range, but it also supports more general kinds of algorithms. A Forward Iterator "points to" something in the same sense that an ordinary C pointer does. Formally, this means that dereferencing a Forward Iterator yields an lvalue.

Since Bidirectional Iterator is a refinement of Forward Iterator and Random Access Iterator a refinement of Bidirectional Iterator, Bidirectional Iterator and Random Access Iterator also support forward traversal, and they, too, support the ordinary C memory model. The difference is that they provide additional forms of traversal. Bidirectional Iterator allows backward traversal, and Random Access Iterator, as the name suggests, allows arbitrary-sized jumps.

These different iterator concepts provide a natural way to classify generic algorithms on ranges. An algorithm can be categorized by the iterator concepts it uses. One important distinction is between *nonmodifying* algorithms, which use constant iterators, and *mutating* algorithms, which use mutable iterators.

All of the iterator concepts are documented in full in Chapter 7. Thus far, we have yet to list all of the requirements for any of the five iterator concepts. This is deliberate. Although we have discussed iterators' basic properties, there is one last requirement of iterators that we haven't yet discussed.

Chapter 3

More about Iterators

Chapter 2 introduced generic algorithms on ranges, iterators, and the STL's five iterator concepts: Input Iterator, Output Iterator, Forward Iterator, Bidirectional Iterator, and Random Access Iterator. It wasn't a complete introduction, however, because it left out some advanced topics that are important when you are writing your own iterator classes or your own generic algorithms. Those topics are the subject of this chapter.

3.1   Iterator Traits and Associated Types

In Section 2.2, we saw that a concept could include associated types. The requirements for a type T are a list of expressions that involve T, and those expressions might also use or return some other types. The five STL iterator concepts do indeed include associated types, and those types are an important part of the iterator requirements.

3.1.1   Value Types

We have already seen that every iterator (except Output Iterators) has at least one associated type. An iterator points to something, and the type of that something is the iterator's *value type*.

The problem is that we haven't yet seen how to refer to the value type. Suppose we have an iterator type I and we need to declare a variable whose type is "the value type of I." This is a reasonable scenario. Certainly, many algorithms require temporary variables. (Consider, for example, a generic algorithm that computes the mean and standard deviation of a list of numbers.) However, the English phrase "the value type of I" doesn't tell us how to express that type in C++.

Sometimes we can use a trick that exploits the C++ type inference mechanism. Suppose we have a generic function f() that takes an argument of type I and we need to declare a temporary variable whose type is I's value type. C++ doesn't let us write something like typeof(*I), but there's a way to get around that limitation. We can turn f() into a mere forwarding function, deferring all of the real work to an internal function f_impl():

```
template <class I, class T>
void f_impl(I iter, T t)
{
  T tmp;                 // T is I's value type.
  ...
}

template <class I> inline void f(I iter)
{
  f_impl(iter, *iter);
}
```

Within the internal function f_impl, we can declare a variable whose type is the same as I's value type. The type inference of template parameters is automatic, so within f_impl the template parameter T is a synonym for the return type of *iter.

This trick is clever and even useful. The STL uses a variant of it in one place. Unfortunately, it isn't always enough. It's adequate (if a bit clumsy) when all we want to do is declare temporary variables, but there's no way to use it to declare a function's return type. The problem, of course, is that f()'s return type needs to be declared in f() itself, and this type inference trick doesn't give us access to the type we need until we get to f_impl().

A second method that you might consider is to declare the value type within the iterator class. C++ allows nested type declarations; so, for example, we could augment the node_wrap iterator class (Section 2.1.3) with a typedef.

```
template <class Node> struct node_wrap {
  typedef Node value_type;
  Node* ptr;
  ...
};
```

If a type I is a node_wrap, this nested type declaration allows us to write I's value type as typename I::value_type.[1] This looks like what we want.

But it isn't. We can't require all iterators to declare nested types. That would be fine for iterator classes like node_wrap, but what about iterators that *aren't* classes? Pointers are iterators, but they aren't classes. If I is (say) an int*, it's impossible to define I::value_type to be int. Relying on nested types would defeat the whole purpose of using iterators. Pointers are models of Random Access Iterator, and we

---

1. We have to include the strange-looking keyword typename because, when I is a template parameter, the compiler doesn't know anything about I until the template is instantiated. In particular, the compiler has no way of knowing whether I::value_type is the name of a type, a member function, or a member variable. See Section A.1.5, and Section C.13.5 of *The C++ Programming Language* [Str97], for more details.

deliberately used pointers as the pattern for other iterators. Whatever requirements we adopt for iterators, it must be possible for pointers to satisfy them.

We can solve our problems by adding one more layer of indirection. The solution is to define a helper class, iterator_traits:

```
template <class Iterator>
struct iterator_traits {
  typedef typename Iterator::value_type value_type;
};
```

We can then refer to an iterator I's value type by writing:

```
typename iterator_traits<I>::value_type
```

This may not seem like any sort of improvement, since iterator_traits still assumes that its template parameter Iterator has a nested type. It is an improvement, though, because we can *specialize* the iterator_traits class by providing an alternate definition for certain template arguments.

C++ allows both full specialization (providing an alternate definition for some specific type, such as int*) and partial specialization (providing an alternate definition that is itself templatized). In this case we need to use partial specialization, since we need an alternate definition for every pointer type:

```
template <class T>
struct iterator_traits<T*> {
  typedef T value_type;
};
```

This is almost complete, and it allows us to refer to the value types of all iterators (including pointers) in a uniform way, but one small detail still needs to be addressed: What is the value type of a constant iterator? Consider, for example,

```
iterator_traits<const int*>::value_type
```

As we have defined iterator_traits, this type is const int, not int. That's because we have specialized iterator_traits for arguments of type T*, and const int* matches T* only if T is const int. Unfortunately, that isn't really what we want. Our goal, after all, is to declare temporary variables whose type is the same as an iterator's value type, and a temporary variable isn't very useful if you can't assign a value to it. The value type of an iterator, even if it is a constant iterator, shouldn't be qualified with a const. The value type of an iterator like const int* is int, not const int. The const is merely a restriction on the operations that you can perform through the iterator itself.

It's easy to solve this problem with another partial specialization:

```
template <class T>
struct iterator_traits<const T*> {
  typedef T value_type;
};
```

We now have three different versions of iterator_traits: one for arguments of type T, one for arguments of type T*, and one for arguments of type const T*. When you write iterator_traits<const int*> it could in principle match any of those three versions, but there's no ambiguity because the C++ compiler will always select the most specific match that it possibly can. Finally, then, we have a mechanism that lets us write algorithms using an iterator's value type. As an example,the following generic function computes the sum of the numbers in a nonempty range:

```
template <class InputIterator>
typename iterator_traits<InputIterator>::value_type
sum_nonempty(InputIterator first, InputIterator last)
{
  typename iterator_traits<InputIterator>::value_type result = *first++;
  for ( ; first != last; ++first)
    result += *first;
  return result;
}
```

This works because of the iterator_traits machinery that we have built up. It works for pointers, because of the specialized versions iterator_traits<const T*> and iterator_traits<T*>, and it works for iterators that define value_type as a nested type within the iterator class itself.

If I is a Input Iterator (this includes the concepts that are refinements of Input Iterator, of course), then iterator_traits<I>::value_type is required to be I's value type. That is, if you're defining a new iterator class, you have to make sure that your class supports iterator_traits. The easiest way to do that is almost always to define value_type as a nested type within your class. That way, you don't have to mention iterator_traits explicitly, and the iterator_traits class that's defined in the library will work correctly with no effort on your part. If for some reason that's impossible or inconvenient, you can specialize iterator_traits for your class as we did for pointers.

Obviously, the iterator_traits mechanism is quite general. We have seen how it works for iterators' value types, but more generally it can be used for any mapping from an iterator type to a type that is associated with it. The iterator concepts of Section 2.3 implicitly have several associated types, and the STL uses iterator_traits for all of them.

3.1.2 Difference Type

If I is a model of Random Access Iterator and p1 and p2 are values of type I, then p2 − p1 is the distance from p1 to p2. If we are to use that distance in a program, we need to know its type. What type does the expression p2 − p1 return?

For pointers, the answer is simple. When you subtract one pointer from another, the return type is ptrdiff_t.[2] So one possible answer might be to require that for all Random Access Iterators, not just for pointers, the return type of p2 - p1 must always be ptrdiff_t.

---

2. The type ptrdiff_t is defined in the C and C++ standards. It is not a distinct type in its own right, but rather a typedef for some other signed integral type, usually int or long.

That answer would be simple, but it would be too restrictive. What if you have a range of iterators that's so large that a ptrdiff_t isn't large enough to store that number of elements in the range? There are situations, such as files, where that's a serious concern. Pointers are 32-bit quantities on most of today's processors, so a ptrdiff_t can usually only represent a number up to about 2^{31}, and, while 2^{31} (more than two billion) may seem like a very large number, it really isn't. Most operating systems allow you to create files that are much larger than that, and terabyte databases are now commonplace. If you're defining an iterator that steps through a very large file, a ptrdiff_t isn't nearly large enough.

For general Random Access Iterators, then, p2 − p1 isn't necessarily a value of type ptrdiff_t. That expression returns some signed integral type: the iterator's *difference type*.

All Input Iterators have difference types. All we're doing when we write p2 − p1 is calculating the number of elements in the range [p1,p2), and that's something that generalizes perfectly well to every kind of Input Iterator. (It doesn't generalize to Output Iterators, which is why an Output Iterator does not necessarily have a difference type.)

As with value types, some algorithms that operate on ranges of iterators have to refer to the iterators' difference types. One of the simplest such algorithms is count (page 214), which counts the number of times that a value x appears in the range [first,last). The return type clearly has to be the iterators' difference type, since count's return value might be as large as the distance from first to last. The obvious solution is to use the same mechanism for both difference_type and value_type. We define difference_type as a nested type in iterator classes and include difference_type in iterator_traits, so that we can refer to every iterator's difference type in exactly the same way:

```
template <class InputIterator, class T>
typename iterator_traits<InputIterator>::difference_type
count(InputIterator first, InputIterator last, const T& x) {
  typename iterator_traits<InputIterator>::difference_type n = 0;
  for ( ; first != last; ++first)
    if (*first == x)
      ++n;
  return n;
}
```

Historically, one of the main motivations for introducing iterator_traits was to provide a mechanism for declaring count's return type.

3.1.3 Reference and Pointer Types

A Forward Iterator points to a specific memory location. If p is a Forward Iterator that points to objects of type T, the expression *p can't normally return a value of type T. Whatever *p returns must be an *lvalue*, "something that refers to an object," to use Stroustrup's definition [Str97].

In C++, a function can return an lvalue by returning a reference. Return by reference is the reason a Forward Iterator can provide both read and write access to the object that it points to. If p is a mutable iterator whose value type is T, *p will normally be of type T&. Similarly, if p is a constant iterator, *p will normally be of type const T&. In general, *p's return type is not the same as p's value type. Instead, it is p's *reference type*.

Pointers and references in C++ are closely related. If it is possible to return an lvalue that refers to the object that p points to, then it must also be possible to refer to that object's address—that is, we must be able to return a pointer to that object.

These types already appear in the simple node_wrap class (Section 2.1.3). The operator* member function returns a Node&, and the operator-> member function,[3] which provides access to Node's fields, returns a Node*. The reference type is Node&, and the pointer type is Node*.

These associated types are also defined in iterator_traits. The two nested types reference and pointer are defined just as value_type and difference_type are.

3.1.4   Dispatching Algorithms and Iterator Tags

The last of the types defined in iterator_traits is more abstract. To understand it, we must look not at iterators themselves, but at algorithms that seem to have nothing to do with iterators' associated types.

It often turns out that an algorithm has a sensible definition for one iterator concept, but there is a different way to define it for a refinement of that concept. Suppose, for example, that we have defined an algorithm for Forward Iterators. It can, of course, be used for Random Access Iterators, since every type that is a model of Random Access Iterator is also a model of Forward Iterator. But just because it's usable, doesn't mean it's optimal. Sometimes we can write a better version specifically for Random Access Iterators, a version that uses such features as an $\mathcal{O}(1)$ operator< and operator+=.

One of the simplest examples is a function that we mentioned briefly in Section 2.3.5: advance. This function isn't very interesting by itself, but other STL algorithms use it as a primitive. It takes two arguments, an iterator p and a number n, and it increments p n times. There are, in fact, three different definitions of advance: one for Input Iterators, one for Bidirectional Iterators, and one for Random Access Iterators.

```
template <class InputIterator, class Distance>
void advance_II(InputIterator& i, Distance n)
{
  for ( ; n > 0; --n, ++i) {}
}
```

---

3. The -> operator doesn't provide any functionality that we don't already have from operator*. The expression p->val is just shorthand for (*p).val. All Input Iterators are required to provide operator-> as well as operator*.

```
template <class BidirectionalIterator, class Distance>
void advance_BI(BidirectionalIterator& i, Distance n)
{
  if (n >= 0)
    for ( ; n > 0; --n, ++i) {}
  else
    for ( ; n < 0; ++n, --i) {}
}

template <class RandomAccessIterator, class Distance>
void advance_RAI(RandomAccessIterator& i, Distance n)
{
  i += n;
}
```

The implementation for Input Iterators decrements n until we get to zero. The implementation for Bidirectional Iterators is essentially the same, except that it allows you to "advance" by a negative quantity. Finally, the implementation for Random Access Iterators uses operator+=. We haven't provided a separate definition for Forward Iterators, because there's no reason to use a different definition for Forward Iterators than for any other kind of Input Iterator.

Which of these three implementations should we use for the iterator primitive advance? Unfortunately, none of them is really suitable. Choosing advance_II would be grossly inefficient for Random Access Iterators; what ought to be an $O(1)$ operation would instead be $O(N)$. Choosing advance_RAI, on the other hand, would make it impossible to use advance with Input Iterators at all.

What we really need is some way to combine these three implementations into one. Conceptually, you could imagine writing something like this:

```
template <class InputIterator, class Distance>
void advance(InputIterator& i, Distance n)
{
  if (is_random_access_iterator(i))
    advance_RAI(i, n);
  else if (is_bidirectional_iterator(i))
    advance_BI(i, n);
  else
    advance_II(i, n);
}
```

We can't implement advance this way, of course. Choosing between these three implementations at runtime is too late. We have to select the right one at compile time. What we're really trying to do here is generalize something that is very familiar to every C++ programmer: function overloading.

In C++ you can define several different functions that all have the same name as long as their argument types are different. When you call an overloaded function, the compiler chooses the version that matches the types you call it with. We're trying to do something similar here, but we're overloading on concepts rather than on types.

The C++ language doesn't directly support overloading on concepts (concepts aren't part of the language), but we can emulate it in terms of ordinary overloading if we can find a way to represent concepts within the C++ type system.

The first step is defining a set of placeholder types, one for each of the iterator concepts. It doesn't really matter what those types are as long as they are unique.

The second step is defining the three implementations of advance as a single name overloaded on these tag types. That overloaded function will take the place of the three functions advance_II, advance_BI, and advance_RAI:

```
template <class InputIterator, class Distance>
void advance(InputIterator& i, Distance n, input_iterator_tag)
{
    // Same implementation as advance_II.
}

template <class ForwardIterator, class Distance>
inline void advance(ForwardIterator& i, Distance n,
                    forward_iterator_tag)
{
    advance(i, n, input_iterator_tag());
}

template <class BidirectionalIterator, class Distance>
void advance(BidirectionalIterator& i, Distance n,
             bidirectional_iterator_tag)
{
    // Same implementation as advance_BI.
}

template <class RandomAccessIterator, class Distance>
void advance(RandomAccessIterator& i, Distance n,
             random_access_iterator_tag)
{
    // Same implementation as advance_RAI.
}
```

We aren't doing anything with the tag arguments. They're placeholders, and the only reason we need them is to distinguish among the different versions of advance. Note also that we now have an implementation for Forward Iterators. It is now explicit that Forward Iterators use the same implementation as other Input Iterators.

Finally, we need to write the top-level function that calls the overloaded advance. It takes two arguments, an iterator i and a distance n. It passes those two arguments to advance along with a third argument, one of the five tag types. The top-level function, then, must be able to deduce a tag type given an iterator type.

This is the same problem we have seen throughout this section, and it has the same solution. Every iterator has an associated *iterator category* type, just as it has a value type. An iterator's category is the tag type that corresponds to the most specific concept that the iterator is a model of. For example, int* is a model of

Random Access Iterator, Bidirectional Iterator, Forward Iterator, Input Iterator, and Output Iterator, but its category is `random_access_iterator_tag`.

Like the other associated types, `iterator_category` is defined as a nested type within `iterator_traits`. This allows us to write advance and other algorithms that must dispatch on the iterator category:

```
template <class InputIter, class Distance>
inline void advance(InputIter& i, Distance n)
{
    advance(i, n, typename iterator_traits<InputIter>::iterator_category());
}
```

The STL defines the five tag types as empty classes.

```
struct input_iterator_tag {};
struct output_iterator_tag {};
struct forward_iterator_tag : public input_iterator_tag {};
struct bidirectional_iterator_tag : public forward_iterator_tag {};
struct random_access_iterator_tag : public bidirectional_iterator_tag {};
```

The fact that these tag types are classes and that the classes use inheritance doesn't matter very much. What's important about the tag types is that they are unique, so they can be used for function overloading. Using inheritance can be convenient. We wrote four versions of advance, for example, but only three are distinct. The version for Forward Iterators just turns around and calls the one for Input Iterators. Since `forward_iterator_tag` inherits from `input_iterator_tag`, we can omit such trivial forwarding functions.

3.1.5 Putting It All Together

Some implications of the `iterator_traits` mechanism are subtle and far-reaching, but its implementation is quite simple:

```
template <class Iterator>
struct iterator_traits {
    typedef typename Iterator::iterator_category iterator_category;
    typedef typename Iterator::value_type        value_type;
    typedef typename Iterator::difference_type    difference_type;
    typedef typename Iterator::pointer            pointer;
    typedef typename Iterator::reference          reference;
};

template <class T>
struct iterator_traits<T*> {
    typedef random_access_iterator_tag iterator_category;
    typedef T                          value_type;
    typedef ptrdiff_t                  difference_type;
    typedef T*                         pointer;
    typedef T&                         reference;
};
```

```
template <class T>
struct iterator_traits<const T*> {
  typedef random_access_iterator_tag iterator_category;
  typedef T                          value_type;
  typedef ptrdiff_t                  difference_type;
  typedef const T*                   pointer;
  typedef const T&                   reference;
};
```

In the end, the only time you ever have to worry about this mechanism is when you're defining your own iterators or algorithms. When you're defining your own algorithm, there are two reasons why you might need to use `iterator_traits`:

- You need to return a value or declare a temporary variable whose type is the same as an iterator's value type, difference type, reference type, or pointer type.

- Your algorithm is like advance in that you need to use a different implementation depending on which category an iterator belongs to. Without this mechanism, you would sometimes be forced to make an impossible choice between an implementation that's general but inefficient and an implementation that's efficient but overly narrow.

Some of the predefined STL algorithms use this mechanism, so whenever you define a new iterator you must make sure that it works properly with `iterator_traits`. Fortunately, this is completely trivial.

Whenever you define a new iterator class I, you must either define the five types `iterator_category`, `value_type`, `difference_type`, `pointer`, and `reference` within that class as nested types, or explicitly specialize `iterator_traits` for your class I in the same way as `iterator_traits` was already specialized for pointers. The first choice is almost always easier, and the STL includes a helper class, the base class `iterator`, to make it even easier still:

```
template <class Category, class Value,
          class Distance = ptrdiff_t,
          class Pointer = Value*,
          class Reference = Value&>
struct iterator {
  typedef Category   iterator_category;
  typedef Value      value_type;
  typedef Distance   difference_type;
  typedef Pointer    pointer;
  typedef Reference  reference;
};
```

The easiest way to ensure that `iterator_traits` is defined appropriately for a new iterator class I is to derive I from iterator. The base class `iterator` contains no member functions or member variables, so inheriting from it ought to incur zero overhead.

3.1.6   Iterator Traits without `iterator_traits`

The `iterator_traits` class is a relatively recent invention, and it was not included in the original HP STL [SL95]. The HP STL did have the notion of value types, difference types, and iterator categories, but it used a different (and clumsier) mechanism to access them. That mechanism is no longer part of the C++ standard, but many STL implementations still provide it for backward compatibility.

This earlier mechanism was a set of iterator query functions: `distance_type`, `value_type`, and `iterator_category`. Each of the iterator query functions takes a single argument, an iterator, and in each case, the information about the iterator's associated type is encoded in the function's return type.

The function `iterator_category` takes a single argument, an iterator, and returns the tag corresponding to that iterator's category. That is, it returns a value of type `random_access_iterator_tag` if its argument is a model of Random Access Iterator, a value of type `bidirectional_iterator_tag` if its argument is a model of Bidirectional Iterator, and so on. Similarly, if `i` is an iterator whose value type is V and whose difference type is D, then `value_type(i)` returns some value of type V* and `difference_type(i)` returns some value of type D*. In all three cases the actual return value is irrelevant. All that matters is the return type.

These functions are less convenient than `iterator_traits` because they don't directly provide types. Using `iterator_traits`, for example, it is easy to write a function that swaps the values of two iterators:

```
template <class ForwardIterator1, class ForwardIterator2>
void iter_swap(ForwardIterator1 p, ForwardIterator2 q)
{
  typename iterator_traits<ForwardIterator1>::value_type tmp = *p;
  *p = *q;
  *q = tmp;
}
```

Using the older mechanism, there is no way to declare tmp directly. The only way to write `iter_swap` using that mechanism is to split it into two separate functions:

```
template <class ForwardIterator1, class ForwardIterator2, class T>
void iter_swap_impl(ForwardIterator1 p, ForwardIterator2 q, T*)
{
  T tmp = *p;
  *p = *q;
  *q = tmp;
}

template <class ForwardIterator1, class ForwardIterator2>
void iter_swap(ForwardIterator1 p, ForwardIterator2 q)
{
  iter_swap_impl(p, q, value_type(p));
}
```

In the original HP STL, these three functions had to be provided for every iterator type. If you were defining a new iterator, the easiest way to make sure the three functions were defined was to derive your iterator class from one of the five base classes `input_iterator`, `output_iterator`, `forward_iterator`, `bidirectional_iterator`, or `random_access_iterator`.

The three iterator query functions and the five iterator base classes are no longer part of the C++ standard. The iterator query functions have been replaced by the `iterator_traits` class, and the iterator base classes have been replaced by the single base class `iterator`. Many STL implementations continue to provide the older mechanism for backward compatibility, and you may see it in older code.

3.2   Defining New Components

The STL is extensible by design. You can use the existing STL algorithms with new iterators that you define, and existing iterators with new algorithms.

The reason for that extensibility should now be obvious. Both iterators and algorithms are written in terms of the iterator requirements. An STL algorithm that works with a range of Forward Iterators uses only the properties guaranteed in the Forward Iterators concept definition, and an iterator that models Forward Iterators must provide all of the functionality required by that concept definition.

Since the iterator concepts are used as an interface both by algorithms and by iterator types, you should use them as a checklist whenever you define a new algorithm or a new iterator—a checklist of functionality that you must provide, in the case of an new iterator, and a checklist of functionality that you may assume to be present in the case of a new algorithm. Chapter 7 presents the iterator concepts in detail.

Fundamentally, an iterator has to do two things: it has to point to something, and it has to be able to step through a range. Once you have defined `operator*` and `operator++`, the rest of the iterator operations usually follow quite easily.

One area that does need some care is making sure that iterators are correctly defined as constant or mutable. This is a common source of errors. This issue is of no concern for Input Iterators, which are read-only, or for Output Iterators, which are write-only, but it is important for other kinds of iterators.

The `node_wrap` class (Section 2.1.3), for example, is a mutable iterator. It lets you modify the value that it points to. "Const correctness" is important in C++. C++ has const pointers precisely so that you don't accidentally change a data structure that is supposed to remain unmodified. When you're defining an iterator that steps through a data structure, you probably shouldn't just be defining *an* iterator. It's usually more appropriate to define *a pair* of iterators, one constant and one mutable, with the same value type and with a conversion from the mutable to the constant (but not the other way around).

You might think that this is unnecessary, that an iterator like `node_wrap` can do double duty as both the constant and the mutable version, but it can't. There are two places where you could imagine putting the const, and both are wrong. A `const node_wrap<T>` isn't a constant iterator. The distinction is whether you can use it to modify the value that it points to, and since `operator*` returns a T& rather than a `const T&`, you can. A `node_wrap<const T>` comes closer (at least `operator*` does return a const T&), but it's still wrong. The value type of a node_wrap<const T> would be const T, but as we found in Section 3.1.1, the value type of an iterator, even a constant iterator, shouldn't be qualified with a const.

The value type, reference type, and pointer type of the mutable iterator class node_wrap<T> are, respectively, T, T&, and T*. For the corresponding constant iterator, those types must be T, const T&, and const T*. We really do need two separate classes for the constant and the mutable versions, although we can use templates or inheritance to factor out the identical parts of the two classes.

The pointer and reference types are the most important difference between the constant and the mutable versions, which suggests that we might be able to make do with a single iterator class that has those types as template parameters. The other difference between the two versions is that you can construct a constant iterator from a mutable iterator but not the other way around, and there's a very simple (albeit subtle) way to deal with that: Define a constructor whose argument is a mutable iterator. For one value of the template parameters it's a copy constructor, and for the other it's the conversion constructor that we need.

This, then, is a complete definition of the node_wrap and const_node_wrap iterator classes. Both classes conform to all of the Forward Iterator requirements. (I made sure it conformed to all of the requirements by looking them up in Chapter 7. You should do the same when you define a new iterator class.)

```
template <class Node, class Reference, class Pointer>
struct node_wrap_base
  : public iterator<forward_iterator_tag, Node,
                    ptrdiff_t, Pointer, Reference>
{
  typedef node_wrap_base<Node, Node&, Node*>              iterator;
  typedef node_wrap_base<Node, const Node&, const Node*> const_iterator;
  Pointer ptr;

  node_wrap_base(Pointer p = 0) : ptr(p) {}
  node_wrap_base(const iterator& x) : ptr(x.ptr) {}

  Reference operator*() const { return *ptr; }
  Pointer operator->() const { return ptr; }

  void incr() { ptr = ptr->next; }

  bool operator==(const node_wrap_base& x) const { return ptr == x.ptr; }
  bool operator!=(const node_wrap_base& x) const { return ptr != x.ptr; }
};

template <class Node>
struct node_wrap : public node_wrap_base<Node, Node&, Node*>
{
  typedef node_wrap_base<Node, Node&, Node*> Base;
  node_wrap(Node* p = 0) : Base(p) {}
  node_wrap(const node_wrap<Node>& x) : Base(x) {}
```

```
    node_wrap& operator++()
      { incr(); return *this; }
    node_wrap  operator++(int)
      { node_wrap tmp = *this; incr(); return tmp; }
};


template <class Node>
struct const_node_wrap
  : public node_wrap_base<Node, const Node&, const Node*>
{
    typedef node_wrap_base<Node, const Node&, const Node*> Base;
    const_node_wrap(const Node* p = 0) : Base(p) {}
    const_node_wrap(const node_wrap<Node>& x) : Base(x) {}

    const_node_wrap& operator++()
      { incr(); return *this; }
    const_node_wrap  operator++(int)
      { const_node_wrap tmp = *this; incr(); return tmp; }
};
```

The base class node_wrap_base almost suffices. The only real reason for deriving node_wrap and const_node_wrap from node_wrap_base instead of making do with the base class alone is that writing node_wrap<T> is much more convenient than having to write node_wrap_base<T, T&, T*>. C++ does not have template typedefs, so we have to use inheritance or containment as a substitute.

If having an inconvenient name doesn't matter or if you're defining another alias anyway, there's no need to bother with those derived classes.

3.2.1 Iterator Adaptors

One useful kind of iterator is an iterator *adaptor*. Broadly speaking, an adaptor is anything that transforms one interface into another. The node_wrap class is in a sense an adaptor, in that it provides an STL interface for a linked list that may have been written without any thought of iterators or the STL.

Another kind of iterator adaptor is one that provides a different interface for an existing STL component. The STL defines several of these iterator adaptors, including front_insert_iterator, back_insert_iterator, and reverse_iterator.

The most interesting of these is reverse_iterator (page 363). It is an adaptor in perhaps the purest sense. It has a single template parameter, a Bidirectional Iterator Iter, and a reverse_iterator<Iter> is just like an Iter except that it steps backward instead of forward. That is, operator++ for a reverse_iterator<Iter> is equivalent to operator-- for an Iter.

If you are defining an iterator adaptor like reverse_iterator, you don't have to explicitly deal with the question of whether it is a constant or mutable iterator. For example, reverse_iterator<Iter> has the same reference type and pointer type as Iter itself, so it is mutable if and only if Iter is mutable.

3.2.2 Advice for Defining an Iterator

- Use the iterator requirements in Chapter 7 as a checklist.

- Be careful about whether the iterator is supposed to be constant or mutable. The main difference is whether the reference type and pointer type are T& and T*, or const T& and const T*. You may want to define a pair of iterators, one constant and one mutable. If you do, you should define a conversion from the mutable iterator to the constant iterator but not one in the opposite direction.

- You must make sure that iterator_traits is defined appropriately for your iterator. That almost always means defining nested types, and the easiest way to do that is to use the class iterator as a base class.

- You should provide as many iterator operations as you can without loss of efficiency. That way, your iterator can be used with as many algorithms as possible. It is better to define it as a model of Random Access Iterator (if practical) than as a model of Bidirectional Iterator alone. If you are defining an iterator that traverses a data structure (as opposed, for example, to an iterator that represents some I/O operator), then it should almost always be at least a Forward Iterator.

- For Forward Iterators in particular, you should make sure to obey the fundamental axiom of iterator equality: Two iterators are equal if and only if they point to the same object.

3.2.3 Advice for Defining an Algorithm

- Assume as little as possible. If you can design your algorithm to work with an Input Iterator or Output Iterator without loss of efficiency, you should. Again, this means that it can be used with as many different kinds of iterators as possible.

- If you are able to write your algorithm to work with Input Iterators, for example, but there is a more efficient way to write it using Forward Iterators, then you should not try to choose between efficiency and generality. Both goals are too important to give up. Instead, you should use the dispatching technique described in Section 3.1.4.

- You should consult the iterator requirements given in Chapter 7 to make sure that you aren't inadvertently assuming more properties about the template parameter than are actually defined by the relevant iterator concept, and when you test your algorithm, you should use a concrete type that adheres as closely as possible to that concept. If you have written an algorithm that works with Input Iterators, for example, you should test it with istream_iterator rather than with int*, and if you have written an algorithm that works with Output Iterators, you should test it with ostream_iterator. If you have written an algorithm that works with Forward Iterators, a good choice for a test case is the iterator defined in the container class slist.

- Pay attention to empty ranges. Most algorithms make sense for empty ranges, and they are an important test case.

3.3   Summary

The central feature of the STL is generic algorithms on ranges. The STL includes many predefined algorithms, documented in Chapters 11–13. These algorithms include operations as diverse as substring matching and random permutations.

All of these algorithms operate on ranges of iterators, where iterators are a family of five pointer-like concepts. Not all algorithms can be used in conjunction with every conceivable data structure. It is hopeless, for example, to expect to perform a quicksort on a singly linked list. Iterators, however, provide a method for classifying which algorithms can be used with which data structures. In this chapter and Chapter 2, we have seen examples of algorithms that operate on each of the different iterator concepts, and even of algorithms that dispatch to multiple implementations depending on what kind of iterator is passed to them.

The STL's five iterator concepts are the glue that binds an algorithm to the data structure it operates on. These concepts make it possible to reuse existing algorithms with new data structures and existing data structures with new algorithms. Iterators, along with function objects (the subject of Chapter 4) allow even simple algorithms to be reused in very diverse contexts.

Chapter 4

Function Objects

As we saw in Chapter 2, many algorithms on ranges can be written solely in terms of iterators. Sometimes, however, that narrow focus is too constraining.

Linear search, the example with which we began Chapter 2, is one such case. In Section 2.1.3 we learned how to write a generic algorithm called `find`, which searches the range [`first, last`) for the first element that's equal to the argument value. This is correct as far as it goes, but it doesn't go far enough. Here is how Knuth defines the general problem of searching, in Chapter 6 of *The Art of Computer Programming* [Knu98b].

> In general, we shall suppose that a set of *N* records has been stored, and the problem is to locate the appropriate one. As in the case of sorting, we assume that each record includes a special field called its *key*. ... Algorithms for searching are presented with a so-called *argument*, *K*, and the problem is to find which record has *K* as its key.

The algorithm `find` isn't general enough because it doesn't fully satisfy this definition. Using Knuth's terminology, `find` is presented with an argument. Rather than searching for a record whose key is equal to that argument, it searches for a record that is identical to the argument in its entirety. That is, `find` satisfies this definition only in the special case where a record's key happens to be the entire record itself.

Suppose, for example, that we are given a collection of records, each of which represents a person. We might want to search by last name or by Social Security number. We can't use `find` for that because `find` can only test for equality. We can use `find` to find the first record that is identical to a particular value, but we can't use it to find the first record that satisfies a looser criterion. We can't use it to test for the equality of last names alone.

4.1 Generalizing Linear Search

In `find`, we have parameterized two different things: the type of object we are searching for and the way that a collection of those objects is organized into a data struc-

49

ture. For full generality we need to be able to specify one more thing: how to determine whether we have found the right element. This requires a new algorithm, find_if:

```
template <class InputIterator, class Predicate>
InputIterator find_if(InputIterator first, InputIterator last,
                      Predicate pred)
{
  while (first != last && !pred(*first))
    ++first;
  return first;
}
```

The algorithm find_if is very much like find. Instead of searching for an element that is equal to an argument T, it searches for an element that satisfies the condition pred. This is clearly more general than find, and in fact it is even more general than Knuth's definition. That definition involves looking for a record that has a particular key, and find_if can be used to look for a record that satisfies a condition that has nothing to do with keys. (It can also, of course, be used for the kind of search that Knuth describes.)

In find_if the test pred isn't declared as a function pointer, as it would have been in C, but as a template parameter Predicate. We saw something like pred in Chapter 1. It is a *function object*, or *functor* (the terms are synonymous). That is, pred is something that can be called in the same way that a function is.

Function objects are useful in many different contexts. In the STL they are used primarily for what Stroustrup [Str97] describes as "using template arguments to specify policy." In this case, for example, the template argument that is passed to find_if determines what kind of search find_if does.

The simplest kind of function object is an ordinary function pointer. Suppose, for example, that you want to find the first even number in an array of integers. You might begin by defining a small function that tests whether an int is even or odd:

```
bool is_even(int x) { return (x & 1) == 0; }
```
You can pass a pointer to is_even as an argument to find_if. If you write:

```
find_if(f, l, is_even)
```
then the return value will be an iterator that points to the first even number in the range [f,l). (The return value will be l if there are no even numbers in the range.) In this case, we are passing find_if a function pointer. A pointer to is_even has the type bool (*)(int). C++ performs the usual process of type deduction, substituting bool (*)(int) for the formal template parameter Predicate.

You don't have to use a function pointer. The function call operator, operator(), can be overloaded, so you can pass any type to find_if as a template argument provided that it defines operator() suitably. You could, for example, define the test as a class, rather than a function:

```
template <class Number> struct even
{
  bool operator()(Number x) const { return (x & 1) == 0; }
};
```

The const in this declaration means that operator() is a const member function. It doesn't alter an even object's state. That's an empty guarantee in this case, since even has no member variables that could possibly be altered, but, as a general rule, it is a good idea to declare a function object's operator() as a const member function whenever possible. It's easy to forget to declare member functions as const when you're defining a trivial class like even, but it's important to do so. If you ever pass a function object by const reference rather than by value, you can't use operator() unless it is a const member function.

We can use the class even in much the same way as we used the function is_even. To find the first even element in a range, we write:

```
find_if(f, l, even<int>())
```

We have to use the slightly odd-looking expression even<int>() for a very straightforward reason: even<int> is a class, so we have to pass an object of that class to find_if. All we're doing is calling a constructor.

The class even isn't a very interesting example of a function object. It's more flexible than the function is_even (it can be used with any integral type, not just int), and it's probably more efficient (using even shouldn't require any function calls, since operator() is declared as an inline member function), but otherwise, it isn't very different. It's just a function wrapped in the form of a class.

Function objects aren't restricted to this simple form. A function object can be a fully general class, and, like any other class, it can have member functions and member variables. That is, you can use function objects to represent the idea of a function that has local state.

We can use local state for the kind of search problem that Knuth describes. For example, we can use it to define a function object that makes it easy to search a collection by last name. We use find_if to search for an element that satisfies a condition. In this case, the condition is that the element's last_name field equals a specific value:

```
struct last_name_is
{
  string value;
  last_name_is(const string& val) : value(val) {}
  bool operator()(const Person& x) const {
    return x.last_name == value;
  }
};
```

We use this function object by writing something like:

```
find_if(first, last, last_name_is("Smith"))
```

A class like last_name_is is an example of a function object in its full generality. It has local state, and it has a constructor, but because of its operator(), an object of type last_name_is also looks like a function, one that takes a single argument of type Person and returns a bool.

It would be difficult to write something like last_name_is in C. Probably the closest you could come would be an ordinary function that referenced a global variable, but that still wouldn't quite be the same because it wouldn't allow multiple instances of that function, each of which searched for a different name. (Some other languages make this even easier. For example, functions with local state are fundamental to Scheme and ML.)

4.2 Function Object Concepts

In Section 4.1 we saw three function objects: is_even, even, and last_name_is. Other than the fact that they can all be called as functions, that all of them have an operator(), the three have very little in common. Clearly, then, the fundamental requirement of any function object concept is that, if f is a function object, it is possible to apply operator() to f.

4.2.1 Unary and Binary Function Objects

The three function objects in Section 4.1 all have the property that if f is any one of those objects, you can write f(x) for some x. That is, f looks like a function that takes a single argument.

That's not the only reasonable kind of function object. There's nothing special about functions that take a single argument. Just as we generalized find by introducing a function object that takes a single argument, we can generalize adjacent_find (Section 2.3.3) by passing it one more argument, a function object that itself takes two arguments:

```
template <class ForwardIterator, class BinaryPredicate>
ForwardIterator
adjacent_find(ForwardIterator first, ForwardIterator last,
              BinaryPredicate pred)
{
  if (first == last)
    return last;
  ForwardIterator next = first;
  while(++next != last) {
    if (pred(*first, *next))
      return first;
    first = next;
  }
  return last;
}
```

The STL overloads adjacent_find. It includes both versions even though, strictly speaking, only the one that uses a function object is really necessary. That's a common theme. When an algorithm takes a function argument as an argument, it's to parameterize some behavior—in this case, the test of the adjacent elements. Usually there's some default behavior that you will want to use most of the time. When that's the case, the STL also includes a version of that algorithm that provides the default behavior.

We have seen an algorithm that uses a function object taking a single argument and one that uses a function object taking two arguments. A few other algorithms, such as generate (page 251), use function objects taking no arguments at all. The basic function object concepts, then, are Generator, Unary Function, and Binary Function. These concepts describe objects that can be called as f(), f(x), and f(x,y), respectively. (Obviously, this list could be extended to ternary function and beyond, but in practice, existing STL algorithms do not require function objects of more than two arguments.) All other function object concepts defined by the STL are refinements of these three.

These three concepts are closely related (all three describe function objects), but there isn't any way to say that all three are refinements of some overarching function object concept. Concept requirements involve specific expressions, and the three expressions f(), f(x), and f(x,y) are inherently distinct.

4.2.2 Predicates and Binary Predicates

Both of the examples we have seen so far in this chapter involve function objects that test some condition—function objects that return true or false. You might wonder whether all function objects are of that form.

They aren't. Function objects are a very general concept, and they can parameterize any sort of operation. Almost every algorithm can be generalized by abstracting some part of its behavior as a function object. This is true even of so mundane an algorithm as copy (page 233), which copies values from one range to another. An obvious generalization is to copy not the values exactly as they appear in the input range but the values after they have passed through some transformation. That is, instead of the operation

$$y_i \leftarrow x_i \tag{4.1}$$

we could perform the operation

$$y_i \leftarrow f(x_i). \tag{4.2}$$

(Equation 4.1 is a special case of Equation 4.2: where f is the identity function id.)

The STL algorithm for this generalized copy is called transform (page 240). Except for the fact that it uses a function object, its implementation looks very much like that of copy.

```
template <class InputIterator, class OutputIterator, class UnaryFunction>
OutputIterator transform(InputIterator first, InputIterator last,
                  OutputIterator result, UnaryFunction f)
{
  while (first != last) *result++ = f(*first++);
  return result;
}
```

Clearly, UnaryFunction isn't restricted to returning true or false. It can return any sort of value, provided that its return type is something you can assign to OutputIterator. You might, for example, use transform to negate a range of numbers.

Function objects that return `bool` are an important special case—they are used more commonly than function objects in their full generality. This kind of function object is useful whenever an algorithm, such as `find_if`, involves some sort of test.

A function object that takes a single argument and returns a `true` or `false` result is called a **Predicate**. This concept is a refinement of Unary Function. Similarly, Binary Predicate is a refinement of Binary Function. A Binary Predicate is a function object that takes two arguments and returns `true` or `false`.

4.2.3 Associated Types

A function object's associated types are the types of its arguments and of its return value. A Generator has one associated type (its return type), a Unary Function has two associated types (its argument type and its return type), and a Binary Function has three associated types (its first argument type, its second argument type, and its return type). The class even<T>, for example, has an argument type T and a return type bool.

As with iterators, it is sometimes useful to be able to access those associated types. We solved that problem for iterators by introducing `iterator_traits` (Section 3.1), and the solution for function objects is similar. Function objects that are defined as classes, like iterators that are defined as classes, can have nested types. We define even<T>::argument_type to be T, and even<T>::result_type to be bool. Again, as with iterators, we define empty base classes unary_function (page 371) and binary_function (page 372), each of which contains nothing but typedefs:

```
template <class Arg, class Result>
struct unary_function {
  typedef Arg argument_type;
  typedef Result result_type;
};


template <class Arg1, class Arg2, class Result>
struct binary_function {
  typedef Arg1 first_argument_type;
  typedef Arg2 second_argument_type;
  typedef Result result_type;
};
```

We could modify even<T> either by declaring these two types explicitly or, more conveniently, by inheriting from unary_function:

```
template <class Number>
struct even : public unary_function<Number, bool>
{
  bool operator()(Number x) const { return (x & 1) == 0; }
};
```

This isn't a complete solution, because it can't be used for one important kind of function object: function pointers, such as bool (*)(int). Function pointers are

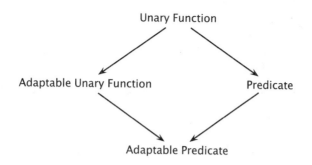

Figure 4.1:   Concepts of single-argument function objects.

built-in types, not classes, so it doesn't make sense to define nested types within them.

We could solve this problem the same way we did with iterators. We could define a traits class, unary_function_traits, and then define a partial specialization of it for function pointers, but the STL has no unary_function_traits class. There's no technical reason for that absence, but, while function objects are important, they are not ubiquitous the way that iterators are. Many of the algorithms that use function objects do not refer explicitly to the argument or return types, so there is no need for every function object to provide a means of accessing those types.

As a result, the STL makes a distinction between function objects and *adaptable function objects*. In general, every function object has an argument type (or argument types, in the case of a Binary Function) and a return type, but there need not be a way for a program to find the names of those types. An adaptable function object does specify what the argument and return types are, and it contains nested typedefs so that those types can be named and used in programs. If a type F1 is a model of Adaptable Unary Function, then it must define F1::argument_type and F1::result_type, and if F2 is a model of Adaptable Binary Function, then it must define F2::first_argument_type, F2::second_argument_type, and F2::result_type. The base classes unary_function and binary_function make it simpler to define Adaptable Unary Functions and Adaptable Binary Functions.

Just as Adaptable Unary Function is a refinement of Unary Function, Adaptable Predicate is a refinement of Predicate. Figure 4.1 shows the various Unary Function concepts. A similar diagram exists for the Binary Function concepts.

None of the algorithms in Chapters 11-13 require adaptable function objects. For example, find_if uses a Predicate and adjacent_find uses a Binary Predicate. Why bother introducing the Adaptable Unary Function and Adaptable Binary Function concepts at all if they are never used?

The answer, of course, is that they are used—just not by the STL's predefined algorithms. They are defined (and named "adaptable") because they are used by function object *adaptors*.

4.3   Function Object Adaptors

An adaptor is any component that transforms one interface into another. For example, `reverse_iterator`, from Section 3.2, is an iterator adaptor. Function object adaptors are particularly tempting.

- Function composition is a basic operation of mathematics and computer science.

- Defining lots of *ad hoc* function object classes is a nuisance. A relatively small number of well-chosen function object adaptors makes it possible to build complicated operations out of simpler ones.

- Many useful function object adaptors are very easy to define. (If you're like me, you'll find that the hardest thing about defining a new function object adaptor usually turns out to be thinking of a good name for it!)

You can, for example, find the first even number in a range of integers by writing:
```
find_if(f, l, even<int>())
```
But what if you want to find the first odd number in a range instead? You could write another function object odd<T>, of course, but that would be silly. The two tests are complementary, and once you have defined one you should not have to define the other. Code should be reused, not rewritten.

The solution, instead, is a function object adaptor—one that is already part of the STL:

```
template <class AdaptablePredicate>
class unary_negate
{
private:
  AdaptablePredicate pred;

public:
  typedef typename AdaptablePredicate::argument_type
          argument_type;
  typedef typename AdaptablePredicate::result_type
          result_type;

  unary_negate(const AdaptablePredicate& x) : pred(x) {}
  bool operator()(const argument_type& x) const {
    return !pred(x);
  }
};
```

If f is a predicate of type F, then `unary_negate<F>(f)` is a predicate that is the negation of f. That is, it is a predicate f_neg with the property that f_neg(x) is `true` if and only if f(x) is `false`.

The template parameter `AdaptablePredicate` must, as the name suggests, be a model of **Adaptable Predicate**. Since unary_negate's argument type is declared to be the same type as `AdaptablePredicate`'s argument type, we must be able to access that type. In turn, unary_negate itself is also a model of Adaptable Predicate because it includes the appropriate nested typedefs. This is typical of function object adaptors, and it is the reason that adaptable function objects are called "adaptable" in the first place.

The only problem with the unary_negate adaptor as it stands is that the expression unary_negate<F>(f) is unnecessarily cumbersome. It's repetitive. We have to provide both the function object f and its type F. Purely for convenience, we can also define a tiny helper function that makes it easier to create unary_negate objects:

```
template <class AdaptablePredicate>
inline unary_negate<AdaptablePredicate>
not1(const AdaptablePredicate& pred) {
  return unary_negate<AdaptablePredicate>(pred);
}
```

You can think of not1 as a higher-order function, or a function that operates on functions. Its argument is a function object, and its return value is that function object's negation. Finally, then, we can find the first odd element in a range by writing:

```
find_if(first, last, not1(even<int>()))
```

By chaining together several different function object adaptors you can construct complicated function objects out of simple predefined components, without ever needing to write a new function or class.

If you need to pass an ordinary function pointer to a function object adaptor, you can use pointer_to_unary_function (page 424) to transform the function pointer into an Adaptable Unary Function. (Note that the pointer_to_unary_function adaptor is necessary *only* if you need to treat a function pointer as an Adaptable Unary Function. As we saw from the example of passing a function pointer to find_if, a function pointer is already a perfectly good Unary Function in its own right.)

```
template <class Arg, class Result>
class pointer_to_unary_function : public unary_function<Arg, Result> {
private:
  Result (*ptr)(Arg);
public:
  pointer_to_unary_function() {}
  pointer_to_unary_function(Result (*x)(Arg)) : ptr(x) {}
  Result operator()(Arg x) const { return ptr(x); }
};

template <class Arg, class Result>
inline pointer_to_unary_function<Arg, Result>
ptr_fun(Result (*x)(Arg)) {
  return pointer_to_unary_function<Arg, Result>(x);
}
```

There is a similar adaptor, pointer_to_binary_function, for binary functions.

The STL defines several other function object adaptors. Some of the most important are binder1st and binder2nd, which transform an Adaptable Binary Function into a Unary Function; the mem_fun_t adaptor and its variants, which are similar to pointer_to_unary_function except that they operate on member functions rather than global functions; and unary_compose, which transforms two function objects f and g into a single function object h such that h(x) is the same as f(g(x)).

4.4   Predefined Function Objects

In addition to adaptors, the STL includes many basic function objects that you can use as building blocks. In particular, the STL includes basic arithmetic operations and it includes comparison operations.

The basic arithmetic operations defined in the STL are plus, minus, multiplies,[1] divides, modulus, and negate. Of these, negate is a model of Adaptable Unary Function, and the others are models of Adaptable Binary Function.

Likewise, the basic comparison operations are equal_to, not_equal_to, greater, less, greater_equal, and less_equal. All are models of Adaptable Binary Function. Of these comparison function objects, the most important by far are equal_to and less. Many algorithms have to test whether two values are the same or whether one value is less than the other. Whenever those operations are parameterized as function objects, equal_to and less are the defaults.

Testing whether one object is less than another is so common and so important that a special concept is devoted to it. The concept Strict Weak Ordering is a refinement of Binary Predicate. A Strict Weak Ordering is a binary predicate that represents a "well-behaved" ordering relation. The formal rules for what makes an ordering relation well-behaved are slightly subtle (you can find them on page 119), but conforming to them isn't difficult. They really are just a formalization of the way that we intuitively expect ordering relations to behave anyway.

4.5   Summary

Function objects are not very useful on their own. A function object is usually a very small class that performs a single specific operation. A function object often has only one member function, operator(), and no member variables.

The reason that function objects are useful is that they allow generic algorithms to be even more general. They make it possible to parameterize policy. A single function, find_if, can search for any kind of object organized in any kind of linear sequence using any search criterion. Similarly, the sorting algorithm sort doesn't have to anticipate every conceivable way that you might want to sort a range. Instead, it uses a function object (which must be a model of Strict Weak Ordering) to define how the range will be sorted.

Function objects, like most of the STL, are useful as an adjunct to algorithms on linear ranges.

---

1. In the original HP STL it was called times. The name was changed to avoid a conflict with one of the functions in the UNIX library.

Chapter 5

Containers

In Chapter 2 we saw how to write generic algorithms in terms of iterators. The iterator abstractions let us decouple an algorithm from the elements that it operates on and make it possible to write algorithms that operate on any sort of linear sequence.

Throughout that chapter and the next two, we begged an important question: Where do those elements come from? Most of the examples in Chapters 2–4 involved ordinary C arrays, and if we're only going to be using these algorithms on arrays, then this generality isn't of much use.

An algorithm that operates on a range of elements is operating on members of some data structure. The reason that algorithms on ranges are important in the first place is that in many cases a data structure can be viewed, in whole or in part, as a linear range. What this means is that to understand generic algorithms on ranges we still need to look at one last aspect of them: the data structures that contain those ranges.

5.1   A Simple Container

The simplest data structure that can contain a range, and the only one that is directly supported by the language itself, is the array. An array holds a collection of elements arranged in sequential order, and it makes it possible to iterate through those elements. The iterators associated with arrays are pointers.

Arrays in C and C++ have a number of obvious advantages, and they are sufficient for many purposes:

- Arrays naturally adhere to the idea of a range (Section 2.1.2). If A is an array with N elements, then A + N is a past-the-end pointer, and all of A's elements are contained in the range [A, A + N).

- Arrays can be allocated on the stack. Most data structures have to use dynamic memory allocation—they have to use `malloc` or `new` to obtain memory—but arrays do not. A declaration like

  ```
  int A[10];
  ```

doesn't involve any dynamic allocation. This is an advantage both because it is faster and because it eliminates the need for checking to determine whether the allocation succeeded.

- Arrays are efficient because accessing an array element doesn't require multiple levels of indirection. Referring to an array element requires very few machine instructions.

- Arrays have a fixed size that is known at compile time. Operations on arrays do not have the potential of incurring resizing overhead, and programs that use arrays don't have to account for the possibility that the size might have changed.

- Arrays have a convenient initialization syntax. You can initialize an array by writing
  ```
  int A[6] = {1, 4, 2, 8, 5, 7};
  ```
  but you can't use that syntax for any of the more complicated container classes.

Arrays in C and C++ also have some equally obvious disadvantages.

- While an array has a fixed size, programs have to explicitly keep track of that size, because arrays don't have a `size()` member function.

- Every array has an iterator that points to the first element and a past-the-end iterator, but there's no direct way to find that past-the-end iterator. You have to find the iterator that points to the beginning of the array, and then use iterator arithmetic to get to the end.

- It is impossible to copy an array directly. Arrays don't have copy constructors or assignment operators. If you want to copy an array, you have to write a loop yourself.

- It is impossible to pass an array to a function by value. In fact, it is difficult to pass an array to a function at all. Whenever you refer to an array in an expression, what you are really referring to is just a pointer to the array's first element. Arrays are part of the C and C++ type systems, but array types usually "decay" to pointer types.

5.1.1 An Array Class

Ordinary C arrays are still widely used, despite the existence of sophisticated container classes. It's easy to define a simple class, `block`,[1] that preserves all of the useful features of the C array while eliminating all of its major defects.

---

1. The name `block` was suggested by Andrew Koenig. Stroustrup [Str97] uses the name `c_array` for a similar (but not identical) class.

```
template <class T, size_t N>
struct block {
  typedef T value_type;

  typedef value_type* pointer;
  typedef const value_type* const_pointer;
  typedef value_type& reference;
  typedef const value_type& const_reference;

  typedef ptrdiff_t difference_type;
  typedef size_t size_type;

  typedef pointer iterator;
  typedef const_pointer const_iterator;

  iterator begin() { return data; }
  iterator end() { return data + N; }

  const_iterator begin() const { return data; }
  const_iterator end() const { return data + N; }

  reference operator[](size_type n) { return data[n]; }
  const_reference operator[](size_type n) const { return data[n]; }

  size_type size() const { return N; }

  T data[N];
};
```

As its name suggests, a block is a simple contiguous block of elements. It is little more than a wrapper around a C array. You declare a block of ten integers as
    block<int,10> A;
and you use ordinary array syntax, such as A[1], to refer to an element.

Some additional machinery is needed to make it easier to use block in generic algorithms. First, block supports iterators and ranges more explicitly than C arrays do. All of the block's elements are contained in the range [A.begin(),A.end()). Second, a container like block has associated types, just as iterators do. We make those types available through nested typedefs.

In C, you can iterate through an array of T using a T* (if you need to modify the values in the array) or using a const T* (if you don't). Since block is a wrapper for an array, it's easy to preserve that distinction. We define two different nested types, iterator and const_iterator. We also have to define two different versions of begin() and of end(). If A is a modifiable block, then [A.begin(),A.end()) is a range of mutable iterators, and if A is a const block, then [A.begin(),A.end()) is a range of constant iterators. Similarly, there are two different versions of the operator[] member function. A[n] returns a modifiable reference if A is modifiable and a const reference if A is const.

The block class thus follows the typical pattern from Section 3.2. It provides a matched pair of iterators, one mutable and one constant, with a conversion from the

mutable to the constant. In this case, of course, those iterators are just the familiar
T* and const T*. For the sake of generality, we define them within block as iterator
and const_iterator.

Those two nested types are the most important ones. Once we know what block's
iterators are, almost everything else about its types follows mechanically. There are
a few more associated types, specifically the types associated with block's iterators.

Since block has two kinds of iterators, and every iterator has a value type, a
difference type, a reference type, and a pointer type, you might think that we need
to define eight more types nested with block. That's almost right, but not quite.
First, some of those eight types must always be identical to each other, so there is
no point in defining them twice. When two iterators form a matched pair like this,
they must always have the same value type and difference type. (Remember that
const T*'s value type is T, not const T.) Second, there's one last nested type that's
not directly associated with either of block's iterators: block's *size type*. Just as you
use the difference type to represent an interval between two iterators, you use the
size type to count elements. The difference type is always signed, and the size type
is always unsigned. (And just as the difference type is almost always ptrdiff_t, the
size type is almost always size_t.)

Here, then, are all of block's nested types.

1. The iterator types, iterator and const_iterator. (In this case, the iterators
    are just pointers.)

2. The value type, value_type. The value type is the type of object stored in the
    block, and it is the same as iterator's value type and const_iterator's value
    type.

3. The difference type, difference_type. It is the same as iterator's difference
    type and const_iterator's difference type.

4. The size type, size_type. It is used to represent the number of elements in a
    block or the index of some particular element. Also, any non-negative value of
    type difference_type can be represented as a size_type. The basic difference
    between the two is that size_type is used for counting and difference_type
    for subtraction.

5. The reference types, reference and const_reference. A reference is a refer-
    ence to an object of type value_type, and it is the same as iterator's refer-
    ence type. It is also the type returned by the non-const version of operator[].
    A const_reference is a const reference to an object of type value_type, and
    it is the same as const_iterator's reference type. It is also the type returned
    by the const version of operator[].

6. The pointer types, pointer and const_pointer. A pointer is a pointer to an
    object of type value_type, and it is the same as iterator's pointer type. A
    const_pointer is a const pointer to an object of type value_type, and it is the
    same as const_iterator's pointer type.

5.1.2   How It Works

The block class is simple. It has only a single member variable, the array data, but in some ways it is a slightly unusual class.

First, the number of elements in a block is part of its type. A block<int,10> is a completely different type from a block<int,12>. The number of elements is fixed at compile time and cannot be changed. You cannot add elements to a block, assign a block<int,12> to a block<int,10>, or pass a block<int,12> as an argument to a function that expects a block<int,10>. The number of elements in a block is one of the block's template arguments, rather than something that is specified in a constructor.

This is an example of a language feature called *nontype template parameters*. The second template parameter isn't a type, but a number. Nontype template parameters have been part of C++ ever since templates were first added to the language, but they are rarely used. This is an example where they are important. Within block, the template parameter N is treated as a compile-time constant. It can be used wherever any other compile-time constant can be used—in this case, as the number of elements in an array. This makes it possible for block's member variable data to be not just a pointer to an array but the array itself. All of block's elements are allocated as a contiguous block of storage, hence the name.

The second way in which block is unusual is that many things seem to be missing: it has no constructors, no destructor, no assignment operator. This is perhaps not terribly surprising, since the default compiler-generated version of each of those member functions is fine. Assigning one block to another just means assigning all of its elements. What is more unusual is that block doesn't even have any public or private declarations. It is declared as a struct, so all of its members, including the array data itself, are public.

This seems to go against the whole idea of encapsulation, but in this particular case, it happens to be harmless. Making data public allows clients to modify the elements of data independently, but clients can already do that anyway. (Either using iterators or using operator[].) That's the whole point of block, after all.

There is a specific reason why making data public is not only harmless but necessary. In C, you can initialize a struct the same way that you can initialize an array: by putting a list of initial values inside a pair of braces. The same is true in C++, but only under a very special restriction. The struct can't have any user-declared constructors, it can't have any virtual member functions, it can't inherit from any other classes, and it can't have any private or protected members.[2] Block satisfies those restrictions, so it is possible to declare a block the same way as you would an array:

```
block<int, 6> A = {1, 4, 2, 8, 5, 7};
```

5.1.3   Finishing Touches

Block satisfies our original goals. It is a container class that can be initialized like an ordinary array, and it is just as efficient as an array, but it is still a "first class"

---

2. The C++ standard refers to a type that satisfies these restrictions as an *aggregate* type.

data type. You can assign one block to another, pass it by value, or get access to its beginning and past-the-end iterators. We can also make a few more enhancements that aren't strictly necessary as far as those original goals are concerned, but that make block more convenient for some purposes.

First and most important, recall that in Section 2.2 we defined a number of very basic concepts that are used in many different concepts and that are modeled by a wide variety of types. We also defined a *regular type* as a type that is a model of all of those concepts.

As we have presently defined it, block is a model of two of those concepts: Assignable and Default Constructible. It is not, however, a model of Equality Comparable or LessThan Comparable. If x and y are two objects of type block<T,N>, you can't write x == y or x < y.

There is no good reason for that omission. Both operator== and operator< have perfectly sensible definitions. Two blocks x and y are equal if they are equal element by element—that is, if each element in x is equal to the corresponding element in y. Similarly, we can use lexicographical, or "dictionary," ordering to tell whether x is less than y. It is less if x[0] < y[0], or if x[0] == y[0] and x[1] < y[1], and so on.[3]

It is easy to implement both operator== and operator< as global (nonmember) functions:

```
template <class T, size_t N>
bool operator==(const block<T,N>& x, const block<T,N>& y)
{
  for (size_t n = 0; n < N; ++n)
    if (x.data[n] != y.data[n])
      return false;
  return true;
}

template <class T, size_t N>
bool operator<(const block<T,N>& x, const block<T,N>& y)
{
  for (size_t n = 0; n < N; ++n)
    if (x.data[n] < y.data[n])
      return true;
    else if (y.data[n] < x.data[n])
      return false;
  return false;
}
```

Strictly speaking, these two functions aren't enough to ensure that block<T,N> is a model of Equality Comparable and LessThan Comparable. They require the ability to

---

3. The generic algorithm lexicographical_compare (page 225) defines the same ordering relation.

apply `operator==` and `operator<` to objects of type T. What they really mean is that block<T,N> is a model of Equality Comparable if and only if T is a model of Equality Comparable and that block<T,N> is a model of LessThan Comparable if and only if T is a model of LessThan Comparable. Or, in plainer language, you can instantiate block with a type that has no `operator==` as long as you never try to compare two such blocks for equality.

The second enhancement we can make is to provide another kind of iterator. If A is a block, then the range [A.begin(),A.end()) contains all of A's elements in the order in which they appear in A. In Section 3.2, we learned about an iterator *adaptor*, `reverse_iterator` (described in full on page 363), that presents elements in the opposite order. A `reverse_iterator<Iter>` is just like an Iter except that `operator++` for a `reverse_iterator<Iter>` means the same thing as `operator--` for an Iter.

We can define two more member functions, `rbegin()` and `rend()`, that return reverse iterators. Then [A.rbegin(),A.rend()) contains all of A's elements just as [A.begin(),A.end()) does, except that [A.rbegin(),A.rend()) contains them in the opposite order. Of course, we need two different versions of `rbegin()` for the same reason that we need two different versions of `begin()`. The expression A.rbegin() must return a constant iterator if A is const, and a mutable iterator otherwise.

```
template <class T, size_t N>
struct block
{
  ...

  typedef reverse_iterator<const_iterator> const_reverse_iterator;
  typedef reverse_iterator<iterator> reverse_iterator;

  reverse_iterator rbegin() { return reverse_iterator(end()); }
  reverse_iterator rend() { return reverse_iterator(begin()); }

  const_reverse_iterator rbegin() const {
    return const_reverse_iterator(end());
  }
  const_reverse_iterator rend() const {
    return const_reverse_iterator(begin());
  }
};
```

There are also a few member functions that are convenient to have, although they are not necessary. They are `swap()`, which exchanges the contents of two blocks; `empty()`, which returns true if and only if the block contains no elements; and `max_size()`, which returns the largest possible number of elements that the block could ever contain. A block can't grow or shrink, so `max_size()` isn't very interesting. It always returns the same value as `size()`. It is really only important for variable-sized containers, and we define it in block in anticipation of that generalization:

```
template <class T, size_t N>
struct block {
  ...

  size_type max_size() const { return N; }
  bool empty() const { return N == 0; }

  void swap(block& x) {
    for (size_t n = 0; n < N; ++n)
      std::swap(data[n], x.data[n]);
  }
};
```

Finally, then, here is the full version of block; even with all of its embellishments it is still much simpler than sophisticated STL data structures like deque and map, but it is useful nonetheless. A simple class like block is often the most appropriate choice.

```
template <class T, size_t N>
struct block {
  typedef T value_type;

  typedef value_type* pointer;
  typedef const value_type* const_pointer;
  typedef value_type& reference;
  typedef const value_type& const_reference;

  typedef ptrdiff_t difference_type;
  typedef size_t size_type;

  typedef pointer iterator;
  typedef const_pointer const_iterator;

  typedef std::reverse_iterator<iterator> reverse_iterator;
  typedef std::reverse_iterator<const_iterator> const_reverse_iterator;

  iterator begin() { return data; }
  iterator end() { return data + N; }

  const_iterator begin() const { return data; }
  const_iterator end() const { return data + N; }

  reverse_iterator rbegin() { return reverse_iterator(end()); }
  reverse_iterator rend() { return reverse_iterator(begin()); }

  const_reverse_iterator rbegin() const {
    return const_reverse_iterator(end());
  }
  const_reverse_iterator rend() const {
    return const_reverse_iterator(begin());
  }
```

```
    reference operator[](size_type n) { return data[n]; }
    const_reference operator[](size_type n) const { return data[n]; }

    size_type size() const { return N; }
    size_type max_size() const { return N; }
    bool empty() const { return N == 0; }

    void swap(block& x) {
      for (size_t n = 0; n < N; ++n)
        std::swap(data[n], x.data[n]);
    }

    T data[N];
};

template <class T, size_t N>
bool operator==(const block<T,N>& x, const block<T,N>& y)
{
  for (size_t n = 0; n < N; ++n)
    if (x.data[n] != y.data[n])
      return false;
  return true;
}

template <class T, size_t N>
bool operator<(const block<T,N>& x, const block<T,N>& y)
{
  for (size_t n = 0; n < N; ++n)
    if (x.data[n] < y.data[n])
      return true;
    else if (y.data[n] < x.data[n])
      return false;
  return false;
}
```

5.2   Container Concepts

By now, the next step should be obvious. We have defined a useful class, block, and it's reasonable to imagine that block is a model of some general concept. The next step is to define that concept. Or, to put it differently, we can imagine defining other block-like classes; just how block-like should they be? When we defined block we didn't distinguish between functionality that all container classes had in common and functionality that was specific to block alone. We now have to disentangle those two categories.

A block has three main areas of functionality. It contains elements, it provides access to those elements, and it supplies the operations that are necessary for a block to be a regular type.

5.2.1 Containment of Elements

It may sound redundant to say that a container contains its elements, but that truism has profound implications. Two blocks can't overlap, and an element can't belong to more than one block. Each element is a subobject contained within the block. It is constructed when the block is constructed, and it is destroyed when the block is destroyed. The lifetime of one of a block's elements is identical to the lifetime of the block itself. You can change the value of an element, but you can't create a new one and you can't destroy an element without destroying the entire block.

A block's element is a part of the block in a very literal sense. A block is a single contiguous region of memory, and every element's address lies within that region. Containment in this literal sense is tied up with block's specific implementation details (we don't want to define containers so narrowly that we end up excluding anything that uses dynamic memory allocation), but we can abstract its most important properties:

1. Two containers can't overlap, and an element can't belong to more than one container. You can put two different copies in two different containers, of course; the restriction is on objects, not values. Ownership, however, can't be shared.

2. An element's lifetime can't extend beyond the lifetime of the container that it is a part of. An element is created no earlier than when the container is constructed, and it is destroyed no later than when the container is destroyed.

3. A container can be a *fixed size* container like block, or it can be a *variable size* container where you can create and/or destroy elements after the container is created. Even a variable size container "owns" its elements, and they are all destroyed by the container's destructor.

Another way to put it is that all containers, like C arrays and like block, have value semantics rather than pointer semantics. The elements of a container are actual objects, not just addresses. This may seem like a serious restriction, but it isn't. Pointers, after all, are objects, and like any other object, they can be stored in containers. You can, for example, have a block<char*, 10>. The block still has value semantics (each char* is a unique object that is stored in the block), but the block "owns" only the pointers themselves rather than whatever it is that they point to. We saw an example of that in Chapter 1, where we created a vector of pointers into a string table.

5.2.2 Iterators

There are three different ways to access a block's elements.

1. The block class defines the nested types iterator and const_iterator, and all of the elements in a block A are contained in the range [A.begin(),A.end()). This form is particularly useful for generic algorithms, since almost all of the STL's generic algorithms operate on ranges of iterators.

2. The nested types reverse_iterator and const_reverse_iterator are reverse iterator types that correspond to iterator and const_iterator, respectively. The range [A.rbegin(),A.rend()) contains the same elements as the range [A.begin(),A.end()) but in reverse order.

3. If n is an integer, the expression A[n] returns the nth element.

Of these three methods, the first is clearly the most fundamental. The second uses an adaptor. The nested types reverse_iterator and const_reverse_iterator are just shorthand for

    reverse_iterator<iterator>

and

    reverse_iterator<const_iterator>.

Similarly, the expression A[n] is shorthand for A.begin()[n], or, for that matter, for *(A.begin() + n).

What is really important about the way that block provides access to its elements is that it defines the iterator types iterator and const_iterator and the member functions begin() and end(). Iterators are just as fundamental to containers as they are to algorithms, and they are important as the primary interface between algorithms and containers.

All containers have iterators. Some of the properties of block's iterators are general, but some are specific to block:

- There are two different iterator types, iterator and const_iterator. The distinction between them is that a mutable block provides a range of iterators, while a const block provides a range of const_iterators. A const block is, by definition, a block whose elements cannot be modified, so a const_iterator is a constant iterator. It does not permit assignment to the value it points to. By contrast, an iterator is a mutable iterator that permits assignment to the value it points to.

  All containers, not just block, define the types iterator and const_iterator and the member functions begin() and end(). The type const_iterator is always, as its name suggests, a constant iterator, and there is always a conversion from a container's iterator to its const_iterator.

  If const_iterator is always a constant iterator it is natural to assume that iterator is always a mutable iterator, as it is in block, and that it must always be possible to modify the value that an iterator points to. That assumption would be wrong. Containers are not required to provide mutable iterators, and iterator might provide either read-write or read-only access. Sometimes, to maintain class invariants, it is necessary to restrict or prohibit write access. This isn't just a hypothetical point. The associative container set (page 461), for example, has no mutable iterators. For a set, iterator and const_iterator can be the very same type.

- The types iterator and const_iterator aren't merely iterators. They are, specifically, Random Access Iterators (which means that they are Bidirectional

Iterators and Forward Iterators as well, since Random Access Iterator is a refinement of Bidirectional Iterator and Bidirectional Iterator is a refinement of Forward Iterator).

The fact that block's iterators are Random Access Iterators is important for two reasons. First, it affects which algorithms you can apply to a block's elements: Random Access Iterators support more algorithms than other kinds of iterators do. For example, you can apply sort (page 292) to a range of Random Access Iterators but not to a range of Forward Iterators. Second, it directly affects which member functions block provides.

The reason that the range [A.begin(),A.end()) makes sense is that block's iterators are Input Iterators (support for ranges is not part of the Output Iterator requirements), and the reason that the range [A.rbegin(),A.rend()) makes sense is that block's iterators are Bidirectional Iterators. Moving backward through a range of iterators is only possible if the iterators support operator--. Finally, accessing a block's element as A[n] is just what "random access" means; this form of access makes sense because block has Random Access Iterators.

We can reasonably require that every container have an iterator type that is a model of Input Iterator, since a container that didn't provide a way to examine its elements wouldn't be very useful, but we can't reasonably require every container's iterator type to be a model of Random Access Iterator. There are simply too many useful data structures where random access is impractical.

5.2.3   The Hierarchy of Containers

Some containers, like block, can and should provide Random Access Iterators. Others, however, can only provide Bidirectional Iterators or Forward Iterators. This suggests that containers aren't a single concept but several different concepts. We can classify containers by the kind of iterator that they provide.

Every type that is a model of Container defines the nested iterator types iterator and const_iterator, both of which are models of Input Iterator. The two types may be the same. In any case, const_iterator is always a constant iterator and there is always a conversion from iterator to const_iterator. (But unless the two types are the same, there must not be a conversion in the opposite direction. A conversion from a constant iterator to a mutable iterator would be a serious violation of "const correctness.") Every Container has the member functions begin() and end(), and all of its elements are contained in the range [begin(),end()).

Every Container also has the ancillary types value_type, pointer, const_pointer, reference, const_reference, difference_type, and size_type. They are defined as a convenience, not a necessity. Except for size_type, they can all be inferred from iterator and const_iterator.

A Forward Container is a Container whose iterators are Forward Iterators, and a Reversible Container is a Forward Container whose iterators are Bidirectional Iterators. A type that is a model of Reversible Container defines two additional nested types, reverse_iterator and const_reverse_iterator, and the member functions rbegin() and rend(). Finally, a Random Access Container is a Reversible Container

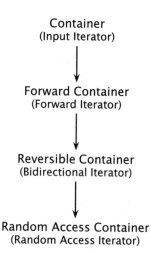

Figure 5.1: The hierarchy of container concepts. Below the name of each container concept is the type of the container's iterator.

whose iterators are Random Access Iterators. A type that is a model of Random Access Container has a member function operator[ ]. Figure 5.1 shows this hierarchy.

All of the STL's predefined container classes are models of Forward Container, and most of them are models of Bidirectional Container. Several, like block, are models of Random Access Container.

5.2.4 The Trivial Container

The block class from Section 5.1 is a very simple container, but it isn't the simplest possible STL container. The simplest possible C++ program is one that does nothing at all:

```
int main() {}
```

Similarly, the simplest possible STL container is one that doesn't actually contain anything.

Every container has member functions begin() and end() that return iterators. The range [begin(), end()) includes all of the container's elements. The "trivial container" is a container where that range is always the empty range, and where the container's size is always zero:

```
template <class T>
struct trivial_container {
  typedef T value_type;

  typedef value_type* pointer;
  typedef const value_type* const_pointer;
  typedef value_type& reference;
  typedef const value_type& const_reference;

  typedef value_type* iterator;
  typedef const value_type* const_iterator;
```

```
    typedef ptrdiff_t difference_type;
    typedef size_t size_type;

    const_iterator begin() const { return 0; }
    const_iterator end() const { return 0; }

    iterator begin() { return 0; }
    iterator end() { return 0; }

    size_type size() const { return 0; }
    bool empty() const { return true; }
    size_type max_size() const { return 0; }

    void swap(trivial_container&) {}
};
```

The trivial container is a curiosity, and it illustrates exactly how much (and how little!) you have to do to satisfy the Container requirements, but it also has two real uses:

- It satisfies all of the Container requirements, so you can use it as a test case for generic algorithms whose arguments are containers.

- As you can see from trivial_container's class definition, an STL container involves extensive "boilerplate." It's easy to forget some detail. When you write a new STL container, you may find it easier to use trivial_container as a starting point than to start with a blank screen.

5.3   Variable Size Container Concepts

The block class is a fixed-size container. The number of elements in a block is a constant that is set when you write your program. This is neither an advantage nor a disadvantage; it's just a fact. Fixed-size containers are sometimes appropriate and sometimes inappropriate. You can't always know how many elements a container will eventually have until after you've started to fill it.

The Container concept (along with Forward Container, Reversible Container, and Random Access Container) allows for the possibility of both fixed-size and variable size containers, but it can't provide any mechanism for adding elements to or deleting them from a container. (If it did provide such a mechanism, then fixed-size containers like block couldn't be models of Container.) What this means, of course, is that variable size containers must be models of some other concept that is a refinement of Container.

The STL defines two different kinds of variable size containers: Sequence[4] and

---

4. The name Sequence is sometimes a source of confusion. The ordinary meaning of the word *sequence*, in computer science and elsewhere, is just a collection of things in some definite order. The STL, however, uses this general-sounding term as the name of a very specific concept. Throughout this book, Sequence, when written as a concept, always has the specific technical meaning rather than the more general meaning.

Associative Container. As with the Container concept itself, each of these concepts is the root of its own conceptual hierarchy.

5.3.1 Sequences

Sequence, a refinement of Forward Container, is the most obvious kind of variable size container. Like all containers, a Sequence presents its elements as a range in strict linear order. Additionally, just as you can refer to any of the elements, you can also add or delete an element at any point in that range. That is, a Sequence doesn't arrange its own elements in a prescribed order. Instead, it gives you the tools so that you can arrange its elements in whatever order you need.

The member functions insert and erase are really all there is to Sequences. If S is a sequence, and p is an iterator that points to some element of S, then S.erase(p) removes that element from S and destroys it. Similarly, S.insert(p, x) creates a new object, a copy of x, and inserts it into S immediately *before* the element that p points to. (Why before p, instead of after? Again, it is because ranges of iterators are asymmetrical. There is a past-the-end element but no before-the-beginning element. You can insert a new element at the very beginning by inserting it before S.begin(), and you can insert a new iterator at the very end by inserting it before S.end(). There's no way you could do that, though, if S.insert(p, x) inserted x after p instead of before.)

Despite the simplicity of these two member functions, they raise two important questions:

- When you insert or erase elements, what happens to the Sequence's other elements? We should expect that their values won't be disturbed, of course. If we start with the values $(1, 2, 3)$ and then insert 7 before the second element, the result had better be $(1, 7, 2, 3)$. Otherwise, the operation would hardly deserve the name insert. But the values are not the only issue.

  An element of a Container isn't just a value: it is an object that exists at a particular location in memory. Although inserting or erasing an element doesn't change any of the other values in the Sequence, it may affect which iterator points to which object.

  One way to make this question concrete is to ask what happens to iterators that point into a Sequence when we insert or erase elements. Suppose, for example, that S is a Sequence and p1 and p2 are iterators that point to two different elements of S. Now suppose we insert a new element before p1, or erase the element that p1 points to. What happens to p2? Does it still point to the same element that it did before? For that matter, does it point to anything at all, or might it be that whatever it once pointed to has now vanished out from under it?

- What is the complexity of insert and erase? Are they simple and fast operations, or are they potentially expensive? Suppose, for example, that you insert or erase an element somewhere in the middle of a thousand-element Sequence. What should you expect about how much time this will take? Should you expect it to be a thousand times slower if it's a million-element Sequence instead?

Both questions have the same answer: It depends. The answers to those questions distinguish one Sequence from another. The STL contains three Sequence classes, vector, list, and deque, and the main differences between them are the kind of iterators they provide, the semantics of iterator invalidation, and the complexity of insert and erase.

The vector class, for example, has Random Access Iterators and stores its elements in a single contiguous region of memory. It is similar to block, except that its size can vary. If you insert a new element in the middle of a vector, then you have to shift the other elements toward the end to make room. This means that it is potentially a slow operation (it is linear in the number of elements from the insertion point to the end) and that it invalidates other iterators that point into the vector. By contrast, list is a node-based container whose iterators are Bidirectional Iterators. Inserting a new element into a list doesn't involve shifting any existing elements, and it doesn't invalidate any iterators.

Other Forms of insert and erase

For a Sequence, insert and erase are overloaded member functions. In addition to the single-element version, a Sequence has other versions that insert or erase an entire range at once. If you do have to insert or erase an entire range, it's usually faster to use one of the multiple-element versions than to call the single-element version multiple times. (At any rate, it's never any slower.) So, for example, if V is a vector and L is a list, you can insert all of L's elements at the beginning of V by writing:

    V.insert(V.begin(), L.begin(), L.end());

Sequences have constructors that are analogous to the multiple-element versions of insert.

Insertion at the Front and Back

Many programs don't have to insert or erase elements at arbitrary positions within a Sequence but only at the very beginning or the very end. (Consider, for example, reading elements into a buffer.) Insertion at the beginning or the end is an important special case.

It's also a special case because it's often much faster to insert an element at the beginning or the end than at some arbitrary position. Inserting an element at the beginning of a vector, for example, is $\mathcal{O}(N)$, where N is the vector's size, but inserting an element at the end is a fast operation. This leads to two more concepts, both refinements of Sequence. A Back Insertion Sequence, like vector, is a Sequence where it is possible to insert or erase an element at the back in amortized constant time. Similarly, a Front Insertion Sequence is a Sequence where it is possible to insert or erase an element at the front in amortized constant time.

Front Insertion Sequences have three special member functions: front, which returns the first element in the container, push_front, which inserts an element at the beginning, and pop_front, which erases the first element. Back Insertion Sequences have the three counterparts back, push_back, and pop_back.

Insertion versus Overwrite Semantics

When you're first learning how to use the STL, one of the most common mistakes is to write something like this:

```
int A[5] = {1, 2, 3, 4, 5};
vector<int> V;
copy(A, A + 5, V.begin());
```

This fragment looks very natural—we're copying five elements into a vector—but it is completely wrong. If you try to do this, your program will crash.

Once you think about it, it's easy to see what the problem is. The copy algorithm copies elements from one range to another. In this case, it copies elements from the range [A, A + 5) to the range [V.begin(), V.begin() + 5). This means it performs the assignment *(V.begin()) = A[0], then the assignment *(V.begin() + 1) = A[1], and so on. But that can't possibly work! The vector V is empty, so the elements we're trying to assign to don't exist.

A slightly different way to look at the problem is that copy has no way of inserting new elements into V because copy never sees V as a whole; it only sees iterators. That is, copying into a range of V's iterators has "overwrite" semantics. It assigns new values to V's existing elements, rather than inserting new elements. To insert a new element into V, you need to call one of V's member functions.

There is actually a way that you can use copy to insert new elements into a Sequence: you can use the insert_iterator adaptor (page 351), or one of the related adaptors front_insert_iterator or back_insert_iterator. An insert_iterator is constructed from a particular Sequence. It is an Output Iterator, and assigning a value through an insert_iterator is equivalent to inserting that value into the base Sequence.

These adaptors allow you to have iterators that provide insert rather than overwrite semantics. Here is the correct way to use copy to insert values into a vector:

```
int A[5] = {1, 2, 3, 4, 5};
vector<int> V;
copy(A, A + 5, back_inserter(V));
```

5.3.2 Associative Containers

A Sequence does not impose a particular ordering: When you insert an element into a Sequence, you can insert it at any position. There's another kind of variable size container, one that guarantees that the elements are always ordered according to its own special rule. With this type of container you don't insert an element at a particular position—you just insert it, and the container places it in whatever position is appropriate.

What reason might there be for having a container that arranges its ordering itself? The most obvious reason is so that you can look up an element faster. If you are looking for a particular element in an ordered range of N elements, then the best you can do is to use linear search: find or find_if. Finding that element is $O(N)$. On average, you have to examine half of the elements in the range before you find the one you're looking for. But if the elements are organized into a data structure that was designed to facilitate efficient searching, you can reduce the complexity from $O(N)$ to $O(\log N)$ or better. If, for example, the elements are always sorted in ascending order, you can use binary search (lower_bound) instead of linear search.

An Associative Container is a variable size container that supports efficient retrieval of elements (values) based on *keys*. Every element in an Associative Container has a key associated with it, and an Associative Container, given a key, has a fast way of finding the element that has that key.

The basic operations on an Associative Container are lookup, insertion, and erasure. You can do all of those things with a Sequence. What distinguishes an Associative Container is first, that it has member functions that explicitly support those operations, and second, that all of those operations are efficient: $O(\log N)$ on average.

Associative Containers are more complicated than Sequences. There are several different ways in which Associative Container classes differ from each other.

- Every element in an Associative Container has a key, and elements are looked up by their keys. Like all containers, an Associative Container has a *value type*. Additionally, it has one more associated type: its *key type*. Every value of type value_type is associated with some value of type key_type.

  There are many ways that values can be associated with keys. The value type could, for example, be a record that has several fields, and the key could be one of those fields. The STL defines two Associative Container concepts that represent two of those ways. A Simple Associative Container is an Associative Container where value_type and key_type are the same type; an element's key is the element itself. A Pair Associative Container is an Associative Container where value_type is of the form pair<const Key, T>; a value in a Pair Associative Container is a pair, and its key is the pair's first field.

  Why pair<const Key, T> instead of just pair<Key, T>? It's for the same reason that you can't insert a new element into an Associative Container at an arbitrary position. An element's position within an Associative Container is determined by its key, so changing the element's key would make the Associative Container inconsistent. In a Pair Associative Container, where an element's key is its first field, that first field must be immutable. In a Simple Associative Container, where an element's key is the element itself, no element's value may ever be changed. Elements may be inserted and erased but not modified in place. A Simple Associative Container provides constant iterators only, not mutable iterators.

- What happens when you insert an element into an Associative Container, but the container already contains another element with the same key? Can an Associative Container ever contain two different elements with the same key?

  A Multiple Associative Container can, but a Unique Associative Container cannot. When you insert an element into a Multiple Associative Container, it is inserted unconditionally. The container doesn't check to see whether there's already an element with the same key. When you insert an element into a Unique Associative Container, the insertion has no effect if the container already has an element with the same key.

- In every Associative Container, the elements are organized by key. Again, there are at least two different refinements of Associative Container that represent two possible ways of organizing the elements. A Hashed Associative Container is an Associative Container where the elements are organized as a hash table. One of its nested types is a function object that is used as a hash function. Similarly, a Sorted Associative Container is an Associative Container whose elements are always sorted in ascending order by key. It also has a nested function object type, a Binary Predicate that is used to determine whether one key is less than another.

These three distinctions are orthogonal. The STL container class set, for example, is a model of Sorted Associative Container, Unique Associative Container, and Simple Associative Container. That is, the elements in a set form a range that is always sorted in ascending order, an element's key is just the element, and no two elements of a set are equal to each other. Similarly, the container class multimap is a model of Sorted Associative Container, Multiple Associative Container, and Pair Associative Container.

An Associative Container, like a Sequence, must define the member functions insert and erase. Also, as with a Sequence, it is possible to insert elements into or erase them from an Associative Container either one at a time or as an entire range. The only real difference is that for a Sequence the member function insert takes an argument that specifies where the element (or range) is inserted, and for an Associative Container it does not. To insert a single element into an Associative Container C you write:

```
C.insert(x);
```

To insert a range you write:

```
C.insert(f, l);
```

As a simple example, suppose that L is a list<int>. You can insert all of L's elements into a set with a single operation by writing:

```
set<int> S;
S.insert(L.begin(), L.end());
```

The set S will contain all of L's elements, but sorted in ascending order and with all of the duplicates removed.

Associative Containers also have member functions to search for elements by key. For example, the expression

```
C.find(k)
```

returns an iterator that points to an element whose key is k (or it returns C.end() if no such element exists), and the expression

```
C.count(k)
```

returns the number of elements whose keys are k. For a Unique Associative Container, the return value is always either zero or one.

5.3.3 Allocators

Many containers—not all, as the example of block shows, but many—use dynamic memory allocation. A list, for example, is a linked list of nodes, and each node is allocated from the free store.

It is occasionally useful to be able to control how a container's memory is allocated. You might, for example, want to choose between a thread-safe allocation scheme and a faster scheme that is only safe in a single-threaded program. Or, instead, you might want to use some preallocated memory pool rather than the ordinary free store.

This is one example of a general problem, that of allowing clients to control some aspect of a class's behavior, and we have already seen the solution: We can encapsulate that behavior as a template parameter. This is similar to the way that algorithms like find_if and sort and container classes like set use function objects.

In this case we can't use a function object, because memory allocation involves several different operations. At a minimum it involves an allocation and a deallocation function, and the two must always be consistent. (You can't allocate memory with new and deallocate it with free.) But the idea is the same: A container's memory management strategy is defined by a template parameter, and that parameter, an Allocator (page 166), is used for all low-level memory allocation and deallocation.

Allocators are not part of the Container requirements (or those of Sequence or Associative Container). All of the predefined STL container classes, however, do allow allocators to be specified as template parameters.

Most of the time, you shouldn't have to think about allocators at all. The predefined containers are parameterized by allocators, but there is a default template parameter. There is rarely any reason to use a nondefault allocator.

5.4 Summary

As Figure 5.2 shows, the full hierarchy of container concepts is quite complicated. You might justifiably wonder whether this complexity is really necessary, whether there's really anything to be gained by defining this conceptual hierarchy and by defining container classes as models of these concepts.

Defining this hierarchy gives us two things. First, it enables a taxonomy of containers. It makes it easy to understand, for example, why the interfaces for vector and list are very similar and also why they can't quite be identical. Second, it allows you to write generic algorithms that operate directly on containers themselves.

5.4.1 Which Container Should You Use?

Because all STL containers are models of a single concept, they provide very similar functionality. You may find that several different container classes seem like reasonable choices. You may even find that you can change which container class your program uses just by changing a single line in your program. (A typedef, for example.)

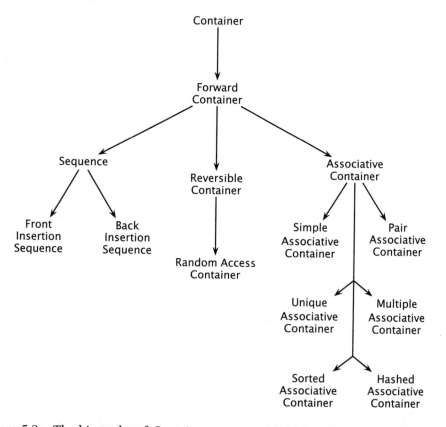

Figure 5.2: The hierarchy of Container concepts, including Sequence and Associative Container concepts.

As a general rule, it's usually best to use the simplest possible container class. If you don't expect insertions into the middle of the container to be frequent, then vector will probably be the most efficient choice. (Or, if you never expect to change the size of the container—if the size is known at compile time—then you could go one step farther and use a block.) If, however, you do expect to be performing insertions frequently, you should use a container like list or slist that is specifically designed for insertion into the middle.

5.4.2 Defining Your Own Container

Sometimes the STL's predefined container classes aren't enough, and you have to write your own. As we saw with block, a container doesn't have to be fancy. The Container concept imposes relatively few requirements. However, the variable size container classes, Sequence and Associative Container, are somewhat more complicated. If you are planning to write a new Sequence or Associative Container you should make sure you understand the specific requirements outlined in Chapter 9.

Part II

Reference Manual:
STL Concepts

Chapter 6

Basic Concepts

The concepts in this chapter are very general. They are applicable to any generic library, not just to the STL. Most of the built-in C++ types and many of the types defined by the STL are models of every one of these concepts.

A *regular type* is defined as a type that is a model of Assignable, Default Constructible, and Equality Comparable. A user-defined type should be regular unless there is a good reason for it not to be a model of one of those concepts.

6.1 Assignable

A type is Assignable if it is possible to copy objects of that type and to assign values to variables of that type.

A copy of an object must be *equivalent* to the original. It must have the same value. You might think this means that equality is a postcondition of assignment. That's almost true, but not quite. The problem is that a type that is a model of Assignable isn't necessarily also a model of Equality Comparable; there isn't necessarily any operator== at all.

If a type is a model of both Assignable and Equality Comparable, then a copy of x should indeed compare equal to x.

Refinement Of

This concept is not a refinement of any other STL concepts.

Notation

X	A type that is a model of Assignable.
x, y	An object of type X.

Valid Expressions

- **Copy constructor**
  X(x)

  Return type: X
  Postcondition: X(x) is a copy of x.

- **Copy constructor**
  X x(y);
  X x = y

  Postcondition: x is a copy of y.

- **Assignment**
  x = y

  Return type: X&
  Postcondition: x is a copy of y.

Models

Almost all of the built-in C++ types are models of Assignable, with the notable exception of const T. For example, int is a model of Assignable (it's possible to copy and assign values of type int), but const int is not. If x is declared to be of type const int, then x = 7 is illegal. You can copy a variable of type const int, but you can't assign to it.

Similarly, the type pair<const int, int> is not Assignable.

6.2 Default Constructible

A type is Default Constructible if it has a default constructor, that is, if it is possible to construct an object of that type without initializing the object to any particular value.

Refinement Of

This concept is not a refinement of any other STL concepts.

Notation

X   A type that is a model of Default Constructible.

x, y   An object of type X.

Valid Expressions

- **Default constructor**
  X()

  Return type: X

- **Default constructor**
  X x;

Note that the form
    X x = X();
is not necessarily a valid expression, since it uses a copy constructor. This form is valid for all regular types, since a regular type is a model of both Default Constructible and Assignable, but it is not valid for a type that is a model of Default Constructible alone.

Models

Almost all of the built-in C++ types are models of Default Constructible. You can, for example, declare a variable of type int without initializing it. Many STL classes, such as vector<int>, are also Default Constructible.

6.3   Equality Comparable

A type is Equality Comparable if objects of that type can be compared for equality using operator== and if operator== is an *equivalence relation*. Equivalence relations are defined below. They are a formalization of the ordinary intuitive properties of equality.

Refinement Of

This concept is not a refinement of any other STL concepts.

Notation

X	A type that is a model of Equality Comparable.
x, y, z	An object of type X.

Valid Expressions

- **Equality**
  x == y

  Return type: Convertible to bool.
  Precondition: x and y are in the domain of operator==. (*Domain* is used here in the ordinary mathematical sense of the word.)

- **Inequality**

  x != y

Return type:	Convertible to bool.
Precondition:	x and y are in the domain of operator==.
Semantics:	Equivalent to !(x == y).

Invariants

Expressions involving Equality Comparable values must satisfy the following invariants, which define an equivalence relation:

- **Identity**

  &x == &y implies x == y.

- **Reflexivity**

  x == x.

- **Symmetry**

  x == y implies y == x.

- **Transitivity**

  x == y and y == z implies x == z.

Equivalence relations are a fundamental concept in mathematics. An equivalence relation is any relation that satisfies the invariants of reflexivity, symmetry, and transitivity.

Models

All of the built-in numeric and pointer types in C++ are models of Equality Comparable. So are many STL types, such as vector<int>. In general, vector<T> is Equality Comparable if and only if T is Equality Comparable.

6.4 Ordering

6.4.1 LessThan Comparable

A type is LessThan Comparable if it is ordered. It must be possible to compare two objects of that type using operator<, and operator< must define a consistent ordering.

Technically, operator< must induce a partial ordering (defined below), but this is not a stringent requirement. A refinement of LessThan Comparable, Strict Weakly Comparable, imposes a stronger requirement on the ordering induced by operator<.

Refinement Of

This concept is not a refinement of any other STL concepts.

Notation

X   A type that is a model of LessThan Comparable.

x, y, z   An object of type X.

Valid Expressions

- **Less**
  x < y

  Return type: Convertible to bool.
  Precondition: x and y are in the domain of operator<. (*Domain* is used here in the ordinary mathematical sense of the word.)

- **Greater**
  x > y

  Return type: Convertible to bool.
  Precondition: x and y are in the domain of operator<.
  Semantics: Equivalent to y < x.

- **Less or equal**
  x <= y

  Return type: Convertible to bool.
  Precondition: x and y are in the domain of operator<.
  Semantics: Equivalent to !(y < x).

- **Greater or equal**
  x >= y

  Return type: Convertible to bool.
  Precondition: x and y are in the domain of operator<.
  Semantics: Equivalent to !(x < y).

Of these four operators, only one is truly fundamental. The others are merely convenient abbreviations. We may choose to regard any one of them as fundamental; the choice is arbitrary. Here, we have chosen to define the other three operators in terms of operator<.

Invariants

Expressions involving LessThan Comparable values must satisfy the following invariants.

- **Irreflexivity**
  x < x must be false.

- **Antisymmetry**
  x < y implies !(y < x).

- **Transitivity**

  x < y and y < z implies x < z.

These invariants are the definition of a *partial ordering*, a relation that is irreflexive and transitive. (Antisymmetry is a theorem, not an axiom. It follows from irreflexivity and transitivity.)

Models

The built-in numeric types in C++ are models of LessThan Comparable. So are the pointer types, even though comparing two arbitrary pointers is not necessarily valid. That's why we require x and y to be in the domain of operator<. In the case of pointers, x and y are in the domain of operator< if they point into the same array.

6.4.2 Strict Weakly Comparable

A type is a model of Strict Weakly Comparable if it is a model of LessThan Comparable and if operator< satisfies not only the requirements of a partial ordering but also the more stringent requirements of a *strict weak ordering*.

   The formal definition of a strict weak ordering is given below. Essentially, a strict weak ordering is one where, if two elements have the property that neither one is less than the other, it makes sense to regard them as in some sense equivalent to each other.

   The definition of a strict weak ordering may seem abstract and complicated, and you may wonder why we bother to define it at all. Strict Weakly Comparable is an important concept for two reasons. First, algorithms that involve some sort of ordering relation (sorting algorithms, for example) do rely on the properties of a strict weak ordering. LessThan Comparable simply doesn't provide strong enough guarantees to allow a sorting algorithm to work correctly. Second, any reasonable ordering relation that you can think of is probably a strict weak ordering anyway.

Refinement Of

LessThan Comparable (page 86)

Notation

  X   A type that is a model of Strict Weakly Comparable.

  x, y, z An object of type X.

Definitions

Two objects x and y are *equivalent* if x < y and y < x are both false. (Note that, because of irreflexivity, any object x is always equivalent to itself. Note also that, if x is equivalent to y, y is equivalent to x.)

   A *total ordering* is an ordering relation with the property that for any two objects x and y, either x < y, or y < x, or else x == y.

Valid Expressions

None, except for those defined in the LessThan Comparable requirements.

Invariants

In addition to the invariants defined in the LessThan Comparable requirements, the following invariant must be satisfied:

- **Transitivity of equivalence**
  If x is equivalent to y, and y is equivalent to z, then x is equivalent to z. Or, to write it out in full,

  ```
  !(x < y) && !(y < x) && !(y < z) && !(z < y)
  ```
  implies that
  ```
  !(x < z) && !(z < x)
  ```

Mathematically, what this means is that "equivalence" deserves its name. It is an equivalence relation. A strict weak ordering divides values into a collection of *equivalence classes*, where all of the values in an equivalence class are equivalent to each other.

A total ordering is a special kind of strict weak ordering. Specifically, it is a strict weak ordering with the special property that each equivalence class contains only a single value.

Models

The built-in numeric types in C++ are all models of Strict Weakly Comparable. Indeed, operator< on integers is a total ordering, not just a strict weak ordering.

Strict weak orderings that are not total orderings are very common—much more common than you might think from the formal definition. Any comparison that looks only at a part of the objects that are being compared is likely to be a strict weak ordering. Case-insensitive string comparison, for example, is a strict weak ordering. Similarly, if a class has two fields first_name and last_name and its operator< looks only at last_name, then it is a model of Strict Weakly Comparable. Whenever two values x and y have the same last name but not the same first name, they are equivalent (x < y and y < x are both false) but not identical.

Chapter 7

Iterators

Iterators are central to the STL. They are a generalization of pointers in that they are objects that point to other objects, and, as the name suggests, they make it possible to iterate through a range of objects.

Iterators are important because they make it possible to decouple containers from the algorithms that operate on them. Most STL algorithms don't operate directly on containers themselves but on ranges of iterators. Since all STL containers have iterators, a single algorithm may apply to many different container types. A container need only provide a way to access its elements using iterators.

The Trivial Iterator concept is an abstraction that represents the notion of an object that points to some other object. The other five concepts in this chapter represent objects that point to other objects and that are also able to iterate through ranges of objects. The main difference between these five concepts is that they support different forms of iteration.

7.1 Trivial Iterator

A Trivial Iterator is an object that may be dereferenced to refer to some other object. Arithmetic operations, such as increment and comparison, are not necessarily supported. A Trivial Iterator is "trivial" because it is an iterator that doesn't iterate!

Refinement Of

Assignable (page 83), Equality Comparable (page 85).

Associated Types

- **Value type**
  The type of the value obtained by dereferencing a Trivial Iterator.

Notation

X	A type that is a model of Trivial Iterator.
T	X's value type.
x, y	Object of type X.
t	Object of type T.

Definitions

- A type that is a model of Trivial Iterator may be *mutable*, meaning that the values referred to by objects of that type may be modified, or *constant*, meaning that they may not. For example, int* is a mutable iterator type, and const int* is a constant iterator type. If an iterator type is mutable its value type is a model of Assignable, but the converse is not necessarily true.

- A Trivial Iterator may have a *singular* value, meaning that the results of most operations, including comparison for equality, are undefined. The only operation that is guaranteed to be supported is assigning a nonsingular iterator to a singular iterator.

- A Trivial Iterator may have a *dereferenceable* value, meaning that dereferencing it yields a well-defined value. Dereferenceable iterators are always nonsingular, but the converse is not true. For example, a past-the-end pointer, the pointer immediately beyond the end of an array, is nonsingular (it is associated with a particular array, and there are well-defined operations on it) even though it is not dereferenceable.

- Invalidating a dereferenceable iterator means performing an operation after which the iterator might be nondereferenceable or singular. For example, if p is a pointer, then delete p invalidates p.

Valid Expressions

In addition to the expressions defined in Assignable and Equality Comparable, the following expressions must be valid:

- **Dereference**

  *x

Precondition:	x is dereferenceable.
Return type:	Convertible to T.[1]

---

1. The requirement for the return type of *x is specified as "convertible to T," rather than simply T, because, in fact, the return type of *x is usually not T but actually a reference or const reference to T. It sometimes even makes sense for an iterator to return some sort of proxy object, rather than the object that the iterator conceptually points to. Proxy objects are implementation details rather than part of an interface, so they do not appear in the Trivial Iterator requirements.

- **Dereference Assignment**
  `*x = t`

  Type requirements: X is a mutable iterator type.
  Precondition: x is dereferenceable.
  Postcondition: *x is a copy of t.

- **Member Access**
  `x->m`

  Type requirements: T is a type for which t.m is defined.
  Precondition: x is dereferenceable.
  Semantics: Equivalent to (*x).m.

The original HP STL did not define operator-> for iterators. The C++ standard does define that operator, but not all STL implementations provide it yet. It depends on features that were added to the C++ language relatively recently and that have not yet been implemented in all C++ compilers. In the meantime, the workaround is just to write (*x).m instead of x->m. The -> operator provides no additional functionality; it is purely an abbreviation.

Complexity Guarantees

The complexity of all of the operations in the Trivial Iterator requirements must be amortized constant time.

Invariants

Expressions involving Trivial Iterator values must satisfy the following invariant, which defines iterator equality:

- **Identity**
  `x == y` if and only if `&*x == &*y`.

Models

The C language actually has Trivial Iterators, although they are not distinguished by the C type system. A pointer to an object that is not part of an array is a Trivial Iterator, because a C pointer may be incremented only if it points into an array. A pointer to an object that is part of an array, however, is a Random Access Iterator (page 103).

All of the iterator types defined in the STL have increment operations—that is, all of the STL's iterator types are models of other iterator concepts as well as Trivial Iterator.

7.2   Input Iterator

An Input Iterator is an iterator that may be dereferenced to refer to some object and that may be incremented to obtain the next iterator in a sequence.

Input Iterators are not required to be mutable, nor are they required to support the ordinary dereference semantics that allows multipass algorithms. It is not guaranteed, for example, that it is possible to pass through the same Input Iterator i twice.

Refinement Of

Trivial Iterator (page 91).

Associated Types

- **Value type**
  typename iterator_traits<X>::value_type
  The type of the value obtained by dereferencing an Input Iterator.

- **Difference type**
  typename iterator_traits<X>::difference_type
  A signed integral type used to represent the distance from one iterator to another or the number of elements in a range.

- **Reference type**
  typename iterator_traits<X>::reference
  Reference to the iterator's value type. It is a mutable reference if the iterator is mutable, and a const reference if the iterator is constant. (If the value type is T, then the reference type is usually T& or const T&.)

- **Pointer type**
  typename iterator_traits<X>::pointer
  Pointer to the iterator's value type. It is a mutable pointer if the iterator is mutable, and a const pointer if the iterator is constant. (If the value type is T, then the pointer type is usually T* or const T*.)

- **Iterator category**
  typename iterator_traits<X>::iterator_category
  One of the iterator tag types: input_iterator_tag, forward_iterator_tag, bidirectional_iterator_tag, or random_access_iterator_tag. An iterator's category is the tag type corresponding to the *most specific* concept that the iterator is a model of. For example, int* is a model of Random Access Iterator. It is also a model of Bidirectional Iterator, Forward Iterator, and so on. Its category is random_access_iterator_tag because Random Access Iterator is the most specific concept that int* is a model of. (Random Access Iterator is a refinement of all of the other iterator concepts.)

Notation

X	A type that is a model of Input Iterator.
T	X's value type.
i, j	Object of type X.
t	Object of type T.

Definitions

- An iterator is *past-the-end* if it points beyond the last element of a container. Past-the-end values are nonsingular and nondereferenceable.

- An iterator is *valid* if it is dereferenceable or past-the-end.

- An iterator i is incrementable if there is a "next" iterator; that is, if ++i is well-defined. Past-the-end iterators are not incrementable.

- An Input Iterator j is *reachable* from an Input Iterator i if, after applying operator++ to i a finite number of times, i == j.[2]

- The notation [i, j) refers to a range of iterators beginning with i and up to but not including j.

- The range [i, j) is a *valid range* if both i and j are valid iterators, and if j is reachable from i. Every iterator in a valid range [i, j) is dereferenceable, and j is either dereferenceable or past-the-end. The fact that every iterator in the range is dereferenceable follows from the fact that incrementable iterators must be dereferenceable.

Valid Expressions

In addition to the expressions defined by Trivial Iterator, the following expressions must be valid:

- **Dereference**
  `*i`

Return type:	Convertible to T.
Semantics:	Returns the element that i points to.
Precondition:	i is incrementable.

- **Preincrement**
  `++i`

Return type:	X&
Precondition:	i is dereferenceable.

---

2. For Input Iterators, i == j does not necessarily imply that ++i == ++j. The Forward Iterator concept removes this restriction.

Postcondition: i is dereferenceable or past the end. After executing ++i,
                      it is not required that copies of the old value of i be deref-
                      erenceable or that they be in the domain of operator==.
                      A type that is a model of Input Iterator need not support
                      more than one active iterator on a single range at once.

- **Postincrement**
  (void) i++

  Precondition: i is dereferenceable.
  Semantics: Equivalent to (void) ++i.
  Postcondition: i is dereferenceable or past the end.

- **Postincrement and dereference**
  *i++

  Return type: T
  Precondition: i is dereferenceable.
  Semantics: Equivalent to:
                      ```
                      T t = *i;
                      ++i;
                      return t;
                      ```
  Postcondition: i is dereferenceable or past the end.

Complexity Guarantees

All operations are amortized constant time.

Models

Almost all of the STL's iterator types are models of Input Iterator, and so are pointers.
A type like deque<int>::iterator, though, is a model of other iterator concepts as
well as Input Iterator.

An example of an iterator type that is a model of Input Iterator and not a model of
any other iterator concept is istream_iterator (page 354). This type really does have
the strange and restrictive semantics that the Input Iterator requirements permit.

7.3   Output Iterator

An Output Iterator is a type that provides a mechanism for storing, but not necessarily accessing, a sequence of values. Output Iterators are in some sense the converse
of Input Iterators, but they have a far more restrictive interface. They do not necessarily support member access or equality, and they do not necessarily have either an
associated difference type or value type.

Additionally, Output Iterators have the same kind of restrictions that Input Iterators do. They do not support multipass algorithms, and it is not guaranteed that it
is possible to pass through the same Output Iterator twice.

Intuitively, you can picture an Output Iterator as a tape: You can write a value to the current location and you can advance to the next location, but you cannot read values and you cannot back up or rewind.

Refinement Of

Assignable (page 83).

Note that Output Iterator is not a refinement of Equality Comparable (page 85): an Output Iterator need not define an operator==. Note also that Output Iterator, unlike all of the other iterator concepts, is not a refinement of Trivial Iterator.

Associated Types

- **Iterator category**
  typename iterator_traits<X>::iterator_category
  One of the iterator tag types: output_iterator_tag, forward_iterator_tag, bidirectional_iterator_tag, or random_access_iterator_tag. See the Input Iterator requirements (page 94) for more details.

Note that Output Iterator does not have many of the associated types that other iterator concepts do. In particular, it does not define an associated value type. Other iterator types, including Trivial Iterator and Input Iterator, define the notion of a value type, the type returned when an iterator is dereferenced. This notion does not apply to Output Iterators since, for Output Iterators, the dereference operator (unary operator*) does not return a usable value. The dereference operator may be used only in the context of assignment, as in *x = t.

Although Input Iterators and Output Iterators are roughly symmetrical concepts, there is an important asymmetry between the operations of accessing and storing values. For an Input Iterator operator* must return some unique type, but, for an Output Iterator, in the expression *x = t, there is no reason why operator= need accept a unique type. Consequently, an Output Iterator need not have any specific "value type."

Notation

X   A type that is a model of Output Iterator.

x, y   Object of type X.

Definitions

- If x is an Output Iterator of type X, then the expression *x = t stores the value t into x. Note that operator=, like other C++ functions, may be overloaded. It may, in fact, even be a function template. In general, then, t may be any of several different types. A type T belongs to the set of value types of X if, for an object t of type T, *x = t is well-defined and does not require any nontrivial conversions to be performed on t.

- An Output Iterator may be *singular*, meaning that the results of most operations, including copying and dereference assignment, are undefined. The only operation on singular iterators that is necessarily supported is assigning a nonsingular iterator to a singular iterator.

- An Output Iterator may be *dereferenceable*, meaning that assignment through it is defined. Dereferenceable iterators are always nonsingular, but nonsingular iterators are not necessarily dereferenceable.

Valid Expressions

In addition to the expressions defined in Assignable, the following expressions must be valid.

- **Copy constructor**
  X y(x);
  X y = x

Precondition:	x is nonsingular.
Postcondition:	The expression *y = t has the same behavior as the expression *x = t. (Note that there should be only one active copy of a particular Output Iterator at any one time. That is, after creating and using a copy y of an Output Iterator x, the original iterator x should no longer be used.)

- **Assignment operator**
  y = x

Return type:	X&
Precondition:	x is nonsingular.
Postcondition:	The expression *y = t has the same behavior as the expression *x = t.

- **Dereference assignment**
  *x = t

Type requirements:	t is convertible to a type in X's set of value types.
Return type:	Result is not used.
Precondition:	x is dereferenceable. If there has been a previous assignment through x, then there has been an intervening increment. (Assignment through an Output Iterator x is expected to alternate with incrementing x, and there must be an assignment through x before x is ever incremented. Any other order of operations results in undefined behavior. For example, *x = t; ++x; *x = t2; ++x is an acceptable sequence of operations, but *x = t; ++x; ++x; *x = t2; is not.)

- **Preincrement**

  ++x

Return type:	X&
Precondition:	x is dereferenceable. There has been a previous assignment through x. If x has previously been incremented, then there has been an intervening assignment through x.
Postcondition:	x points to the next location into which a value may be stored.

- **Postincrement**

  (void) x++

Return type:	void
Precondition:	x is dereferenceable. There has been a previous assignment through x. If x has previously been incremented, then there has been an intervening assignment through x.
Semantics:	Equivalent to (void) ++x.
Postcondition:	x points to the next location into which a value may be stored.

- **Postincrement and assign**

  *x++ = t

Type requirements:	t is convertible to a type in X's set of value types.
Return type:	Result is not used.
Precondition:	x is dereferenceable. If there has been a previous assignment through x, then there has been an intervening increment.
Semantics:	Equivalent to:

  ```
  *x = t;
  ++x;
  ```

Postcondition:	x points to the next location into which a value may be stored.

Note that the expression *x = t is required to be defined, but that the expression *x, by itself, doesn't necessarily have any useful value. That is, an Output Iterator doesn't necessarily point to anything; it is nothing but a handle that can be used for assignment.

If you are implementing an Output Iterator class X, one sensible way to implement the expression *x = t is to define X::operator* so that it returns an object of some private class X_proxy and to define the member function X_proxy::operator= appropriately. Note that you may overload X_proxy::operator= or define it as a member template. Doing so allows assignment of more than one type through an Output Iterator of class X.

Complexity Guarantees

All operations are amortized constant time.

Models

The following types are example of Output Iterators:

- `front_insert_iterator` (page 345)
- `back_insert_iterator` (page 348)
- `insert_iterator` (page 351)
- `ostream_iterator` (page 357)

7.4   Forward Iterator

A Forward Iterator is an iterator that corresponds to the usual intuitive notion of a linear sequence of values. It is possible to use Forward Iterators (unlike Input Iterators and Output Iterators) in multipass algorithms. Forward Iterators do not, however, allow stepping backward through a range but only, as the name suggests, forward.

A type that is a model of Forward Iterator may be either *mutable* or *constant*, as defined in the Trivial Iterator requirements (page 91).

Refinement Of

Default Constructible (page 84), Input Iterator (page 94), Output Iterator (page 96).

Associated Types

The same as for Input Iterator.

Notation

X	A type that is a model of Forward Iterator.
T	X's value type.
i, j	Object of type X.
t	Object of type T.

Valid Expressions

Forward Iterator does not define any new expressions beyond those defined in Input Iterator and Default Constructible. However, some of the restrictions described in Input Iterator are relaxed. In particular, incrementing a Forward Iterator does not invalidate copies of the old value, and it is guaranteed, if i and j are dereferenceable and i == j, that ++i == ++j. Consequently, it is possible to pass through the same Forward Iterator twice.

- **Default constructor**

  X x;

  X()

  Postcondition: x may be singular.

- **Preincrement**

  ++i

  Return type: X&

  Precondition: i is dereferenceable.

  Semantics: i is modified to point to the next value.

  Postcondition: i is dereferenceable or past the end. &i == &++i. If i == j, then ++i == ++j.

- **Postincrement**

  i++

  Return type: X

  Precondition: i is dereferenceable.

  Semantics: Equivalent to

  ```
  X tmp = i;
  ++i;
  return tmp;
  ```

  Postcondition: i is dereferenceable or past the end.

- **Dereference**

  *i

  Return type: If X is a mutable iterator type, then the return type is a modifiable lvalue. If X is a constant iterator type, then the return type is an rvalue or a const lvalue. (The return type is X's reference type, usually T& or const T&.)

  Semantics: Returns the element that i points to.

  Precondition: i is incrementable.

Complexity Guarantees

The complexity of operations on Forward Iterators is guaranteed to be amortized constant time.

Models

The following types are examples of Forward Iterators:

- slist<int>::iterator
- slist<double>::const_iterator

- `hash_set<string>::iterator`
- `char*` (also a model of Bidirectional Iterator and of Random Access Iterator)

7.5   Bidirectional Iterator

A Bidirectional Iterator is an iterator that can be both incremented and decremented. The requirement that a Bidirectional Iterator can be decremented is the only thing that distinguishes Bidirectional Iterators from Forward Iterators.

Refinement Of

Forward Iterator (page 100).

Associated Types

The same as for Forward Iterator.

Notation

X	A type that is a model of Bidirectional Iterator.
T	X's value type.
i, j	Object of type X.
t	Object of type T.

Valid Expressions

In addition to the expressions defined in Forward Iterator, the following expressions must be valid:

- **Predecrement**
  `--i`

Return type:	X&
Precondition:	i is dereferenceable or past the end. There exists a dereferenceable iterator j such that i == ++j.
Semantics:	i is modified to point to the previous value.
Postcondition:	i is dereferenceable. &i == &--i. If i == j, then --i == --j. If j is dereferenceable and i == ++j, then --i == j.

- **Postdecrement**
  `i--`

Return type:	X
Precondition:	i is dereferenceable or past the end. There exists a dereferenceable iterator j such that i == ++j.

Semantics: Equivalent to:

```
X tmp = i;
--i;
return tmp;
```

Complexity Guarantees

The complexity of operations on Bidirectional Iterators is guaranteed to be amortized constant time.

Invariants

Expressions involving Bidirectional Iterator values must satisfy the following invariant:

- **Symmetry of increment and decrement**
  If i is dereferenceable, then
      ++i; --i;
  is a null operation. Similarly, if --i is well-defined, then
      --i; ++i;
  is a null operation.

Models

The following types are examples of Bidirectional Iterators:

- list<int>::iterator
- set<string>::iterator
- char* (also a model of Random Access Iterator)

7.6 Random Access Iterator

A Random Access Iterator is an iterator that provides both increment and decrement (just like a Bidirectional Iterator) and that also provides constant-time methods for moving forward and backward in arbitrary-sized steps and for comparing two iterators.

Random Access Iterators provide all of the operations of familiar C pointer arithmetic.

Refinement Of

Bidirectional Iterator (page 102), Strict Weakly Comparable (page 88).

Associated Types

The same as for Bidirectional Iterator.

Notation

X	A type that is a model of Random Access Iterator.
T	X's value type.
D	X's difference type.
i, j	Object of type X.
t	Object of type T.
n	Object of type D.

Valid Expressions

In addition to the expressions defined in Bidirectional Iterator, the following expressions must be valid:

- **Iterator addition**
  i += n

Return type:	X&
Precondition:	Including i itself, there must be n dereferenceable or past-the-end iterators following i (if n is positive), or -n preceding i (if n is negative).
Semantics:	If n > 0, equivalent to executing ++i n times. If n < 0, equivalent to executing --i |n| times. If n == 0, i += n is a null operation. (Note that "equivalent to" merely means that i += n yields the same iterator as if i had been incremented (decremented) n times. It does not mean that this is how operator+= should be implemented; in fact, that wouldn't even be a permissible implementation. It is guaranteed that i += n is amortized constant time, regardless of the magnitude of n.)
Postcondition:	i is dereferenceable or past the end.

- **Iterator addition**
  i + n
  n + i

Return type:	X
Precondition:	Same as for i += n.

Semantics:	Equivalent to:
	    `X tmp = i;`
	    `return tmp += n;`
	The two forms i + n and n + i are identical.

Postcondition:	The result is dereferenceable or past the end.

- **Iterator subtraction**
  i -= n

Return type: X&

Precondition: Including i itself, there must be n dereferenceable or past-the-end iterators preceding i (if n is positive), or −n following i (if n is negative).

Semantics: Equivalent to i += (-n).

Postcondition: i is dereferenceable or past the end.

- **Iterator subtraction**
  i − n

Return type: X

Precondition: Same as for i -= n.

Semantics: Equivalent to:
```
X tmp = i;
return tmp -= n;
```

Postcondition: The result is dereferenceable or past the end.

- **Difference**
  i − j

Return type: D

Precondition: Either i is reachable from j, or j is reachable from i, or both.

Semantics: Returns a number n such that i == j + n.

- **Less**
  i < j

Return type: Convertible to bool.

Precondition: Either i is reachable from j, or j is reachable from i, or both. (It is instructive to compare this to the precondition given in Strict Weakly Comparable, that i and j are in the domain of operator<. Essentially, then, this is a definition of that domain. It is the set of pairs of iterators such that one iterator is reachable from the other. This corresponds closely to the ordinary C rule that two pointers may be compared only if they point into the same array.)

Semantics: As described in Strict Weakly Comparable. All of the other comparison operators (>, <=, and >=) are defined in terms of operator<, so they, too, have the semantics described in Strict Weakly Comparable.

- **Element access**
  i[n]

Return type: Convertible to T.

Precondition: i + n exists, and is dereferenceable.

Semantics: Equivalent to $*(\texttt{i} + \texttt{n})$.[3]

- **Element assignment**
  i[n] = t

  Type requirements: X is a mutable iterator type.
  Return type: Convertible to T.
  Precondition: i + n exists, and is dereferenceable.
  Semantics: Equivalent to $*(\texttt{i} + \texttt{n}) = \texttt{t}$.
  Postcondition: i[n] is a copy of t.

Complexity Guarantees

All operations on Random Access Iterators are amortized constant time. This complexity guarantee is the only reason Random Access Iterator exists as a distinct concept. Every operation in iterator arithmetic can be defined for Bidirectional Iterators— which is exactly what the algorithms distance (page 181) and advance (page 183) do. The distinction is simply that the Bidirectional Iterator implementations are linear time, while Random Access Iterators are required to support random access to elements in amortized constant time. This has major implications for the kind of algorithms that can sensibly be written using the two types of iterators.

Invariants

Expressions involving Random Access Iterator values must satisfy the following invariants:

- **Symmetry of addition and subtraction**
  If i + n is well-defined, then
      i += n; i -= n;
  and
  (i + n) − n
  are null operations. Similarly, if i − n is well-defined, then
      i -= n; i += n;
  and
  (i − n) + n
  are null operations.

- **Relation between addition and distance**
  If i − j is well-defined, then i == j + (i − j).

- **Distance and reachability**
  If i is reachable from j, then i − j ≥ 0.

---

3. The C language has a minor syntactic oddity: If p is a pointer, then p[n] and n[p] are equivalent. This equivalence is not guaranteed, however, for general Random Access Iterators. Only i[n] need be supported. That isn't an important restriction since the equivalence of p[n] and n[p] has no use outside of obfuscated C contests.

Models

Any pointer type models Random Access Iterator. Pointers are the most important models of Random Access Iterator. Additionally, the following types are also models of Random Access Iterator:

- vector<int>::iterator
- vector<int>::const_iterator
- deque<int>::iterator
- deque<int>::const_iterator

Chapter 8

Function Objects

A *function object*, or *functor* (the terms are synonymous), is any object that can be called using ordinary function call syntax. A function pointer is a function object, and so is an object of any class that has an `operator()` member function. By contrast, a pointer to a nonstatic member function is not a function object.

The basic function object concepts are Generator, Unary Function, and Binary Function: these describe objects that can be called as `f()`, `f(x)`, and `f(x,y)`, respectively. (This list could, of course, be extended to ternary functions and beyond, but in practice no STL algorithms require function objects of more than two arguments.) All other function object concepts defined by the STL are refinements of these three.

Function objects that return `bool` are an important special case. A Unary Function whose return type is `bool` is called a Predicate, and a Binary Function whose return type is `bool` is called a Binary Predicate.

There is an important but somewhat subtle distinction between function objects and *adaptable function objects*. In general, a function object has restrictions on the type of its argument. The type restrictions need not be simple. For example, `operator()` may be overloaded, a member template, or both. There doesn't have to be a way for a program to determine what those restrictions are.

An adaptable function object does specify what the argument and return types are, and it contains nested type declarations so that those types can be named and used in programs. If a type F0 is a model of Adaptable Generator, it must define the nested type `F0::result_type`. Similarly, if F1 is a model of Adaptable Unary Function, it must define the nested types `F1::argument_type` and `F1::result_type`; and if F2 is a model of Adaptable Binary Function, it must define the nested types `F2::first_argument_type`, `F2::second_argument_type`, and `F2::result_type`.

Adaptable function objects are called "adaptable" because they can be used by function object *adaptors*, function objects that transform or manipulate other function objects. The STL defines many different function object adaptors, including `unary_negate`, `unary_compose`, and `bind1st` and `bind2nd`.

8.1   Basic Function Objects

8.1.1   Generator

A function object is an object that is called as if it were an ordinary C++ function, and a Generator is a function object that is called with no arguments.

Refinement Of

Assignable (page 83).

Associated Types

- **Result type**
  The type returned when the Generator is called.

Notation

F	A type that is a model of Generator.
Result	F's result type.
f	Object of type F.

Definitions

- The *range* of a Generator is the set of all possible values that it may return.

Valid Expressions

- **Function call**
  f()

Return type:	Result
Semantics:	Returns some value of type Result. Note that two different invocations of f may return different results. A Generator may refer to local state, perform I/O, and so on. The expression f() is even permitted to change f's state—that is, operator() is not necessarily a const member function. For example, f might represent a pseudo-random number generator.
Postcondition:	The return value is in f's range.

Models

Any function that returns a value and that takes no arguments behaves as a Generator. For example, a function pointer of type

    int (*)()

is a model of Generator.

8.1.2 Unary Function

A function object is an object that is called as if it were an ordinary C++ function, and a Unary Function is a function object that is called with a single argument.

Refinement Of

Assignable (page 83).

Associated Types

- **Argument type**
  The type of the Unary Function's argument.

- **Result type**
  The type returned when the Unary Function is called.

Notation

F	A type that is a model of Unary Function.
X	F's argument type.
Result	F's result type.
f	Object of type F.
x	Object of type X.

Definitions

- The *domain* of a Unary Function is the set of all permissible values for its argument.

- The *range* of a Unary Function is the set of all possible values that it may return.

Valid Expressions

- **Function call**
  f(x)

Return type:	Result
Precondition:	x is in f's domain.
Semantics:	Calls f with x as an argument, and returns a value of type Result. Note that two different invocations of f may return different results, even if f is called with the same argument both times. A Unary Function may refer to local state, perform I/O, and so on. The expression f(x) is even permitted to change f's state—that is, operator() is not necessarily a const member function.
Postcondition:	The return value is in f's range.

Models

Any function that takes a single argument and returns a value behaves as a Unary Function. For example, a function pointer of type

```
double (*)(double)
```

is a model of Unary Function.

A more interesting example is the subtractive_rng class (page 402). An object of type subtractive_rng has local state, and two successive calls to a subtractive_rng usually do not return the same result.

8.1.3 Binary Function

A function object is an object that is called as if it were an ordinary C++ function, and a Binary Function is a function object that is called with two arguments.

Refinement Of

Assignable (page 83).

Associated Types

- **First argument type**
  The type of the Binary Function's first argument.

- **Second argument type**
  The type of the Binary Function's second argument.

- **Result type**
  The type returned when the Binary Function is called.

Notation

F	A type that is a model of Binary Function.
X	F's first argument type.
Y	F's second argument type.
Result	F's result type.
f	Object of type F.
x	Object of type X.
y	Object of type Y.

Definitions

- The domain of a Binary Function is the set of all ordered pairs (x, y) that are permissible values for its arguments.

- The range of a Binary Function is the set of all possible values that it may return.

Valid Expressions

- **Function call**
  f(x,y)

Return type:	Result
Precondition:	The ordered pair (x, y) is in f's domain.
Semantics:	Calls f with x and y as arguments, and returns a value of type Result. Note that two different invocations of f may return different results, even if f is called with the same argument both times. A Binary Function may refer to local state, perform I/O, and so on. The expression f(x, y) is even permitted to change f's state—that is, operator() is not necessarily a const member function.
Postcondition:	The return value is in f's range.

Models

Any function that takes two arguments and returns a value behaves as a Binary Function. For example, a function pointer of type

    double (*)(double, double)

is a model of Binary Function.

8.2 Adaptable Function Objects

8.2.1 Adaptable Generator

An Adaptable Generator is a Generator with a nested typedef that defines its result type. This nested typedef makes it possible to use function object adaptors, and it is the only difference between an Adaptable Generator and any other Generator. For example, a function pointer T (*f)() is a model of Generator but not of Adaptable Generator: The expression f::result_type makes no sense if f is a function pointer.

Refinement Of

Generator (page 110).

Associated Types

- **Result type**
  F::result_type
  The type returned when the Adaptable Generator is called.

Notation

F	A type that is a model of Adaptable Generator

Valid Expressions

None except for those defined by Generator.

Models

The STL does not include any types that are models of Adaptable Generator. Here is an example of a user-defined Adaptable Generator:

```
struct counter
{
  typedef int result_type;

  counter(result_type init = 0) : n(init) {}
  result_type operator()() { return n++; }

  result_type n;
};
```

8.2.2 Adaptable Unary Function

An Adaptable Unary Function is a Unary Function with nested typedefs that define its argument type and result type. These nested typedefs make it possible to use function object adaptors, such as unary_negate and unary_compose, and they are the only difference between an Adaptable Unary Function and any other Unary Function. For example, a function pointer T (*f)(X) is a Unary Function but not an Adaptable Unary Function. The expressions f::argument_type and f::result_type make no sense if f is a function pointer.

When you define a class that is a model of Adaptable Unary Function, you must define these nested types. The easiest way to do that is to derive the class from the base class unary_function. This is an empty class, with no member functions or member variables, only type declarations. The only reason it exists is to make defining Adaptable Unary Functions more convenient. The unary_function class is very similar to the base class iterator.

Refinement Of

Unary Function (page 111).

Associated Types

- **Argument type**
  F::argument_type
  The type of F's argument.

- **Result type**
  F::result_type
  The type returned when the Adaptable Unary Function is called.

Notation

F   A type that is a model of Adaptable Unary Function.

Valid Expressions

None except for those defined by Unary Function.

Models

The following types are examples of Adaptable Unary Functions:

- negate
- identity
- pointer_to_unary_function

The pointer_to_unary_function adaptor is particularly interesting because it allows a function pointer to be used as an Adaptable Unary Function. A function pointer Result (*f)(Arg) is not an Adaptable Unary Function, but ptr_fun(f) is.

8.2.3 Adaptable Binary Function

An Adaptable Binary Function is a Binary Function with nested typedefs that define its argument types and result type. These nested typedefs make it possible to use function object adaptors, such as binder1st and binder2nd, and they are the only difference between an Adaptable Binary Function and any other Binary Function. For example, a function pointer T (*f)(X,Y) is a Binary Function but not an Adaptable Binary Function.

When you define a class that is a model of Adaptable Binary Function, you must provide these typedefs. The easiest way to do that is to derive the class from the base class binary_function. This is an empty class with no member functions or member variables, only type declarations. The only reason it exists is to make defining Adaptable Binary Functions more convenient. The binary_function class is very similar to the base class iterator.

Refinement Of

Binary Function (page 112).

Associated Types

- **First argument type**
  F::first_argument_type
  The type of F's first argument.

- **Second argument type**
  F::second_argument_type
  The type of F's second argument.

- **Result type**
  F::result_type
  The type returned when the Adaptable Binary Function is called.

Notation

F   A type that is a model of Adaptable Binary Function.

Valid Expressions

None except for those defined by Binary Function.

Models

The STL includes many predefined Adaptable Binary Functions, mainly to represent arithmetic or logical operations. The following types are examples of Adaptable Binary Functions:

- plus
- multiplies
- less
- equal_to
- pointer_to_binary_function

8.3   Predicates

8.3.1   Predicate

A Predicate is a Unary Function whose result represents the truth or falsehood of some condition. One example of a Predicate is a function that takes an argument of type int and returns true if the argument is positive.

Refinement Of

Unary Function (page 111).

Associated Types

Predicate has the same associated types as Unary Function, but with one additional restriction: A Predicate's result type must be convertible to bool.

Notation

F   A type that is a model of Predicate.

X   F's argument type.

f   Object of type F.

x   Object of type X.

Valid Expressions

- **Function call**
  f(x)

Return type:	Convertible to bool.
Precondition:	x is in f's domain.
Semantics:	Returns true if the condition that f represents is satisfied, and false if it is not.
Postcondition:	The return value is either true or false.

Models

A function that takes a single argument and returns true or false, such as one of the character classification functions in the standard C library, is a Predicate. For example, the function pointer type

    bool (*)(char)

is a model of Predicate.

8.3.2 Binary Predicate

A Binary Predicate is a Binary Function whose result represents the truth or falsehood of some condition. One example of a Binary Predicate is a function that takes two arguments and tests whether they are equal.

Binary Predicates are important because many different STL algorithms parameterize some aspect of their behavior as Binary Predicates. Such algorithms include, for example, search_n (page 211) and mismatch (page 222).

Refinement Of

Binary Function (page 112).

Associated Types

Binary Predicate has the same associated types as Binary Function, but with one additional restriction: A Binary Predicate's result type must be convertible to bool.

Notation

F	A type that is a model of Binary Predicate.
X	F's first argument type.
Y	F's second argument type.
f	Object of type F.
x	Object of type X.
y	Object of type Y.

Valid Expressions

- **Function call**
  f(x,y)

Return type:	Convertible to bool.
Precondition:	The ordered pair (x, y) is in f's domain.
Semantics:	Returns true if the condition that f represents is satisfied, and false if it is not.
Postcondition:	The return value is either true or false.

Models

The following types are examples of Binary Predicate. The first is a function pointer type, and the other two are function object classes defined by the STL:

- bool (*)(int, int)
- equal_to<string>
- less_equal<double>

8.3.3   Adaptable Predicate

An Adaptable Predicate is a Predicate that is also an Adaptable Unary Function. That is, it is a Unary Function whose return type is convertible to bool and that contains nested typedefs defining its argument type and return type.

Refinement Of

Predicate (page 116), Adaptable Unary Function (page 114).

Associated Types

None except for those associated with Predicate and Adaptable Unary Function. An Adaptable Predicate must have a nested type result_type, and that result type must be convertible to bool.

Valid Expressions

None except for those defined by the Predicate and Adaptable Unary Function requirements.

Models

The following STL function object classes are examples of Adaptable Predicate:

- logical_not<bool>
- binder1st<equal_to<int> >

A function pointer is not a model of Adaptable Predicate. Function pointers aren't classes, so they can't have nested types.

8.3.4 Adaptable Binary Predicate

An Adaptable Binary Predicate is a Binary Predicate that is also an Adaptable Binary Function. That is, it is a Binary Function whose return type is convertible to bool and that includes nested typedefs defining its argument type and return type.

Refinement Of

Binary Predicate (page 117), Adaptable Binary Function (page 115).

Associated Types

None except for those associated with Binary Predicate and Adaptable Binary Function. An Adaptable Binary Predicate must have a nested type result_type, and that result type must be convertible to bool.

Valid Expressions

None except for those defined by the Binary Predicate and Adaptable Binary Function requirements.

Models

The STL defines many classes that are models of Adaptable Binary Predicate; these classes represent tests of some kind of relation between two values. The following are a few of the STL's Adaptable Binary Predicate classes:

- less<T>
- greater<T>
- equal_to<T>
- logical_and<T>

8.3.5 Strict Weak Ordering

A Strict Weak Ordering is a Binary Predicate that compares two objects, returning true if the first precedes the second. This predicate must satisfy the standard mathematical definition of a *strict weak ordering*. The precise requirements are stated below, but roughly what they mean is that a Strict Weak Ordering has to satisfy the same properties that an ordinary ordering relation like "less than" does. For example, if *a* is less than *b*, then *b* is not less than *a*.

The concept Strict Weak Ordering and the concept Strict Weakly Comparable both deal with strict weak orderings, but in slightly different forms. One is a set of requirements on the ordering defined by operator< (the requirements are on the type that is being used as operator<'s arguments), and the other is a set of requirements on the ordering defined by a function object.

The two concepts are complementary because algorithms that use ordering relations often come in pairs, where one version compares values using operator< and the other uses a user-supplied function object. In such cases, the first version uses the Strict Weakly Comparable concept, and the second uses Strict Weak Ordering.

Refinement Of

Binary Predicate (page 117).

Associated Types

Strict Weak Ordering has the same associated types as Binary Predicate with one additional restriction: The first argument type and second argument type must be the same type.

Notation

F	A type that is a model of Strict Weak Ordering.
X	The type of F's arguments.
f	Object of type F.
x, y, z	Objects of type X.

Definitions

- Two objects x and y are *equivalent* if both f(x, y) and f(y, x) are false. Note that an object is always (by the irreflexivity invariant, stated below) equivalent to itself.

Valid Expressions

- **Function call**
  f(x,y)

Return type:	Convertible to bool.
Precondition:	The ordered pair (x, y) is in f's domain.
Semantics:	Returns true if x precedes y, and false otherwise.
Postcondition:	The return value is either true or false.

Invariants

Expressions involving Strict Weak Ordering values must satisfy the following invariants.

- **Irreflexivity**
  f(x, x) must be false.

- **Antisymmetry**
  f(x, y) implies !f(y, x).

- **Transitivity**
  f(x, y) and f(y, z) implies f(x, z).

- **Transitivity of equivalence**
  Equivalence (as defined above) is transitive. If x is equivalent to y and y is equivalent to z, then x is equivalent to z. This means that equivalence does in fact satisfy the mathematical definition of an equivalence relation.

The first three axioms, irreflexivity, antisymmetry, and transitivity, are the definition of a partial ordering. Transitivity of equivalence is required by the definition of a strict weak ordering. A total ordering is one that satisfies an even stronger condition: Equivalence the same as equality.

The definition of a total ordering is very simple, but despite that simplicity, no STL algorithms use total orderings. The total ordering requirements would be unnecessarily strong and unduly restrictive. Strict weak orderings that aren't total orderings are quite ordinary. One of the most familiar is case-insensitive string comparison.

Models

The following types are examples of Strict Weak Ordering:

- less<int>
- greater<int>
- less<string>
- greater<string>

This is general. The function objects less and greater are the link between the two concepts Strict Weak Ordering and Strict Weakly Comparable. The classes less<T> and greater<T> are models of Strict Weak Ordering if and only if T is a model of Strict Weakly Comparable.

Note that less_equal<T> and greater_equal<T> are *not* models of Strict Weak Ordering. A strict weak ordering is an ordering that behaves like "less than," not like "less than or equal to." A Strict Weak Ordering f must satisfy the property that f(x, x) is false.

8.4   Specialized Concepts

8.4.1   Random Number Generator

A Random Number Generator is a function object that can be used to generate a random sequence of integers. That is, if f is a Random Number Generator and N is a positive integer, then f(N) returns an integer less than N and greater than or equal to 0. If f is called many times with the same value of N, it yields a sequence of numbers that is uniformly distributed in the range [0,N).[1]

Random number generators are a very subtle subject. A good random number generator must satisfy many statistical properties beyond uniform distribution. See Section 3.4 of Knuth [Knu98a] for a discussion of what it means for a sequence to be random, and Section 3.2 for several algorithms that may be used to write random number generators.

Refinement Of

Unary Function (page 111).

Associated Types

- **Argument type**
  The type of the Random Number Generator's argument. It must be an integral type.

- **Result type**
  The type returned when the Random Number Generator is called. It must be the same as the argument type.

Notation

F	A type that is a model of Random Number Generator.
Integer	F's argument type.
f	Object of type F.
N	Value of type Integer.

Definitions

- The *domain* of a Random Number Generator (the set of permissible values for its argument) is the set of numbers that are greater than zero and less than some maximum value.

- The *range* of a Random Number Generator is the set of nonnegative integers that are less than the Random Number Generator's argument.

---

1. Uniform distribution means that all of the numbers in the range [0,N) appear with equal frequency. The probability for obtaining any particular value is $1/N$.

Invariants

Expressions involving Random Number Generator values must satisfy the following invariant:

- **Uniformity**
  In the limit as f is called many times with the same argument N, every integer in the range $[0, N)$ will appear an equal number of times.

8.4.2 Hash Function

A Hash Function is a Unary Function that is used by Hashed Associative Containers (page 161). It takes a single argument, and maps that argument to a result of type size_t. A Hash Function must be deterministic, meaning that the return value must depend only on the argument and that equal arguments must yield equal results.

The performance of a Hashed Associative Container depends crucially on its hash function. It is important for a Hash Function to minimize collisions, where a collision is defined as two different arguments that hash to the same value. It is also important for the distribution of hash values to be uniform. The probability that a Hash Function returns any particular value of type size_t should be roughly the same as the probability that it returns any other value. Finally, it is important for the Hash Function to be fast. There is naturally some tension among these three goals.

The goals of uniformity and minimization of collisions make sense only in the context of a specific distribution of input values. To take a simple example, suppose that the values being hashed are the six strings "aardvark", "trombone", "history", "diamond", "forthright", and "reasonable". In this case, one reasonable (and fast) hash function would be the first character of each string. On the other hand, suppose that the values are instead "aaa1001", "aaa1010", "aaa0011", "aaa1100", "aaa0101", and "aaa0110". In this case, a different hash function would be more appropriate. That's why Hashed Associative Containers are parameterized by the hash function: No one hash function is best for every application.

Note also that a Hash Function does not know the number of "buckets" that the Hashed Associative Container will eventually use. A Hash Function is responsible only for mapping its argument to a number—possibly a very large number. It is the Hashed Associative Container's responsibility to turn that large number into the address of a particular bucket.

Refinement Of

Unary Function (page 111).

Associated Types

None beyond those defined in Unary Function. However, there is one additional restriction: The result type must be size_t.

Invariants

In addition to the invariants defined in the Unary Function requirements, the following invariant must be satisfied:

- **Deterministic function**
  The return value depends only on the argument, as opposed to the past history of the Hash Function object. For any particular Hash Function object, the return value is always the same whenever the argument is the same.

Models

The only Hash Function that is predefined by the STL is the class hash (page 400).

Chapter 9

Containers

Containers are objects that contain and manage other objects and provide iterators that allow the contained objects (*elements*) to be addressed.

The STL's container concepts fall into three broad categories. First, there is the very general Container concept itself and three other slightly less general concepts, which classify containers by the type of iterators that they provide. All STL containers are models of Container. Second is the Sequence concept, which describes dynamically sized containers where elements can be inserted or removed at any position. Third, the Associative Container concept describes containers that are specially optimized for looking up elements by value.

Finally, some containers are parameterized by their memory allocation scheme, and many of these containers use the Allocator concept. Allocator is not a refinement of Container, but it is included in this chapter because of its close connection with containers.

9.1 General Container Concepts

9.1.1 Container

A Container is an object that stores other objects (its elements) and that has methods for accessing its elements. In particular, every type that is a model of Container has an associated iterator type that can be used to iterate through the Container's elements. All of the elements in a Container are accessible through a range of iterators.

Container concepts can be classified by their associated iterator types. Container itself, the most general container concept, requires only that the associated iterator type be a model of Input Iterator. Accordingly, you shouldn't assume anything more about a Container's iterators than you would about any other Input Iterators.

There is no guarantee that the elements of a Container are stored in any definite order. In fact, the order might be different upon each iteration through the Container. Nor is there a guarantee that more than one iterator into a Container may be active at any one time. (Other container concepts, such as Forward Container (page 131), provide stronger guarantees.)

A Container "owns" its elements: the lifetime of an element stored in a container cannot exceed that of the Container itself. This may seem like a severe restriction, but it isn't. If you need more relaxed ownership semantics, all you have to do is use a container of pointers. Pointers, after all, are objects, and, like any other objects, you can put them in a Container. The Container still owns its elements—the pointers themselves—but not the things that they point to.

Refinement Of

Assignable (page 83).

Associated Types

- **Value type**

  X::value_type

  The type of the object stored in a Container. The value type must be Assignable, but it need not be Default Constructible.

- **Reference type**

  X::reference

  A type that behaves as a reference to the Container's value type. The reference type is usually just value_type&. ("Smart references," user-defined reference types that provide some sort of extra functionality, are usually not a viable option. It is impossible for a user-defined type to have the same semantics as C++ references. The C++ language does not support redefining operator., the member access operator.)

- **Const reference type**

  X::const_reference

  A type that behaves as a const reference to the Container's value type. Usually, it is const value_type&.

- **Pointer type**

  X::pointer

  A type that behaves as a pointer to the Container's value type. The pointer type is usually value_type*. (The pointer type is required to have the same semantics as an ordinary C++ pointer, but it need not actually be a pointer. "Smart pointers," unlike smart references, are possible. The C++ language does permit user-defined types to define operator* and operator->, the dereference operator and the pointer member access operator.)

- **Const pointer type**

  X::const_pointer

  A type that behaves as a const pointer to the Container's value type. Usually, it is const value_type*.

- **Iterator type**
  X::iterator
  An iterator that points to the Container's elements. The iterator's value type is expected to be the Container's value type, and its reference and pointer types are the Container's reference and pointer types. The iterator type must be a model of Input Iterator (page 94).

  Note that the iterator type need only be an Input Iterator, which provides a very weak set of guarantees. In particular, all algorithms on Input Iterators must be "single pass." The Forward Container concept provides the stronger guarantee that the iterator type is a model of Forward Iterator.

- **Constant iterator type**
  X::const_iterator
  A constant iterator that points to the Container's elements. The constant iterator's value type is expected to be the Container's value type, and its reference and pointer types are the Container's const reference and const pointer types. Like the iterator type, the constant iterator type must also be a model of Input Iterator. The iterator type and constant iterator type must have the same difference type and the same iterator category, and a conversion from the iterator type to the constant iterator type must exist.

  Note that a Container's iterator type and constant iterator type may be the same. There is no requirement that every Container type have an associated mutable iterator type. The set and hash_set classes, for example, do not provide mutable iterators.

  If iterator and const_iterator are the same type, it follows that reference and const_reference—and, similarly, pointer and const_pointer—must also be the same types.

- **Difference type**
  X::difference_type
  A signed integral type used to represent the distance between two of the Container's iterators. This type must be the same as the iterators' difference type.

- **Size type**
  X::size_type
  An unsigned integral type that can represent any nonnegative value of the Container's difference type.

Notation

X	A type that is a model of Container.
a, b	Object of type X.
T	X's value type.

Definitions

- The *size* of a Container is the number of elements it contains. A Container's size is a nonnegative number.

- The *area* of a Container is the total number of bytes that it occupies. More specifically, it is the sum of the elements' areas plus whatever overhead is associated with the Container itself. If a Container's value type T is a simple type (as opposed to a container type), then the Container's area is bounded above by a constant times the container's size times sizeof(T). That is, if a is a container with a simple value type, then a's area is $O(\text{a.size()})$.

- A *variable-sized* container is one that provides methods for inserting and/or removing elements. Its size may vary during the container's lifetime. A *fixed-size* container is one where the size is constant throughout the container's lifetime. The size of some fixed-size container types is determined at compile time.

Valid Expressions

In addition to the expressions defined in Assignable, the following expressions must be valid.

- **Copy constructor**
  X(a)

Return type:	X
Postcondition:	X().size() == a.size(). X() contains a copy of each of a's elements.

- **Copy constructor**
  X b(a);

Postcondition:	b.size() == a.size(). b contains a copy of each of a's elements.

- **Assignment operator**
  b = a

Type requirements:	b is mutable.
Return type:	X&
Postcondition:	b.size() == a.size(). b contains a copy of each of a's elements.

- **Destructor**
  a.~X()

Semantics:	Each of a's elements has its destructor called, and memory allocated for them, if any, is deallocated.

- **Beginning of range**
  a.begin()

Return type:	iterator if a is mutable, otherwise const_iterator.
Semantics:	Returns an iterator pointing to the first element in the container.
Postcondition:	a.begin() is either dereferenceable or past the end. It is past the end if and only if a.size() == 0.

- **End of range**
  a.end()

Return type:	iterator if a is mutable, otherwise const_iterator.
Semantics:	Returns an iterator pointing one past the last element in the container.
Postcondition:	a.end() is past the end. The two iterators a.begin() and a.end() are equal if and only if a.size() == 0.

- **Size**
  a.size()

Return type:	size_type
Semantics:	Returns the size of the container a, that is, the number of elements it contains.
Postcondition:	$0 \leq$ a.size() $\leq$ a.max_size().

- **Maximum size**
  a.max_size()

Return type:	size_type
Semantics:	Returns an upper bound on the container's size. Note that max_size returns an upper bound, but not necessarily a strict upper bound. That is, there is no guarantee that you can actually create a container of type X whose size is a.max_size(), only that you cannot create a container whose size is greater than max_size().
	For a fixed-size container, a.size() and a.max_size() are equal.
Postcondition:	$0 \leq$ a.size() $\leq$ a.max_size().

- **Empty**
  a.empty()

Return type:	Convertible to bool.
Semantics:	Equivalent to a.size() == 0. (But possibly faster. One reason this member function exists is that a.size() need only be $\mathcal{O}(N)$, while empty is guaranteed to be $\mathcal{O}(1)$.)

- **Swap**
  a.swap(b)

Type requirements: Both a and b are mutable.

Return type: void

Semantics: Equivalent to:
                            `X tmp = a;`
                            `a = b;`
                            `b = tmp;`
(But almost always faster. If a and b each have N elements, swapping the two containers using `operator=` requires $3N$ assignments. Usually, however, it is possible to implement a Container's swap member function so that `a.swap(b)` is $\mathcal{O}(1)$ rather than $\mathcal{O}(N)$.)

Complexity Guarantees

- The copy constructor, the assignment operator, and the destructor are linear in the container's size.

- `begin()` and `end()` are amortized constant time.

- `size()` is linear in the container's size. (For many containers, such as `vector` and `deque`, `size()` is $\mathcal{O}(1)$. This satisfies the requirement that it be $\mathcal{O}(N)$.)

- `max_size()` and `empty()` are amortized constant time.

- `swap()` is linear in the container's size. (For most containers, however, it is amortized constant time. It should be defined to be $\mathcal{O}(1)$ unless there is a strong reason why that would be impossible.)

Invariants

Expressions involving Container values must satisfy the following invariants:

- **Valid range**
  For any Container a, [`a.begin()`, `a.end()`) is a valid range. (Note, though, that it is only required to be a range of Input Iterators, and that the order of elements within that range is unspecified. The Forward Container concept provides Forward Iterators, and introduces additional ordering guarantees.)

- **Range size**
  `a.size() == distance(a.begin(), a.end())`.

- **Completeness**
  An algorithm that iterates through the range [`a.begin()`, `a.end()`) will pass through each element of a exactly once.

Models

Every STL container class is a model of Container. These classes include `vector`, `slist`, and `map`.

All of the STL's container classes are, in fact, also models of Forward Container. The STL does not define any classes that are models of Container alone. One example of a class that is a model of Container but not Forward Container would be a self-adjusting array, or in Knuth's terminology [Knu98b], a "self-organizing file": a class that automatically moves frequently requested elements toward the front.

9.1.2 Forward Container

A Forward Container is a Container whose elements are arranged in a definite order. The ordering will not change spontaneously from iteration to iteration. The guarantee of a definite ordering allows the definition of element-by-element equality (if the container's element type is Equality Comparable) and of lexicographical ordering (if the container's element type is LessThan Comparable).

Iterators into a Forward Container satisfy the Forward Iterator requirements. Consequently, Forward Containers support multipass algorithms and allow multiple iterators into the same container to be active at the same time.

Refinement Of

Container (page 125), Equality Comparable (page 85), LessThan Comparable (page 86).

Associated Types

No additional types beyond those defined in Container, but the requirements for the iterator type are strengthened. The iterator type must be a model of Forward Iterator (page 100).

Notation

X	A type that is a model of Forward Container.
a, b	Object of type X.
T	X's value type.

Valid Expressions

In addition to the expressions defined in Container, the following expressions must be valid:

- **Equality**
  a == b

  Type requirements: T is Equality Comparable.
  Return type: Convertible to bool.
  Semantics: Returns true if a.size() == b.size() and if each element of a compares equal to the corresponding element of b. Otherwise, returns false.

- **Inequality**
  ```
  a != b
  ```

  Type requirements: T is Equality Comparable.
  Return type: Convertible to bool.

- **Less**
  ```
  a < b
  ```

  Type requirements: T is LessThan Comparable.
  Return type: Convertible to bool.
  Semantics: Equivalent to:
  ```
  lexicographical_compare(a.begin(), a.end(),
                                        b.begin(), b.end())
  ```

- **Greater**
  ```
  a > b
  ```

  Type requirements: T is LessThan Comparable.
  Return type: Convertible to bool.

- **Less or equal**
  ```
  a <= b
  ```

  Type requirements: T is LessThan Comparable.
  Return type: Convertible to bool.

- **Greater or equal**
  ```
  a >= b
  ```

  Type requirements: T is LessThan Comparable.
  Return type: Convertible to bool.

Complexity Guarantees

The comparison operations are linear in the container's size.

Invariants

In addition to the invariants defined in the Container requirements, the following invariant must be satisfied:

- **Ordering**
  Two different iterations through a Forward Container will access its elements in the same order, providing that there have been no intervening mutative operations.

Models

All of the STL's container classes are models of Forward Container. The following types are examples:

- `vector`
- `list`
- `slist`
- `deque`
- `set`
- `hash_set`
- `map`
- `hash_map`
- `multiset`
- `hash_multiset`
- `multimap`
- `hash_multimap`

9.1.3 Reversible Container

A Reversible Container is a Forward Container whose iterators are Bidirectional Iterators. It includes additional member functions and nested types that allow backward iteration through the container as well as forward.

Refinement Of

Forward Container (page 131).

Associated Types

Two new types are introduced. In addition, the iterator type and the constant iterator type must satisfy a more stringent requirement than for a Forward Container. The iterator and reverse iterator types must be Bidirectional Iterators, not merely Forward Iterators.

- **Reverse iterator type**
  `X::reverse_iterator`
  A reverse iterator adaptor (page 363) whose base iterator type is `X::iterator`. Incrementing an object of type `reverse_iterator` moves backward through the container. The reverse iterator adaptor maps `operator++` to `operator--`.

- **Constant reverse iterator type**
  `X::const_reverse_iterator`
  A reverse iterator adaptor whose base iterator type is `X::const_iterator`. (Note that a Container's iterator type and constant iterator type may be the

same type. A container need not provide mutable iterators. It follows from this
that the reverse iterator type and the constant reverse iterator type may also
be the same.)

Notation

X	A type that is a model of Reversible Container.
a, b	Object of type X.

Valid Expressions

In addition to the expressions defined in Forward Container, the following expressions must be valid:

- **Beginning of range**
  a.rbegin()

Semantics:	Equivalent to X::reverse_iterator(a.end()).
Postcondition:	a.rbegin() is dereferenceable or past the end. It is past the end if and only if a.size() == 0.

- **End of range**
  a.rend()

Semantics:	Equivalent to X::reverse_iterator(a.begin()).
Postcondition:	a.rend() is past the end.

Complexity Guarantees

The runtime complexity of rbegin() and rend() is amortized constant time.

Invariants

In addition to the invariants defined in the Forward Container requirements, the following invariants must be satisfied:

- **Valid range**
  [a.rbegin(),a.rend()) is a valid range.

- **Equivalence of ranges**
  The distance from a.begin() to a.end() is the same as the distance from a.rbegin() to a.rend(), and the two ranges contain the same elements.

Models

The following types are examples of Reversible Containers:

- vector<double>

- list<string>

- set<int>

9.1.4 Random Access Container

A Random Access Container is a Reversible Container whose iterator type is a Random Access Iterator. It provides amortized constant time access to arbitrary elements, both through its iterators and directly through an operator[] member function.

Refinement Of

Reversible Container (page 133).

Associated Types

No additional types beyond those defined in Reversible Container, but the requirements for the iterator type are strengthened: It must be a Random Access Iterator.

Notation

X	A type that is a model of Random Access Container.
a, b	Object of type X.
T	X's value type.

Valid Expressions

- **Element access**
  a[n]

Type requirements:	n is convertible to size_type.
Return type:	reference if a is mutable, const_reference if it is not.
Precondition:	$0 \leq n < a.size()$.
Semantics:	Returns the nth element from the beginning of the container. The element returned by a[n] is the same as the one obtained by incrementing a.begin() n times and then dereferencing the resulting iterator.

Complexity Guarantees

The runtime complexity of element access is amortized constant time.

Models

The STL containers vector and deque are models of Random Access Container and so is the block class from Section 5.1. By contrast, linked list classes like list and slist are not models of Random Access Container. Those classes do not have operator[] member functions, and their iterators are not Random Access Iterators.

9.2   Sequences

9.2.1   Sequence

A Sequence is a variable-sized Container whose elements are arranged in a strict
linear order. The Sequence concept introduces many new member functions that
support insertion and deletion of elements—both individual elements and ranges—
at arbitrary positions.

Refinement Of

Forward Container (page 131), Default Constructible (page 84).

Associated Types

None, except for those of Forward Container.

Notation

X	A type that is a model of Sequence.
a, b	Object of type X.
T	X's value type.
t	Object of type T.
p, q	Object of type X::iterator.
n	Object of a type convertible to X::size_type.

Definitions

- If a is a Sequence, then p is a *valid iterator in* a if it is a valid iterator that is
  reachable from a.begin().

- If a is a Sequence, then [p,q) is a *valid range in* a if [p,q) is a valid range and
  p is a valid iterator in a.

Valid Expressions

In addition to the expressions defined in Forward Container, the following expressions must be valid:

- **Fill constructor**
  X(n, t)

Return type:	X
Precondition:	$n \geq 0$.
Semantics:	Creates a sequence with n copies of t.
Postcondition:	The sequence's size is equal to n. Every element in the se-quence is a copy of t.

- **Fill constructor**
  X(n)

  Type requirements: T is Default Constructible.

Return type:	X
Precondition:	$n \geq 0$.
Semantics:	Equivalent to X(n, T()). That is, it creates a sequence with n elements initialized to a default value.
Postcondition:	The sequence's size is equal to n. Every element in the sequence is a copy of T().

- **Default constructor**
  X()

Return type:	X
Semantics:	Equivalent to X(0, t). That is, it creates a sequence that contains no elements.
Postcondition:	The sequence's size is zero.

- **Range constructor**
  X(i, j)

  Type requirements: i and j are Input Iterators whose value type is convertible to T.

Return type:	X
Precondition:	[i,j) is a valid range.
Semantics:	Creates a sequence that is a copy of the range [i,j).
Postcondition:	The resulting sequence's size is equal to distance(i, j). Every element in the sequence is equal to the corresponding element from the input range.

- **Insert**
  a.insert(p,t)

Type requirements:	a is mutable.
Return type:	X::iterator
Precondition:	p is a valid iterator in a. a.size() < a.max_size().
Semantics:	Inserts a copy of t before p. There are two important special cases: a.insert(a.begin(), t) inserts t at the beginning (before the first element) and a.insert(a.end(), t) appends t at the end.
Postcondition:	a.size() is incremented by 1. *(a.insert(p,t)) is a copy of t. The relative order of elements already in the sequence is unchanged. *Warning*: This postcondition does not mean that a valid iterator on a is guaranteed to remain valid after an insertion or an erasure. For example, it is not guaranteed that p, the iterator passed to insert, will remain valid.

In some cases iterators do remain valid and continue to point to the same elements they did before. In other cases, inserting an element into a sequence rearranges the existing elements to make room, and an iterator that used to point into the sequence might point to a different element than it did before or to no element at all. The details are different for each sequence class.

- **Fill insert**
  `a.insert(p, n, t)`

  Type requirements: a is mutable.

  Return type: void

  Precondition: p is a valid iterator in a. n >= 0.
  `a.size() + n <= a.max_size()`.

  Semantics: Inserts n copies of t before p. It is guaranteed that this is no slower than calling `insert(p, t)` n times. In some cases, it may be significantly faster.

  Postcondition: `a.size()` is incremented by n. The relative order of elements already in the sequence is unchanged.

- **Range insert**
  `a.insert(p, i, j)`

  Type requirements: a is mutable. i and j are Input Iterators whose value type is convertible to T.

  Return type: void

  Precondition: p is a valid iterator in a. [i,j) is a valid range.
  `a.size() + distance(i, j) <= a.max_size()`.

  Semantics: Inserts a copy of the range [i,j) before p.

  Postcondition: `a.size()` is incremented by `distance(i,j)`. The relative order of elements already in the sequence is unchanged.

- **Erase**
  `a.erase(p)`

  Type requirements: a is mutable.

  Return type: `iterator`

  Precondition: p is a dereferenceable iterator in a.

  Semantics: Destroys the element that p points to, and removes it from the sequence. The return value is an iterator that points to the element immediately following the one that was removed, or else `a.end()` if there is no such element.

  Postcondition: `a.size()` is decremented by 1. The relative order of the other elements in the sequence is unchanged. Note that, as in the case of insert, erase might invalidate iterators that point into the sequence. Certainly, a.erase(p) affects p itself, but it might affect other iterators as well. Erasing an element, like inserting one, might involve rearranging the sequence's other elements. One implication of this fact is that you should not assume that the return value of a.erase(p) is p + 1.

- **Range erase**
  a.erase(p, q)

  Type requirements: a is mutable.

Return type:	iterator
Precondition:	[p, q) is a valid range in a.
Semantics:	Destroys all of the elements in the range [p, q), and removes them from a. The return value is an iterator pointing to the element immediately following the ones that were removed or a.end() if no such element exists. (As with the single-element version of erase, you should not assume that the return value is necessarily q.)
Postcondition:	a.size() is decremented by distance(p, q). The relative order of the other elements in the sequence is unchanged.

- **Front**
  a.front()

Return type:	reference if a is mutable, and const_reference otherwise.
Precondition:	!a.empty().
Semantics:	Equivalent to *(a.begin()).

Two of these expressions involve ranges of general Input Iterators. So, for example, you can insert all of the elements in a list<> into a vector<> by writing:

    V.insert(V.begin(), L.begin(), L.end())

Since this must work with any Input Iterator type, the insert member function must be a *member template,* a member function that is defined as a template.

The obvious solution when you're defining a Sequence class is to define two different versions of insert, an ordinary member function that inserts n copies of a value t and a member template that inserts a range [i, j):

```
template <class T>
class my_sequence {
    ...
public:
    void insert(iterator p, size_type n, const value_type& t);
    template <class InputIterator>
    void insert(iterator p, InputIterator first, InputIterator last);
};
```

This is basically the right idea, but there's one technical detail that makes it a little more complicated. (You only have to worry about this detail if you're planning to implement a new Sequence yourself.)

Suppose that you're dealing with a Sequence whose value type is int—for example, vector<int>. Now suppose that you write:

```
V.insert(V.begin(), 100, 0);
```

The intention, clearly, is to insert 100 copies of 0. That's also what the Sequence requirements say should happen; this is the fill version of insert. Unfortunately, actually implementing a Sequence so that this works correctly is rather tricky. Given the two versions of insert defined earlier, a C++ compiler will choose the second instead of the first.

The reason is that 100 and 0 are both of type int. The first version, which takes a size_t, is not an exact match, but the second, which takes any two arguments of the same type, is. The problem, fundamentally, is that the C++ compiler doesn't know anything about concepts. The range version of insert has a template parameter named InputIterator, but there's nothing special about that name. The compiler doesn't know that insert's arguments really do have to be Input Iterators.

There are two ways to implement insert so that this works correctly. First, you could just overload it for more types. In addition to

```
void insert(iterator, size_t, const value_type&);
```

you would also define

```
void insert(iterator, int, const value_type&);
void insert(iterator, long, const value_type&);
```

and so on for every integral type. This is straightforward but tedious. Second, you could use a variation of the type dispatching that some algorithms perform. Test whether insert's argument is an integer, and if it is, don't attempt to use the range version.

The numeric_limits class, from the standard C++ library, lets you check whether a type is an integer. It returns that information as a value of type bool, and you can convert that value to a type by means of a dummy class with a nontype template parameter:

```
template <bool x> struct dummy {};

template <class T>
class my_sequence {
  ...
private:
  void fill_insert(iterator, size_type, const value_type&);

  template <class InputIter>
  void range_insert(iterator, InputIter, InputIter);

  template <class Number>
  void insert(iterator p, Number n, Number t, dummy<true>) {
    fill_insert(p, n, t);
  }
```

```
      template <class InputIter>
      void insert(iterator p, InputIter f, InputIter l, dummy<false>) {
        range_insert(p, f, l);
      }
  public:
      void insert(iterator p, size_type n, const value_type& t) {
        fill_insert(p, n, t);
      }
      template <class InputIter>
      void insert(iterator p, InputIter f, InputIter l) {
        insert(p, f, l,
               dummy<std::numeric_limits<InputIter>::is_integer>());
      }
  };
```

Complexity Guarantees

- The fill constructor, default fill constructor, and range constructor are linear.

- The runtime complexity of the single-element forms of `insert` and `erase` are sequence-dependent.

- The multiple-element forms of `insert` and `erase` are linear.

- The member function `front` is amortized constant time.

Models

The STL containers `vector`, `deque`, `list`, and `slist` are models of Sequence. They differ from each other mainly in the types of their iterators (`vector` and `deque` provide Random Access Iterators, `list` provides Bidirectional Iterators, `slist` provides Forward Iterators) and in the runtime complexity of `insert` and `erase`.

The best choice is usually `vector`. It is the simplest of the standard container classes, and accordingly, it has the smallest time overhead for iterator and element access. Since insertion into a `vector` is linear in the number of elements from the insertion point to the end, however, other sequences are sometimes preferable in the case of frequent insertions. A `deque` may be a good choice if you are performing many insertions at both the beginning and end of the sequence, and a `list` or an `slist` may be a good choice if you are performing many insertions into the middle. In almost all other situations, `vector` is more efficient.

9.2.2 Front Insertion Sequence

A Front Insertion Sequence is a Sequence where it is possible to insert an element at the beginning or to access the first element, in amortized constant time. Front Insertion Sequences have special member functions as a shorthand for those operations.

Refinement Of

Sequence (page 136).

Associated Types

None, except for those of Sequence.

Notation

X	A type that is a model of Front Insertion Sequence.
a	Object of type X.
T	X's value type.
t	Object of type T.

Valid Expressions

In addition to the expressions defined in Sequence, the following expressions must be valid:

- **Front**[1]
  a.front()

Return type:	reference if a is mutable, otherwise const_reference.
Precondition:	!a.empty()
Semantics:	Equivalent to *(a.begin()).

- **Push front**
  a.push_front(t)

Type requirements:	a is mutable.
Return type:	void
Semantics:	Equivalent to a.insert(a.begin(), t).

- **Pop front**
  a.pop_front(t)

Type requirements:	a is mutable.
Return type:	void
Precondition:	!a.empty().
Semantics:	Equivalent to a.erase(a.begin(), t).

You may wonder why pop_front() has void as the return type. Don't books on data structures often define pop as an operation that removes a value from the a data

---

1. front is actually defined in Sequence, since it is always possible to implement it in amortized constant time. Its definition is repeated here, along with push_front and pop_front, in the interest of clarity.

structure and then returns that value? There are two reasons why we don't define pop_front to do that. First, it's unnecessary. If you want to examine the value that you're removing, then you can just call front first. Second, it would be inefficient. Unlike front, pop_front couldn't return a reference, because there isn't anything left that a reference could refer to after the element is removed. It would have to return by value, which would involve an unnecessary and potentially expensive copy.

Complexity Guarantees

The three operations introduced by Front Insertion Sequence, front, push_front, and pop_front, are all amortized constant time.

This complexity guarantee is the only reason for Front Insertion Sequence to be defined as a concept. Except for the complexity guarantee, these three operations provide no additional functionality beyond begin, insert, and erase. Not every sequence must define these operations, but it is guaranteed that they are efficient if they exist at all.

Invariants

In addition to the invariants defined in the Sequence requirements, the following invariant must be satisfied:

- **Symmetry of push and pop**
  push_front followed by pop_front is a null operation.

Models

The STL containers list, slist, and deque are models of Front Insertion Sequence. By contrast, the STL container vector is not. It has a front member function, but it does not have push_front or pop_front. Insertion or erasure at the beginning of a vector is not a constant time operation.

9.2.3 Back Insertion Sequence

A Back Insertion Sequence is a Sequence where it is possible to append an element to the end or to access the last element, in amortized constant time. Back Insertion Sequences have special member functions as a shorthand for those operations.

Refinement Of

Sequence (page 136).

Associated Types

None, except for those of Sequence.

Notation

X	A type that is a model of Back Insertion Sequence.
a	Object of type X.
T	X's value type.
t	Object of type T.

Valid Expressions

In addition to the expressions defined in Sequence, the following expressions must be valid:

- **Back**
  `a.back()`

Return type:	reference if a is mutable, otherwise const_reference.
Precondition:	!a.empty()
Semantics:	Equivalent to *(--a.end()).

- **Push back**
  `a.push_back(t)`

Type requirements:	a is mutable.
Return type:	void
Semantics:	Equivalent to a.insert(a.end(), t).

- **Pop back**
  `a.pop_back(t)`

Type requirements:	a is mutable.
Return type:	void
Precondition:	!a.empty().
Semantics:	Equivalent to a.erase(--a.end()).

As with pop_front and Front Insertion Sequence (page 141), pop_back is defined to return void rather than to return the element that was removed. If pop_back did return a value, it would have to make an otherwise unnecessary copy. It couldn't return by reference, since it's destroying the element that the reference would refer to.

Complexity Guarantees

All three of the operations introduced by Back Insertion Sequence, back, push_back, and pop_back, are amortized constant time.

   This complexity guarantee is the only reason that Back Insertion Sequence is defined as a concept. Except for the complexity guarantee, these three operations provide no additional functionality beyond end, insert, and erase. Not every sequence must define these operations, but it is guaranteed that they are efficient if they exist at all.

Invariants

In addition to the invariants defined in the Sequence requirements, the following invariant must be satisfied:

- **Symmetry of push and pop**
  push_back followed by pop_back is a null operation.

Models

The STL containers vector, list, and deque are models of Back Insertion Sequence. By contrast, the STL container slist is not. It does not have the member functions back, push_back, or pop_back. It is a singly linked list that provides Forward Iterators rather than Bidirectional Iterators, and access to the last element of an slist is not a constant time operation.

9.3   Associative Containers

9.3.1   Associative Container

An Associative Container is a variable-sized Container that supports efficient retrieval of elements (values) based on keys. It supports insertion and removal of elements but differs from a Sequence in that it does not provide a mechanism for inserting an element at a specific position.

The reason there is no such mechanism is that the way in which elements are arranged in an Associative Container is typically a class invariant. Elements in a Sorted Associative Container, for example, are always stored in ascending order, and elements in a Hashed Associative Container are always stored according to the hash function. It would make no sense to allow the position of an element to be chosen arbitrarily.

Like all containers, an Associative Container contains elements whose type is value_type. Additionally, each element in an Associative Container has a *key* of type key_type. In some Associative Containers, Simple Associative Containers, the value type and key type are the same; elements are their own keys. In others, the key is some specific part of the value. Since elements are stored according to their keys, it is essential that the key associated with each element is immutable. In Simple Associative Containers this means that you can never change an element once it has been put in the container, while in other types of Associative Containers, such as Pair Associative Containers, the elements themselves are mutable but the part of an element that is its key cannot be modified. This means that an Associative Container's value type is not necessarily Assignable.

This fact has an important consequence. Since the elements in an Associative Container can't be modified arbitrarily, it follows that an Associative Container can't have mutable iterators. The problem is that a mutable iterator must, by definition, allow assignment (it supports the expression *i = t), but that would violate the immutability of keys.

In Simple Associative Containers, where the elements are the keys, the nested types `iterator` and `const_iterator` have exactly the same functionality (and might even be the same type). You can remove an element from a Simple Associative Container, but there is no way to modify an element in place. Other types of Associative Containers do have mutable elements and do provide iterators through which elements can be modified. You can change an element's value as long as you don't change its key. Pair Associative Containers, for example, have two different nested types, `iterator` and `const_iterator`. Even here `iterator` isn't a mutable iterator, since you can't write `*i = t`, but it also isn't completely constant. If, for example, `i` is of type `map<int, double>::iterator`, then you can write `i->second = 3`.

In Unique Associative Containers, it is guaranteed that no two elements have the same key. In Multiple Associative Containers, multiple elements with the same key are permitted.

(What it means for keys to be "the same" depends on the type of the Associative Container. It doesn't necessarily mean that the keys are equal, since the Associative Containers concept doesn't require keys to be Equality Comparable. In Sorted Associative Containers, for example, where elements are sorted in ascending order by some Strict Weak Ordering, two keys are considered to be the same if neither is less than the other.)

There are many different ways of organizing elements into data structures in such a way that it is easy to look up an element by its key. Two of the most important such data structures are binary search trees and hash tables.

Refinement Of

Forward Container (page 131).

Associated Types

One new type is introduced, in addition to the types defined in the Forward Container requirements.

- **Key type**
  `X::key_type`
  The type of the key associated with `X::value_type`. Note that the key type and value type might be the same. (For a Simple Associative Container they are always the same.)

Notation

X	A type that is a model of Associative Container.
a	Object of type X.
T	X's value type.
t	Object of type `X::value_type`.
k	Object of type `X::key_type`.
p, q	Object of type `X::iterator`.

Definitions

- If a is an Associative Container, then p is a *valid iterator in* a if it is a valid iterator that is reachable from a.begin().

- If a is an Associative Container, then [p, q) is a *valid range in* a if [p, q) is a valid range and p is a valid iterator in a.

Valid Expressions

- **Default constructor**
  X()
  X a;

Semantics:	Creates an empty container.
Postcondition:	The size of the container is zero.

- **Find**
  a.find(k)

Return type:	iterator if a is mutable, otherwise const_iterator.
Semantics:	Returns an iterator pointing to an element whose key is k. (Note that there may be more than one such element. If so, it is unspecified which one the return value points to.) The return value is a.end() if no such element exists.
Postcondition:	Either the return value is a.end(), or it is an iterator pointing to an element whose key is k.

- **Count**
  a.count(k)

Return type:	size_type
Semantics:	Returns the number of elements in a whose keys are k.
Postcondition:	The return value is non-negative, and is less than or equal to a.size(). (For a Unique Associative Container, the return value is always either 0 or 1.)

- **Equal range**
  a.equal_range(k)

Return type:	pair<iterator, iterator> if a is mutable, and pair<const_iterator, const_iterator> otherwise.
Semantics:	Returns all elements whose keys are k. Specifically, returns a pair P such that the range [P.first, P.second) contains all of the elements whose keys are k. (Note the implication of this member function: If two elements have the same key, there must be no intervening elements with different keys. The requirement that elements with the same key be stored contiguously is an Associative Container invariant.)

	If a doesn't contain any such elements, then the return value is an empty range.
Postcondition:	distance(P.first, P.second) is equal to a.count(k). If p is a dereferenceable iterator in [P.first, P.second), then p points to an element whose key is k. If q is a dereferenceable iterator in a, then either q lies in the range [P.first, P.second) or else q points to an element whose key is not k.

- **Erase key**
  a.erase(k)

Return type:	void
Semantics:	Destroys all elements whose keys are k, and removes them from the container.
Postcondition:	a's size is decremented by a.count(k). a contains no elements whose keys are k.

- **Erase element**
  a.erase(p)

Return type:	void
Precondition:	p is a dereferenceable iterator in a.
Semantics:	Destroys the element that p points to, and removes it from a.
Postcondition:	a's size is decremented by 1.

- **Erase range**
  a.erase(p,q)

Return type:	void
Precondition:	[p, q) is a valid range in a.
Semantics:	Destroys the elements in the range [p, q), and removes them from a.
Postcondition:	a's size is decremented by distance(p, q).

You might wonder why this list contains methods for looking up elements and for erasing elements but none for inserting them. The reason is that inserting an element means something very different for a Unique Associative Container than it does for a Multiple Associative Container. The methods for inserting elements are defined in those two concepts.

Complexity Guarantees

- Average complexity for Find and Equal range is at most logarithmic.

- Average complexity for Count is at most $\mathcal{O}(\log(\texttt{size())} + \texttt{count(k)})$.

- Average complexity for Erase key is at most $\mathcal{O}(\log(\texttt{size())} + \texttt{count(k)})$.

- Average complexity for Erase element is amortized constant time.

- Average complexity for Erase range is at most $\mathcal{O}(\log(\texttt{size())} + N)$, where N is the number of elements in the range.

Note that these are average complexity requirements, not worst case. Some associative container concepts strengthen them to worst case requirements.

Invariants

In addition to the invariants defined in the Forward Container requirements, the following invariants must be satisfied:

- **Contiguous storage**
  All elements with the same key are adjacent to each other. That is, if p and q are iterators that point to elements that have the same key, and if p precedes q, then every element in the range [p, q) has the same key as every other.

- **Immutability of keys**
  Every element of an Associative Container has an immutable key. Objects may be inserted and erased, but an element in an Associative Container is never modified in such a way as to change its key.

Models

The following container classes are models of Associative Container:

- set
- multiset
- hash_set
- hash_multiset
- map
- multimap
- hash_map
- hash_multimap

9.3.2 Unique Associative Container

A Unique Associative Container is an Associative Container with the property that each key in the container is unique. No two elements in a Unique Associative Container have the same key.

What this means is that "inserting" an element t into a Unique Associative Container is always conditional: t doesn't get inserted into the container if an element with t's key is already present.

Refinement Of

Associative Container (page 145).

Associated Types

None, except for those defined in Associative Container.

Notation

X	A type that is a model of Unique Associative Container.
a	Object of type X.
T	X's value type.
t	Object of type X::value_type.
k	Object of type X::key_type.
p, q	Object of type X::iterator.

Valid Expressions

In addition to the expressions defined in Associative Container, the following expressions must be valid:

- **Range constructor**
  ```
  X(i, j)
  X a(i, j);
  ```

Type requirements:	i and j are Input Iterators whose value type is convertible to T.
Precondition:	[i, j) is a valid range.
Semantics:	Creates an associative container that contains all of the elements in [i, j) that have unique keys.
Postcondition:	size() is less than or equal to distance(i, j). ("Less than or equal to," not "equal to," because [i, j) may have several elements with the same key. If so, only the first such element will be inserted.)

- **Insert element**
  ```
  a.insert(t)
  ```

Return type:	pair<X::iterator, bool>
Semantics:	Inserts t into a if and only if a does not already contain an element whose key is the same as t's key. The return value is a pair P, whose second element is of type bool. If a already contained an element whose key is the same as that of t, then P.first is an iterator pointing to that element and P.second is false. If a did not already contain such an

element, then P.first is an iterator pointing to the newly inserted element and P.second is true. That is, P.second is true if and only if t is actually inserted into a.

Postcondition: P.first is a dereferenceable iterator pointing to an element whose key is the same as that of t. The size of a is incremented by 1 if and only if P.second is true.

- **Insert range**
  a.insert(i, j)

  Type requirements: i and j are Input Iterators whose value type is convertible to T.

  Return type: void

  Precondition: [i, j) is a valid range.

  Semantics: Equivalent to a.insert(t) for each object t in the range [i, j). That is, each object in that range is inserted into a provided that a does not already contain an element with the same key.

  Postcondition: a's size is incremented by at most distance(i, j).

Complexity Guarantees

- Average complexity for insertion of a single element is at most logarithmic.

- Average complexity for insertion of a range is at most $\mathcal{O}\,(N \log(\texttt{size}() + N))$, where N is the number of elements in the range.

Invariants

In addition to the invariants defined in the Associative Container requirements, the following invariant must be satisfied:

- **Uniqueness**
  No two elements have the same key. Equivalently, this means that, for every value k of type key_type, a.count(k) is either zero or one.

Models

The following STL container classes are models of Unique Associative Container:

- set
- map
- hash_set
- hash_map

9.3.3 Multiple Associative Container

A Multiple Associative Container is an Associative Container that may contain more than one element with the same key. That is, it is an Associative Container that does not have the restrictions of a Unique Associative Container.

Insertion into a Multiple Associative Container is unconditional, just like insertion into a Sequence: insert does not check to see whether or not the container already contains any elements whose keys are the same as the element that is being inserted.

Refinement Of

Associative Container (page 145).

Associated Types

None, except for those defined in Associative Container.

Notation

X	A type that is a model of Multiple Associative Container.
a	Object of type X.
T	X's value type.
t	Object of type X::value_type.
k	Object of type X::key_type.
p, q	Object of type X::iterator.

Valid Expressions

In addition to the expressions defined in Associative Container, the following expressions must be valid:

- **Range constructor**
  X(i, j)
  X a(i, j);

Type requirements:	i and j are Input Iterators whose value type is convertible to T.
Precondition:	[i, j) is a valid range.
Semantics:	Creates an associative container that contains all of the elements in the range [i, j).
Postcondition:	The container's size is equal to the distance(i, j). Each element from the range [i, j) is present in the container.

- **Insert element**
  a.insert(t)

Return type:	X::iterator

Semantics:	Inserts t into a, unconditionally. The return value is an iterator pointing to the newly inserted element.
Postcondition:	a's size is incremented by 1. The value of a.count(t) is incremented by 1.

- **Insert range**
  a.insert(i, j)

Type requirements:	i and j are Input Iterators whose value type is convertible to T.
Return type:	void
Precondition:	[i, j) is a valid range.
Semantics:	Equivalent to a.insert(t) for each object t in the range [i, j). That is, each object in that range is inserted into a.
Postcondition:	a's size is incremented by distance(i, j).

Complexity Guarantees

- Average complexity for insertion of a single element is at most logarithmic.

- Average complexity for insertion of a range is at most $\mathcal{O}\left(N \log(\texttt{size}() + N)\right)$, where N is the number of elements in the range.

Models

The following STL container classes are models of Multiple Associative Container:

- multiset
- multimap
- hash_multiset
- hash_multimap

9.3.4 Simple Associative Container

A Simple Associative Container is an Associative Container whose elements are their own keys. A value stored in a Simple Associative Container is just a key, not a key plus some additional piece of data.

Refinement Of

Associative Container (page 145).

Associated Types

None, except for those described in the Associative Container requirements. Simple Associative Container does, however, introduce two new type restrictions:

- **Key type**
  X::key_type
  The type of the key associated with X::value_type. The types key_type and value_type must be the same type.

- **Iterator**
  X::iterator
  The type of iterator used to iterate through a Simple Associative Container's elements. The types X::iterator and X::const_iterator must have the same behavior and may even be the same type. A Simple Associative Container does not provide mutable iterators. This is a consequence of the fact that an Associative Container's keys are always immutable. Keys may never be modified, and values in a Simple Associative Container are themselves keys, so it immediately follows that values in a Simple Associative Container may not be modified at all.

Notation

X	A type that is a model of Simple Associative Container.
a	Object of type X.
k	Object of type X::key_type.
p, q	Object of type X::iterator.

Valid Expressions

None, except for those defined in the Associative Container requirements.

Invariants

- **Immutability of elements**
  Elements of a Simple Associative Container are immutable. Objects may be inserted and erased, but they may never be modified in place. Every Associative Container has immutable keys. In a Simple Associative Container the keys are the elements themselves, so the elements are immutable.

Models

The following container classes are models of Simple Associative Container:

- set
- multiset
- hash_set
- hash_multiset

9.3.5 Pair Associative Container

A Pair Associative Container is an Associative Container that associates a key with some other object. The value type of a Pair Associative Container is of the form pair<const key_type, mapped_type>, where key_type is the container's key type.

Refinement Of

Associative Container (page 145).

Associated Types

One new type is introduced, in addition to the types defined in the Associative Container requirements. Pair Associative Container also introduces a new type restriction.

- **Key type**
  X::key_type
  The type of an element's key.

- **Mapped type**
  X::mapped_type
  The type of an element's data. A Pair Associative Container can be thought of as an associative array that stores values of type mapped_type or as a mapping from values of type key_type to values of type mapped_type. The mapped type is sometimes also called the *data type*.

- **Value type**
  X::value_type
  The type of object stored in the container. The value type is required to be pair<const key_type, mapped_type>.

The reason that the value type is pair<const key_type, mapped_type>, rather than pair<key_type, mapped_type>, is the invariant that the keys of an Associative Container must be immutable. The mapped_type part of an object in a Pair Associative Container may be modified, but the key_type part may not be. Note the implication of this fact: a Pair Associative Container cannot provide mutable iterators (as defined in the Trivial Iterator requirements) because the value type of a mutable iterator must be Assignable, and pair<const key_type, mapped_type> is not Assignable. However, a Pair Associative Container can and does provide iterators that are not completely constant, iterators that allow you to write an expression like i->second = d.

Notation

X	A type that is a model of Pair Associative Container.
a	Object of type X.
t	Object of type X::value_type.
k	Object of type X::key_type.

d   Object of type X::mapped_type.

p, q   Object of type X::iterator.

Valid Expressions

None, except for those defined in the Associative Container requirements.

Models

The following container classes are models of Pair Associative Container:

- map
- multimap
- hash_map
- hash_multimap

9.3.6 Sorted Associative Container

A Sorted Associative Container is a type of Associative Container that sorts elements in ascending order by key, using a Strict Weak Ordering. Since a Strict Weak Ordering induces an equivalence relation, we can define two keys as the same if neither one is less than the other.

Sorted Associative Containers guarantee that the complexity of the basic Associative Container operations is never worse than logarithmic.

Refinement Of

Associative Container (page 145), Reversible Container (page 133).

Associated Types

Two new types are introduced, in addition to the types defined in the Associative Container and Reversible Container requirements:

- **Key comparison**
  X::key_compare
  A function object type: a Strict Weak Ordering used to compare keys. Its argument type is X::key_type.

- **Value comparison**
  X::value_compare
  The type of a Strict Weak Ordering used to compare values. Its argument type is X::value_type. The value comparison is the ordering induced by the key comparison. It compares two objects of value_type by passing the keys associated with those objects to a function object of type key_compare.

Notation

X	A type that is a model of Associative Container.
a	Object of type X.
T	X's value type, X::value_type.
t	Object of type X::value_type.
k	Object of type X::key_type.
p, q	Object of type X::iterator.
c	Object of type X::key_compare.

Valid Expressions

In addition to the expressions defined in Associative Container and Reversible Container, the following expressions must be valid:

- **Default constructor**
  ```
  X()
  X a;
  ```

  Semantics: Creates an empty container using key_compare() as the comparison function.

- **Default constructor with compare**
  ```
  X(c)
  X a(c);
  ```

  Semantics: Creates an empty container using c as the comparison function.

- **Range constructor**
  ```
  X(i, j)
  X a(i, j);
  ```

  Type requirements: i and j are Input Iterators whose value type is convertible to T.

  Precondition: [i, j) is a valid range.

  Semantics: Equivalent to:
  ```
  X a;
  a.insert(i, j);
  ```
  (The effect of insert—that is, whether it inserts all of the elements in [i, j) or only the unique elements—depends on whether X is a model of Multiple Associative Container or of Unique Associative Container.)

- **Range constructor with compare**
  ```
  X(i, j, c)
  X a(i, j, c);
  ```

Type requirements: i and j are Input Iterators whose value type is convertible to T.

Precondition: [i, j) is a valid range.

Semantics: Equivalent to:
```
X a(c);
a.insert(i, j);
```

- **Key comparison**
  a.key_comp()

  Return type: key_compare

  Semantics: Returns a's key comparison object. (The key comparison object is set when a is constructed and cannot be changed subsequently.)

- **Value comparison**
  a.value_comp()

  Return type: value_compare

  Semantics: Returns the value comparison object that is induced by a's key comparison object.

  Postcondition: If t1 and t2 are objects of type value_type, and k1 and k2 are the keys associated with them, then
  ```
  a.value_comp()(t1, t2)
  ```
  is equivalent to
  ```
  a.key_comp()(k1, k2)
  ```

- **Lower bound**
  a.lower_bound(k)

  Return type: iterator if a is mutable, and const_iterator otherwise.

  Semantics: Returns an iterator pointing to the first element whose key is not less than k. Returns a.end() if no such element exists.

  Postcondition: If a contains any elements whose key is k, lower_bound's return value points to the first such element.

- **Upper bound**
  a.upper_bound(k)

  Return type: iterator if a is mutable, and const_iterator otherwise.

  Semantics: Returns an iterator pointing to the first element whose key is greater than k. Returns a.end() if no such element exists.

  Postcondition: If a contains any elements whose key is k, upper_bound's return value points to element immediately following the last such element.

- **Equal range**

  a.equal_range(k)

Return type:	pair<iterator,iterator> if a is mutable, and pair<const_iterator,const_iterator> otherwise.
Semantics:	Returns a pair P such that P.first is a.lower_bound(k) and P.second is a.upper_bound(k).
	This definition is consistent with the semantics described in the Associative Container requirements, but it strengthens those requirements. If a contains no elements with the key k, then a.equal_range(k) returns an empty range that indicates the position where those elements would have been if they did exist. Associative Container, however, merely requires in this situation that the return value be some arbitrary empty range.
Postcondition:	All of the elements whose keys are equal to k are contained in the range [P.first,P.second).

- **Insert with hint**

  a.insert(p, t)

Return type:	iterator
Precondition:	p is a nonsingular iterator in a.
Semantics:	Same as a.insert(t). If X is a model of Multiple Associative Container then the insertion is unconditional, and the return value is an iterator pointing to the newly inserted element. If X is a model of Unique Associative Container then t is inserted into a only if there is not already an element with the same key. The return value is an iterator pointing to the newly inserted element (if it was inserted), or to the element whose key was the same as t's. The argument p is a hint. It should point to the location where t is to be inserted. The hint has no effect on correctness, only on performance.

Complexity Guarantees

Sorted Associative Container has significantly stronger complexity guarantees than Associative Container does. The guarantees in Associative Container only apply to average complexity. Worst-case complexity is allowed to be greater. Sorted Associative Container, however, provides an upper limit on worst-case complexity.

- The range constructor, and range constructor with compare, are in general $\mathcal{O}(N \log N)$, where N is the size of the range used to construct the container. However, they are linear in N if the range is already sorted in ascending order by value_comp().

- `key_comp()` and `value_comp()` are constant time.

- Insert with hint is logarithmic in general, but it is amortized constant time if the hint is correct—that is, if t is inserted immediately before p.

- Insert range is in general $\mathcal{O}(N \log N)$, where N is the size of the range. However, it is linear in N if the range that is being inserted is already sorted in ascending order by `value_comp()`.

- Erase element is amortized constant time.

- Erase key is $\mathcal{O}(\log(\texttt{size}()) + \texttt{count(k)})$.

- Erase range is $\mathcal{O}(\log(\texttt{size}()) + N)$, where N is the length of the range that is being erased.

- Find is logarithmic.

- Count is $\mathcal{O}(\log(\texttt{size}()) + \texttt{count(k)})$.

- Lower bound, upper bound, and equal range are logarithmic.

Invariants

In addition to the invariants defined in the Associative Container requirements, the following invariants must be satisfied.

- **Definition of value compare**
  If t1 and t2 are objects of type X::value_type and k1 and k2 are the keys associated with those objects, then a.value_comp() returns a function object such that a.value_comp()(t1, t2) is equivalent to a.key_comp()(k1, k2).

- **Ascending order**
  The elements in a Sorted Associative Container are always arranged in ascending order by key. If a is a Sorted Associative Container, then
      is_sorted(a.begin(), a.end(), a.value_comp())
  is always true. This is the reason for the name "sorted associative container."

Models

The following STL container classes are models of Sorted Associative Container:

- set
- map
- multiset
- multimap

9.3.7 Hashed Associative Container

A Hashed Associative Container is an Associative Container whose implementation is a hash table. The elements of a Hashed Associative Container are not guaranteed to be in any meaningful order. In particular, they are not sorted. The worst-case complexity of most operations on Hashed Associative Containers is linear in the size of the container, but the average case complexity is constant time. This means that for applications where values are simply stored and retrieved and where ordering is unimportant, Hashed Associative Containers are usually much faster than Sorted Associative Containers.

There is an extensive literature dealing with hash tables. See, for example, Section 6.4 of Knuth [Knu98b].

Refinement Of

Associative Container (page 145).

Associated Types

Two new types are introduced, in addition to the types defined in the Associative Container requirements:

- **Hash function**
  X::hasher
  A function object type: a model of Hash Function (page 123). X::hasher's argument type is X::key_type.

- **Key equality**
  X::key_equal
  A Binary Predicate whose argument type is X::key_type. An object of type key_equal returns true if its arguments are the same key, and false otherwise. X::key_equal must be an equivalence relation. Additionally, the hash function and the key equality function must be consistent. If two keys are equal according to the key equality function, then both keys must hash to the same value.

Notation

X	A type that is a model of Associative Container.
a	Object of type X.
T	X's value type.
t	Object of type X::value_type.
k	Object of type X::key_type.
p, q	Object of type X::iterator.
n	Object of type X::size_type.
h	Object of type X::hasher.
c	Object of type X::key_equal.

Definitions

- A *hash function* for a Hashed Associative Container X is a Unary Function whose argument type is X::key_type and whose return type is size_t. A hash function must be deterministic (it must always return the same value whenever it is called with the same argument), but return values of the hash function should be as uniform as possible. Ideally, no two keys ever hash to the same value.

  A poor hash function—one where many different keys hash to the same value—will hurt performance. The worst case is where every key hashes to the same value. If that happens then the runtime complexity of most Hashed Associative Container operations will be $\mathcal{O}(N)$ instead of $\mathcal{O}(1)$.

- Elements in a Hashed Associative Container are grouped into *buckets*. A Hashed Associative Container uses the value of the hash function to determine which bucket an element is assigned to.

- The number of elements in a Hashed Associative Container divided by the number of buckets is called the *load factor*. In general, a Hashed Associative Container with a small load factor is faster than one with a large load factor.

Valid Expressions

In addition to the expressions defined in Associative Container, the following expressions must be valid:

- **Default constructor**
  ```
  X()
  X a;
  ```

  Semantics: Creates an empty container, using hasher() as the hash function and key_equal() as the key equality function.

  Postcondition: The size of the container is 0. The bucket count is an unspecified default value. The hash function is hasher(), and the key equality function is key_equal().

- **Default constructor with bucket count**
  ```
  X(n)
  X a(n);
  ```

  Semantics: Creates an empty container with at least n buckets, using hasher() as the hash function and key_equal() as the key equality function.

  Postcondition: The size of the container is 0. The bucket count is greater than or equal to n. The hash function is hasher(), and the key equality function is key_equal().

- **Default constructor with hash function**
  ```
  X(n, h)
  X a(n, h);
  ```

Semantics:	Creates an empty container with at least n buckets, using h as the hash function and key_equal() as the key equality function.
Postcondition:	The size of the container is 0. The bucket count is greater than or equal to n. The hash function is h, and the key equality function is key_equal().

- **Default constructor with key equality**
  ```
  X(n, h, k)
  X a(n, h, k);
  ```

Semantics:	Creates an empty container with at least n buckets, using h as the hash function and k as the key equality function.
Postcondition:	The size of the container is 0. The bucket count is greater than or equal to n. The hash function is h, and the key equality function is k.

- **Range constructor**
  ```
  X(i, j)
  X a(i, j);
  ```

Type requirements:	i and j are Input Iterators whose value type is convertible to T.
Precondition:	[i, j) is a valid range.
Semantics:	Equivalent to:

  ```
      X a;
      a.insert(i, j);
  ```
  (The effect of insert—that is, whether it inserts all of the elements in [i, j) or only the unique elements—depends on whether X is a model of Multiple Associative Container or of Unique Associative Container.)

- **Range constructor with bucket count**
  ```
  X(i, j, n)
  X a(i, j, n);
  ```

Type requirements:	i and j are Input Iterators whose value type is convertible to T.
Precondition:	[i, j) is a valid range.
Semantics:	Equivalent to:

  ```
      X a(n);
      a.insert(i, j);
  ```

- **Range constructor with hash function**
  ```
  X(i, j, n, h)
  X a(i, j, n, h);
  ```

Type requirements: i and j are Input Iterators whose value type is convertible
to T.

Precondition: [i, j) is a valid range.

Semantics: Equivalent to:

```
X a(n, h);
a.insert(i, j);
```

- **Range constructor with key equality**
  X(i, j, n, h, k)
  X a(i, j, n, h, k);

  Type requirements: i and j are Input Iterators whose value type is convertible
  to T.

  Precondition: [i, j) is a valid range.

  Semantics: Equivalent to:

  ```
  X a(n, h, k);
  a.insert(i, j);
  ```

- **Hash function**
  a.hash_funct()

  Return type: X::hasher

  Semantics: Returns a's hash function.

- **Key equality**
  a.key_eq()

  Return type: X::key_equal

  Semantics: Returns a's key equality function.

- **Bucket count**
  a.bucket_count()

  Return type: X::size_type

  Semantics: Returns a's bucket count.

- **Resize**
  a.resize(n)

  Semantics: Increases a's bucket count.

  Postcondition: a's bucket count will be at least n. All iterators pointing to
                         a's elements will remain valid.

                         Note that although resizing does not invalidate iterators,
                         it does in general change the ordering relations between
                         iterators. If i and j are iterators that point into a Hashed

Associative Container, and j is i's successor, then there is no guarantee that j will still be i's successor after the container is resized. The only guarantee about ordering is the contiguous storage invariant: Elements with the same key are always adjacent to each other.

As a general rule, Hashed Associative Containers try to maintain their load factors within some fairly narrow range. (This is necessary to satisfy the complexity constraints. If the load factor were allowed to grow without bound, then Hashed Associative Containers would scale poorly as the number of elements increased.)

When you insert elements into a Hashed Associative Container, you may trigger an automatic resizing. This automatic resizing affects iterators and ranges just the same way as the resize member function does. It preserves iterators' validity, but it does not necessarily preserve the ordering relations between iterators. This, of course, is one reason why resize exists, and why there are constructors that let you specify a bucket count. If you know in advance how large a Hashed Associative Container will eventually grow, then it is more efficient for you to set the bucket count while the container is still empty.

Complexity Guarantees

Hashed Associative Container strengthens the average-case complexity guarantees defined in Associative Container. However, Hashed Associative Container still has weak worst-case guarantees. Worst-case performance usually corresponds to a poor choice of hash function.

- The default constructor, constructor with bucket count, constructor with hash function, and constructor with key equal, are all amortized constant time. (Worst case.)

- The range constructor, range constructor with bucket count, range constructor with hash function, and range constructor with key equal, are all $\mathcal{O}(N)$, where N is the size of the range used to construct the container. (Average case.)

- The expressions to obtain the hash function and key equality function are constant time.

- Erasing a single element, erase(p), is amortized constant time. (Worst case.)

- Average complexity for erase(k) (erasing all elements whose key is k) is $\mathcal{O}(n)$, where n is count(k). Worst case is $\mathcal{O}(N)$, where N is the size of the container.

- Average complexity for erase(p, q) (erasing a range) is $\mathcal{O}(n)$, where n is the length of the range being erased. Worst case is $\mathcal{O}(N)$, where N is the size of the container.

- Average complexity for find(k) (lookup by key) is $\mathcal{O}(1)$. Worst case is $\mathcal{O}(N)$, where N is the number of elements in the container.

- Average complexity for equal_range(k) (finding all elements whose key is k) is $\mathcal{O}(\text{count(k)})$. Worst case is $\mathcal{O}(N)$, where N is the number of elements in the container.

- Average complexity for count(k) (counting the number of elements whose key is k) is $\mathcal{O}(\text{count(k)})$. Worst case is $\mathcal{O}(N)$, where N is the number of elements in the container.

- Bucket count is $\mathcal{O}(1)$. (Worst case.)

- Resize is $\mathcal{O}(N)$, where N is the number of elements in the container. (Worst case.)

Models

The following STL container classes are models of Hashed Associative Container:

- hash_set
- hash_map

9.4 Allocator

An Allocator is a class that encapsulates some of the details of memory allocation and deallocation. All of the STL's predefined container classes use Allocators for their memory management. When you instantiate the vector template, for example, you can specify which Allocator class it uses.

There are three facts about allocators that are far more important than any technical details.

First, and most important, you probably don't need to know about Allocators at all. You don't need to know about Allocators to use the STL's predefined container classes because those container classes use default template parameters to hide the use of Allocators. By default, for example, vector<int> means the same thing as vector<int, allocator<int> >. You don't even need to know about Allocators to write a new container class. A container class doesn't have to use sophisticated memory management techniques. In fact, as we saw with the block class (Section 5.1), a container class doesn't necessarily need to perform any sort of dynamic memory allocation.

Second, allocators are one of the least portable aspects of the STL. The C++ standard does describe the Allocator concept, but as of 1998, several nonstandard versions of allocators are still in common use. (This is partly because standard allocators use several language features that are not yet universally available.)

Third, while containers are parameterized by allocators, this does not mean that you have control over every conceivable aspect of a container's memory management. The Allocator concept is completely unrelated to how many elements are contained in a deque's node, whether a container's elements are stored contiguously, or how a vector grows when it reallocates itself.

Fundamentally, what Allocator does encapsulate is the way in which memory is obtained from or returned to the free store. If you request memory from an Allocator then that Allocator might use `malloc`, or `new`, or some other method that's specific to your operating system. The Allocator might maintain a "free list," since it is often faster to allocate a single large block than many small blocks. All of this complexity, though, is internal. An Allocator should be efficient even for allocating small objects, and containers should not have to maintain their own class-specific free lists. (This is one way in which the C++ standard is simpler than the original HP STL.)

In general, two objects of the same Allocator class need not be equivalent. If `a1` and `a2` are both objects of type `My_Allocator`, then `a1` and `a2` might not allocate memory in the same way. Your operating system might, for example, support allocation through several distinct pools of memory. If it does, then you can write an Allocator class where different objects of that class represent different memory pools. If you create a container of type `vector<int, My_Allocator<int> >`, then you can specify which memory pool that `vector` will use. Like all of the standard containers, `vector` lets you specify in its constructor which allocator object it will use.

(All of the standard containers use default parameters. You don't have to bother specifying an allocator object unless you need to use something other than the default. And if you're using the default Allocator class `allocator`, it doesn't matter anyway, since all objects of class `allocator` are the same.)

Like a container class, every Allocator class has a *value type*, the type of object for which it allocates storage. If an Allocator's value type is `T`, then calling the member function `allocate(n)` is a request for enough storage to contain n objects of type `T`. Also like container classes, Allocator classes contain the nested types `pointer`, `reference`, and so on. In principle, these types can define an alternate memory model, where `pointer` isn't actually `T*` but instead some other pointer-like type. In practice, however, the freedom to define alternate memory models is limited, since the C++ language does not provide any satisfactory way of defining a reference-like type other than the ordinary `T&`.

Since Allocator classes have value types, there must be a way of converting from one value type to another. Consider a linked list class, for example. A `list<int>` has an Allocator whose value type is `int`, but internally, `list` doesn't allocate objects of type `int`; it allocates list nodes. The `list` class, then, has to be able to convert from an allocator class with one value type to an allocator class with a different value type, and it has to convert an allocator object of one class to an object of the second class. It can use Allocator's `rebind` mechanism for the first of those tasks, and Allocator's "generalized copy constructor" for the second.

One final reminder. It's likely that you don't have to worry about allocators at all, and it's even more likely that you don't have to use advanced features like alternate memory models and distinct allocator instances. If you do plan to use advanced allocator features, you should read your implementation's documentation closely because Section 20.1.5 of the C++ standard [ISO98] contains a very important caveat:

> Implementations of containers described in this International Standard are permitted to assume that their Allocator template parameter meets the following two additional requirements beyond those in Table 32.

- All instances of a given allocator type are required to be
  interchangeable and always compare equal to each other.
- The typedef members `pointer`, `const_pointer`, `size_type`,
  and `difference_type` are required to be `T*`, `T const*`,
  `size_t`, and `ptrdiff_t`, respectively.

Implementors are encouraged to supply libraries that can accept allocators that encapsulate more general memory models and that support
non-equal instances. In such implementations, any requirements imposed
on allocators by containers beyond those requirements that appear in
Table 32, and the semantics of containers and algorithms when allocator
instances compare non-equal, are implementation-defined.

This means that while the C++ standard requires Allocators to have syntactic hooks
for alternate memory models and distinct allocator instances, it doesn't guarantee
that you can use those features with the containers that your implementation provides.

Refinement Of

Equality Comparable (page 85), Default Constructible (page 84). Allocator is not a
refinement of Assignable because, while it defines a copy constructor, it does not
define an assignment operator.

Associated Types

- **Value type**
  `X::value_type`
  The type that the allocator manages.

- **Pointer type**
  `X::pointer`
  A pointer (not necessarily a built-in C++ pointer) to `X::value_type`. The pointer
  type is required to be convertible to the const pointer type, to `void*`, and to
  `value_type*`.

- **Const pointer type**
  `X::const_pointer`
  A const pointer (not necessarily a built-in C++ pointer) to `X::value_type`.

- **Reference type**
  `X::reference`
  A reference to `X::value_type`. Since C++ does not make alternate reference
  types possible, `X::reference` must be `X::value_type&`.

- **Const reference type**
  `X::const_reference`
  A const reference to `X::value_type`. As with the reference type, the const
  reference type must be const `X::value_type&`.

- **Difference type**

  X::difference_type

  A signed integral type that represents the difference between two values of type X::pointer.

- **Size type**

  X::size_type

  An unsigned integral type that can represent any non-negative value of type X::difference_type.

- **Alternate allocator type**

  X::rebind<U>::other[2]

  For any type U, X::rebind<U>::other is an allocator whose value type is U. The type X::rebind<X::value_type>::other is identical to X itself.

Notation

T, U	Any types.
X	An Allocator whose value type is T.
Y	The corresponding Allocator whose value type is U.
a, b	Object of type X.
y	Object of type Y.
t	Object of type T.
p	Object of type X::pointer.
n	Value of type X::size_type.

Valid Expressions

- **Default constructor**

  X()
  X a;

Return type:	X
Semantics:	Creates a default instance of X.

- **Copy constructor**

  X b(a)
  X(a);

Return type:	X
Semantics:	Creates a copy of a.
Postcondition:	The copy compares equal to a.

---

2. This awkward syntax is in part because C++ does not support "template typedefs." Thus other is a typedef within the nested template class rebind.

- **Generalized copy constructor**
  ```
  X a(y)
  X(y);
  ```

Return type:	X
Semantics:	Creates a copy of y, an Allocator whose value type is U.
Postcondition:	`Y(X(y)) == y`.

- **Comparison**
  ```
  a == b
  ```

Return type:	Convertible to bool.
Semantics:	Returns true if and only if storage allocated using a can be deallocated using b, and *vice versa*.

- **Allocate**
  ```
  a.allocate(n)
  ```

Return type:	X::pointer
Precondition:	$0 < n \le$ a.max_size().
Semantics:	Allocates n * sizeof(T) bytes of memory.
Postcondition:	The return value is a pointer to an uninitialized block of memory that is large enough to contain n objects of type T.

- **Allocate with hint**
  ```
  a.allocate(n, q)
  ```

Type requirements:	q is a value of type Y::const_pointer for some Y.
Return type:	X::pointer
Precondition:	$0 < n \le$ a.max_size(). q is either a null pointer or a pointer that was obtained by a previous call to allocate.
Semantics:	Allocates n * sizeof(T) bytes of memory. The pointer argument q is a hint. An allocator might use it as an aid to locality, or it might ignore the hint entirely.
Postcondition:	The return value is a pointer to an uninitialized block of memory that is large enough to contain n objects of type T.

- **Deallocate**
  ```
  a.deallocate(p, n)
  ```

Return type:	void
Precondition:	p is a pointer to memory that was obtained via a previous call to allocate, and n is the argument that was passed to allocate. p is non-null, and n is nonzero.
Semantics:	Deallocates the memory that p points to.

- **Maximum size**
  `a.max_size()`

Return type:	`X::size_type`
Semantics:	Returns the maximum value that can be passed as an argument to `allocate`.

- **Construct**
  `a.construct(p, t)`

Return type:	`void`
Precondition:	`p` points to an uninitialized region of memory whose size is at least `sizeof(T)`.
Semantics:	Equivalent to `new((void*) p) T(t);`

- **Destroy**
  `a.destroy(p)`

Return type:	`void`
Precondition:	`p` points to an object of type `T`.
Semantics:	Equivalent to `((T*) p)->~T();`

- **Address**
  `a.address(r)`

Type requirements:	`r` is of type `T&` or of type `const T&`.
Return type:	`pointer` if `r` is of type `T&`, and `const_pointer` if `r` is of type `const T&`.
Precondition:	`r` is a reference to an object that was allocated using `a`.
Semantics:	Returns a pointer to `r`.

Models

- `allocator` (page 187).

Part III

Reference Manual:
Algorithms and Classes

Chapter 10

Basic Components

The types and functions in this chapter are building blocks that are used in many different parts of the library. For the most part, they are extremely simple. Some of them, however, are very low level and specialized and are only useful if you are implementing a new container.

10.1 pair

pair<T1, T2>

The class pair<T1,T2> is a heterogeneous pair. It holds one object of type T1 and one of type T2. A pair is much like a Container, in that it "owns" its elements (they are destroyed when the pair itself is destroyed), but it is not actually a model of Container because it does not support the standard methods (such as iterators) for accessing Container elements.

Functions that need to return two values often return a pair.

Example

```
pair<bool, double> result = do_a_calculation();
if (result.first)
  do_something_more(result.second);
else
  report_error();
```

Where Defined

In the HP implementation, pair was defined in the header <pair.h>. According to the C++ standard, it is declared in the header <utility>.

Template Parameters

T1   The type of the first element stored in the pair.

T2   The type of the second element stored in the pair.

Model Of

Assignable (page 83) if and only if T1 and T2 are both Assignable, Default Constructible (page 84) if and only if T1 and T2 are both Default Constructible, Equality Comparable (page 85) if and only if T1 and T2 are both Equality Comparable, and LessThan Comparable (page 86) if and only if T1 and T2 are both LessThan Comparable.

Type Requirements

None.

Public Base Classes

None.

Members

Some of pair's members are not defined in the Assignable, Default Constructible, Equality Comparable, or LessThan Comparable requirements, but are specific to pair. These special members are flagged with the symbol ∗.

∗ `pair::first_type`
   The type of the pair's first component T1.

∗ `pair::second_type`
   The type of the pair's second component T2.

∗ `pair::pair(const T1& x, const T2& y)`
   The constructor. Constructs a pair such that first is constructed from x and second is constructed from y.

   `pair::pair(const pair&)`
   The copy constructor.
   (Described in Assignable.)

∗ `template <class U1, class U2>`
   `pair::pair(const pair<U1, U2>& p)`
   Generalized copy constructor. If T1 has a constructor that takes a single argument of type U1 and T2 has a constructor that takes a single argument of type U2, then constructs a pair such that first is initialized from p.first and second is initialized from p.second.

   `pair& pair::operator=(const pair&)`
   The assignment operator.
   (Described in Assignable.)

∗ `pair::first`
   Public member variable of type first_type: the pair's first element.

∗ `pair::second`
   Public member variable of type second_type: the pair's second element.

```
bool operator==(const pair&, const pair&)
```
The equality operator.
(Described in Equality Comparable.)

```
bool operator<(const pair& x, const pair& y)
```
The comparison operator. The expression x < y is true if x.first is less than y.first, or if x.second is less than y.second and x.first and y.first are the same.
(Described in LessThan Comparable.)

* ```
  template <class T1, class T2>
  pair<T1, T2> make_pair(const T1& x, const T2& y)
  ```
  Helper function for creating a pair. Equivalent to pair<T1, T2>(x, y), but often more convenient.

10.2 Iterator Primitives

10.2.1 iterator_traits

iterator_traits<Iterator>

As discussed in Section 3.1, all iterators have associated types. One such is the value type, the type of object that the iterator points to. The iterator also has an associated difference type, a signed integral type that can be used to represent the distance between two iterators. For a pointer of type int*, for example, the value type is int and the difference type is ptrdiff_t.

As part of the iterator requirements, the STL defines a mechanism for accessing these associated types. For example, if II is a model of Input Iterator, its value type is iterator_traits<II>::value_type. The STL's own predefined iterators satisfy this requirement by defining three versions of a class template iterator_traits: a general version, a specialized version for pointers, and an even more specialized version for const pointers.

This is an example of *partial specialization*, since the two specialized versions are themselves templates:

```
template <class Iterator>
struct iterator_traits {
  typedef typename Iterator::iterator_category iterator_category;
  typedef typename Iterator::value_type        value_type;
  typedef typename Iterator::difference_type   difference_type;
  typedef typename Iterator::pointer           pointer;
  typedef typename Iterator::reference         reference;
};

template <class T>
struct iterator_traits<T*> {
  typedef random_access_iterator_tag iterator_category;
  typedef T                          value_type;
  typedef ptrdiff_t                  difference_type;
  typedef T*                         pointer;
  typedef T&                         reference;
};
```
```

```
template <class T>
struct iterator_traits<const T*> {
  typedef random_access_iterator_tag iterator_category;
  typedef T                          value_type;
  typedef ptrdiff_t                  difference_type;
  typedef const T*                   pointer;
  typedef const T&                   reference;
};
```

When you write a new iterator type I, you must ensure that iterator_traits<I> is defined properly. There are two ways to do this. First, you can define your iterator so that it has nested types I::value_type, I::difference_type, and so on. Second, you can explicitly specialize iterator_traits for your type. The first way is more convenient, though, especially since you can do it simply by inheriting from the base class iterator (page 185).

The iterator_traits class is a relatively new addition to the STL. It was not part of the original HP implementation. (It couldn't have been, since partial specialization was not available at the time.) The HP STL had a different way of querying iterators' associated types: three functions called value_type, distance_type, and iterator_category. (See Section 3.1.6.) These functions are no longer part of the C++ standard.

Example

This generic function returns the last element in a nonempty range. There is no way to define a function with this interface in terms of the old value_type function because the function's return type must be declared to be the iterator's value type:

```
template <class InputIter>
typename iterator_traits<InputIter>::value_type
last_value(InputIter first, InputIter last) {
  typename iterator_traits<InputIter>::value_type result = *first;
  for (++first; first != last; ++first)
    result = *first;
}
```

(Note: This is a simple example of how to use iterator_traits. It is not a recommended way of writing this generic algorithm. There are better ways to find the last element in a range of Bidirectional Iterators or even Forward Iterators.)

Where Defined

The iterator_traits class was not part of the HP implementation. According to the C++ standard, it is declared in the header <iterator>.

Template Parameters

Iterator   The iterator type whose associated types are being accessed.

Model Of

Default Constructible (page 84), Assignable (page 83).

Type Requirements

- `Iterator` is a model of an iterator concept, Input Iterator (page 94) or Output Iterator (page 96).

Public Base Classes

None.

Members

All of `iterator_traits`'s members are nested `typedef`s.

> `iterator_traits::iterator_category`
> A tag type: either `input_iterator_tag`, `output_iterator_tag`, `forward_iterator_tag`, `bidirectional_iterator_tag`, or `random_access_iterator_tag`. An iterator's category is the *most specific* iterator concept that the iterator is a model of.

> `iterator_traits::value_type`
> Iterator's value type, as defined in the Input Iterator requirements. Note that this member may be used only if `Iterator` is a model of Input Iterator; an Output Iterator need not have a value type.

> `iterator_traits::difference_type`
> Iterator's difference type, as defined in the Input Iterator requirements. Note that an Output Iterator need not have a difference type.

> `iterator_traits::pointer`
> Iterator's pointer type, as defined in the Input Iterator requirements. Note that an Output Iterator need not have a pointer type.

> `iterator_traits::reference`
> Iterator's reference type, as defined in the Input Iterator requirements. Note that an Output Iterator need not have a reference type.

10.2.2 Iterator Tag Classes

```
struct output_iterator_tag {};
struct input_iterator_tag {};
struct forward_iterator_tag : public input_iterator_tag {};
struct bidirectional_iterator_tag : public forward_iterator_tag {};
struct random_iterator_tag : public bidirectional_iterator_tag {};
```

The five *iterator tag* classes are completely empty. They have no member functions, member variables, or nested types. As their names suggest, they are used solely as tags, representations of the five iterator concepts within the C++ type system.

The iterator tag classes are closely related to `iterator_traits`. For any iterator type I, `iterator_traits<I>::iterator_category` is defined to be one of the tag classes.

In general, an iterator's category is the *most specific* iterator concept that that iterator is a model of. For example, int* is a model of Random Access Iterator. It is also a model of Bidirectional Iterator, Forward Iterator, and so on. The most specific of these concepts, however, is Random Access Iterator (it is a refinement of all of the other iterator concepts), so iterator_traits<int*>::iterator_category is random_access_iterator_tag.

Example

The generic algorithm reverse (page 264) can be implemented for Bidirectional Iterators, but there is a more efficient version for Random Access Iterators. Consequently, reverse uses iterator_traits and tag classes to select whichever algorithm is appropriate for the iterator type. This dispatch takes place at compile time, and does not incur any runtime penalty.

```
template <class BI>
void __reverse(BI first, BI last, bidirectional_iterator_tag) {
  while (true)
      if (first == last || first == --last)
        return;
      else
        iter_swap(first++, last);
}

template <class RAI>
void __reverse(RAI first, RAI last, random_access_iterator_tag) {
  while (first < last)
    iter_swap(first++, --last);
}

template <class BI>
inline void reverse(BI first, BI last) {
  __reverse(first, last,
          typename iterator_traits<BI>::iterator_category());
}
```

Where Defined

In the HP STL, the iterator tag classes were declared in the header <iterator.h>. According to the C++ standard, they are declared in the header <iterator>.

Template Parameters

None.

Model Of

Default Constructible, Assignable.

Public Base Classes

The iterator tag structs form an inheritance hierarchy: `forward_iterator_tag` is derived from `input_iterator_tag`, `bidirectional_iterator_tag` is derived from `forward_iterator_tag`, and similarly `random_access_iterator_tag` is derived from `bidirectional_iterator_tag`.

You might wonder why `forward_iterator_tag` has `input_iterator_tag` as a base class but not `output_iterator_tag`. Fundamentally, the answer is that it doesn't matter very much that these tag classes use inheritance at all. The inheritance hierarchy of iterator tag classes has no deep significance. It is nothing more than a minor convenience that sometimes makes it easier to write generic algorithms that dispatch on iterator category. Inheritance from `output_iterator_tag` is left out because it is unnecessary for that purpose.

10.2.3 `distance`

① `template <class InputIterator>`
`typename iterator_traits<InputIterator>::difference_type`
`distance(InputIterator first, InputIterator last);`

② `template <class InputIterator, class Distance>`
`void distance(InputIterator first, InputIterator last, Distance& n);`

The algorithm `distance` is an iterator primitive that is used in other STL algorithms. It finds the distance between `first` and `last`, that is, the number of times that `first` must be incremented until it is equal to `last`.[1] The values in [`first,last`) are irrelevant, because `distance` only operates on the iterators themselves. None of the iterators are dereferenced.

The two versions of `distance` do exactly the same thing, using two different interfaces. Version 2 was defined in the original HP release of the STL [SL95], but the interface was changed during the standardization process. The C++ standard [ISO98] includes only version 1. At present (1998) some STL implementations include only version 1, some include only version 2, and some include both to provide a transition from the old interface to the new. Version 1 simply returns the distance between `first` and `last`; version 2 increments n by that distance.

The interface of version 2 is quite cumbersome. To find the distance from `first` to `last` you must create a local variable, initialize that value to 0, and then call `distance`. This is inconvenient and error-prone (forgetting to initialize the local variable to 0 is a common mistake), which is why the interface was changed to that of version 1.

The reason the original STL used that inconvenient interface is that declaring `distance`'s return type is slightly tricky. If we're counting the number of elements in

---

1. This is the reason that `distance` is not defined for Output Iterators. It is not necessarily possible to compare two Output Iterators for equality.

[first,last) that are equal to value, then the return type has to be an integral type that is large enough to store that number. Each iterator type has an associated type, its *difference type*, that can represent the distance between any two iterators of that type. For example, the difference type for built-in pointers is ptrdiff_t. The type of the value that distance calculates is InputIterator's difference type.

The mechanism for declaring this return type is the iterator_traits class (Section 3.1). If I is a model of Input Iterator, then the nested type

```
    iterator_traits<I>::difference_type
```
is I's difference type.

The original HP STL used a different method, because iterator_traits did not exist at the time. Version 2 stores the return value in a variable provided by the user. The type Distance, in version 2, must be at least as large as InputIterator's difference type.

Where Defined

In the HP implementation, distance was declared in the header <algo.h>. According to the C++ standard, it is declared in the header <iterator>.

Requirements on Types

For version 1:

- InputIterator is a model of Input Iterator.

For version 2:

- InputIterator is a model of Input Iterator.
- Distance is an integral type that is large enough to represent non-negative values of InputIterator's distance type.

Preconditions

For version 1:

- [first,last) is a valid range.

For version 2:

- [first,last) is a valid range.
- The number of elements in [first,last) does not exceed the maximum value of type Distance.

Complexity

Constant time if InputIterator is a model of Random Access Iterator; otherwise, linear time.

Example

This artificial example shows how to use version 1 of distance:

```
int main() {
  list<int> L;
  L.push_back(0);
  L.push_back(1);

  assert(distance(L.begin(), L.end()) == L.size());
}
```

The real reason that distance exists isn't for such trivial examples but as a primitive used by other generic algorithms. For example, the implementation of lower_bound (page 308) uses distance:

```
template <class ForwardIterator, class T>
ForwardIterator lower_bound(ForwardIterator first, ForwardIterator last,
                            const T& value) {
  iterator_traits<ForwardIterator>::difference_type len
        = distance(first, last);
  iterator_traits<ForwardIterator>::difference_type half;
  ForwardIterator middle;

  while (len > 0) {
    half = len / 2;
    middle = first;
    advance(middle, half);
    if (*middle < value) {
      first = middle;
      ++first;
      len = len - half - 1;
    } else
      len = half;
  }
  return first;
}
```

10.2.4 advance

```
template <class InputIterator, class Distance>
void advance(InputIterator& i, Distance n);
```

The expression advance(i, n) increments the iterator i by the distance n. If n > 0 it is equivalent to executing ++i n times (although it will be much faster if the type InputIterator is a model of **Random Access Iterator**), and if n < 0 it is equivalent to executing --i n times. If n == 0, the call has no effect.

A negative value is permitted only if the type InputIterator is a model of Bidirectional Iterator.

Where Defined

In the HP implementation, advance was declared in the header <algo.h>. According to the C++ standard, it is declared in the header <iterator>.

Requirements on Types

- InputIterator is a model of Input Iterator.
- Distance is an integral type that is convertible to InputIterator's difference type.

Preconditions

- i is nonsingular.
- Every iterator between i and i + n (inclusive) is nonsingular.
- If InputIterator is a model of Input Iterator but not a model of Bidirectional Iterator, n must be non-negative. If InputIterator is a model of Bidirectional Iterator (including the case where it is a model of Random Access Iterator), this precondition does not apply.

Complexity

Constant time if the type InputIterator is a model of Random Access Iterator; otherwise, linear time.

Example

This contrived example shows how you can use advance to increment a Forward Iterator n times:

```
int main()
{
  slist<int> L;
  L.push_front(0);
  L.push_front(1);

  slist<int>::iterator i = L.begin();
  advance(i, 2);
  assert(i == L.end());
}
```

As with distance (page 181), though, the real reason that advance exists is so that it can be used in the implementation of other generic algorithms. For example, lower_bound is written in terms of both distance and advance. An implementation of lower_bound is shown on page 183.

10.2.5   Iterator Base Class

`iterator<Category, T, Distance, Pointer, Reference>`

The `iterator` class is an empty base class. It has no member functions or member variables, only nested `typedef`s.

You have no reason to care about the `iterator` class unless you are defining your own iterator class. In fact, you do not necessarily have to use `iterator` even when you are defining an iterator class. It is only one of several options.

When you write a new iterator class, you must ensure that it works properly with `iterator_traits`. The easiest way to do that is for your class to contain the five nested types `iterator_category`, `value_type`, `difference_type`, `pointer`, and `reference`. You can define those `typedef`s explicitly or you can derive your iterator class from `iterator`, which makes its template arguments available as those five `typedef`s.

Note that the HP STL did not include `iterator`. Instead, it included five different iterator base classes: `input_iterator`, `output_iterator`, `forward_iterator`, `bidirectional_iterator`, and `random_access_iterator`. Those five classes are no longer part of the C++ standard. In the HP STL you can define a new Output Iterator by inheriting from

```
output_iterator
```
and a new Forward Iterator by inheriting from

```
forward_iterator<T>.
```
In standard C++, you can instead define a new Output Iterator by inheriting from

```
iterator<output_iterator_tag, void, void, void, void>
```
and a new Forward Iterator by inheriting from

```
iterator<forward_iterator_tag, T>.
```


Example

```
class my_forward_iterator :
    public std::iterator<forward_iterator_tag, double>
{
  ...
};
```

This declares `my_forward_iterator` to be a Forward Iterator whose value type is double, whose difference type is `ptrdiff_t`, and whose pointer and reference types are double* and double&.

You can do exactly the same thing without using `iterator`, by defining the nested types in `my_forward_iterator` itself:

```
class my_forward_iterator
{
public:
  typedef forward_iterator_tag  iterator_category;
  typedef double                value_type;
```

```
        typedef ptrdiff_t            difference_type;
        typedef double*              pointer;
        typedef double&              reference;
        ...
    };
```

Defining the nested types explicitly is slightly more verbose, but it is also slightly clearer. Additionally, you can sometimes get better performance by defining them explicitly. On many compilers, empty base classes do take up some space. (The C++ standard neither requires nor forbids this.) If you are using such a compiler, and if you derive my_forward_iterator from iterator, then you will be wasting a few bytes every time you create a my_forward_iterator object.

Where Defined

The iterator class was not part of the HP implementation. According to the C++ standard, it is declared in the header <iterator>.

Template Parameters

Category   An iterator tag struct (page 179) that represents the iterator's category: input_iterator_tag, output_iterator_tag, forward_iterator_tag, bidirectional_iterator_tag, or random_access_iterator_tag. An iterator's category is the *most specific* concept that the iterator is a model of. Also defined as the nested type iterator_category.

T   The iterator's value type, the type of object that the iterator points to. Also defined as the nested type value_type.

Distance   The iterator's difference type, a signed integral type that is able to represent the distance between two iterators. Also defined as the nested type difference_type.
           Default: ptrdiff_t

Pointer   Pointer to the iterator's value type. The pointer type is almost always either T* or const T*, the former for a mutable iterator and the latter for a constant iterator. Also defined as the nested type pointer.
           Default: T*

Reference Reference to the iterator's value type. The reference type is almost always either T& or const T&, the former for a mutable iterator and the latter for a constant iterator. Also defined as the nested type reference.
           Default: T&

Model Of

Default Constructible, Assignable.

Public Base Classes

None.

10.3 allocator

`allocator<T>`

Example

There is rarely any reason to use the `allocator` class directly.

Unless you are writing a new container class, the only place you will ever see an Allocator (page 166) is as a container's template parameter—and the only time you ever have to mention that template parameter is when you want to use something other than the `allocator` class.

All of the predefined STL containers have a template parameter that models Allocator, and that template parameter defaults to `allocator`. For example, `vector<int>` is just the same as `vector<int, allocator<int> >`.

If you are writing a new container class and you want to parameterize the way that the class performs dynamic memory allocation, you can follow the pattern of giving the class a template parameter whose default is `allocator`.

Where Defined

In the HP implementation, a very different version of `allocator` was defined in the header `<allocator.h>`. According to the C++ standard, `allocator` is defined in the header `<memory>`.

Template Parameters

T   The `allocator`'s value type, the type of object for which it allocates and deallocates storage.

Model Of

Allocator (page 166).

Type Requirements

None.

Public Base Classes

None.

Members

The following members are defined for the general case of `allocator<T>`. There is also a specialization `allocator<void>` that contains only the members `value_type`, `pointer`, `const_pointer`, and `rebind`. (Those are the only members that make any sense for `allocator<void>`.)

The class `allocator` has no special members. All of its members are defined in the Allocator requirements.

`allocator::value_type`
The allocator's value type, T
(Described in Allocator.)

`allocator::pointer`
The allocator's pointer type, T*
(Described in Allocator.)

`allocator::const_pointer`
The allocator's const pointer type, const T*
(Described in Allocator.)

`allocator::reference`
The allocator's reference type, T&
(Described in Allocator.)

`allocator::const_reference`
The allocator's const reference type, const T&
(Described in Allocator.)

`allocator::size_type`
An unsigned integral type: size_t
(Described in Allocator.)

`allocator::difference_type`
A signed integral type: ptrdiff_t
(Described in Allocator.)

`allocator::rebind`
A nested class template. The class rebind<U> has a single member, other, which is a typedef for allocator<U>.
(Described in Allocator.)

`allocator::allocator()`
The default constructor.
(Described in Allocator.)

`allocator::allocator(const allocator&)`
The copy constructor. Since all instances of class allocator are equivalent to each other, the difference between the default constructor and the copy constructor is purely syntactic.
(Described in Allocator.)

`template <class U>`
`allocator::allocator(const allocator<U>&)`
The generalized copy constructor.
(Described in Allocator.)

`allocator::~allocator()`
The destructor.
(Described in Allocator.)

`pointer allocator::address(reference x) const`
Returns the address of an object. The expression a.address(x) is equivalent to &x.
(Described in Allocator.)

> `const_pointer allocator::address(const_reference x) const`
> Returns the address of a const object. The expression a.address(x) is equivalent to &x.
> (Described in Allocator.)
>
> `pointer allocator::allocate(size_type n, const void* = 0)`
> Allocates a block of memory large enough to store n objects of type T. The second argument is a hint. The implementation might use it as an aid to locality, or it might ignore it entirely.
> (Described in Allocator.)
>
> `void allocator::deallocate(pointer p, size_type n)`
> Deallocates a block of memory that was previously allocated with allocate.
> (Described in Allocator.)
>
> `size_type allocator::max_size() const`
> Returns the largest value for which allocate might succeed.
> (Described in Allocator.)
>
> `void allocator::construct(pointer p, const T& x)`
> Equivalent to new((const void*) p) T(x)
> (Described in Allocator.)
>
> `void allocator::destroy(pointer p)`
> Equivalent to p->~T().
> (Described in Allocator.)

10.4 Memory Management Primitives

The "algorithms" in this section are unlike all other STL algorithms. They operate on uninitialized storage, rather than on actual C++ objects. These low-level operations are chiefly useful for implementing container classes.

The three most important algorithms in this section are uninitialized_copy, uninitialized_fill, and uninitialized_fill_n. They correspond closely to the algorithms copy (page 233), fill (page 249), and fill_n (page 250). The only real difference is that copy, fill, and fill_n assign new values to objects that already exist, while the low-level algorithms uninitialized_copy, uninitialized_fill, and uninitialized_fill_n construct new objects.

10.4.1 construct

```
template <class T1, class T2>
void construct(T1* p, const T2& value);
```

In C++, the operator new allocates memory for an object and then creates an object at that location by calling a constructor. Occasionally, it is useful to separate those two operations. (In particular, it's useful when you are implementing a container class.)

If p is a pointer to memory that has been allocated but not initialized, then construct(p, value) creates an object of type T1 at the location pointed to by p. The argument value is passed as an argument to T1's constructor.

The expression construct(p, value) is essentially equivalent to the expression new(p) T1(value).

Where Defined

In the HP implementation construct was declared in the header <algo.h>, and in the SGI implementation it is declared in the header <memory>. The C++ standard does not include construct.

Requirements on Types

- T1 has a constructor that takes a single argument of type T2.

Preconditions

- p is a valid pointer that points to a region of memory whose size is at least sizeof(T1).
- The memory pointed to by p is uninitialized. That is, no object has been constructed at the location p.

Example

```
string* sptr = (string*) malloc(sizeof(string));
construct(sptr, "test");
assert(strcmp(sptr->c_str(), "test") == 0);
```

10.4.2 destroy

① template <class T> void destroy(T* pointer);

② template <class ForwardIterator>
  void destroy(ForwardIterator first, ForwardIterator last);

In C++ the operator delete destroys an object by calling its destructor and then deallocates the memory where that object was stored. Occasionally, it is useful to separate those two operations. (In particular, it is useful when you are implementing a container class. A container usually manages memory some of which contains C++ objects and some of which is uninitialized storage.) You can call an object's destructor, without deallocating the memory where the object was stored, by using destroy.

Version 1 of destroy destroys the object that pointer points to by calling the destructor T::~T(). The memory where the object was stored is not deallocated and can be reused for some other object.

Version 2 destroys all of the objects in the range of elements [first, last). It is equivalent to calling destroy(&*i) for every iterator i in [first, last).

Where Defined

In the HP implementation destroy was declared in the header <algo.h>, and in the SGI implementation it is declared in the header <memory>. The C++ standard does not include destroy.

Requirements on Types

For version 1:

- T's destructor, ~T(), is accessible.

For version 2:

- ForwardIterator is a model of Forward Iterator.
- ForwardIterator is mutable.
- ForwardIterator's value type has an accessible destructor.

Preconditions

For version 1:

- pointer points to a valid object of type T.

For version 2:

- [first,last) is a valid range.
- Each iterator in [first,last) points to a valid object.

Complexity

The runtime complexity of version 2 is linear: it calls the destructor exactly last − first times.

Example

```
class Int {
public:
  Int(int x) : val(x) {}
  int get() { return val; }
private:
  int val;
};

int main()
{
  Int A[] = { Int(1), Int(2), Int(3) };

  destroy(A, A + 3);
  construct(A + 0, Int(10));
```

```
    construct(A + 1, Int(11));
    construct(A + 2, Int(12));
}
```

10.4.3 uninitialized_copy

```
template <class InputIterator, class ForwardIterator>
ForwardIterator
uninitialized_copy(InputIterator first, InputIterator last,
                   ForwardIterator result);
```

The algorithm uninitialized_copy is one of the low-level STL components that make it possible to decouple memory allocation and object construction. If each iterator in the output range [result, result + (last − first)) points to uninitialized memory, then uninitialized_copy uses the copy constructor to create a copy of the objects [first, last) in the output range. That is, for each iterator i in the input range, uninitialized_copy creates a copy of *i in the corresponding location in the output range by calling construct(&*(result + (i - first)), *i).

Functions like uninitialized_copy are useful when you are implementing a container class. For example, a container's range constructor usually has two steps.

1. Allocate a block of uninitialized storage that is large enough to contain all of the elements in the range.

2. Use uninitialized_copy to create the container's elements in that memory block.

Because uninitialized_copy is mainly intended to be used in containers, it has an unusual burden: It must be possible to use uninitialized_copy to write exception-safe code. In particular, it must be possible to write a container class that won't cause a memory leak if one of the constructors that uninitialized_copy calls throws an exception. The C++ standard requires uninitialized_copy to have *commit or rollback* semantics. Either it constructs all elements as requested, or if any of the copy constructors fail, it constructs none at all. Here is one plausible implementation:

```
template <class InputIterator, class ForwardIterator>
ForwardIterator
uninitialized_copy(InputIterator first, InputIterator last,
                   ForwardIterator result)
{
  ForwardIterator cur = result;
  try {
    for ( ; first != last; ++first, ++cur)
      construct(&*cur, *first);
    return cur;
  }
  catch(...) {
    destroy(result, cur);
    throw;
```

```
    }
}
```

Where Defined

In the HP implementation, `uninitialized_copy` was declared in the header `<algo.h>`. According to the C++ standard, it is declared in the header `<memory>`.

Requirements on Types

- `InputIterator` is a model of Input Iterator.
- `ForwardIterator` is a model of Forward Iterator.
- `ForwardIterator` is mutable.
- `ForwardIterator`'s value type has a constructor that takes a single argument whose type is `InputIterator`'s value type.

Preconditions

- [first, last) is a valid range.
- [result, result + (last − first)) is a valid range.
- Each iterator in [result, result + (last − first)) points to a region of uninitialized memory that is large enough to contain a value of `ForwardIterator`'s value type.

Complexity

Linear. Exactly last − first constructor calls.

Example

```
class Int {
public:
  Int(int x) : val(x) {}
  // Int has no default constructor.
  int get() { return val; }
private:
  int val;
};

int main()
{
  int A1[] = {1, 2, 3, 4, 5, 6, 7};
  const int N = sizeof(A1) / sizeof(int);

  Int* A2 = (Int*) malloc(N * sizeof(Int));
  uninitialized_copy(A1, A1 + N, A2);
}
```

10.4.4 `uninitialized_fill`

```
template <class ForwardIterator, class T>
void uninitialized_fill(ForwardIterator first, ForwardIterator last,
                        const T& x);
```

Like `uninitialized_copy` (page 192), `uninitialized_fill` is one of the low-level STL algorithms that make it possible to decouple memory allocation from object construction. If each iterator in the range [first, last) points to uninitialized memory, then `uninitialized_fill` creates copies of the value x in that range. That is, for each iterator i in the range [first, last), `uninitialized_copy` creates a copy of x in that location by calling `construct(&*i, x)`.

Just as `uninitialized_copy` is useful when you are implementing a constructor that creates a container given a range of elements, so `uninitialized_fill` is useful when you are implementing a constructor that creates a container each of whose elements is initialized to the value x. Like `uninitialized_copy`, `uninitialized_fill` must have commit or rollback semantics. It must create all of the elements or none. If any of the copy constructors throws an exception, `uninitialized_fill` must clean up by destroying whatever elements it succeeded in creating.

Where Defined

In the HP implementation, `uninitialized_fill` was declared in the header `<algo.h>`. According to the C++ standard, it is declared in the header `<memory>`.

Requirements on Types

- `ForwardIterator` is a model of **Forward Iterator**.
- `ForwardIterator` is mutable.
- `ForwardIterator`'s value type has a constructor that takes a single argument of type T.

Preconditions

- [first, last) is a valid range.
- Each iterator in [first, last) points to a region of uninitialized memory that is large enough to contain a value of `ForwardIterator`'s value type.

Complexity

Linear. Exactly last − first constructor calls.

Example

```
class Int {
public:
  Int(int x) : val(x) {}
```

```
  // Int has no default constructor
  int get() { return val; }
private:
  int val;
};

int main()
{
  const int N = 137;

  Int val(46);
  Int* A = (Int*) malloc(N * sizeof(Int));
  uninitialized_fill(A, A + N, val);
}
```

10.4.5 uninitialized_fill_n

```
template <class ForwardIterator, class Size, class T>
ForwardIterator
uninitialized_fill_n(ForwardIterator first, Size n, const T& x);
```

The algorithm uninitialized_fill_n is similar to uninitialized_fill. It is one of the low-level STL algorithms that make it possible to decouple memory allocation from object construction. It initializes elements in a range to a copy of the same value. The difference between the two is that uninitialized_fill operates on a range denoted by a pair of iterators, while uninitialized_fill_n operates on a range denoted by a single iterator and an element count. This allows uninitialized_fill_n to work with Output Iterators.

If each iterator in the range [first, first + n) points to uninitialized memory, uninitialized_fill_n creates copies of x in that range using the copy constructor. That is, for each iterator i in the range [first, first + n), uninitialized_fill_n creates a copy of x in that location by calling construct(&*i, x).

Like uninitialized_copy and uninitialized_fill, uninitialized_fill_n has commit or rollback semantics. It creates all of the elements or none. If any of the copy constructors throws an exception, uninitialized_fill_n must clean up by destroying whatever elements it succeeded in creating.

Where Defined

In the HP implementation, uninitialized_fill_n was declared in <algo.h>. According to the C++ standard, it is declared in the header <memory>.

Requirements on Types

- ForwardIterator is a model of Forward Iterator.
- ForwardIterator is mutable.

- Size is an integral type that is convertible to ForwardIterator's difference type.
- ForwardIterator's value type has a constructor that takes a single argument of type T.

Preconditions

- n is nonnegative.
- [first, first + n) is a valid range.
- Each iterator in [first, first + n) points to a region of uninitialized memory that is large enough to contain a value of ForwardIterator's value type.

Complexity

Linear. Exactly n constructor calls.

Example

```
class Int {
public:
  Int(int x) : val(x) {}
  // Int has no default constructor
  int get() { return val; }
private:
  int val;
};

int main()
{
  const int N = 137;

  Int val(46);
  Int* A = (Int*) malloc(N * sizeof(Int));
  uninitialized_fill_n(A, N, val);
}
```

10.5 Temporary Buffers

Some algorithms, such as stable_sort and inplace_merge, are *adaptive*. They attempt to allocate extra temporary storage for intermediate results. If the allocation succeeds, the adaptive algorithms switch to alternate methods that have better runtime complexity.

One mechanism you can use, if you are writing an adaptive algorithm yourself, is the pair of functions get_temporary_buffer and return_temporary_buffer. As the names suggest, get_temporary_buffer allocates an uninitialized block of memory and return_temporary_buffer deallocates it. (It is unspecified whether get_temporary_buffer uses malloc, or operator new, or some other method.)

These functions should only be used for memory that truly is temporary. If a function allocates memory using `get_temporary_buffer`, it must deallocate that memory, using `return_temporary_buffer`, before it returns.

Unfortunately, `get_temporary_buffer` and `return_temporary_buffer` are not actually as useful as they might seem. Using these functions is a complicated process. The memory you obtain from `get_temporary_buffer` is uninitialized, so you must initialize it with `uninitialized_fill` (or some similar function). Similarly, you must destroy all of the objects in the buffer before you use `return_temporary_buffer` to deallocate it.

Partly because of this complicated multistep process, it is very difficult to write exception-safe code using `get_temporary_buffer` and `return_temporary_buffer`. If you are writing an adaptive algorithm and exception safety is important to you, you should almost certainly use a temporary buffer class instead. The constructor should allocate a buffer with `get_temporary_buffer` and initialize the elements in the buffer, and the destructor should destroy the elements and deallocate the buffer.

10.5.1 `get_temporary_buffer`

```
template <class T>
pair<T*, ptrdiff_t> get_temporary_buffer(ptrdiff_t len);
```

The function `get_temporary_buffer` allocates temporary storage. The argument `len` is the requested size of the buffer. For example, `get_temporary_buffer<T>(len)` requests a buffer that is aligned for objects of type `T` and that is large enough to hold `len` objects of type `T`.

This calling sequence is unusual: the template parameter `T` must be provided explicitly because it can't be deduced from `get_temporary_buffer`'s argument. This is called *explicit specification* of function template arguments, and it is a relatively new language feature. As of 1998 not all compilers support it.

If your compiler does not yet support explicit specification you may be able to use the HP STL's version of `get_temporary_buffer`, which is no longer part of the standard but which is commonly provided for backward compatibility. That version takes two arguments, where the second one is a dummy argument of type `T*` used only for template parameter deduction. To request a buffer that can hold `len` objects of type `T`, you would write `get_temporary_buffer(len, (T*) 0)`.

In either case the argument `len` is a request, not a requirement. The buffer that gets allocated might be smaller. The intention is that `get_temporary_buffer` will return as large a buffer as can be allocated without hurting performance.

The return value is a pair `P` whose first component is a pointer to the memory that was allocated and whose second argument indicates how large the buffer is. The buffer pointed to by `P.first` is large enough to hold `P.second` objects of type `T`. One of the postconditions is that $0 \leq P.second \leq len$. If `P.second` is zero, no buffer was allocated. In that case, `P.first` is a null pointer.

Note that `P.first` is a pointer to uninitialized memory rather than to actual objects of type `T`. You can create objects in the buffer using `uninitialized_copy`, `uninitialized_fill`, or some similar method.

Where Defined

In the HP STL, get_temporary_buffer was defined in <tempbuf.h>, which is included into <algo.h>. According to the C++ standard, it is defined in <memory>.

Preconditions

- len is greater than zero.

Example

```
int main()
{
  pair<int*, ptrdiff_t> P = get_temporary_buffer<int>(10000);
  int* buf = P.first;
  ptrdiff_t N = P.second;
  uninitialized_fill_n(buf, N, 42);
  int* result = find_if(buf, buf + N,
                        bind2nd(not_equal_to<int>(), 42));
  assert(result == buf + N);
  return_temporary_buffer(buf);
}
```

10.5.2 return_temporary_buffer

```
template <class T> void return_temporary_buffer(T* p);
```

The function return_temporary_buffer is used to deallocate memory that was allocated using get_temporary_buffer.

Where Defined

In the HP STL, return_temporary_buffer was defined in <tempbuf.h>, which is included into <algo.h>. According to the C++ standard, it is defined in <memory>.

Preconditions

- The argument p is a pointer to a block of memory that was allocated using get_temporary_buffer(ptrdiff_t, T*).
- Any objects that were constructed in this block of memory have been destroyed prior to the call to return_temporary_buffer.

Chapter 11

Nonmutating Algorithms

This chapter describes basic STL algorithms that operate on a range of iterators without changing the elements that those iterators point to. These algorithms return some information about the elements in the range. They are algorithms for inspection, rather than modification.

11.1 Linear Search

11.1.1 find

```
template<class InputIterator, class EqualityComparable>
InputIterator find(InputIterator first, InputIterator last,
                   const EqualityComparable& value);
```

The algorithm find performs linear search for a specific value through a range of iterators. Specifically, it returns the first iterator i in the range [first,last) such that *i == value. If no such value exists, the return value is last.

Linear search (or, to use Knuth's terminology [Knu98b], sequential search) is the most straightforward way to find a particular value in a range. The procedure is to test the first element to see if it has the desired value. If it does, stop. Otherwise, advance to the next element. Repeat until there are no more elements to test.

Sometimes linear search is written a bit differently. If you put a "sentinel element" at the end that's equal to value, it's guaranteed that the search will always terminate, and you can omit the test for the end of the range. The variation is unsuitable for a fully generic algorithm, however, because it relies on the assumption that the search procedure can modify its input range—and the STL can't make that assumption. Perhaps there is no element beyond the range [first,last), or perhaps the range consists of constant iterators. The STL's version of find doesn't use the sentinel technique.

Where Defined

In the HP implementation, find was declared in the header <algo.h>. According to the C++ standard, it is declared in the header <algorithm>.

Requirements on Types

- EqualityComparable is a model of Equality Comparable.
- InputIterator is a model of Input Iterator.
- Equality is defined between objects of type EqualityComparable and objects of InputIterator's value type.

Preconditions

- [first,last) is a valid range.

Complexity

Linear. At most last – first comparisons for equality.

Example

```
int main()
{
  list<int> L;
  L.push_back(3);
  L.push_back(1);
  L.push_back(7);

  list<int>::iterator result = find(L.begin(), L.end(), 7);
  assert(result == L.end() || *result == 7);
}
```

11.1.2 find_if

```
template<class InputIterator, class Predicate>
InputIterator find_if(InputIterator first, InputIterator last,
                      Predicate pred);
```

The algorithm find_if, like find (page 199), performs linear search through a range of iterators. The difference is that find_if is more general. Instead of searching for a particular value, it searches for an element that satisfies some condition. The return value is the first iterator i in the range [first,last) such that pred(*i) is true. If no such iterator exists, the return value is last.

Note that you can use find_if to find the first element that is equal to a particular value. The function object pred can, after all, test to see if its argument is equal to that value. That isn't very useful by itself, since it's just a more cumbersome way of doing the same thing as find, but a slight generalization is more interesting.

One very common operation is looking for an element that has a particular *key* (for example, looking for a person by last name or looking for an operating system process by its process ID number). Many books about algorithms, including Knuth [Knu98b], define searching as looking for an unknown element with a known key. You can't use find for this, since it can test only for object equality, but you can use find_if. You can use a function object that extracts its argument's key and then compares that key for equality with the desired value.

(Since find and find_if are so similar you might legitimately wonder why they have two different names. Why not just have two overloaded versions of find? The reason is purely technical. Both algorithms take the same number of arguments, and in both cases the type of the third argument is a template parameter. If the two algorithms had the same name, there would be no way to call them. The compiler wouldn't be able to tell which one you meant.)

Where Defined

In the HP implementation, find_if was declared in the header <algo.h>. According to the C++ standard, it is declared in the header <algorithm>.

Requirements on Types

- Predicate is a model of **Predicate**.
- InputIterator is a model of **InputIterator**.
- InputIterator's value type is convertible to Predicate's argument type.

Preconditions

- [first,last) is a valid range.
- For each iterator i in the range [first,last), *i is in the domain of Predicate.

Complexity

Linear. At most last − first applications of Pred.

Example

Find the first zero in an array of integers. Here, find_if is just being used as a less convenient version of find.

```
int main()
{
  int A[] = {4, 1, 0, 3, 2, 0, 6};
  const int N = sizeof(A) / sizeof(int);

  int* p = find_if(A, A + N,
                   bind2nd(equal_to<int>(), 0));
  cout << "Index of first zero = " << p - A << endl;
}
```

Find the first element whose key is equal to 2. In this example the elements are pairs, and the first component of the pair is treated as the key. More generally, you could use any field of a data structure as a key; all you need is a function object to extract that field.

```
int main()
{
  typedef pair<int, char*> Pair;

  vector<Pair> V;
  V.push_back(Pair(3, "A"));
  V.push_back(Pair(7, "B"));
  V.push_back(Pair(2, "C"));
  V.push_back(Pair(0, "D"));
  V.push_back(Pair(6, "E"));

  vector<Pair>::iterator p =
    find_if(V.begin(), V.end(),
            compose1(bind2nd(equal_to<int>(), 2), select1st<Pair>()));
  cout << "Found: "
       << "<" << (*p).first << "," << (*p).second << ">"
       << endl;
}
```

Find the first positive element in a list of integers. This is an example showing find_if in its full generality. It doesn't involve looking for a specific value or even for a value with a specific key.

```
int main()
{
  list<int> L;
  L.push_back(-3);
  L.push_back(0);
  L.push_back(3);
  L.push_back(-2);
  L.push_back(7);

  list<int>::iterator result = find_if(L.begin(), L.end(),
                                       bind2nd(greater<int>(), 0));
  assert(result == L.end() || *result > 0);
}
```

11.1.3 adjacent_find

① ```
template <class ForwardIterator>
ForwardIterator
adjacent_find(ForwardIterator first, ForwardIterator last);
```
```

② `template <class ForwardIterator, class BinaryPredicate>`
`ForwardIterator`
`adjacent_find(ForwardIterator first, ForwardIterator last,`
`             BinaryPredicate binary_pred);`

The `adjacent_find` algorithm, like `find` (page 199), performs linear search through a range of iterators. The difference between them is that `find` searches for a single element, while `adjacent_find` searches for two adjacent elements.

There are two versions of `adjacent_find`. Version 1 searches for two adjacent elements that are equal. Version 2 is more general. It searches for two adjacent elements that satisfy some condition, where that condition is defined by a **Binary Predicate**.

Version 1 of `adjacent_find` returns the first iterator i such that i and i+1 are both valid iterators in [`first`,`last`) and such that `*i == *(i+1)`. It returns `last` if no such iterator exists.

Version 2 returns the first iterator i such that i and i+1 are both valid iterators in [`first`,`last`) and such that `binary_pred(*i, *(i+1))` is true. Again, it returns `last` if no such iterator exists.

Where Defined

In the HP implementation, `adjacent_find` was declared in the header `<algo.h>`. According to the C++ standard, it is declared in the header `<algorithm>`.

Requirements on Types

For version 1:

- `ForwardIterator` is a model of **Forward Iterator**.
- `ForwardIterator`'s value type is **Equality Comparable**.

For version 2:

- `ForwardIterator` is a model of **Forward Iterator**.
- `ForwardIterator`'s value type is convertible to `BinaryPredicate`'s first argument type and to its second argument type.

Preconditions

- [`first`,`last`) is a valid range.

Complexity

Linear in the number of elements. Specifically, if the range [`first`,`last`) is nonempty, then `adjacent_find` performs at most `last` − `first` − 1 comparisons. If [`first`,`last`) is empty, it performs no comparisons.

Example

Find the first duplicated element. This example uses version 1:

```
int main()
{
  int A[] = {1, 2, 3, 3, 4, 5};
  const int N = sizeof(A) / sizeof(int);

  const int* p = adjacent_find(A, A + N);

  if (p != A + N)
    cout << "Duplicate element: " << *p << endl;
}
```

Find the first element that is greater than its successor—that is, the first place where the range fails to be sorted in ascending order. This example uses version 2.

```
int main()
{
  int A[] = {1, 2, 3, 4, 6, 5, 7, 8};
  const int N = sizeof(A) / sizeof(int);

  const int* p = adjacent_find(A, A + N, greater<int>());

  if (p == A + N)
    cout << "The range is sorted in ascending order." << endl;
  else
    cout << "Element " << p - A << " is out of order: "
         << *p << " > " << *(p + 1) << "." << endl;
}
```

11.1.4 find_first_of

① template <class InputIterator, class ForwardIterator>
   InputIterator
   find_first_of(InputIterator first1, InputIterator last1,
                 ForwardIterator first2, ForwardIterator last2);

② template <class InputIterator, class ForwardIterator,
             class BinaryPredicate>
   InputIterator
   find_first_of(InputIterator first1, InputIterator last1,
                 ForwardIterator first2, ForwardIterator last2,
                 BinaryPredicate comp);

The algorithm find_first_of is similar to find (page 199). It performs linear search through a range of Input Iterators. The difference is that while find searches for one particular value, find_first_of searches for any of several values. Specifically, find_first_of searches for the first occurrence in the range [first1, last1) of any of the elements in [first2, last2).

Just as find is like strchr from the standard C library, so is find_first_of like strpbrk.

The two versions of find_first_of differ in how they compare elements for equality. Version 1 uses operator==, and version 2 uses an arbitrary user-supplied function object comp. Version 1 returns the first iterator i in [first1,last1) such that, for some iterator j in [first2,last2), *i == *j. Version 2 returns the first iterator i in [first1,last1) such that, for some iterator j in [first2,last2), the expression comp(*i, *j) is true.

As usual, both versions return last1 if no such iterator i exists. As a consequence, if either [first1,last1) or [first2,last2) is an empty range then find_first_of will necessarily return last1.

Where Defined

The HP implementation did not include find_first_of. According to the C++ standard find_first_of is declared in the header <algorithm>.

Requirements on Types

For version 1:

- InputIterator is a model of Input Iterator.[1]
- ForwardIterator is a model of Forward Iterator.
- InputIterator's value type is Equality Comparable, and can be compared for equality with ForwardIterator's value type.

For version 2:

- InputIterator is a model of Input Iterator.
- ForwardIterator is a model of Forward Iterator.
- BinaryPredicate is a model of Binary Predicate.
- InputIterator's value type is convertible to BinaryPredicate's first argument type.
- ForwardIterator's value type is convertible to BinaryPredicate's second argument type.

Preconditions

- [first1,last1) is a valid range.
- [first2,last2) is a valid range.

Complexity

At most (last1 − first1) × (last2 − first2) comparisons.

---

1. According to the C++ standard both iterator types are required to be models of Forward Iterator, but this is unnecessarily strict. It is possible to implement find_first_of such that the second iterator type is a model of Forward Iterator and the first is any kind of Input Iterator.

Example

Like strpbrk, one of the uses of first_first_of is to find whitespace in a string. Space, tab, and newline are all whitespace characters.

```
int main()
{
    const char* WS = " \t\n";
    const int n_WS = strlen(WS);

    char* s1 = "This sentence contains five words.";
    char* s2 = "OneWord";


    char* end1 = find_first_of(s1, s1 + strlen(s1),
                               WS, WS + n_WS);
    char* end2 = find_first_of(s2, s2 + strlen(s2),
                               WS, WS + n_WS);

    printf("First word of s1: %.*s\n", end1 - s1, s1);
    printf("First word of s2: %.*s\n", end2 - s2, s2);
}
```

11.2   Subsequence Matching

11.2.1   search

① template <class ForwardIterator1, class ForwardIterator2>
ForwardIterator1
search(ForwardIterator1 first1, ForwardIterator1 last1,
       ForwardIterator2 first2, ForwardIterator2 last2);

② template <class ForwardIterator1, class ForwardIterator2,
            class BinaryPredicate>
ForwardIterator1
search(ForwardIterator1 first1, ForwardIterator1 last1,
       ForwardIterator2 first2, ForwardIterator2 last2,
       BinaryPredicate binary_pred);

The algorithm search is similar to find (page 199) and find_if (page 200) in that it performs a search through a range of elements. The difference is that while find and find_if each attempts to find a single element, search attempts to find an entire subrange of elements; it attempts to find the range [first2,last2) within [first1,last1). That is, search looks for a subsequence of [first1,last1) that is identical to [first2,last2) when compared element by element. It returns an iterator pointing to the beginning of that subsequence or last1 if no such subsequence exists.

Version 1 returns the first iterator i in the range [first1, last1 − (last2 − first2)) such that, for every iterator j in the range [first2, last2), *(i + (j − first2)) == *j. (This condition looks very complicated. What it means is simply that every element in the subrange beginning with i must be the same as the corresponding element in [first2, last2).)

The reason that this range is [first1, last1 − (last2 − first2)), instead of just [first1, last1), is that we are looking for a subrange that is equal to the *entire* range [first2, last2). A subrange can't be longer than the entire range, so an iterator i can't be the beginning of such a subsequence unless last1 − i ≥ last2 − first2. You may call search with arguments such that last1 − first1 < last2 − first2, but such a search will always fail.

Version 2 is identical, except for the way in which it determines whether two elements are the same. Version 1 uses operator==, and version 2 uses the user-supplied function object binary_pred. Version 2 returns the first iterator i in [first1, last1 − (last2 − first2)) such that, for every iterator j in [first2, last2), the expression binary_pred(*(i + (j − first2)), *j) is true.

Where Defined

In the HP implementation, search was declared in the header <algo.h>. According to the C++ standard, it is declared in the header <algorithm>.

Requirements on Types

For version 1:

- ForwardIterator1 is a model of Forward Iterator.
- ForwardIterator2 is a model of Forward Iterator.
- ForwardIterator1's value type is a model of EqualityComparable.
- ForwardIterator2's value type is a model of EqualityComparable.
- Objects of ForwardIterator1's value type can be compared for equality with objects of ForwardIterator2's value type.

For version 2:

- ForwardIterator1 is a model of Forward Iterator.
- ForwardIterator2 is a model of Forward Iterator.
- BinaryPredicate is a model of Binary Predicate.
- ForwardIterator1's value type is convertible to BinaryPredicate's first argument type.
- ForwardIterator2's value type is convertible to BinaryPredicate's second argument type.

Preconditions

- [first1, last1) is a valid range.
- [first2, last2) is a valid range.

Complexity

Worst-case complexity is linear in both the length of the text and of the pattern to be searched for (search performs at most (last1 − first1) × (last2 − first2) comparisons), but this behavior is very unlikely. Average complexity is linear in last1 − first1.

Example

Search for a substring in a string of characters. This is one of the main uses of search:

```
int main()
{
  const char S1[] = "Hello, world!";
  const char S2[] = "world";
  const int N1 = strlen(S1);
  const int N2 = strlen(S2);

  const char* p = search(S1, S1 + N1, S2, S2 + N2);
  if (p != S1 + N1)
    printf("Found substring \"%s\" at character %d of string \"%s\".\n",
           S2, p - S1, S1);
  else
    printf("Couldn't find substring.\n");
}
```

Find a subsequence of three numbers whose last digits are 1, 2, and 3, respectively.

```
template <class Integer>
struct congruent {
  congruent(Integer mod) : N(mod) {}
  bool operator()(Integer a, Integer b) const {
    return (a - b) % N == 0;
  }

  Integer N;
};

int main()
{
  int A[10] = {23, 46, 81, 2, 43, 19, 14, 98, 72, 51};
  int digits[3] = {1, 2, 3};

  int* seq = search(A, A + 10, digits, digits + 3,
                    congruent<int>(10));
  if (seq != A + 10) {
    cout << "Subsequence: ";
    copy(seq, seq + 3, ostream_iterator<int>(cout, " "));
    cout << endl;
```

```
    }
    else
      cout << "Subsequence not found" << endl;
  }
  // The printed output is
  // Subsequence: 81 2 43
```

11.2.2 find_end

① template <class ForwardIterator1, class ForwardIterator2>
ForwardIterator1
find_end(ForwardIterator1 first1, ForwardIterator1 last1,
         ForwardIterator2 first2, ForwardIterator2 last2);

② template <class ForwardIterator1, class ForwardIterator2,
            class BinaryPredicate>
ForwardIterator1
find_end(ForwardIterator1 first1, ForwardIterator1 last1,
         ForwardIterator2 first2, ForwardIterator2 last2,
         BinaryPredicate comp);

The algorithm find_end is misnamed. It is much more like search (page 206) than like find, and a more accurate name would have been search_end.

Like search, find_end looks for a subsequence within the range [first1,last1) that is identical to [first2,last2). The difference is that while search looks for the first such subsequence, find_end looks for the *last* such subsequence. It returns an iterator pointing to the beginning of that subsequence, or last1 if no such subsequence exists.

Version 1 returns the last iterator i in the range [first1,last1−(last2−first2)) such that, for every iterator j in the range [first2,last2), $*(i+(j-first2))$ == $*j$. (This condition looks very complicated. What it means is simply that every element in the subrange beginning with i must be the same as the corresponding element in [first2,last2).)

As with search, the reason that this range is [first1,last1 − (last2 − first2)) instead of [first1,last1) is that we are looking for a subrange that is equal to the *entire* range [first2,last2). A subrange can't be longer than the entire range, so an iterator i can't be the beginning of such a subsequence unless last1 − i ≥ last2 − first2. You may call find_end with arguments such that last1 − first1 < last2 − first2, but the return value in that case will always be last1.

Version 2 is identical, except for the way in which it determines whether two elements are the same: Version 1 uses operator==, and version 2 uses the user-supplied function object binary_pred. Version 2 returns the last iterator i in [first1,last1 − (last2 − first2)) such that, for every iterator j in [first2,last2), the expression binary_pred($*(i + (j - first2))$, $*j$) is true.

Where Defined

The algorithm find_end was not part of the HP implementation. According to the C++ standard it is declared in the header <algorithm>.

Requirements on Types

For version 1:

- ForwardIterator1 is a model of **Forward Iterator**.
- ForwardIterator2 is a model of **Forward Iterator**.
- ForwardIterator1's value type is **Equality Comparable**.
- ForwardIterator2's value type is **Equality Comparable**.
- Objects of ForwardIterator1's value type can be compared for equality with objects of ForwardIterator2's value type.

For version 2:

- ForwardIterator1 is a model of **Forward Iterator**.
- ForwardIterator2 is a model of **Forward Iterator**.
- BinaryPredicate is a model of **Binary Predicate**.
- ForwardIterator1's value type is convertible to BinaryPredicate's first argument type.
- ForwardIterator2's value type is convertible to BinaryPredicate's second argument type.

Preconditions

- [first1,last1) is a valid range.
- [first2,last2) is a valid range.

Complexity

The number of comparisons is proportional to $(last1 - first1) \times (last2 - first2)$. If both ForwardIterator1 and ForwardIterator2 are models of **Bidirectional Iterator**, then the average complexity is linear and the worst case is at most $(last1 - first1) \times (last2 - first2)$ comparisons.

Example

```
int main()
{
  char* s = "executable.exe";
  char* suffix = "exe";

  const int N = strlen(s);
  const int N_suf = strlen(suffix);
```

```
      char* location = find_end(s, s + N, suffix,
                                suffix + N_suf);

   if (location != s + N) {
     cout << "Found a match for " << suffix << " within " << s
          << endl;
     cout << s << endl;

     int i;
     for (i = 0; i < (location - s); ++i)
        cout << ' ';
     for (i = 0; i < N_suf; ++i)
        cout << '^';
     cout << endl;
   }
   else
     cout << "No match for " << suffix << " within " << s << endl;
 }
```

11.2.3 search_n

① template <class ForwardIterator, class Integer, class T>
ForwardIterator search_n(ForwardIterator first, ForwardIterator last,
                         Integer count, const T& value);

② template <class ForwardIterator, class Integer, class T,
            class BinaryPredicate>
ForwardIterator search_n(ForwardIterator first, ForwardIterator last,
                         Integer count, const T& value,
                         BinaryPredicate binary_pred);

The algorithm search_n searches for a subsequence of count consecutive elements in the range [first, last), all of which are equal to value. It returns an iterator pointing to the beginning of the first such subsequence or last if no such subsequence exists.

Note that count is permitted to be zero. A subsequence of zero elements is well defined. No matter what value is, every range contains a subrange of zero consecutive elements that are equal to value. When search_n is called with count equal to zero, the search always succeeds and the return value is always first.

The two versions of search_n differ in how they determine whether two elements are the same. Version 1 uses operator ==, and version 2 uses the user-supplied function object binary_pred.

Version 1 returns the first iterator i in the range [first, last − count) such that, for every iterator j in the range [i, i + count), *j == value. Version 2 returns the first iterator i in the range [first, last − count) such that, for every iterator j in the range [i, i + count), binary_pred(*j, value) is true.

As with search (page 206), the reason that this range is [first, last − count), instead of just [first, last), is that we are looking for a subrange of length count. A subrange can't be longer than the entire range, so an iterator i can't be the beginning of such a subsequence unless last − i ≥ count. You may call search_n with arguments such that last − first < count, but such a search will always fail.

Where Defined

The algorithm search_n was not part of the HP implementation. According to the C++ standard it is declared in the header <algorithm>.

Requirements on Types

For version 1:

- ForwardIterator is a model of Forward Iterator.
- Integer is an integral type.
- T is a model of Equality Comparable.
- ForwardIterator's value type is a model of Equality Comparable.
- Objects of ForwardIterator's value type can be compared for equality with objects of type T.

For version 2:

- ForwardIterator is a model of Forward Iterator.
- Integer is an integral type.
- T is a model of Equality Comparable.
- BinaryPredicate is a model of Binary Predicate.
- ForwardIterator's value type is convertible to BinaryPredicate's first argument type.
- T is convertible to BinaryPredicate's second argument type.

Preconditions

- [first, last) is a valid range.
- count ≥ 0.

Complexity

Linear: search_n performs at most last − first comparisons.[2]

---

2. The C++ standard imposes an upper bound of count × (last − first) comparisons, but this is unnecessarily lax. Regardless of the value of count, there is no reason for search_n to examine any element in [first, last) more than once.

Example

```
bool eq_nosign(int x, int y) { return abs(x) == abs(y); }

void lookup(int* first, int* last, size_t count, int val) {
  cout << "Searching for a sequence of "
       << count
       << " '" << val << "'"
       << (count != 1 ? "s: " : ":  ");
  int* result = search_n(first, last, count, val);
  if (result == last)
    cout << "Not found" << endl;
  else
    cout << "Index = " << result - first << endl;
}

void lookup_nosign(int* first, int* last, size_t count, int val) {
  cout << "Searching for a (sign-insensitive) sequence of "
       << count
       << " '" << val << "'"
       << (count != 1 ? "s: " : ":  ");
  int* result = search_n(first, last, count, val, eq_nosign);
  if (result == last)
    cout << "Not found" << endl;
  else
    cout << "Index = " << result - first << endl;
}

int main() {
  const int N = 10;
  int A[N] = {1, 2, 1, 1, 3, -3, 1, 1, 1, 1};

  lookup(A, A+N, 1, 4);
  lookup(A, A+N, 0, 4);
  lookup(A, A+N, 1, 1);
  lookup(A, A+N, 2, 1);
  lookup(A, A+N, 3, 1);
  lookup(A, A+N, 4, 1);

  lookup(A, A+N, 1, 3);
  lookup(A, A+N, 2, 3);
  lookup_nosign(A, A+N, 1, 3);
  lookup_nosign(A, A+N, 2, 3);
}
```

The output is

```
Searching for a sequence of 1 '4':  Not found
Searching for a sequence of 0 '4's: Index = 0
Searching for a sequence of 1 '1':  Index = 0
Searching for a sequence of 2 '1's: Index = 2
```

```
Searching for a sequence of 3 '1's: Index = 6
Searching for a sequence of 4 '1's: Index = 6
Searching for a sequence of 1 '3':  Index = 4
Searching for a sequence of 2 '3's: Not found
Searching for a (sign-insensitive) sequence of 1 '3':  Index = 4
Searching for a (sign-insensitive) sequence of 2 '3's: Index = 4
```

11.3   Counting Elements

11.3.1   count

① `template <class InputIterator, class EqualityComparable>`
`typename iterator_traits<InputIterator>::difference_type`
`count(InputIterator first, InputIterator last,`
`      const EqualityComparable& value);`

② `template <class InputIterator, class EqualityComparable, class Size>`
`void count(InputIterator first, InputIterator last,`
`           const EqualityComparable& value,`
`           Size& n);`

The algorithm `count` computes the number of elements in [first,last) that are
equal to value.

The two versions of `count` do exactly the same thing (count the number of elements that are equal to value), but they use two different interfaces. Version 2 was
defined in the original HP release of the STL [SL95], but the interface was changed during the standardization process. The C++ standard [ISO98] includes version 1 only.
At present (1998) some STL implementations include only version 1, some include
only version 2, and some include both.

Version 1 returns the number of elements in [first,last) that are equal to value.
Version 2 has a more complicated interface; it adds to n the number of iterators i in
[first,last) such that *i == value.

The interface of version 2 is quite cumbersome. If you want to count the number
of elements that are equal to some value, you must create a local variable, initialize
that variable to 0, and then call `count`. This is clearly inconvenient and error-prone
(forgetting to initialize the local variable to 0 is a common mistake), which is why the
interface was changed to that of version 1.

As in the case of `distance` (page 181), the reason the original STL used such an
inconvenient interface is that the original HP STL did not include `iterator_traits`
(Section 3.1).

Where Defined

In the HP implementation, `count` was declared in the header <algo.h>. According to
the C++ standard, it is declared in the header <algorithm>.

Requirements on Types

For version 1:

- InputIterator is a model of Input Iterator.
- EqualityComparable is a model of Equality Comparable.
- InputIterator's value type is a model of Equality Comparable.
- An object of InputIterator's value type can be compared for equality with an object of EqualityComparable's value type.

For version 2:

- InputIterator is a model of Input Iterator.
- EqualityComparable is a model of Equality Comparable.
- Size is an integral type that is large enough to represent non-negative values of InputIterator's distance type.
- InputIterator's value type is a model of Equality Comparable.
- An object of InputIterator's value type can be compared for equality with an object of EqualityComparable's value type.

Preconditions

For version 1:

- [first,last) is a valid range.

For version 2:

- [first,last) is a valid range.
- n plus the number of elements equal to value does not exceed the maximum value of type Size.

Complexity

Linear. Exactly last − first comparisons.

Example

Count the number of zeros in a range, using the old interface (version 2).

```
int main()
{
  int A[] = { 2, 0, 4, 6, 0, 3, 1, -7 };
  const int N = sizeof(A) / sizeof(int);

  int result = 0;
  count(A, A + N, 0, result);
  cout << "Number of zeros: " << result << endl;
}
```

Do exactly the same thing using the new interface (version 1).

```
int main()
{
  int A[] = { 2, 0, 4, 6, 0, 3, 1, -7 };
  const int N = sizeof(A) / sizeof(int);

  cout << "Number of zeros: " <<  count(A, A + N, 0) << endl;
}
```

11.3.2   count_if

① template <class InputIterator, class Predicate>
typename iterator_traits<InputIterator>::difference_type
count_if(InputIterator first, InputIterator last,
         Predicate pred);

② template <class InputIterator, class Predicate, class Size>
  void count_if(InputIterator first, InputIterator last,
                Predicate pred,
                Size& n);

The algorithm count_if is very similar to count (page 214), but is more general. Instead of computing the number of elements that are equal to a particular value, count_if computes the number of elements in [first, last) that satisfy some condition. The condition is a user-supplied function object pred, and count_if computes the number of iterators i in that range such that pred(*i) is true.

There are two count_if interfaces for the same reason that there are two count interfaces. Version 2 was defined in the original HP release of the STL [SL95] and version 1 is defined in the C++ standard [ISO98]. Some STL implementations include only the old interface, some include only the new, and some include both.

Version 1 returns the number of elements that satisfy pred—that is, it returns the number of iterators i in [first, last) such that pred(*i) is true. Version 2 adds to n the number of iterators i in [first, last) such that pred(*i) is true.

Where Defined

In the HP implementation, count_if was declared in the header <algo.h>. According to the C++ standard, it is declared in the header <algorithm>.

Requirements on Types

For version 1:

- InputIterator is a model of Input Iterator.
- Predicate is a model of Predicate.
- InputIterator's value type is convertible to Predicate's argument type.

For version 2:

- `InputIterator` is a model of Input Iterator.
- `Predicate` is a model of **Predicate**.
- `Size` is an integral type that can hold values of `InputIterator`'s distance type.
- `InputIterator`'s value type is convertible to `Predicate`'s argument type.

Preconditions

For version 1:

- `[first,last)` is a valid range.

For version 2:

- `[first,last)` is a valid range.
- n plus the number of elements that satisfy `pred` does not exceed the maximum value of type `Size`.

Complexity

Linear. Exactly `last − first` applications of `pred`.

Example

Count the number of zeros in a range using the old interface (version 2). There is no reason to use `count_if` for this, since `count` does the same thing but more conveniently. The only reason for presenting this example is to illustrate that `count` is a special case of `count_if`.

```
int main()
{
  int A[] = { 2, 0, 4, 6, 0, 3, 1, -7 };
  const int N = sizeof(A) / sizeof(int);

  int result = 0;
  count_if(A, A + N, bind2nd(equal_to<int>(), 0), result);
  cout << "Number of zeros: " << result << endl;
}
```

Do exactly the same thing, but using the new interface (version 1).

```
int main()
{
  int A[] = { 2, 0, 4, 6, 0, 3, 1, -7 };
  const int N = sizeof(A) / sizeof(int);

  cout << "Number of zeros: " <<
          << count_if(A, A + N, bind2nd(equal_to<int>(), 0))
          << endl;
}
```

As in the case of find_if (page 200), counting the number of elements equal to some value has an interesting generalization: Counting the number of elements whose *key* is equal to some value. In this example the elements are pairs. The first component of the pair is treated as the key.

```
int main()
{
   typedef pair<int, char*> Pair;

   vector<Pair> V;
   V.push_back(Pair(3, "A"));
   V.push_back(Pair(7, "B"));
   V.push_back(Pair(2, "C"));
   V.push_back(Pair(3, "D"));
   V.push_back(Pair(0, "E"));
   V.push_back(Pair(6, "E"));

   cout << "Number of elements with key equal to 3: "
        << count_if(V.begin(), V.end(),
                       compose1(bind2nd(equal_to<int>(), 3),
                                  select1st<Pair>()))
        << endl;
}
```

Count the number of even elements in a range.

```
int main()
{
   int A[] = { 2, 0, 4, 6, 0, 3, 1, -7 };
   const int N = sizeof(A) / sizeof(int);

   cout << "Number of even elements: "
        << count_if(A, A + N,
                       compose1(bind2nd(equal_to<int>(), 0),
                                  bind2nd(modulus<int>(), 2)))
        << endl;
}
```

11.4 for_each

```
template <class InputIterator, class UnaryFunction>
UnaryFunction for_each(InputIterator first, InputIterator last,
                        UnaryFunction f);
```

The algorithm for_each applies the function object f to each element in the range [first, last), discarding f's return value (if any). Applications are performed in forward order, that is, from first to last. The return value is the function object after it has been applied to each element.

The return value is often ignored, since for_each is commonly used just to perform a sequence of actions. Occasionally, however, the return value is useful. A function object is not necessarily a simple function pointer, but it may be a user-defined class. In particular, a function object might have local state. This means that for_each isn't just a way to perform a sequence of actions, but more generally, it is a way to perform a sequence of actions while potentially accumulating information. The function object might, for example, count the number of times that it is called, or it might have a status flag to indicate whether or not every call succeeded.

Where Defined

In the HP implementation, for_each was declared in the header <algo.h>. According to the C++ standard, it is declared in the header <algorithm>.

Requirements on Types

- InputIterator is a model of Input Iterator.
- UnaryFunction is a model of Unary Function.
- InputIterator's value type is convertible to UnaryFunction's argument type.

Preconditions

- [first,last) is a valid range.

Complexity

Linear. Exactly last − first applications of UnaryFunction.

Example

Print a sequence of elements, using a unary function object that prints its argument.

```
template<class T> struct print : public unary_function<T, void>
{
  print(ostream& out) : os(out), count(0) {}
  void operator() (T x) { os << x << ' '; ++count; }
  ostream& os;
  int count;
};

int main()
{
  int A[] = {1, 4, 2, 8, 5, 7};
  const int N = sizeof(A) / sizeof(int);

  print<int> P = for_each(A, A + N, print<int>(cout));
  cout << endl << P.count << " objects printed." << endl;
}
```

This example isn't very interesting because it's possible to achieve the same effect with an `ostream_iterator`.

A somewhat more sophisticated example uses the `system` function, from the standard C library, to execute a list of operating system commands one after another. In this case, the function object we pass to `for_each` is a function pointer.

```
int main()
{
  char* commands[] = {"uptime", "pwd", "ls"};
  const int N = sizeof(commands) / sizeof(char*);

  for_each(commands, commands + N, system);
}
```

This example can be extended almost indefinitely. For example, instead of using the `system` function directly, we might use a function object that checks `system`'s return value to test whether the call succeeded. On an even more ambitious level, we might use a function object that encapsulates the differences between various operating systems.

11.5   Comparing Two Ranges

11.5.1   `equal`

① `template <class InputIterator1, class InputIterator2>`
`bool equal(InputIterator1 first1, InputIterator1 last1,`
`          InputIterator2 first2);`

② `template <class InputIterator1, class InputIterator2,`
`             class BinaryPredicate>`
`bool equal(InputIterator1 first1, InputIterator1 last1,`
`          InputIterator2 first2, BinaryPredicate binary_pred);`

The algorithm `equal` returns `true` if the ranges $[first1, last1)$ and $[first2, first2 + (last1 - first1))$ are identical when compared element by element, and otherwise returns `false`.

The two versions of `equal` differ in that the first one compares elements using `operator==` and the second uses a user-supplied function object `binary_pred`.

Version 1 returns `true` if and only if, for every iterator i in $[first1, last1)$, `*i == *(first2 + (i - first1))`. Version 2 returns `true` if and only if, for every iterator i in $[first1, last1)$, `binary_pred(*i, *(first2 + (i - first1))` is `true`.

Where Defined

In the HP implementation, `equal` was declared in the header `<algo.h>` and defined in `<algobase.h>`. According to the C++ standard, it is declared in `<algorithm>`.

Requirements on Types

For version 1:

- InputIterator1 is a model of Input Iterator.
- InputIterator2 is a model of Input Iterator.
- InputIterator1's value type is a model of Equality Comparable.
- InputIterator2's value type is a model of Equality Comparable.
- Objects of InputIterator1's value type can be compared for equality with objects of InputIterator2's value type.

For version 2:

- InputIterator1 is a model of Input Iterator.
- InputIterator2 is a model of Input Iterator.
- BinaryPredicate is a model of Binary Predicate.
- InputIterator1's value type is convertible to BinaryPredicate's first argument type.
- InputIterator2's value type is convertible to BinaryPredicate's second argument type.

Preconditions

- [first1, last1) is a valid range.
- [first2, first2 + (last2 − last1)) is a valid range.

Complexity

Linear. At most last1 − first1 comparisons.

Example

Compare two ranges for equality.

```
int main()
{
  int A1[] = { 3, 1, 4, 1, 5, 9, 3 };
  int A2[] = { 3, 1, 4, 2, 8, 5, 7 };
  const int N = sizeof(A1) / sizeof(int);

  if (equal(A1, A1 + N, A2))
    cout << "Equal" << endl;
  else
    cout << "Not equal" << endl;
}
```

Compare two strings for equality, ignoring case.

```
inline bool eq_nocase(char c1, char c2) {
  return toupper(c1) == toupper(c2);
}

int main()
{
  const char* s1 = "This is a Test";
  const char* s2 = "this is a test";
  const int N = strlen(s1);

  if (equal(s1, s1 + N, s2, eq_nocase))
    cout << "Equal" << endl;
  else
    cout << "Not equal" << endl;
}
```

11.5.2 mismatch

① template <class InputIterator1, class InputIterator2>
pair<InputIterator1, InputIterator2>
mismatch(InputIterator1 first1, InputIterator1 last1,
         InputIterator2 first2);

② template <class InputIterator1, class InputIterator2,
            class BinaryPredicate>
pair<InputIterator1, InputIterator2>
mismatch(InputIterator1 first1, InputIterator1 last1,
         InputIterator2 first2,
         BinaryPredicate binary_pred);

The algorithm mismatch returns the first position where the ranges [first1, last1) and [first2, first2 + (last1 − first1)) differ. That position can be described by an iterator in the range [first1, last1) and a corresponding iterator in the range [first2, first2 + (last1 − first1)), and mismatch returns a pair of those two iterators.[3]

The two versions of mismatch differ in how they test whether elements are equal: Version 1 tests for equality using operator==, and version 2 uses a user-supplied function object binary_pred.

---

3. Note how similar this is to equal (page 220). The only real difference is what happens when the two ranges differ: equal just returns a boolean result, but mismatch tells where they differ. The expression equal(f1, l1, f2) is equivalent to the expression mismatch(f1, l1, f2).first == l1, and this is a reasonable way to implement equal.

Version 1 finds the first iterator i in [first1,last1) such that *i != *(first2 + (i − first1)). The return value is a pair whose first element is i and whose second element is first2 + (i − first1). If no such iterator i exists, the return value is a pair whose first element is last1 and whose second element is first2 + (last1 − first1).

Version 2 finds the first iterator i in [first1,last1) such that binary_pred(*i, *(first2 + (i − first1)) is false. The return value is a pair whose first element is i and whose second element is first2 + (i − first1). If no such iterator i exists, the return value is a pair whose first element is last1 and whose second element is first2 + (last1 − first1).

Where Defined

In the HP implementation, mismatch was declared in the header <algo.h> and defined in <algobase.h>. According to the C++ standard, it is declared in the header <algorithm>.

Requirements on Types

For version 1:

- InputIterator1 is a model of Input Iterator.
- InputIterator2 is a model of Input Iterator.
- InputIterator1's value type is a model of Equality Comparable.
- InputIterator2's value type is a model of Equality Comparable.
- An object of InputIterator1's value type can be compared for equality with an object of InputIterator2's value type.

For version 2:

- InputIterator1 is a model of Input Iterator.
- InputIterator2 is a model of Input Iterator.
- BinaryPredicate is a model of Binary Predicate.
- InputIterator1's value type is convertible to BinaryPredicate's first argument type.
- InputIterator2's value type is convertible to BinaryPredicate's second argument type.

Preconditions

- [first1,last1) is a valid range.
- [first2,first2 + (last2 − last1)) is a valid range.

Complexity

Linear. At most last1 − first1 comparisons.

Example

Find the first position where two sequences differ.

```
int main()
{
  int A1[] = { 3, 1, 4, 1, 5, 9, 3 };
  int A2[] = { 3, 1, 4, 2, 8, 5, 7 };
  const int N = sizeof(A1) / sizeof(int);

  pair<int*, int*> result = mismatch(A1, A1 + N, A2);
  if (result.first == A1 + N)
    cout << "The two ranges do not differ." << endl;
  else {
    cout << "First mismatch is in position "
         << result.first - A1 << endl;
    cout << "Values: " << *(result.first) << ", "
                       << *(result.second) << endl;
  }
}
```

Find the first position where two strings differ, ignoring case.

```
inline bool eq_nocase(char c1, char c2) {
  return toupper(c1) == toupper(c2);
}

int main()
{
  const char* s1 = "This is a Test";
  const char* s2 = "this is a test";
  const int N = strlen(s1);

  pair<const char*, const char*> result =
    mismatch(s1, s1 + N, s2, eq_nocase)

  if (result.first == s1 + N)
    cout << "The two strings do not differ" << endl;
  else {
    cout << "The strings differ starting at character "
         << result.first - s1 << endl;
    cout << "Trailing part of s1: " << result.first << endl;
    cout << "Trailing part of s2: " << result.second << endl;
  }
}
```

11.5.3 `lexicographical_compare`

① `template <class InputIterator1, class InputIterator2>`
  `bool`
  `lexicographical_compare(InputIterator1 first1, InputIterator1 last1,`
  `                        InputIterator2 first2, InputIterator2 last2);`

② `template <class InputIterator1, class InputIterator2,`
  `          class BinaryPredicate>`
  `bool`
  `lexicographical_compare(InputIterator1 first1, InputIterator1 last1,`
  `                        InputIterator2 first2, InputIterator2 last2,`
  `                        BinaryPredicate comp);`

The algorithm `lexicographical_compare` returns true if the range [`first1,last1`) is lexicographically less than the range [`first2,last2`), and `false` otherwise.

Lexicographical comparison means "dictionary" (element-by-element) ordering. That is, [`first1,last1`) is less than [`first2,last2`) if `*first1` is less than `*first2`, and greater if `*first1` is greater than `*first2`. If the two first elements are equivalent then `lexicographical_compare` compares the two second elements, and so on. As with ordinary dictionary order, the first range is considered to be less than the second if every element in the first range is equal to the corresponding element in the second but the second contains more elements.

The two ranges [`first1,last1`) and [`first2,last2`) do not necessarily have the same number of elements. This is unusual. Most STL algorithms that operate on two ranges, such as `equal` (page 220) and `copy` (page 233), do require the two ranges to be of equal length. Most algorithms specify two ranges using three iterators, rather than the four iterators in `lexicographical_compare`'s arguments.

The two versions of `lexicographical_compare` differ in how they define whether one element is less than another. Version 1 compares objects using `operator<`, and version 2 compares objects using a user-supplied function object `comp`.

Where Defined

In the HP implementation, `lexicographical_compare` was declared in the header `<algo.h>` and defined in `<algobase.h>`. According to the C++ standard, it is declared in the header `<algorithm>`.

Requirements on Types

For version 1:

- `InputIterator1` is a model of Input Iterator.
- `InputIterator2` is a model of Input Iterator.
- `InputIterator1`'s value type is a model of LessThan Comparable.

- InputIterator2's value type is a model of LessThan Comparable.
- If v1 is a value of InputIterator1's value type and v2 is of InputIterator2's value type, then both v1 < v2 and v2 < v1 are defined.

For version 2:

- InputIterator1 is a model of Input Iterator.
- InputIterator2 is a model of Input Iterator.
- BinaryPredicate is a model of Binary Predicate.
- InputIterator1's value type is convertible to BinaryPredicate's first argument type and second argument type.
- InputIterator2's value type is convertible to BinaryPredicate's first argument type and second argument type.

Preconditions

- [first1,last1) is a valid range.
- [first2,last2) is a valid range.

Complexity

Linear. At most $2 \min(\text{last1} - \text{first1}, \text{last2} - \text{first2})$ comparisons.

Example

Compare two ranges of numbers in dictionary order.

```
int main()
{
  int A1[] = {3, 1, 4, 1, 5, 9, 3};
  int A2[] = {3, 1, 4, 2, 8, 5, 7};
  int A3[] = {1, 2, 3, 4};
  int A4[] = {1, 2, 3, 4, 5};

  const int N1 = sizeof(A1) / sizeof(int);
  const int N2 = sizeof(A2) / sizeof(int);
  const int N3 = sizeof(A3) / sizeof(int);
  const int N4 = sizeof(A4) / sizeof(int);

  bool C12 = lexicographical_compare(A1, A1 + N1,
                                     A2, A2 + N2);

  bool C34 = lexicographical_compare(A3, A3 + N3,
                                     A4, A4 + N4);

  cout << "A1[] < A2[]: " << (C12 ? "true" : "false") << endl;
  cout << "A3[] < A4[]: " << (C34 ? "true" : "false") << endl;
}
```

Compare two strings in dictionary order, ignoring case.

```
inline bool lt_nocase(char c1, char c2) {
  return toupper(c1) < toupper(c2);
}

int main()
{
  const char* s1 = "abc";
  const char* s2 = "ABC";
  const char* s3 = "abcDEF";
  const int N1 = 3, N2 = 3, N3 = 6;

  printf("%s < %s : %c\n",
         s1, s2,
         lexicographical_compare(s1, s1 + N1,
                                 s2, s2 + N2,
                                 lt_nocase) ? 't' : 'f');

  printf("%s < %s : %c\n",
         s2, s3,
         lexicographical_compare(s2, s2 + N2,
                                 s3, s3 + N3,
                                 lt_nocase) ? 't' : 'f');
}
// The printed output is:
// abc < ABC : f
// ABC < abcDEF : t
```

11.6 Minimum and Maximum

11.6.1 min

① `template <class LessThanComparable>`
`const LessThanComparable& min(const LessThanComparable& a,`
`                              const LessThanComparable& b);`

② `template <class T, class BinaryPredicate>`
`const T& min(const T& a, const T& b, BinaryPredicate comp);`

Most STL algorithms operate on ranges of elements; min is one of the few that instead operate on individual objects passed as arguments. Specifically, min returns the lesser of its two arguments. It returns the first argument if neither is less than the other.

The two versions of min differ in how they define whether one element is less than another. Version 1 compares objects using operator<, and version 2 compares objects using the function object comp.

Where Defined

In the HP implementation, `min` was declared in the header `<algo.h>` and defined in `<algobase.h>`. According to the C++ standard, it is declared in `<algorithm>`.

Requirements on Types

For version 1:

- `LessThanComparable` is a model of LessThan Comparable.

For version 2:

- `BinaryPredicate` is a model of Binary Predicate.
- `T` is convertible to `BinaryPredicate`'s first argument type and to its second argument type.

Example

```
int main()
{
  const int x = min(3, 9);
  assert(x == 3);

  int a = 3;
  int b = 3;

  const int& result = min(a, b);
  assert(&result == &a);
}
```

11.6.2 max

① template <class LessThanComparable>
  const LessThanComparable& max(const LessThanComparable& a,
                                const LessThanComparable& b);

② template <class T, class BinaryPredicate>
  const T& max(const T& a, const T& b, BinaryPredicate comp);

Most STL algorithms operate on ranges of elements; `max` is one of the few that instead operate on individual objects passed as arguments. Specifically, `max` returns the greater of its two arguments. It returns the first argument if neither is greater than the other.

The two versions of `max` differ in how they define whether one element is less than another. Version 1 compares objects using `operator<`, and version 2 compares objects using the function object `comp`.

Where Defined

In the HP implementation, max was declared in the header <algo.h> and defined in <algobase.h>. According to the C++ standard, it is declared in <algorithm>.

Requirements on Types

For version 1:

- LessThanComparable is a model of LessThan Comparable.

For version 2:

- BinaryPredicate is a model of Binary Predicate.
- T is convertible to BinaryPredicate's first argument type and to its second argument type.

Example

```
int main() {
    const int x = max(3, 9);
    assert(x == 9);

    int a = 3;
    int b = 3;

    const int& result = max(a, b);
    assert(&result == &a);
}
```

11.6.3 min_element

① template <class ForwardIterator>
ForwardIterator
min_element(ForwardIterator first, ForwardIterator last);

② template <class ForwardIterator, class BinaryPredicate>
ForwardIterator
min_element(ForwardIterator first, ForwardIterator last,
            BinaryPredicate comp);

The algorithm min_element finds the smallest element in the range [first,last). It returns the first iterator i in [first,last) such that no other iterator in the range points to a value smaller than *i.[4] The return value is last if and only if [first,last) is an empty range.

---

4. We can't say "an iterator pointing to the smallest element in [first,last)" because there might not be a unique smallest element. The smallest value might appear more than once in the range. For example, if every element in [first,last) is equal, then min_element will always return first. This is a generalization of min, which returns its first argument if the two are equal.

The two versions of `min_element` differ in how they define whether one element is less than another. Version 1 compares objects using `operator<`, and version 2 compares objects using a function object `comp`.

Version 1 returns the first iterator i in [first,last) such that, for every iterator j in [first,last), *j < *i is false. Version 2 returns the first iterator i in [first,last) such that, for every iterator j in [first, last), comp(*j, *i) is false.

Where Defined

In the HP implementation, `min_element` is declared in the header `<algo.h>`. According to the C++ standard, it is declared in the header `<algorithm>`.

Requirements on Types

For version 1:

- `ForwardIterator` is a model of Forward Iterator.
- `ForwardIterator`'s value type is LessThan Comparable.

For version 2:

- `ForwardIterator` is a model of Forward Iterator.
- `BinaryPredicate` is a model of Binary Predicate.
- `ForwardIterator`'s value type is convertible to `BinaryPredicate`'s first argument type and second argument type.

Preconditions

- [first,last) is a valid range.

Complexity

Linear. For a nonempty range, exactly (last − first) − 1 comparisons.

Example

```
int main()
{
  list<int> L;
  generate_n(front_inserter(L), 1000, rand);

  list<int>::const_iterator it = min_element(L.begin(), L.end());
  cout << "The smallest element is " << *it << endl;
}
```

11.6.4 max_element

① template <class ForwardIterator>
ForwardIterator
max_element(ForwardIterator first, ForwardIterator last);

② template <class ForwardIterator, class BinaryPredicate>
ForwardIterator
max_element(ForwardIterator first, ForwardIterator last,
            BinaryPredicate comp);

The algorithm max_element finds the largest element in the range [first,last). It returns the first iterator i in [first,last) such that no other iterator in the range points to a value greater than *i.[5] The return value is last if and only if [first,last) is an empty range.

The two versions of max_element differ in how they define whether one element is less than another. Version 1 compares objects using operator<, and version 2 compares objects using a function object comp.

Version 1 returns the first iterator i in [first,last) such that, for every iterator j in [first,last), *i < *j is false. Version 2 returns the first iterator i in [first,last) such that, for every iterator j in [first,last), comp(*i, *j) is false.

Where Defined

In the HP implementation, max_element is declared in the header <algo.h>. According to the C++ standard, it is declared in the header <algorithm>.

Requirements on Types

For version 1:

- ForwardIterator is a model of Forward Iterator.
- ForwardIterator's value type is LessThan Comparable.

For version 2:

- ForwardIterator is a model of Forward Iterator.
- BinaryPredicate is a model of Binary Predicate.
- ForwardIterator's value type is convertible to BinaryPredicate's first argument type and second argument type.

---

5. We can't say "an iterator pointing to the largest element in [first,last)" because there might not be a unique largest element. The largest value might appear more than once in the range. For example, if every element in [first,last) is equal, then max_element will always return first. This is a generalization of max, which returns its first argument if the two are equal.

Preconditions

- [first, last) is a valid range.

Complexity

Linear. For a nonempty range, exactly (last − first) − 1 comparisons.

Example

```
int main()
{
  list<int> L;
  generate_n(front_inserter(L), 1000, rand);

  list<int>::const_iterator it = max_element(L.begin(), L.end());
  cout << "The largest element is " << *it << endl;
}
```

Chapter 12

Basic Mutating Algorithms

This chapter describes the basic algorithms that, unlike the "inspection" algorithms of Chapter 11, operate on one or more ranges of iterators by modifying some of the elements that those iterators point to. The basic modifying algorithms include copying elements from one range to another, assigning a value to every iterator in a range, and replacing one value with another.

The algorithms in this chapter all share an important property. They modify the *values* pointed to by a range of iterators, rather than the iterators themselves (or, to put it differently, these algorithms modify a range of elements rather than a range of iterators). If you pass the range [first, last) to one of the algorithms in this chapter, then, even though the algorithm might change *first, it cannot change first itself. It cannot change the fact that the iterator first + 1 comes immediately after first, nor can it change the number of elements in the range [first, last).

This property may seem obvious when you see it stated like this, but in the context of specific algorithms it sometimes has unexpected implications.

Some of the algorithms in this chapter, such as partition, operate on a single range. Others, such as copy, operate on two distinct ranges: an input range, whose values are not modified, and an output range, to which the results of the algorithm are assigned.

Sometimes the STL provides both forms of the same algorithm. For example, reverse reverses a range in place, while reverse_copy copies the input range, in reverse order, to the output range. This naming convention is consistent. An algorithm named X_copy is always the copying form of the algorithm X.

12.1 Copying Ranges

12.1.1 copy

```
template <class InputIterator, class OutputIterator>
OutputIterator copy(InputIterator first, InputIterator last,
                    OutputIterator result);
```

The algorithm copy copies elements from the input range [first,last) to the output range [result,result + (last − first)). That is, it performs the assignments *result = *first, *(result + 1) = *(first + 1), and so on. The return value is result + (last − first).

The requirements that copy imposes on its template arguments are very weak. Its input range need only consist of Input Iterators, and its output range need only consist of Output Iterators. This means that you can use copy to copy values from almost any sort of source to almost any sort of destination.

For every integer n from 0 up to (but not including) last − first, copy performs the assignment *(result+n) = *(first+n). Assignments are performed in forward order, *i.e.* in order of increasing n.[1]

As with all of the algorithms in this chapter, copy modifies only the values pointed to by the range of iterators [result,result + (last − first)), not the iterators themselves. It acts by assigning new values to elements in the output range, rather than by creating new elements. It can't change the number of iterators in the output range. One consequence of this fact is that copy can't directly be used to insert elements into an empty Container.

If you want to insert elements into a Sequence, you can either use its insert member function explicitly, or else you can use copy along with the insert_iterator adaptor (page 351).

Where Defined

In the HP implementation, copy was declared in the header <algo.h> and defined in <algobase.h>. According to the C++ standard, it is declared in <algorithm>.

Requirements on Types

- InputIterator is a model of Input Iterator.
- OutputIterator is a model of Output Iterator.
- InputIterator's value type is convertible to a type in OutputIterator's set of value types.

Preconditions

- [first,last) is a valid range.
- result is not an iterator within the range [first,last).

---

1. The order of assignments matters when the input and output ranges overlap. It implies that copy may not be used if result is in the range [first,last). That is, it may not be used if the beginning of the output range overlaps with the input range, but it may be used if the end of the output range overlaps with the input range; copy_backward has opposite restrictions. (If the two ranges are completely nonoverlapping, of course, then either algorithm may be used.) The order of assignments also matters if result is an ostream_iterator (page 357), or some other iterator whose semantics depends on the order of assignments.

- There is enough space to hold all of the elements being copied. More formally, the requirement is that $[\text{result}, \text{result} + (\text{last} - \text{first}))$ is a valid range.

Complexity

Linear. Exactly $\text{last} - \text{first}$ assignments are performed.

Example

Copy elements from a vector to an slist. In this example, we explicitly create an slist that is large enough to hold all of the vector's elements.

```
int main()
{
  char A[] = "abcdefgh";
  vector<char> V(A, A + strlen(A));

  slist<char> L(V.size());
  copy(V.begin(), V.end(), L.begin());
  assert(equal(V.begin(), V.end(), L.begin()));
}
```

Fill an empty list with the elements from a vector. It's impossible to do that by copying directly into the list (there aren't any elements in the list that we could assign into), so instead, we use copy into an output iterator adaptor that appends elements to the list.

```
int main()
{
  char A[] = "abcdefgh";
  vector<char> V(A, A + strlen(A));

  list<char> L;
  copy(V.begin(), V.end(), back_inserter(L));
  assert(equal(V.begin(), V.end(), L.begin()));
}
```

Copy the elements of a list to standard output, using ostream_iterator (page 357).

```
int main()
{
  list<int> L;
  L.push_back(1);
  L.push_back(3);
  L.push_back(5);
  L.push_back(7);

  copy(L.begin(), L.end(),
       ostream_iterator<int>(cout, "\n"));
}
```

12.1.2 `copy_backward`

```
template <class BidirectionalIterator1, class BidirectionalIterator2>
BidirectionalIterator2 copy_backward(BidirectionalIterator1 first,
                                     BidirectionalIterator1 last,
                                     BidirectionalIterator2 result);
```

The algorithm `copy_backward`, like copy (page 233), copies elements from an input range to an output range. The input range is $[first, last)$, and the output range is $[result - (last - first), result)$. It performs the assignments $*(result - 1) = *(last - 1)$, $*(result - 2) = *(last - 2)$, and so on. For every integer n from 0 up to (but not including) $last - first$, `copy_backward` performs the assignment $*(result - n - 1) = *(last - n - 1)$. Assignments are performed from the end of the input sequence to the beginning, that is, in order of increasing n.[2]

The return value is $result - (last - first)$.

The algorithms copy and `copy_backward` differ in three ways. First, copy requires only that its input range consist of Input Iterators and its output range of Output Iterators. By contrast, `copy_backward` imposes much more stringent requirements. It requires that both its input and output ranges consist of Bidirectional Iterators. Second, the two algorithms perform assignments in the opposite order; copy copies ranges from front to back, and `copy_backward`, as the name suggests, copies ranges from back to front. Third, copy, like most STL algorithms, denotes the output range by an iterator that points to the beginning of the range. In the case of `copy_backward`, however, the iterator `result` points to the *end* of the output range. This is highly unusual. It is the only STL algorithm where a range is described by a single iterator pointing to the end of the range.

Where Defined

In the HP implementation, `copy_backward` was declared in the header `<algo.h>` and defined in `<algobase.h>`. According to the C++ standard, it is declared in the header `<algorithm>`.

Requirements on Types

- `BidirectionalIterator1` and `BidirectionalIterator2` are models of Bidirectional Iterator.
- Values of `BidirectionalIterator1`'s value type are convertible to values of `BidirectionalIterator2`'s value type.

---

2. The order of assignments matters when the input and output ranges overlap. It implies that `copy_backward` may not be used if `result` is in the range $[first, last)$. That is, it may not be used if the end of the output range overlaps with the input range, but it may be used if the beginning of the output range overlaps with the input range; copy has opposite restrictions. If the two ranges are completely nonoverlapping, of course, then either algorithm may be used.

Preconditions

- [first,last) is a valid range.
- result is not an iterator within the range [first,last).
- There is enough space to hold all of the elements being copied. More formally, the requirement is that [result − (last − first),result) is a valid range.

Complexity

Linear. Exactly last − first assignments are performed.

Example

The only important difference between copy and copy_backward is the order of assignment. The order matters if the input and output ranges overlap. In this example we copy elements from one part of an array to another, overlapping part.

```
int main() {
    int A[15] = {1, 2, 3, 4, 5, 6, 7, 8, 9, 10, 11, 12, 13, 14, 15};
    copy_backward(A, A + 10, A + 15);

    copy(A, A + 15, ostream_iterator<int>(cout, " "));
    cout << endl;
    // The output is "1 2 3 4 5 1 2 3 4 5 6 7 8 9 10".
}
```

12.2 Swapping Elements

12.2.1 swap

```
template <class Assignable>
void swap(Assignable& a, Assignable& b);
```

The algorithm swap is one of the few STL algorithms that operate on individual objects passed as arguments, rather than on ranges of elements. It exchanges the values of a and b, assigning the contents of a to b and the contents of b to a. The swap operation is a primitive used by many other algorithms.

The only completely general way of implementing swap is with a temporary variable. This method makes one call to a copy constructor and two calls to an assignment operator, and it should be expected to take about the same amount of time as three assignments. In many cases, it is possible to write a specialized version of swap that is far more efficient. For example, consider swapping two vector<double>s each of which has N elements. The fully general version requires three vector assignments, hence $3N$ assignments of double. A specialized version written just for vector would just need to swap a few pointers.

This is important because swap is used as a primitive operation by many other STL algorithms and because containers of containers (such as vector<string>) are very common. The STL includes specialized versions of swap for all container classes. User-defined types should also provide specialized versions of swap whenever it is possible to write one that is more efficient than the general version.

Where Defined

In the HP implementation, swap was declared in the header <algo.h> and defined in <algobase.h>. According to the C++ standard, it is declared in <algorithm>.

Requirements on Types

- Assignable is a model of Assignable.

Preconditions

None.

Complexity

Amortized constant time.[3]

Example

```
int main()
{
  int x = 1;
  int y = 2;
  assert(x == 1 && y == 2);
  swap(x, y);
  assert(x == 2 && y == 1);
}
```

12.2.2   iter_swap

```
template <class ForwardIterator1, class ForwardIterator2>
inline void iter_swap(ForwardIterator1 a, ForwardIterator2 b);
```

If a and b are iterators, then iter_swap(a, b) is equivalent to swap(*a, *b).

There is rarely any good reason for using iter_swap. You should just use swap instead. The iter_swap algorithm is now almost entirely vestigial. It was included in the original HP STL [SL95] for purely technical reasons (specifically, to support iterators with nonstandard reference types), and it remained in later implementations and was included in the C++ standard to preserve backward compatibility.

Where Defined

In the HP implementation, iter_swap was declared in the header <algo.h> and defined in <algobase.h>. According to the C++ standard, it is declared in the header <algorithm>.

---

3. The time required to swap two objects of type T will obviously depend on their type. "Constant time" does not mean that performance will be the same for an 8-bit char as for a 128-bit complex<double>.

Requirements on Types

- `ForwardIterator1` and `ForwardIterator2` are models of Forward Iterator.
- `ForwardIterator1` and `ForwardIterator2` are mutable.
- `ForwardIterator1` and `ForwardIterator2` have the same value type.

Preconditions

- `ForwardIterator1` and `ForwardIterator2` are dereferenceable.

Complexity

Amortized constant time.

Example

```
int main()
{
  int x = 1;
  int y = 2;
  assert(x == 1 && y == 2);
  iter_swap(&x, &y);
  assert(x == 2 && y == 1);
}
```

12.2.3 swap_ranges

```
template <class ForwardIterator1, class ForwardIterator2>
ForwardIterator2
swap_ranges(ForwardIterator1 first1, ForwardIterator1 last1,
            ForwardIterator2 first2);
```

The algorithm `swap_ranges` exchanges the contents of two ranges of equal size. It exchanges each value in the range [`first1`, `last1`) with the corresponding element in the range [`first2`, `first2` + (`last1` − `first1`)). That is, for each integer n in the range $0 \le n <$ (`last1` − `first1`), it swaps *(`first1` + n) and *(`first2` + n). The return value is `first2` + (`last1` − `first1`).

Where Defined

In the HP implementation, `swap_ranges` was declared in the header `<algo.h>`. According to the C++ standard, it is declared in the header `<algorithm>`.

Requirements on Types

- `ForwardIterator1` and `ForwardIterator2` are models of Forward Iterator.
- The value types of `ForwardIterator1` and `ForwardIterator2` are convertible to each other.

Preconditions

- [first1, last1) is a valid range.
- [first2, first2 + (last1 − first1)) is a valid range.
- The two ranges [first1, last1) and [first2, first2 + (last1 − first1)) do not overlap.

Complexity

Linear. Exactly last1 − first1 swaps are performed.

Example

```
int main()
{
  vector<int> V1;
  V1.push_back(1);
  V1.push_back(2);

  vector<int> V2;
  V2.push_back(3);
  V2.push_back(4);

  assert(V1[0] == 1 && V1[1] == 2 && V2[0] == 3 && V2[1] == 4);
  swap_ranges(V1.begin(), V1.end(), V2.begin());
  assert(V1[0] == 3 && V1[1] == 4 && V2[0] == 1 && V2[1] == 2);
}
```

12.3 transform

```
① template <class InputIterator, class OutputIterator,
            class UnaryFunction>
  OutputIterator transform(InputIterator first, InputIterator last,
                     OutputIterator result, UnaryFunction op);


② template <class InputIterator1, class InputIterator2,
            class OutputIterator,
            class BinaryFunction>
  OutputIterator transform(InputIterator1 first1, InputIterator1 last1,
                     InputIterator2 first2, OutputIterator result,
                     BinaryFunction binary_op);
```

The algorithm transform is very similar to for_each (page 218), in that it performs some operation (supplied as a function object) on a range of objects. The difference is that for_each discards the function object's return values, while transform copies the return values into another range.[4] This is the reason for transform's name: It *transforms* one range into another by performing some operation on the range's elements.

There are two versions of transform. One applies a Unary Function to a single input range, and one applies a Binary Function to two input ranges of equal size.

Version 1 performs the operation op(*i) for every iterator i in the input range [first,last) and assigns the result of that expression to *o, where o is the output iterator that corresponds to i. That is, for each n in the range $0 \le n <$ last – first, it performs the assignment *(result + n) = op(*(first + n)). The return value is result + (last – first).

Version 2 uses a Binary Function instead of a Unary Function. It performs the operation op(*i1, *i2) for each iterator i1 in the range [first1,last1) and assigns the result to *o, where i2 is the corresponding iterator in the second input range and where o is the corresponding output iterator. That is, for each n in the range $0 \le n <$ last1 – first1, it performs the assignment *(result + n) = op(*(first1 + n), *(first2 + n)). The return value is result + (last1 – first1).

Note that transform may be used to modify a sequence "in place." It is permissible for the iterators first and result to be the same. While the input and output ranges may be identical, they may not otherwise overlap. The Output Iterator result may not be the same as any of the Input Iterators in the range [first,last), with the exception of first itself.

Where Defined

In the HP implementation, transform was declared in the header <algo.h>. According to the C++ standard, it is declared in the header <algorithm>.

Requirements on Types

For version 1:

- InputIterator is a model of Input Iterator.
- OutputIterator is a model of Output Iterator.
- UnaryFunction is a model of Unary Function.
- InputIterator's value type is convertible to UnaryFunction's argument type.
- UnaryFunction's result type is convertible to a type in OutputIterator's set of value types.

For version 2:

- InputIterator1 and InputIterator2 are models of Input Iterator.
- OutputIterator is a model of Output Iterator.
- BinaryFunction is a model of Binary Function.

---

4. If you are a lisp programmer, you may find this familiar: for_each and transform are related in the same way as mapc and mapcar.

- `InputIterator1`'s and `InputIterator2`'s value types are convertible, respectively, to `BinaryFunction`'s first and second argument types.
- `UnaryFunction`'s result type must be convertible to a type in `OutputIterator`'s set of value types.

Preconditions

For version 1:

- `[first,last)` is a valid range.
- `result` is not an iterator within the range `[first + 1, last)`.
- There is enough space to hold all of the elements being copied. More formally, the requirement is that `[result, result + (last − first))` is a valid range.

For version 2:

- `[first1,last1)` is a valid range.
- `[first2, first2 + (last1 − first1))` is a valid range.
- `result` is not an iterator within the range `[first1 + 1, last1)` or `[first2 + 1, first2 + (last1 − first1))`.
- There is enough space to hold all of the elements being copied. More formally, the requirement is that `[result, result + (last1 − first1))` is a valid range.

Complexity

Linear. The operation is applied exactly `last − first` times in the case of version 1 or `last1 − first1` in the case of version 2.

Example

Version 1 of `transform` is a generalization of `copy` (page 233). It takes values from one range, performs some operation on them, and writes them to another range. We can recover exactly the same behavior as `copy` if that operation is the identity function.

```
int main()
{
    const int N = 7;
    double A[N] = {4, 5, 6, 7, 1, 2, 3};
    list<double> L(N);

    transform(A, A + N, L.begin(), identity<double>());
    copy(L.begin(), L.end(), ostream_iterator<double>(cout, "\n"));
}
```

A more conventional example is replacing every number in an array with its negative.

```
int main()
{
  const int N = 10;
  double A[N] = {1, 2, 3, 4, 5, 6, 7, 8, 9, 10};

  transform(A, A+N, A, negate<double>());
  copy(A, A+N, ostream_iterator<double>(cout, "\n"));
}
```

Version 2 operates on two different input ranges. In this case, we use it to calculate the sum of a vector and an array. The output range doesn't have to be a list or a vector. It can be any sort of Output Iterator, including an Output Iterator that isn't associated with any container at all.

```
int main()
{
  const int N = 10;

  vector<int> V(N);
  fill(V.begin(), V.end(), 75);

  int A[N] = {10, 9, 8, 7, 6, 5, 4, 3, 2, 1};

  transform(V.begin(), V.end(), &A[0],
            ostream_iterator<int>(cout, "\n"),
            plus<int>());
}
```

12.4 Replacing Elements

12.4.1 replace

```
template <class ForwardIterator, class T>
void replace(ForwardIterator first, ForwardIterator last,
             const T& old_value, const T& new_value)
```

The algorithm replace examines every element in a range, replacing every occurrence of old_value with new_value. Elements that are not equal to old_value are unaffected.

More formally, for every iterator i in the range [first,last), replace compares *i to old_value. If *i == old_value, it performs the assignment *i = new_value.

As with find (page 199), there is an obvious generalization of replace. Instead of testing to see whether elements are equal to old_value, let the user control the test by supplying a general Predicate. For technical reasons, it is impossible for this more general version also to be called replace. Both versions have the same number of arguments, and both are template functions. The general version must instead have a different name: replace_if.

Where Defined

In the HP implementation, `replace` was declared in the header `<algo.h>`. According to the C++ standard, it is declared in the header `<algorithm>`.

Requirements on Types

- `ForwardIterator` is a model of Forward Iterator.
- `ForwardIterator` is mutable.
- `T` is convertible to `ForwardIterator`'s value type.
- `T` is Assignable.
- `T` is EqualityComparable and may be compared for equality with objects of `ForwardIterator`'s value type.

Preconditions

- [`first,last`) is a valid range.

Complexity

Linear. Exactly `last − first` comparisons for equality and at most `last − first` assignments.

Example

Replace apples with oranges.

```
int main()
{
  vector<string> fruits;
  fruits.push_back("cherry");
  fruits.push_back("apple");
  fruits.push_back("peach");
  fruits.push_back("plum");
  fruits.push_back("pear");

  replace(fruits.begin(), fruits.end(),
          string("apple"), string("orange"));
  copy(fruits.begin(), fruits.end(),
       ostream_iterator<string>(cout, "\n"));
}
```

12.4.2   replace_if

```
template <class ForwardIterator, class Predicate, class T>
void replace(ForwardIterator first, ForwardIterator last,
             Predicate pred,
             const T& new_value);
```

The algorithm `replace_if` is a generalization of `replace`. It examines every element in a range, replacing every element for which the **Predicate** `pred` returns `true`. The elements for which `pred` is `true` are replaced by the value `new_value`. Elements for which `pred` is `false` are unaffected.

More formally, for every iterator `i` in the range [`first`,`last`), `replace_if` evaluates `pred(*i)`. If `pred(*i)` is `true`, then `replace_if` performs the assignment `*i = new_value`.

Many STL algorithms have two versions, one that performs a default operation and one that takes a general user-supplied operation. The two versions usually have the same name. The algorithms `replace` and `replace_if` have two different names for purely technical reasons. Both are template functions and both have the same number of arguments, so there would have been ambiguities if the name `replace` had been used for both versions.

Where Defined

In the HP implementation, `replace_if` was declared in the header `<algo.h>`. According to the C++ standard, it is declared in the header `<algorithm>`.

Requirements on Types

- `ForwardIterator` is a model of **Forward Iterator**.
- `ForwardIterator` is mutable.
- `Predicate` is a model of **Predicate**.
- `ForwardIterator`'s value type is convertible to `Predicate`'s argument type.
- `T` is convertible to `Forward Iterator`'s value type.
- `T` is **Assignable**.

Preconditions

- [`first`,`last`) is a valid range.

Complexity

Linear. Exactly `last` − `first` applications of `pred` and at most `last` − `first` assignments.

Example

One common use of `replace_if` is to make sure that all values in a range obey some sort of constraint. The values that don't obey it are replaced with a value that does. In this example, all negative numbers are replaced by 0.

```
int main()
{
  vector<double> V;
  V.push_back(1);
```

```
    V.push_back(-3);
    V.push_back(2);
    V.push_back(-1);

    replace_if(V.begin(), V.end(),
               bind2nd(less<double>(), 0),
               0.);
    assert(V[1] == 0 && V[3] == 0);
}
```

Similarly, we can replace all strings whose length is greater than 6 with the overflow indicator "******".

```
struct string_length_exceeds
{
  string_length_exceeds(int n) : limit(n) {}
  bool operator()(const string& s) const { return s.size() > limit; }

  int limit;
};

int main()
{
  string A[7] = {"oxygen", "carbon", "nitrogen", "iron",
                 "sodium", "hydrogen", "silicon"};

  replace_if(A, A + 7,
             string_length_exceeds(6),
             "******");
  copy(A, A + 7, ostream_iterator<string>(cout, "\n"));
}
```

12.4.3 replace_copy

```
template <class InputIterator, class OutputIterator, class T>
OutputIterator replace_copy(InputIterator first, InputIterator last,
                            OutputIterator result, const T& old_value,
                            const T& new_value);
```

The algorithm replace_copy copies elements from the range [first, last) to the range [result, result + (last − first)), replacing old_value with new_value during the copy. The range [first, last) is not modified.

More precisely, for every integer n such that $0 \le n <$ last − first, replace_copy performs the assignment *(result + n) = new_value if *(first + n) == old_value, and *(result + n) = *(first + n) otherwise.

As is usual for algorithms named *_copy, replace_copy is very similar to copy followed by replace. One difference is that replace_copy is more efficient, and another is that replace_copy can be used with an output range of Output Iterators.

Where Defined

In the HP implementation, `replace_copy` was declared in the header `<algo.h>`. According to the C++ standard, it is declared in the header `<algorithm>`.

Requirements on Types

- `InputIterator` is a model of Input Iterator.
- `OutputIterator` is a model of Output Iterator.
- `T` is EqualityComparable and may be compared for equality with objects of `InputIterator`'s value type.
- `T` is Assignable.
- `T` is convertible to a type in `OutputIterator`'s set of value types.

Preconditions

- $[first, last)$ is a valid range.
- There is enough space in the output range to store the copied values. That is, $[result, result + (last - first))$ is a valid range.
- `result` is not an iterator within the range $[first, last)$.

Complexity

Linear. Exactly $last - first$ comparisons for equality and exactly $last - first$ assignments.

Example

Replace all occurrences of 1 with 99.

```
int main()
{
  vector<int> V1;
  V1.push_back(1);
  V1.push_back(2);
  V1.push_back(3);
  V1.push_back(1);

  vector<int> V2(V1.size());
  replace_copy(V1.begin(), V1.end(), V2.begin(), 1, 99);
  assert(V2[1] == V1[1] && V2[2] == V1[2]);
  assert(V2[0] == 99 && V2[3] == 99);
}
```

12.4.4 `replace_copy_if`

```
template <class InputIterator, class OutputIterator,
         class Predicate, class T>
OutputIterator replace_copy_if(InputIterator first, InputIterator last,
                               OutputIterator result, Predicate pred,
                               const T& new_value);
```

The algorithm `replace_copy_if` is the copying variation of `replace_if`, just as the algorithm `replace_copy` is the copying variation of `replace`. That is, it is very much like `replace_if` except that it operates on an input range and an output range rather than modifying a single range "in place."

As usual for the copying forms of algorithms, `replace_copy_if` is similar to copy followed by `replace_if`. It copies elements from the range [first, last) to the range [result, result + (last − first)), replacing any elements for which pred is true with the value new_value.

Specifically, for every integer n such that $0 \le n <$ last − first, `replace_copy_if` performs the assignment `*(result + n) = new_value` if `pred(*(first + n))`, and `*(result + n) = *(first + n)` otherwise.

Where Defined

In the HP implementation, `replace_copy_if` was declared in the header `<algo.h>`. According to the C++ standard, it is declared in the header `<algorithm>`.

Requirements on Types

- `InputIterator` is a model of Input Iterator.
- `OutputIterator` is a model of Output Iterator.
- `Predicate` is a model of Predicate.
- `T` is convertible to `Predicate`'s argument type.
- `T` is Assignable.
- `T` is convertible to a type in `OutputIterator`'s set of value types.

Preconditions

- [first, last) is a valid range.
- There is enough space in the output range to store the copied values. That is, [result, result + (last − first)) is a valid range.
- result is not an iterator within the range [first, last).

Complexity

Linear. Exactly last − first applications of pred and exactly last − first assignments.

Example

Copy elements from a vector to the standard output, replacing all negative numbers with 0.

```
int main()
{
  vector<int> V;
  V.push_back(1);
  V.push_back(-1);
  V.push_back(-5);
  V.push_back(2);

  replace_copy_if(V.begin(), V.end(), ostream_iterator<int>(cout, "\n"),
                  bind2nd(less<int>(), 0),
                  0);
}
```

12.5 Filling Ranges

12.5.1 fill

```
template <class ForwardIterator, class T>
void fill(ForwardIterator first, ForwardIterator last, const T& value);
```

The algorithm fill assigns value to every element in the range [first,last). That is, for every iterator i in [first,last), it performs the assignment *i = value.

Where Defined

In the HP implementation, fill was declared in the header <algo.h> and defined in <algobase.h>. According to the C++ standard, it is declared in <algorithm>.

Requirements on Types

- ForwardIterator is a model of Forward Iterator.[5]
- ForwardIterator is mutable.
- T is Assignable.
- T is convertible to ForwardIterator's value type.

Preconditions

- [first,last) is a valid range.

---

5. The argument must be a mutable Forward Iterator rather than an Output Iterator because fill uses a range [first,last) of iterators. There is no sensible way to describe a range of Output Iterators because it is impossible to compare two Output Iterators for equality. By contrast, fill_n has an interface that does permit use of an Output Iterator.

Complexity

Linear. Exactly last − first assignments.

Example

Assign the value 137 to every element of a vector.

```
int main()
{
  vector<double> V(4);
  fill(V.begin(), V.end(), 137);
  assert(V[0] == 137 && V[1] == 137 && V[2] == 137 && V[3] == 137);
}
```

12.5.2 fill_n

```
template <class OutputIterator, class Size, class T>
OutputIterator fill_n(OutputIterator first, Size n, const T& value);
```

The algorithm fill_n assigns the value value to every element in [first, first + n).
That is, for every iterator i in the range [first, first + n), it performs the assignment
*i = value. The return value is first + n.

Where Defined

In the HP implementation, fill_n was declared in the header <algo.h> and defined in <algobase.h>. According to the C++ standard, it is declared in the header
<algorithm>.

Requirements on Types

- OutputIterator is a model of Output Iterator.
- Size is an integral type (either signed or unsigned).
- T is Assignable.
- T is convertible to a type in OutputIterator's set of value types.

Preconditions

- $n \geq 0$.
- There is enough space to hold n values. That is, [first, first + n) is a valid
  range.

Complexity

Linear. Exactly n assignments.

Example

Append three copies of the value 137 to the end of a vector.

```
int main()
{
  vector<double> V(2, 128.);
  fill_n(back_inserter(V), 3, 137.);
  assert(V.size() == 5 &&
         V[2] == 137 && V[3] == 137 && V[4] == 137);
}
```

12.5.3 generate

```
template <class ForwardIterator, class Generator>
void generate(ForwardIterator first, ForwardIterator last,
              Generator gen);
```

The algorithm generate assigns the result of invoking gen, a function object that takes no arguments, to each element in the range [first,last). That is, for each iterator i in the range [first,last), it performs the operation *i = gen().

The function object gen is invoked for each iterator in the range [first,last), as opposed to just being invoked a single time outside the loop. This distinction is important because a Generator need not return the same result each time it is invoked. It is permitted to read from a file, refer to and modify local state, and so on.

If you want to invoke a function object once and assign the result to every element in a range, you can do that with fill.

Where Defined

In the HP implementation, generate was declared in the header <algo.h>. According to the C++ standard, it is declared in the header <algorithm>.

Requirements on Types

- ForwardIterator is a model of Forward Iterator.[6]
- ForwardIterator is mutable.
- Generator is a model of Generator.
- Generator's result type is convertible to ForwardIterator's value type.

Preconditions

- [first,last) is a valid range.

---

6. The argument must be a mutable Forward Iterator rather than an Output Iterator because it generates a range [first,last) of iterators. There is no sensible way to describe a range of Output Iterators because it is impossible to compare two Output Iterators for equality. The generate_n algorithm has an interface that does permit use of an Output Iterator.

Complexity

Linear. Exactly last − first invocations of gen.

Example

Fill a vector with random numbers, using the standard C library function rand.

```
int main()
{
  vector<int> V(100);
  generate(V.begin(), V.end(), rand);
}
```

12.5.4 generate_n

```
template <class OutputIterator, class Size, class Generator>
OutputIterator generate_n(OutputIterator first, Size n, Generator gen);
```

The algorithm generate_n assigns the result of invoking gen, a function object that takes no arguments, to each element in the range [first, first + n). That is, for each iterator i in the range [first, first + n), it performs the assignment *i = gen().

The return value is first + n.

The function object gen is invoked n times (once for each iterator in the range [first, first + n)), as opposed to just being invoked a single time outside the loop. This distinction is important because a Generator need not return the same result each time it is invoked. It is permitted to read from a file, refer to and modify local state, and so on.

Where Defined

In the HP implementation, generate_n was declared in the header <algo.h>. According to the C++ standard, it is declared in the header <algorithm>.

Requirements on Types

- OutputIterator is a model of Output Iterator.
- Size is an integral type (either signed or unsigned).
- Generator is a model of Generator.
- Generator's result type is convertible to a type in OutputIterator's set of value types.

Preconditions

- $n \geq 0$.
- There is enough space to hold n values. That is, [first, first + n) is a valid range.

Complexity

Linear. Exactly n invocations of gen.

Example

Print 100 random numbers, using the C standard library function rand.

```
int main()
{
    generate_n(ostream_iterator<int>(cout, "\n"), 100, rand);
}
```

12.6   Removing Elements

12.6.1   remove

```
template <class ForwardIterator, class T>
ForwardIterator remove(ForwardIterator first, ForwardIterator last,
                       const T& value);
```

The algorithm remove removes the value value from the range [first, last).

The meaning of *removal*, however, is somewhat subtle. The most important point to realize is that none of the mutating algorithms in this chapter, including remove, destroy any iterators or change the distance between first and last (see page 233). There's no way that they could do anything of the sort. Suppose, for example, that A is a C array of type int[10]. If you write remove(A, A + 10, 3), it is impossible for remove to actually change the number of elements in A: C arrays can't be resized. The expression A + 10 will always refer to a location that is 10 elements beyond A.

Removal has to mean something other than actually changing the size of a container, since the algorithms in this chapter do not operate on containers but only on iterators: They can do nothing but assign to the elements that the iterators point to.

The actual meaning of removal, in this context, is that remove returns an iterator new_last such that the range [first, new_last) contains no elements equal to value. That is, value has been removed from the range [first, new_last). This procedure remove is stable, meaning that the relative order of the elements that are left behind is unchanged.

The iterators in the range [new_last, last) are all still dereferenceable, but the values they point to are unspecified. Those elements are of no interest, and may be discarded.

If you are removing elements from a Sequence, you may simply erase the elements that follow new_last. A reasonable way to remove elements from a Sequence S—to really remove them and change the Sequence's size—is to write:

```
S.erase(remove(S.begin(), S.end(), x), S.end());
```

Where Defined

In the HP implementation, remove was declared in the header <algo.h>. According to the C++ standard, it is declared in the header <algorithm>.

Requirements on Types

- ForwardIterator is a model of Forward Iterator.
- ForwardIterator is mutable.
- T is Equality Comparable.
- Values of type T can be compared for equality with values of ForwardIterator's value type.

Preconditions

- [first, last) is a valid range.

Complexity

Linear. Exactly last − first comparisons for equality.

Example

Remove all elements equal to 1 from a vector. Note that the vector's size is unchanged after the call to remove. When the vector is printed for the second time, immediately after the call to remove, it still has nine elements. None of the elements in the range [V.begin(), new_end), however, are equal to 1.

The size of the vector does not change until the explicit call to the member function erase().

```
template<class Container>
void print_container(const Container& C)
{
  cout << C.size() << " elements: ";
  copy(C.begin(), C.end(),
       ostream_iterator<typename Container::value_type>(cout, " "));
  cout << endl;
}

int main() {
  const int A[9] = {3, 1, 4, 1, 5, 9, 2, 6, 5};

  vector<int> V(A, A + 9);
  print_container(V);

  vector<int>::iterator new_end = remove(V.begin(), V.end(), 1);
  print_container(V);

  V.erase(new_end, V.end());
```

```
    print_container(V);
}
```

12.6.2 remove_if

```
template <class ForwardIterator, class Predicate>
ForwardIterator remove_if(ForwardIterator first, ForwardIterator last,
                          Predicate pred);
```

The algorithm remove_if removes all elements for which pred is true from the range [first,last). It corresponds to remove in the same way that replace_if corresponds to replace. The algorithms remove and remove_if have two different names for purely technical reasons. Both are template functions and both have the same number of arguments, so it would have been ambiguous if the name remove had been used for both versions.

As with remove, the meaning of *removal* is somewhat subtle. It does not mean changing the number of elements in the range [first,last). (See page 253 for a detailed discussion of why it can't mean that.)

As with remove, remove_if returns an iterator new_last such that the range [first,new_last) contains no elements for which pred is true. That is, the elements that satisfy pred have been removed from the range [first,new_last). This operation is stable, meaning that the relative order of the elements in [first,new_last) is unchanged from the order of those elements in [first,last).

All the iterators in the range [new_last,last) are still dereferenceable, but the values that they point to are unspecified.

Where Defined

In the HP implementation, remove_if was declared in the header <algo.h>. According to the C++ standard, it is declared in the header <algorithm>.

Requirements on Types

- ForwardIterator is a model of Forward Iterator.
- ForwardIterator is mutable.
- Predicate is a model of Predicate.
- ForwardIterator's value type is convertible to Predicate's argument type.

Preconditions

- [first,last) is a valid range.

Complexity

Linear. Exactly last − first applications of pred.

Example

Remove all even numbers from a vector. As with remove (page 253), remove_if does not change the number of elements in the vector. The size of the vector does not change until the explicit call to the member function erase().

```
int main()
{
  vector<int> V;
  V.push_back(1);
  V.push_back(4);
  V.push_back(2);
  V.push_back(8);
  V.push_back(5);
  V.push_back(7);

  copy(V.begin(), V.end(), ostream_iterator<int>(cout, " "));
      // The output is "1 4 2 8 5 7"

  vector<int>::iterator new_end =
          remove_if(V.begin(), V.end(),
                    compose1(bind2nd(equal_to<int>(), 0),
                             bind2nd(modulus<int>(), 2)));
  V.erase(new_end, V.end());

  copy(V.begin(), V.end(), ostream_iterator<int>(cout, " "));
      // The output is "1 5 7".
}
```

12.6.3 remove_copy

```
template <class InputIterator, class OutputIterator, class T>
OutputIterator remove_copy(InputIterator first, InputIterator last,
                           OutputIterator result, const T& value);
```

The algorithm remove_copy copies elements from the range [first,last) to a range beginning at result, except that elements that are equal to value are not copied. The return value is the end of the resulting range. If there are n elements in [first,last) that are not equal to result, then the return value is result + n.

This operation is stable, meaning that the relative order of the elements that are copied is the same as in the range [first,last).

Where Defined

In the HP implementation, remove_copy was declared in the header <algo.h>. According to the C++ standard, it is declared in the header <algorithm>.

Requirements on Types

- InputIterator is a model of Input Iterator.
- OutputIterator is a model of Output Iterator.
- InputIterator's value type is convertible to a type in OutputIterator's set of value types.
- T is Equality Comparable.
- Objects of type T can be compared for equality with objects of InputIterator's value type.

Preconditions

- [first, last) is a valid range.
- There is enough space in the output range to store the copied values. If there are n elements in [first, last) that are not equal to value, [result, result + n) is a valid range.
- result is not an iterator in the range [first, last).

Complexity

Linear. Exactly last – first comparisons for equality and at most last – first assignments.

Example

Print all of the nonempty strings in a vector.

```
int main()
{
  vector<string> V;

  V.push_back("one");
  V.push_back("");
  V.push_back("four");
  V.push_back("");
  V.push_back("");
  V.push_back("ten");

  remove_copy(V.begin(), V.end(),
              ostream_iterator<string>(cout, "\n"),
              string(""));
}
```

The printed output is:

```
one
four
ten
```

12.6.4 `remove_copy_if`

```
template <class InputIterator, class OutputIterator, class Predicate>
OutputIterator
remove_copy_if(InputIterator first, InputIterator last,
               OutputIterator result, Predicate pred);
```

The algorithm `remove_copy_if` copies elements from the range [first, last) to a range beginning at `result`, except that elements for which `pred` is `true` are not copied. The return value is the end of the resulting range. If there are n elements in [first, last) for which pred is not true, then the return value is `result` + n.

This operation is stable, meaning that the relative order of the elements that are copied is the same as in the range [first, last).

Where Defined

In the HP implementation, `remove_copy_if` was declared in the header `<algo.h>`. According to the C++ standard, it is declared in the header `<algorithm>`.

Requirements on Types

- `InputIterator` is a model of Input Iterator.
- `OutputIterator` is a model of Output Iterator.
- `InputIterator`'s value type is convertible to a type in `OutputIterator`'s set of value types.
- `Predicate` is a model of Predicate.
- `InputIterator`'s value type is convertible to `Predicate`'s argument type.

Preconditions

- [first, last) is a valid range.
- There is enough space in the output range to store the copied values. That is, if there are n elements in [first, last) that do not satisfy pred, then the output range [result, result + n) is a valid range.
- `result` is not an iterator in the range [first, last).

Complexity

Linear. Exactly last − first applications of `pred` and at most last − first assignments.

Example

Fill a vector with the non-negative elements of another vector.

```
int main()
{
  vector<int> V1;
  V.push_back(-2);
  V.push_back(0);
  V.push_back(-1);
  V.push_back(0);
  V.push_back(1);
  V.push_back(2);

  vector<int> V2;
  remove_copy_if(V1.begin(), V1.end(), back_inserter(V2),
                 bind2nd(less<int>(), 0));
}
```

Many people have suggested that the STL should include an algorithm copy_if, which would be the exact opposite of remove_copy_if. While remove_copy_if copies all of the elements that don't satisfy some condition, copy_if would copy all of the elements that *do* satisfy a condition.

It is trivial to implement copy_if in terms of remove_copy_if:

```
template <class InputIterator, class OutputIterator, class Predicate>
OutputIterator copy_if(InputIterator first, InputIterator last,
                   OutputIterator result, Predicate pred)
{
  return remove_copy_if(first, last, result, not1(pred));
}
```

12.6.5 unique

① template <class ForwardIterator>
ForwardIterator unique(ForwardIterator first, ForwardIterator last);

② template <class ForwardIterator, class BinaryPredicate>
ForwardIterator unique(ForwardIterator first, ForwardIterator last,
                   BinaryPredicate binary_pred);

The algorithm unique removes duplicate elements. Whenever a consecutive group of duplicate elements appears in the range [first, last), unique removes all but the first element in each such group.

Note that unique removes only duplicate elements that are adjacent to each other. If you want to remove all duplicate elements, you must ensure that duplicates are always adjacent. For that reason, unique is especially useful when combined with sort (page 292).

Like all of the algorithms in this chapter, unique can't actually change the number of elements in the range [first, last). See page 253 for a discussion of what *removal* means for algorithms that do not change the number of elements in a range.

The algorithm unique returns an iterator new_last such that [first, new_last) contains no consecutive elements that are duplicates. That is, duplicates have been removed from the range [first, new_last). This operation is stable, meaning that the relative order of elements that are not removed is unchanged.

The iterators in the range [new_last, last) are all still dereferenceable, but the elements that they point to are unspecified.

There are two different versions of unique because there are two different definitions of what it means for a consecutive group of elements to be duplicates. In version 1 the test is simple equality. The elements in a range [f, l) are duplicates if, for every iterator i in that range other than the first, *i == *(i-1). In version 2, the test is an arbitrary Binary Predicate binary_pred. The elements in [f, l) are duplicates if, for every iterator i in that range other than the first, binary_pred(*i, *(i-1)) is true.

Where Defined

In the HP implementation, unique was declared in the header <algo.h>. According to the C++ standard, it is declared in the header <algorithm>.

Requirements on Types

For version 1:

- ForwardIterator is a model of Forward Iterator.
- ForwardIterator is mutable.
- ForwardIterator's value type is Equality Comparable.

For version 2:

- ForwardIterator is a model of Forward Iterator.
- ForwardIterator is mutable.
- BinaryPredicate is a model of Binary Predicate.[7]
- ForwardIterator's value type is convertible to BinaryPredicate's first argument type and to BinaryPredicate's second argument type.

Preconditions

- [first, last) is a valid range.

Complexity

Linear. For nonempty ranges, exactly (last − first) − 1 applications of operator== (for version 1) or of binary_pred (for version 2). For empty ranges, no applications of operator== or of binary_pred.

---

7. BinaryPredicate is not required to be an equivalence relation, but you should be cautious about using unique with a Binary Predicate that is not an equivalence relation: You could easily get unexpected results.

Example

Remove the duplicate values from consecutive groups of equal ints. As with remove (page 253), note that the size of the vector is unchanged until the explicit call to the member function erase().

```
int main() {
  vector<int> V;
  V.push_back(1);
  V.push_back(3);
  V.push_back(3);
  V.push_back(3);
  V.push_back(2);
  V.push_back(2);
  V.push_back(1);

  vector<int>::iterator new_end = unique(V.begin(), V.end());
  V.erase(new_end, V.end());
  copy(V.begin(), V.end(), ostream_iterator<int>(cout, " "));
  cout << endl;
  // The output is "1 3 2 1".
}
```

Strictly speaking, version 1 of unique is redundant: Calling version 2, with an object of class equal_to as the Binary Predicate argument, is exactly equivalent. Here, we use version 2 of unique as a less convenient replacement for version 1.

```
int main() {
  int A[8] = {7, 7, 1, 4, 6, 6, 6, 3};

  int* new_end = unique(A, A + 8, equal_to<int>());
  copy(A, new_end, ostream_iterator<int>(cout, "\n"));
}
```

A more useful example of version 2 is removing duplicate characters from a vector, ignoring case. First we sort the vector, and then we remove duplicates from consecutive groups.

```
inline bool eq_nocase(char c1, char c2) {
  return tolower(c1) == tolower(c2);
}
inline bool lt_nocase(char c1, char c2) {
  return tolower(c1) < tolower(c2);
}

int main()
{
  const char init[] = "The Standard Template Library";
  vector<char> V(init, init + sizeof(init));
  sort(V.begin(), V.end(), lt_nocase);
  copy(V.begin(), V.end(), ostream_iterator<char>(cout));
```

```
    cout << endl;
    vector<char>::iterator new_end = unique(V.begin(), V.end(), eq_nocase);
    copy(V.begin(), new_end, ostream_iterator<char>(cout));
    cout << endl;
    // The output is:
    //    aaaabddeeehiLlmnprrrStTtTy
    //    abdehiLmnprSty
}
```

12.6.6 unique_copy

① `template <class InputIterator, class OutputIterator>`
  `OutputIterator unique_copy(InputIterator first, InputIterator last,`
                             `OutputIterator result);`

② `template <class InputIterator, class OutputIterator,`
          `class BinaryPredicate>`
  `OutputIterator unique_copy(InputIterator first, InputIterator last,`
                             `OutputIterator result,`
                             `BinaryPredicate binary_pred);`

The algorithm `unique_copy` copies elements from the range `[first,last)` to a range beginning with `result`, except that in a consecutive group of duplicate elements only the first one is copied. The return value is the end of the range to which the elements are copied.[8]

As usual for algorithms whose names are of the form `*_copy`, `unique_copy` is the copying version of `unique` (page 259). It is similar to `copy` followed by `unique`. As with `unique`, it only removes duplicate elements when they are adjacent to each other. Duplicates separated by other elements are not removed.

There are two different versions of `unique_copy` because there are two different definitions of what it means for a consecutive group of elements to be duplicates. In version 1, the test is simple equality: the elements in a range `[f,l)` are duplicates if, for every iterator i in that range other than the first, `*i == *(i-1)`. In version 2, the test is an arbitrary Binary Predicate `binary_pred`: the elements in `[f,l)` are duplicates if, for every iterator i in that range other than the first, `binary_pred(*i, *(i-1))` is true.

Where Defined

In the HP implementation, `unique_copy` was declared in the header `<algo.h>`. According to the C++ standard, it is declared in the header `<algorithm>`.

---

8. This behavior is similar to the UNIX filter `uniq`.

Requirements on Types

For version 1:

- InputIterator is a model of Input Iterator.
- InputIterator's value type is Equality Comparable.
- OutputIterator is a model of Output Iterator.
- InputIterator's value type is convertible to a type in OutputIterator's set of value types.

For version 2:

- InputIterator is a model of Input Iterator.
- BinaryPredicate is a model of Binary Predicate.[9]
- InputIterator's value type is convertible to BinaryPredicate's first argument type and to BinaryPredicate's second argument type.
- OutputIterator is a model of Output Iterator.
- InputIterator's value type is convertible to a type in OutputIterator's set of value types.

Preconditions

- [first, last) is a valid range.
- There is enough space to hold all of the elements being copied. More formally, if there are n elements in the range [first, last) after duplicates are removed from consecutive groups, then [result, result + n) must be a valid range.

Complexity

Linear. Exactly last − first applications of operator== (in the case of version 1) or of binary_pred (in the case of version 2), and at most last − first assignments.

Example

Print all of the numbers in an array, but only print the first one in a consecutive group of identical numbers. The output still has duplicates—the numbers 2 and 8 both appear twice—but the output contains no adjacent duplicate elements, which is all that unique or unique_copy guarantees.

```
int main() {
  const int A[] = {2, 7, 7, 7, 1, 1, 8, 8, 8, 2, 8, 8};
  unique_copy(A, A + sizeof(A) / sizeof(int),
```

---

9. BinaryPredicate is not required to be an equivalence relation, but you should be cautious about using unique_copy with a Binary Predicate that is not an equivalence relation. You could easily get unexpected results.

```
                    ostream_iterator<int>(cout, " "));
    cout << endl;
      // The output is "2 7 1 8 2 8".
  }
```

Fill a vector with numbers from an array but only taking one number from the range 0-9, one from the range 10-19, and so on.

```
struct eq_div {
  eq_div(int divisor) : n(divisor) {}
  bool operator()(int x, int y) const { return x / n == y / n; }

  int n;
};

int main() {
  int A[] = {1, 5, 8, 15, 23, 27, 41, 42, 43, 44, 67, 83, 89};
  const int N = sizeof(A) / sizeof(int);

  vector<int> V;
  unique_copy(A, A + N, back_inserter(V), eq_div(10));

  copy(V.begin(), V.end(), ostream_iterator<int>(cout, "\n"));
  // The output is 1 15 23 41 67 83
}
```

12.7 Permuting Algorithms

A permutation of a range of elements is a reordering of those elements. It doesn't eliminate any values or introduce any new ones, it just puts the values in the input range into a different order. Many important algorithms on ranges are permutations. (Sorting a range is a type of permutation. Sorting is so important, though, that all of Chapter 13 will be devoted to sorting algorithms.)

12.7.1 reverse

```
template <class BidirectionalIterator>
void reverse(BidirectionalIterator first, BidirectionalIterator last);
```

The algorithm reverse reverses a range in place. That is, for every n in the range $0 \leq n \leq (\text{last} - \text{first})/2$, it exchanges the values $*(\text{first} + n)$ and $*(\text{last} - (n+1))$.

Note that reverse, like all algorithms in this chapter, reverses the *values* pointed to by a range of iterators, rather than the iterators themselves.

Where Defined

In the HP implementation, reverse was declared in the header <algo.h>. According to the C++ standard, it is declared in the header <algorithm>.

Requirements on Types

- BidirectionalIterator is a model of Bidirectional Iterator.
- BidirectionalIterator is mutable.

Preconditions

- [first,last) is a valid range.

Complexity

Linear. Exactly (last − first)/2 invocations of swap (page 237).

Example

```
int main() {
  vector<int> V;
  V.push_back(0);
  V.push_back(1);
  V.push_back(2);
  copy(V.begin(), V.end(), ostream_iterator<int>(cout, " "));
  cout << endl;
              // Output: 0 1 2
  reverse(V.begin(), V.end());
  copy(V.begin(), V.end(), ostream_iterator<int>(cout, " "));
  cout << endl;
              // Output: 2 1 0
}
```

12.7.2 reverse_copy

```
template <class BidirectionalIterator, class OutputIterator>
OutputIterator reverse_copy(BidirectionalIterator first,
                            BidirectionalIterator last,
                            OutputIterator result);
```

The algorithm reverse_copy copies elements from the range [first,last) to the range [result,result + (last − first)) such that the copy is a reverse of the original range. That is, for every n in the range $0 \leq n <$ (last − first), reverse_copy performs the assignment *(result + (last − first) − n) = *(first + n).

The return value is the end of the resulting range: result + (last − first).

As the name suggests, reverse_copy is the copying version of reverse. Its effects are similar to copy followed by reverse.

Where Defined

In the HP implementation, reverse_copy was declared in the header <algo.h>. According to the C++ standard, it is declared in the header <algorithm>.

Requirements on Types

- `BidirectionalIterator` is a model of Bidirectional Iterator.
- `OutputIterator` is a model of Output Iterator.
- `BidirectionalIterator`'s is convertible to a type in `OutputIterator`'s set of value types.

Preconditions

- `[first, last)` is a valid range.
- There is enough space to hold all of the elements being copied. More formally, the requirement is that `[result, result + (last − first))` is a valid range.
- The ranges `[first, last)` and `[result, result + (last − first))` do not overlap.

Complexity

Linear. Exactly `last − first` assignments.

Example

```
int main() {
  vector<int> V;
  V.push_back(0);
  V.push_back(1);
  V.push_back(2);
  copy(V.begin(), V.end(), ostream_iterator<int>(cout, " "));
  cout << endl;
                // Output: 0 1 2
  reverse_copy(V.begin(), V.end(), ostream_iterator<int>(cout, " "));
  cout << endl;
                // Output: 2 1 0
}
```

12.7.3 rotate

```
template <class ForwardIterator>
inline void rotate(ForwardIterator first, ForwardIterator middle,
                ForwardIterator last);
```

The algorithm `rotate` rotates the elements in a range. That is, it moves the element at the position `middle` to the position `first`, it moves the element pointed to by `middle + 1` to the position `first + 1`, and so on. Formally, for every integer n in the range $0 \leq n < last − first$, the element $*(first + n)$ is assigned to $*(first + (n + (last − middle)) \% (last − first))$.

Because of this formidable definition, you might think that `rotate` is obscure or specialized. In fact, there's a much simpler way to understand what `rotate` does. It exchanges the two ranges `[first, middle)` and `[middle, last)`.

One of the uses for `rotate` is to "swap" ranges in a way that is impossible to do with `swap_ranges` (page 239). You can use `swap_ranges` to exchange two ranges that are exactly the same length, but you can use `rotate` to exchange two adjacent ranges whose lengths are different.

Where Defined

In the HP implementation, `rotate` was declared in the header `<algo.h>`. According to the C++ standard, it is declared in the header `<algorithm>`.

Requirements on Types

- `ForwardIterator` is a model of **Forward Iterator**.
- `ForwardIterator` is mutable.

Preconditions

- [`first,middle`) and [`middle,last`) are valid ranges. (It follows that the range [`first,last`) is also a valid range.)

Complexity

Linear: `rotate` invokes swap (page 237) at most `last − first` times. (The exact number of assignments depends on whether `rotate`'s arguments are Forward Iterators, Bidirectional Iterators, or Random Access Iterators. The complexity is linear in all three cases.)

Example

In this example, we rotate an array of integers. We begin by moving the first element to the end of the array (that is, we exchange the range that contains only the first element, and the range that contains all the other elements). Next, we reverse the operation (that is, we exchange the range that contains only the last element, and the range containing all the others). Finally, we move the first three elements of the array to the end.

```
int main()
{
  int A[] = {1, 2, 3, 4, 5, 6, 7};
  const int N = sizeof(A) / sizeof(int);

  copy(A, A + N, ostream_iterator<int>(cout, " "));
  cout << endl;
                        // Output: 1 2 3 4 5 6 7

  rotate(A, A + 1, A + N);
  copy(A, A + N, ostream_iterator<int>(cout, " "));
  cout << endl;
                        // Output: 2 3 4 5 6 7 1
```

```
    rotate(A, A + N - 1, A + N);
    copy(A, A + N, ostream_iterator<int>(cout, " "));
    cout << endl;
                            // Output: 1 2 3 4 5 6 7

    rotate(A, A + 3, A + N);
    copy(A, A + N, ostream_iterator<int>(cout, " "));
    cout << endl;
                            // Output: 4 5 6 7 1 2 3

}
```

12.7.4 `rotate_copy`

```
template <class ForwardIterator, class OutputIterator>
OutputIterator
rotate_copy(ForwardIterator first, ForwardIterator middle,
            ForwardIterator last, OutputIterator result);
```

The algorithm `rotate_copy` is the copying version of `rotate`. It is similar to `copy` followed by `rotate`. Instead of rotating its input range in place, `rotate_copy` creates a rotated copy in the range that begins with the iterator `result`.

As with `rotate`, you can think of this operation as the exchange of two ranges: `rotate_copy` copies elements from the input range [`first`, `last`) to the output range [`result`, `result` + (`last` − `first`)), but with [`first`, `middle`) and [`middle`, `last`) reversed. That is, `*middle` is copied to `*result`, `*(middle + 1)` is copied to `*(result + 1)`, and so on. Formally, for every integer n in the range $0 \leq n <$ `last` − `first`, `rotate_copy` performs the assignment `*(result` + (n + (`last` − `middle`)) % (`last` − `first`))` = *(first` + n)`.

The return value is the end of the output range, `result` + (`last` − `first`).

Where Defined

In the HP implementation, `rotate_copy` was declared in the header `<algo.h>`. According to the C++ standard, it is declared in the header `<algorithm>`.

Requirements on Types

- `ForwardIterator` is a model of **Forward Iterator**.
- `OutputIterator` is a model of **Output Iterator**.
- `ForwardIterator`'s value type is convertible to a type in `OutputIterator`'s set of value types.

Preconditions

- [`first`, `middle`) and [`middle`, `last`) are valid ranges. (It follows that the range [`first`, `last`) is also a valid range.)
- There is enough space to hold all of the elements being copied. More formally, the requirement is that [`result`, `result` + (`last` − `first`)) is a valid range.

- The ranges [first, last) and [result, result + (last − first)) do not overlap.

Complexity

Linear. Exactly last − first assignments.

Example

In this example, the array A consists of a series of 1's followed by a series of 2's. We copy that array to the standard output but reverse the order of the two parts.

```
int main()
{
  int A[] = {1, 1, 1, 2, 2, 2, 2};
  const int N = sizeof(A) / sizeof(int);

  rotate_copy(A, A + 3, A + N, ostream_iterator<int>(cout, " "));
  cout << endl;
                          // Output: 2 2 2 2 1 1 1
}
```

12.7.5 next_permutation

① template <class BidirectionalIterator>
bool next_permutation(BidirectionalIterator first,
                      BidirectionalIterator last);

② template <class BidirectionalIterator, class StrictWeakOrdering>
bool next_permutation(BidirectionalIterator first,
                      BidirectionalIterator last,
                      StrictWeakOrdering comp);

Given any two ranges whose elements are LessThan Comparable, it is always possible to compare them in dictionary order using lexicographical_compare (page 225). In particular it is possible to compare two distinct permutations of the same range, such as $(1, 2, 3)$ and $(1, 3, 2)$.

For any range of n elements, there are a finite number of distinct permutations, at most $n!$.[10] Conceptually, you can imagine arranging all of those permutations into a table, sorted by lexicographical ordering. For each permutation in the table, there is an unambiguous definition of the previous and the next permutation.

The algorithm next_permutation transforms the range of elements [first, last) into the next permutation in that table, that is, the lexicographically next greater permutation of the elements.

---

10. If all of the elements in that range are distinct, then there are exactly $n!$ permutations. If some elements are the same as each other, though, then there are fewer. There are, for example, only three $(3!/2)$ permutations of the elements $(1, 2, 2)$.

If such a permutation exists, `next_permutation` transforms `[first,last)` into that permutation and returns `true`. Otherwise, it transforms `[first,last)` into the lexicographically smallest permutation (which, by definition, is sorted in ascending order) and returns `false`.

The postcondition is that the new permutation of elements is lexicographically greater than the old (as determined by `lexicographical_compare`) if and only if the return value is `true`.

The two versions of `next_permutation` differ in how they define whether one element is less than another, hence how they determine which of two ranges is lexicographically less than the other. Version 1 compares objects using `operator<`, and version 2 compares objects using the user-supplied function object `comp`.

Where Defined

In the HP implementation, `next_permutation` was declared in the header `<algo.h>`. According to the C++ standard, it is declared in the header `<algorithm>`.

Requirements on Types

For version 1:

- `BidirectionalIterator` is a model of Bidirectional Iterator.
- `BidirectionalIterator` is mutable.
- `BidirectionalIterator`'s value type is Strict Weakly Comparable.

For version 2:

- `BidirectionalIterator` is a model of Bidirectional Iterator.
- `BidirectionalIterator` is mutable.
- `StrictWeakOrdering` is a model of Strict Weak Ordering.
- `BidirectionalIterator`'s value type is convertible to `StrictWeakOrdering`'s argument type.

Preconditions

- `[first,last)` is a valid range.

Complexity

Linear. At most `(last − first)/2` invocations of swap (page 237).

Example

Enumerate every permutation of the elements $(1, 2, 3, 4)$. This program produces $4! = 24$ lines of output. The first permutation is $(1, 2, 3, 4)$, and the last is $(4, 3, 2, 1)$.

```
int main() {
  const int N = 4;
  int A[N] = {1, 2, 3, 4};

  do {
    copy(A, A + N, ostream_iterator<int>(cout, " "));
    cout << endl;
  } while (next_permutation(A, A + N));
}
```

Enumerating every permutation of a range is the basis of the worst known deterministic sorting algorithm. Most good sorting algorithms are $\mathcal{O}(N \log(N))$, and even most bad algorithms are only $\mathcal{O}(N^2)$. This silly example demonstrates an $\mathcal{O}(N!)$ sorting algorithm:

```
template <class BidirectionalIterator, class StrictWeakOrdering>
void snail_sort(BidirectionalIterator first, BidirectionalIterator last,
                StrictWeakOrdering comp)
{
  while (next_permutation(first, last, comp)) {}
}
```

12.7.6 prev_permutation

① `template <class BidirectionalIterator>`
`bool prev_permutation(BidirectionalIterator first,`
                     `BidirectionalIterator last);`

② `template <class BidirectionalIterator, class StrictWeakOrdering>`
`bool prev_permutation(BidirectionalIterator first,`
                     `BidirectionalIterator last,`
                     `StrictWeakOrdering comp);`

The permutations of a set of elements may be arranged in dictionary order (that is, lexicographical ordering); see page 269 for a full discussion. Since there are a finite number of distinct permutations, lexicographical ordering yields an unambiguous definition of the next and the previous permutation.

The algorithm prev_permutation transforms the range of elements [first, last) into the lexicographically previous permutation of the same elements.

If such a permutation exists, prev_permutation transforms [first, last) into that permutation and returns true. Otherwise (that is, if every permutation of the elements in [first, last) would be greater than the original range [first, last)), it transforms [first, last) into the lexicographically greatest permutation (which, by definition, is sorted in descending order) and returns false.

The postcondition is that the new permutation of elements is lexicographically less than the old (as determined by lexicographical_compare) if and only if the return value is true.

The two versions of prev_permutation differ in how they define whether one element is less than another, hence how they determine which of two ranges is lexicographically less than the other. Version 1 compares objects using operator<, and version 2 compares objects using the user-supplied function object comp.

Where Defined

In the HP implementation, prev_permutation was declared in the header <algo.h>. According to the C++ standard, it is declared in the header <algorithm>.

Requirements on Types

For version 1:

- BidirectionalIterator is a model of Bidirectional Iterator.
- BidirectionalIterator is mutable.
- BidirectionalIterator's value type is Strict Weakly Comparable.

For version 2:

- BidirectionalIterator is a model of Bidirectional Iterator.
- BidirectionalIterator is mutable.
- StrictWeakOrdering is a model of Strict Weak Ordering.
- BidirectionalIterator's value type is convertible to StrictWeakOrdering's argument type.

Preconditions

- [first,last) is a valid range.

Complexity

Linear. At most (last − first)/2 invocations of swap (page 237).

Example
```
int main()
{
  int A[] = {2, 3, 4, 5, 6, 1};
  const int N = sizeof(A) / sizeof(int);

  cout << "Initially:                ";
  copy(A, A+N, ostream_iterator<int>(cout, " "));
  cout << endl;

  prev_permutation(A, A+N);
  cout << "After prev_permutation: ";
  copy(A, A+N, ostream_iterator<int>(cout, " "));
  cout << endl;
```

```
    next_permutation(A, A+N);
    cout << "After next_permutation: ";
    copy(A, A+N, ostream_iterator<int>(cout, " "));
    cout << endl;
}
```

12.8 Partitions

12.8.1 partition

```
template <class BidirectionalIterator, class Predicate>
BidirectionalIterator partition(BidirectionalIterator first,
                                BidirectionalIterator last,
                                Predicate pred);
```

The algorithm partition reorders the elements in the range [first,last) based on the function object pred, such that the elements that satisfy pred precede the elements that fail to satisfy it.

The postcondition of partition is that, for some iterator middle in the range [first,last), pred(*i) is true for every iterator i in the range [first,middle) and false for every iterator i in the range [middle,last). Note that partition does not necessarily preserve the relative order of elements. It is guaranteed that the elements in [first,middle) satisfy pred and the elements in [middle,last) do not, but there are no guarantees about the order of elements within [first,middle) or [middle,last). A different algorithm, by contrast, stable_partition (page 274), does preserve the relative order.

The return value is the iterator middle.

Where Defined

In the HP implementation, partition was declared in the header <algo.h>. According to the C++ standard, it is declared in the header <algorithm>.

Requirements on Types

- BidirectionalIterator is a model of Bidirectional Iterator.
- Predicate is a model of Predicate.
- BidirectionalIterator's value type is convertible to Predicate's argument type.

Preconditions

- [first,last) is a valid range.

Complexity

Linear. Exactly last − first applications of pred and at most (last − first)/2 invocations of swap (page 237).

Example

Reorder a sequence so that even numbers precede odd numbers. Note that although the initial range is sorted, neither the even numbers nor the odd numbers are sorted afterward: partition, unlike stable_partition, does not preserve the relative order of elements.

```
int main()
{
  int A[] = {1, 2, 3, 4, 5, 6, 7, 8, 9, 10};
  const int N = sizeof(A)/sizeof(int);
  partition(A, A + N,
            compose1(bind2nd(equal_to<int>(), 0),
                     bind2nd(modulus<int>(), 2)));
  copy(A, A + N, ostream_iterator<int>(cout, " "));
  // The output is "10 2 8 4 6 5 7 3 9 1".
}
```

12.8.2   stable_partition

```
template <class ForwardIterator, class Predicate>
ForwardIterator
stable_partition(ForwardIterator first, ForwardIterator last,
                 Predicate pred);
```

The algorithm stable_partition is much like partition. It reorders the elements in the range [first,last) based on the function object pred, such that all of the elements that satisfy pred precede the elements that fail to satisfy it.

Like partition, stable_partition has the postcondition that, for some iterator middle in the range [first,last), pred(*i) is true for every iterator i in the range [first,middle) and false for every iterator i in the range [middle,last).

The return value is the iterator middle.

The difference between the algorithms partition and stable_partition is that stable_partition has one additional postcondition: It preserves relative order. If x and y are elements in [first,last) such that pred(x) == pred(y), and if x precedes y, then, afterward, x will still precede y.

The preservation of relative order is the only semantic difference between the algorithms stable_partition and partition. Since partition is faster, you should never use stable_partition unless the guarantee of stability is important for your application.

Where Defined

In the HP implementation, stable_partition was declared in the header <algo.h>. According to the C++ standard, it is declared in the header <algorithm>.

Requirements on Types

- ForwardIterator is a model of Forward Iterator.[11]
- Predicate is a model of Predicate.
- ForwardIterator's value type is convertible to Predicate's argument type.

Preconditions

- [first, last) is a valid range.

Complexity

Unlike partition, stable_partition is an *adaptive* algorithm: it attempts to allocate a temporary memory buffer, and its runtime complexity depends on how much memory is available. Worst-case behavior (if no auxiliary memory is available) is at most $N \log(N)$ invocations of swap (page 237), where N is last − first, and best case (if a large enough auxiliary memory buffer is available) is linear in N. In either case, pred is applied exactly N times.

Note that partition is faster. It uses no temporary buffer and is always linear.

Example

Reorder a sequence so that even numbers precede odd numbers. The sequence is initially sorted. After it is partitioned, the even numbers and the odd numbers are both still sorted. This is because stable_partition, unlike partition (page 273), preserves the relative order of elements.

```
int main()
{
  int A[] = {1, 2, 3, 4, 5, 6, 7, 8, 9, 10};
  const int N = sizeof(A)/sizeof(int);
  stable_partition(A, A + N, compose1(bind2nd(equal_to<int>(), 0),
                                      bind2nd(modulus<int>(), 2)));
  copy(A, A + N, ostream_iterator<int>(cout, " "));
}
// The output is "2 4 6 8 10 1 3 5 7 9"
```

12.9   Random Shuffling and Sampling

The first algorithm in this section, random_shuffle, is a permuting algorithm. Like the algorithms in Section 12.7, it reorders the values in a range while preserving all of the initial values. Neither of the other two algorithms in this section are permutations. Instead of randomly reordering a range, they perform the closely related task of selecting a random subset from an input range.

---

11. According to the C++ standard the iterator type is required to be a model of Bidirectional Iterator, but this is unnecessarily strict. It is possible to implement stable_partition for any Forward Iterator.

12.9.1 `random_shuffle`

① `template <class RandomAccessIterator>`
`void random_shuffle(RandomAccessIterator first,`
`                    RandomAccessIterator last);`

② `template <class RandomAccessIterator, class RandomNumberGenerator>`
`void random_shuffle(RandomAccessIterator first,`
`                    RandomAccessIterator last,`
`                    RandomNumberGenerator& rand)`

The algorithm `random_shuffle` randomly rearranges the range [`first`, `last`). That is, it randomly picks one of the $N!$ possible permutations of the elements, where N is `last` − `first`.

There are $N!$ ways of arranging a sequence of N elements, and `random_shuffle` yields uniformly distributed results. The probability of any particular permutation is $1/N!$. The reason this comment is important is that a number of algorithms seem at first sight to implement random shuffling of a sequence, but do not in fact produce a uniform distribution over the $N!$ possible permutations. It's easy to get random shuffle wrong.

This algorithm is described in Section 3.4.2 of Knuth [Knu98a]. Knuth credits Moses and Oakford [MO63] and Durstenfeld [Dur64].

The two versions of `random_shuffle` differ in how they obtain random numbers. Version 1 uses an internal random number generator, and version 2 uses a Random Number Generator, a special kind of function object, that is explicitly passed as an argument. (It is passed by reference, rather than by value, because the whole point of a Random Number Generator is that its local state is modified each time it is called.)

When using random numbers it is sometimes important to be able to set the "seed" of the random number generator explicitly. If that sort of control is important for your application, you must use version 2.

Where Defined

In the HP implementation, `random_shuffle` was declared in the header `<algo.h>`. According to the C++ standard, it is declared in the header `<algorithm>`.

Requirements on Types

For version 1:

- `RandomAccessIterator` is a model of Random Access Iterator

For version 2:

- `RandomAccessIterator` is a model of Random Access Iterator
- `RandomNumberGenerator` is a model of Random Number Generator
- The difference type of `RandomAccessIterator` is convertible to the argument type of `RandomNumberGenerator`.

Preconditions

- [first,last) is a valid range.
- last − first is less than rand's maximum value.

Complexity

Linear in last − first. For nonempty ranges, random_shuffle invokes swap exactly (last − first) − 1 times.

Example

```
int main()
{
  const int N = 8;
  int A[] = {1, 2, 3, 4, 5, 6, 7, 8};
  random_shuffle(A, A + N);
  copy(A, A + N, ostream_iterator<int>(cout, " "));
  cout << endl;
  // The printed result might be 7 1 6 3 2 5 4 8,
  //   or any of 40,319 other possibilities.
}
```

12.9.2 `random_sample`

① template <class InputIterator, class RandomAccessIterator>
RandomAccessIterator
random_sample(InputIterator first, InputIterator last,
              RandomAccessIterator ofirst, RandomAccessIterator olast)

② template <class InputIterator, class RandomAccessIterator,
            class RandomNumberGenerator>
random_sample(InputIterator first, InputIterator last,
              RandomAccessIterator ofirst, RandomAccessIterator olast,
              RandomNumberGenerator& rand)

The algorithm random_sample randomly copies a sample of the elements from the range [first,last) into the range [ofirst,olast). It copies n elements, where n is min(last − first, olast − ofirst). Each element from the input range appears at most once in the output range, and samples are chosen with uniform probability.

The return value is ofirst + n.

Ignoring the order of elements, there are $N!/(n!(N-n)!)$ ways to select a sample of n elements from a set of N elements. This algorithm yields uniformly distributed results. The probability of selecting any particular element is n/N, and the probability of any particular sampling (not considering order of elements) is $n!(N-n)!/N!$.

Elements might appear in any order in the output range. Relative order within the input range is not guaranteed to be preserved.[12]

This is "Algorithm R" from Section 3.4.2 of Knuth [Knu98a]. Knuth credits Alan Waterman.

The two versions of random_sample differ in how they obtain random numbers. Version 1 uses an internal random number generator, while version 2 uses a **Random Number Generator**, a special kind of function object, that is explicitly passed as an argument.

When using random numbers it is sometimes important to be able to set the "seed" of the random number generator explicitly. If that sort of control is important for your application, you must use version 2.

Where Defined

The algorithm random_sample is not present in the original HP implementation of the STL, or in the C++ standard. In the SGI implementation, it is declared in the header <algorithm>.

Requirements on Types

For version 1:

- InputIterator is a model of Input Iterator
- RandomAccessIterator is a model of Random Access Iterator.
- RandomAccessIterator is mutable.
- InputIterator's value type is convertible to RandomAccessIterator's value type.

For version 2:

- InputIterator is a model of Input Iterator
- RandomAccessIterator is a model of Random Access Iterator
- RandomAccessIterator is mutable.
- RandomNumberGenerator is a model of Random Number Generator
- InputIterator's value type is convertible to RandomAccessIterator's value type.
- The difference type of RandomAccessIterator is convertible to the argument type of RandomNumberGenerator.

Preconditions

- [first,last) is a valid range.
- [ofirst,olast) is a valid range.

---

12. If preservation of the relative ordering within the input range is important for your application, you should use random_sample_n (page 279) instead. The main restriction of random_sample_n is that the input range must consist of Forward Iterators instead of Input Iterators.

- [first, last) and [ofirst, olast) do not overlap.
- last − first is less than rand's maximum value.

Complexity

Linear in last − first. At most last − first elements are copied from the input range to the output range.

Example

```
int main()
{
  const int N = 10;
  const int n = 4;
  int A[] = {1, 2, 3, 4, 5, 6, 7, 8, 9, 10};
  int B[n];

  random_sample(A, A+N, B, B+n);
  copy(B, B + n, ostream_iterator<int>(cout, " "));
  // The printed output might be 1 6 3 5,
  //   or any of 5039 other possibilities.
}
```

12.9.3 random_sample_n

① template <class ForwardIterator, class OutputIterator, class Distance>
OutputIterator
random_sample_n(ForwardIterator first, ForwardIterator last,
              OutputIterator out, Distance n)

② template <class ForwardIterator, class OutputIterator, class Distance,
            class RandomNumberGenerator>
OutputIterator
random_sample_n(ForwardIterator first, ForwardIterator last,
              OutputIterator out, Distance n,
              RandomNumberGenerator& rand)

The algorithm random_sample_n randomly copies some of the elements from the range [first, last) into the range [out, out + n). The number of elements it copies is m, where m is min(last − first, n). Each element in the input range appears at most once in the output range, and samples are chosen with uniform probability.

The return value is out + m.

Ignoring the order of elements, there are $N!/(n!(N − n)!)$ ways to select a sample of n elements from a range of N elements. This algorithm yields uniformly distributed results. The probability of selecting any particular element is n/N, and the probability of any particular sampling is $n!(N − n)!/N!$.

One of the important differences between random_sample and random_sample_n is that random_sample_n preserves the relative order of the elements in its input range, while `random_sample` does not. The other major distinction between the two algorithms is that `random_sample_n` requires its input range to be Forward Iterators and requires its output range only to be Output Iterators, while `random_sample` requires its input range only to be Input Iterators and requires its output range to be Random Access Iterators.

This is "Algorithm S" from Section 3.4.2 of Knuth [Knu98a]. Knuth credits Fan, Muller, and Rezucha [FMR62] and T. G. Jones.

The two versions of `random_sample` differ in how they obtain random numbers. Version 1 uses an internal random number generator, and version 2 a Random Number Generator, a special kind of function object, that is explicitly passed as an argument.

Where Defined

The algorithm `random_sample_n` is not present in the original HP implementation of the STL, or in the C++ standard. In the SGI implementation, it is declared in the header `<algorithm>`.

Requirements on Types

For version 1:

- `ForwardIterator` is a model of Forward Iterator.
- `OutputIterator` is a model of Output Iterator.
- `ForwardIterator`'s value type is convertible to a type in `OutputIterator`'s set of value types.
- `Distance` is an integral type that is large enough to represent the value `last − first`.

For version 2:

- `ForwardIterator` is a model of Forward Iterator.
- `OutputIterator` is a model of Output Iterator.
- `RandomNumberGenerator` is a model of Random Number Generator.
- `Distance` is an integral type that is large enough to represent the value `last − first`.
- `ForwardIterator`'s value type is convertible to a type in `OutputIterator`'s set of value types.
- `Distance` is convertible to `RandomNumberGenerator`'s argument type.

Preconditions

- `[first,last)` is a valid range.
- n is non-negative.
- `[first,last)` and `[out,out + n)` do not overlap.

- There is enough space to hold all of the elements being copied. More formally, the requirement is that $[out, out + min(n, last - first))$ is a valid range.
- $last - first$ is less than rand's maximum value.

Complexity

Linear in $last - first$. At most $last - first$ elements from the input range are examined and exactly $min(n, last - first)$ elements are copied to the output range.

Example

```
int main()
{
  const int N = 10;
  int A[] = {1, 2, 3, 4, 5, 6, 7, 8, 9, 10};

  random_sample_n(A, A+N, ostream_iterator<int>(cout, " "), 4);
  cout << endl;
  // The printed output might be 3 5 6 10,
  //   or any of 209 other possibilities.
}
```

12.10 Generalized Numeric Algorithms

12.10.1 accumulate

① template <class InputIterator, class T>
  T accumulate(InputIterator first, InputIterator last, T init);

② template <class InputIterator, class T, class BinaryFunction>
  T accumulate(InputIterator first, InputIterator last, T init,
               BinaryFunction binary_op);

The algorithm accumulate is a generalization of summation. It computes the sum (or some other binary operation) of init and all of the elements in [first, last).

Note that accumulate's interface is slightly awkward. You must always provide an initial value init. (One reason for this is so there can be a well-defined value when [first, last) is an empty range.) If, for example, you want to compute the sum of all of the numbers in the range [first, last), you should provide 0 as the initial value.

The binary operation is not required to be commutative or associative. The order of all of accumulate's operations is specified. The result is first initialized to init. Then, for each iterator i in [first, last), in order from beginning to end, it is updated by result = result + *i (in version 1) or result = binary_op(result, *i) (in version 2).

Where Defined

In the HP implementation, accumulate was declared in the header <algo.h>. According to the C++ standard, it is declared in the header <numeric>.

Requirements on Types

For version 1:

- InputIterator is a model of Input Iterator.
- T is a model of Assignable.
- If x is an object of type T and y is an object of InputIterator's value type, then x + y is defined.
- The return type of x + y is convertible to T.

For version 2:

- InputIterator is a model of Input Iterator.
- T is a model of Assignable.
- BinaryFunction is a model of Binary Function.
- T is convertible to BinaryFunction's first argument type.
- The value type of InputIterator is convertible to BinaryFunction's second argument type.
- BinaryFunction's return type is convertible to T.

Preconditions

- [first, last) is a valid range.

Complexity

Linear. Exactly last − first invocations of the binary operation.

Example

Calculate the sum, and the product, of all of the elements in a range. This example demonstrates both version 1 and version 2 of accumulate. Since addition and multiplication have different identity elements, we provide 0 as the initial element when we're computing the sum and 1 when we're computing the product.

```
int main()
{
  int A[] = {1, 2, 3, 4, 5};
  const int N = sizeof(A) / sizeof(int);

  cout << "The sum of all elements in A is "
       << accumulate(A, A + N, 0)
```

```
            << endl;

    cout << "The product of all elements in A is "
         << accumulate(A, A + N, 1, multiplies<int>())
         << endl;
}
```

For nonempty ranges, it's easy to define a wrapper for `accumulate` that lets you avoid having to provide the `init` argument. (You can't use this wrapper if [first, last) is an empty range because there wouldn't be a good choice for the return value.)

```
template <class InputIterator>
typename iterator_traits<InputIterator>::value_type
accumulate_nonempty(InputIterator first, InputIterator last)
{
  assert(first != last);
  typename iterator_traits<InputIterator>::value_type sum = *first++;
  return accumulate(first, last, sum);
}

template <class InputIterator, class BinaryFunction>
typename iterator_traits<InputIterator>::value_type
accumulate_nonempty(InputIterator first, InputIterator last,
                    BinaryFunction binary_op)
{
  assert(first != last);
  typename iterator_traits<InputIterator>::value_type init = *first++;
  return accumulate(first, last, init, binary_op);
}
```

12.10.2 inner_product

```
① template <class InputIterator1, class InputIterator2, class T>
  T inner_product(InputIterator1 first1, InputIterator1 last1,
                  InputIterator2 first2,
                  T init);


② template <class InputIterator1, class InputIterator2, class T,
            class BinaryFunction1, class BinaryFunction2>
  T inner_product(InputIterator1 first1, InputIterator1 last1,
                  InputIterator2 first2, T init,
                  BinaryFunction1 binary_op1,
                  BinaryFunction2 binary_op2);
```

The algorithm `inner_product` calculates a generalized inner product of the two ranges [first1, last1) and [first2, first2 + (last1 − first1)).

Note that `inner_product`'s interface is slightly awkward. You must always provide an initial value `init`. (One reason for this is so there can be a well-defined value when [`first,last`) is an empty range.) If, for example, you want to compute the ordinary inner product of two vectors, you should provide 0 as the initial value.

Version 1 calculates `init` plus the inner product of the two ranges. That is, it first initializes the result to `init`, and then, for each iterator `i` in [`first1,last1`), in order from the beginning to the end of the range, it updates the result by `result = result + (*i) * *(first2 + (i - first1))`.

Version 2 of `inner_product` is identical, except that it uses two user-supplied function objects instead of `operator+` and `operator*`. That is, it first initializes the result to `init`, and then for each iterator `i` in [`first1,last1`), in order from the beginning to the end of the range, it updates the result by `result = binary_op1(result, binary_op2(*i, *(first2 + (i - first1))))`.

Neither binary operation is required to be associative or commutative. The order of all operations is specified.

Where Defined

In the HP implementation, `inner_product` was declared in the header `<algo.h>`. According to the C++ standard, it is declared in the header `<numeric>`.

Requirements on Types

For version 1:

- `InputIterator1` is a model of Input Iterator.
- `InputIterator2` is a model of Input Iterator.
- `T` is Assignable.
- If x is an object of type `T`, y is an object of `InputIterator1`'s value type, and z is an object of `InputIterator2`'s value type, then x + y * z is defined.
- The type of x + y * z is convertible to `T`.

For version 2:

- `InputIterator1` is a model of Input Iterator.
- `InputIterator2` is a model of Input Iterator.
- `T` is Assignable.
- `BinaryFunction1` is a model of Binary Function.
- `BinaryFunction2` is a model of Binary Function.
- `InputIterator1`'s value type is convertible to `BinaryFunction2`'s first argument type.
- `InputIterator2`'s value type is convertible to `BinaryFunction2`'s second argument type.
- `T` is convertible to `BinaryFunction1`'s first argument type.

- BinaryFunction2's return type is convertible to BinaryFunction1's second argument type.
- BinaryFunction1's return type is convertible to T.

Preconditions

- [first1, last1) is a valid range.
- [first2, first2 + (last1 − first1)) is a valid range.

Complexity

Linear. Exactly last1 − first1 applications of each binary operation.

Example

```
int main()
{
  int A1[] = {1, 2, 3};
  int A2[] = {4, 1, -2};
  const int N1 = sizeof(A1) / sizeof(int);

  cout << "The inner product of A1 and A2 is "
       << inner_product(A1, A1 + N1, A2, 0)
       << endl;
}
```

12.10.3 partial_sum

① template <class InputIterator, class OutputIterator>
  OutputIterator partial_sum(InputIterator first, InputIterator last,
                       OutputIterator result);

② template <class InputIterator, class OutputIterator,
            class BinaryFunction>
  OutputIterator partial_sum(InputIterator first, InputIterator last,
                       OutputIterator result,
                       BinaryFunction binary_op);

The algorithm partial_sum calculates a generalized partial sum. It assigns the value *first to *result, the sum of *first and *(first + 1) to *(result + 1), and so on. Note that result is permitted to be the same iterator as first. This is useful for computing partial sums in place.

The running sum is first initialized to *first and assigned to *result. For each iterator i in [first + 1, last), in order from beginning to end, the sum is updated by sum = sum + *i (in version 1) or sum = binary_op(sum, *i) (in version 2) and is assigned to *(result + (i − first)). The binary operation is not required to be associative or commutative. The order of all operations is specified.

The return value is the end of the output range, result + (last − first).

Where Defined

In the HP implementation, partial_sum was declared in the header <algo.h>. According to the C++ standard, it is declared in the header <numeric>.

Requirements on Types

For version 1:

- InputIterator is a model of Input Iterator.
- OutputIterator is a model of Output Iterator.
- If x and y are objects of InputIterator's value type, then x + y is defined.
- The return type of x + y is convertible to InputIterator's value type.
- InputIterator's value type is convertible to a type in OutputIterator's set of value types.

For version 2:

- InputIterator is a model of Input Iterator.
- OutputIterator is a model of Output Iterator.
- BinaryFunction is a model of Binary Function.
- InputIterator's value type is convertible to BinaryFunction's first argument type and second argument type.
- BinaryFunction's result type is convertible to InputIterator's value type.
- InputIterator's value type is convertible to a type in OutputIterator's set of value types.

Preconditions

- [first, last) is a valid range.
- [result, result + (last − first)) is a valid range.

Complexity

Linear. Zero applications of the binary operation if [first, last) is an empty range; otherwise, exactly (last − first) − 1 applications.

Example

```
int main()
{
    const int N = 10;
```

```
    int A[N];

    fill(A, A+N, 1);
    cout << "A:                    ";
    copy(A, A+N, ostream_iterator<int>(cout, " "));
    cout << endl;

    cout << "Partial sums of A: ";
    partial_sum(A, A+N, ostream_iterator<int>(cout, " "));
    cout << endl;
}
```

12.10.4 adjacent_difference

① `template <class InputIterator, class OutputIterator>`
   `OutputIterator`
   `adjacent_difference(InputIterator first, InputIterator last,`
                       `OutputIterator result);`

② `template <class InputIterator, class OutputIterator,`
            `class BinaryFunction>`
   `OutputIterator`
   `adjacent_difference(InputIterator first, InputIterator last,`
                       `OutputIterator result,`
                       `BinaryFunction binary_op);`

The algorithm `adjacent_difference` calculates the differences of adjacent elements in the range [`first,last`). That is, it assigns the value `*first` to `*result`, and, for each iterator i in the range [`first + 1,last`), it assigns the difference of `*i` and `*(i − 1)` to `*(result + (i − first))`.

Note that `result` is permitted to be the same iterator as `first`. You can use `adjacent_difference` to compute differences in place.

The reason it is useful to store the value of the first element, as well as simply storing the differences, is that doing so provides enough information to reconstruct the input range. If addition and subtraction have the usual arithmetic definitions, then `adjacent_difference` and `partial_sum` are inverses of each other.

Version 1 uses `operator-` to calculate differences, and version 2 uses a user-supplied binary function. In version 1, for each iterator i in the range [`first + 1,last`), `*i − *(i − 1)` is assigned to `*(result + (i − first))`. In version 2, the value that is assigned to `*(result + (i − first))` is instead `binary_op(*i, *(i − 1))`.

Where Defined

In the HP implementation, `adjacent_difference` is declared in the header `<algo.h>`. According to the C++ standard, it is declared in the header `<numeric>`.

Requirements on Types

For version 1:

- `ForwardIterator` is a model of Forward Iterator.
- `OutputIterator` is a model of Output Iterator.
- If x and y are objects of `ForwardIterator`'s value type, then x − y is defined.
- `InputIterator`'s value type is convertible to a type in `OutputIterator`'s set of value types.
- The return type of x − y is convertible to a type in `OutputIterator`'s set of value types.

For version 2:

- `ForwardIterator` is a model of Forward Iterator.
- `OutputIterator` is a model of Output Iterator.
- `BinaryFunction` is a model of Binary Function.
- `InputIterator`'s value type is convertible to `BinaryFunction`'s first argument type and second argument type.
- `InputIterators` value type is convertible to a type in `OutputIterator`'s set of value types.
- `BinaryFunction`'s result type is convertible to a type in `OutputIterator`'s set of value types.

Preconditions

- [`first,last`) is a valid range.
- [`result,result + (last − first)`) is a valid range.

Complexity

Linear. Zero applications of the binary operation if [`first,last`) is an empty range; otherwise, exactly (`last − first`) − 1 applications.

Example

In this example, we form the adjacent differences of an array of integers and then use `partial_sum` to reconstruct the original array.

```
int main()
{
    int A[] = {1, 4, 9, 16, 25, 36, 49, 64, 81, 100};
    const int N = sizeof(A) / sizeof(int);
    int B[N];

    cout << "A[]:          ";
    copy(A, A + N, ostream_iterator<int>(cout, " "));
```

```
    cout << endl;

    adjacent_difference(A, A + N, B);
    cout << "Differences: ";
    copy(B, B + N, ostream_iterator<int>(cout, " "));
    cout << endl;

    cout << "Reconstruct: ";
    partial_sum(B, B + N, ostream_iterator<int>(cout, " "));
    cout << endl;
}
```

Chapter 13

Sorting and Searching

Some of the most important algorithms in computer science deal with the general problem of sorting a range of values. This chapter describes the STL algorithms that sort ranges (either wholly or in part) and algorithms that operate on sorted ranges.

Throughout this chapter, a "sorted" range is one that is arranged in ascending order—or more precisely, since a range might contain duplicate elements, one that is arranged in nondescending order. Nevertheless, all of the algorithms in this chapter are completely general. All have versions that are parameterized by function objects, so it is always possible for you to use any ordering that happens to be appropriate for your application.

Even saying that a range might contain duplicate elements isn't precise enough. What is really relevant is that a range might contain several *equivalent* elements.

The reason equivalence is important, and the reason it is not necessarily the same as equality, is that all of the algorithms in this chapter compare elements using a *strict weak ordering*. As discussed in the Strict Weakly Comparable requirements (page 88), whenever you define a strict weak ordering you are also implicitly defining a notion of equivalence. Two elements are equivalent if neither is less than the other. If, for example, you are sorting a list of people by last name, then two people are equivalent if their last names happen to be the same.

The word *equivalent* is used in this sense throughout this chapter. None of the algorithms in this chapter ever compare elements for equality.

13.1   Sorting Ranges

This section contains the STL's sorting algorithms, that is, the algorithms that sort ranges. A sorting algorithm is a type of permuting algorithm: like the algorithms in Section 12.7, it rearranges the values in a range rather than introducing new values.

In addition to the algorithms in this section, the STL contains three other forms of sorting. First, the Containers list (page 441) and slist (page 448) each have a member function sort that sorts the entire container. Second, the Sorted Associative Containers (page 156) have the property that their elements are always arranged in a sorted range. Third, you can sort any range by using the *heap sort* algorithm. First construct a heap by calling make_heap (page 336), and then transform the heap into a sorted range by calling sort_heap (page 342).

There is no such thing as a sorting algorithm that is always best. Because sorting is an important and potentially time-consuming operation, you should choose your sorting algorithm carefully; sort is often a good choice, but other methods are sometimes more appropriate.

13.1.1 sort

① template <class RandomAccessIterator>
  void sort(RandomAccessIterator first, RandomAccessIterator last);

② template <class RandomAccessIterator, class StrictWeakOrdering>
  void sort(RandomAccessIterator first, RandomAccessIterator last,
            StrictWeakOrdering comp);

The algorithm sort sorts the elements in [first, last) into ascending order (or more strictly, nondescending order), meaning that if i and j are any two dereferenceable iterators in [first, last) such that i precedes j, then *j is guaranteed not to be less than *i.

Note that sort is not necessarily a *stable* sorting algorithm. Suppose that *i and *j are equivalent: neither is less than the other. It is not guaranteed that the relative order of these two elements will be preserved by sort.

Stability is often an irrelevant criterion. It only matters when a range contains elements that are equivalent but not identical,[1] and when the ordering of those elements within the initial range is significant.

One case where stability does sometimes matter is when you are sorting records that have multiple fields. You might want to sort first by one field and then by another, and in that case it is quite important that the second sorting operation be stable. The algorithm stable_sort (page 294), as its name suggests, preserves the relative ordering of equivalent elements.

The two versions of sort differ in how they define whether one element is less than another. Version 1 compares objects using operator<, and version 2 compares objects using a function object comp. Version 1 has the postcondition that is_sorted(first, last) (page 303) is true, and version 2 has the postcondition that is_sorted(first, last, comp) is true.

Where Defined

In the HP implementation, sort was declared in the header <algo.h>. According to the C++ standard, it is declared in the header <algorithm>.

---

1. One example is sorting a list of people by last name. Two entries with the same last name are equivalent for the purposes of the sorting, but since the first names might not be the same, they are not necessarily equal.

Requirements on Types

For version 1:

- RandomAccessIterator is a model of Random Access Iterator.
- RandomAccessIterator is mutable.
- RandomAccessIterator's value type is Strict Weakly Comparable.

For version 2:

- RandomAccessIterator is a model of Random Access Iterator.
- RandomAccessIterator is mutable.
- StrictWeakOrdering is a model of Strict Weak Ordering.
- RandomAccessIterator's value type is convertible to StrictWeakOrdering's argument type.

Preconditions

- [first,last) is a valid range.

Complexity

According to the C++ standard, sort is required to perform $O(N \log N)$ comparisons on average but has worst-case complexity of $O(N^2)$, where N is last − first.

This latitude, however, is unnecessary. It is possible to implement sort so that the number of comparisons, both average and worst-case, is only $O(N \log N)$. The SGI implementation of the STL, as well as some other implementations, do make that guarantee.

The reason that earlier versions of sort had quadratic worst-case complexity is that they used the *quicksort* algorithm [Hoa62] using a pivot chosen by median of three [Sin69]. Quicksort has $O(N \log N)$ average complexity, but quadratic worst-case complexity. See Section 5.2.2 of Knuth [Knu98b].

More recent versions of sort use the *introsort* algorithm [Mus97], whose worst-case complexity is $O(N \log N)$. Introsort is very similar to median-of-three quicksort, and it is at least as fast as quicksort on average.

Example

Sort a range of integers into ascending order. This is the simplest way to use sort.

```
int main()
{
  int A[] = {1, 4, 2, 8, 5, 7};
  const int N = sizeof(A) / sizeof(int);
  sort(A, A + N);
  assert(is_sorted(A, A + N));
  copy(A, A + N, ostream_iterator<int>(cout, " "));
  cout << endl;
```

```
  // The output is "1 2 4 5 7 8".
}
```

In the preceding example, we sorted a range of integers into ascending order. It's just as easy to sort a range into descending order. We simply pass the appropriate function object to version 2 of sort. The function object greater (page 386) is a Strict Weak Ordering, so it is a perfectly reasonable choice. By definition, if a range is sorted according to greater, it is sorted in descending order.

```
int main() {
  vector<string> fruits;
  fruits.push_back("apple");
  fruits.push_back("banana");
  fruits.push_back("pear");
  fruits.push_back("grapefruit");
  fruits.push_back("cherry");
  fruits.push_back("orange");
  fruits.push_back("watermelon");
  fruits.push_back("mango");

  sort(fruits.begin(), fruits.end(),
       greater<string>());
  assert(is_sorted(fruits.begin(), fruits.end(),
         greater<string>()));

  copy(fruits.begin(), fruits.end(),
       ostream_iterator<string>(cout, "\n"));
}
```

13.1.2 stable_sort

① template <class RandomAccessIterator>
  void
  stable_sort(RandomAccessIterator first, RandomAccessIterator last);

② template <class RandomAccessIterator, class StrictWeakOrdering>
  void stable_sort(RandomAccessIterator first, RandomAccessIterator last,
                   StrictWeakOrdering comp);

The algorithm stable_sort is much like sort (page 292). It sorts the elements in [first,last) into ascending order (or more strictly, into nondescending order).

There are two important differences between stable_sort and sort. First, they have different runtime complexities. Usually sort is much faster. Second, as the name suggests, stable_sort is stable. It preserves the relative ordering of equivalent elements. If x and y are elements in [first,last) such that x precedes y, and if the two elements are equivalent (neither one is less than the other), then stable_sort has an additional postcondition beyond sort's postconditions: x still precedes y.

The guarantee of stability is important because under some orderings two elements may be equivalent without being identical. One common example is sorting a sequence of names by last name. If two people have the same last name but different first names, they are equivalent for the purpose of the comparison (neither is less than the other) even though they are not equal. This is one reason that `stable_sort` is sometimes useful. If you are sorting a sequence of records that have several different fields, you may want to sort it by one field without completely destroying the ordering that you previously obtained from sorting it by a different field. You might, for example, sort by first name and then do a stable sort by last name.

The two versions of `stable_sort` differ in how they define whether one element is less than another. Version 1 compares objects using `operator<`, and version 2 compares objects using a function object `comp`.

Version 1 has the postcondition that `is_sorted(first, last)` is true, and version 2 has the postcondition that `is_sorted(first, last, comp)` is true. Both versions have the postcondition that equivalent elements have the same relative ordering after `stable_sort` as they did before.

Internally, `stable_sort` is implemented in terms of the *merge sort* algorithm; see page 316, and Section 5.2.4 of Knuth [Knu98b].

Where Defined

In the HP implementation, `stable_sort` was declared in the header `<algo.h>`. According to the C++ standard, it is declared in the header `<algorithm>`.

Requirements on Types

For version 1:

- `RandomAccessIterator` is a model of **Random Access Iterator**.
- `RandomAccessIterator` is mutable.
- `RandomAccessIterator`'s value type is **Strict Weakly Comparable**.

For version 2:

- `RandomAccessIterator` is a model of **Random Access Iterator**.
- `RandomAccessIterator` is mutable.
- `StrictWeakOrdering` is a model of **Strict Weak Ordering**.
- `RandomAccessIterator`'s value type is convertible to `StrictWeakOrdering`'s argument type.

Preconditions

- [`first`, `last`) is a valid range.

Complexity

Unlike sort, stable_sort is an *adaptive* algorithm. It attempts to allocate a temporary memory buffer, and its runtime complexity depends on how much memory is available. Worst-case behavior (if no auxiliary memory is available) is $\mathcal{O}(N(\log N)^2)$ comparisons, where N is last − first, and best case (if a large enough auxiliary memory buffer is available) is $\mathcal{O}(N(\log N))$. Both sort and stable_sort are $\mathcal{O}(N(\log N))$, but sort is faster by a constant factor.

Example

Sort a sequence of characters, ignoring their case. Note that the relative order of characters that differ only by case is preserved.

```
inline bool lt_nocase(char c1, char c2) {
  return tolower(c1) < tolower(c2);
}

int main()
{
  char A[] = "fdBeACFDbEac";
  const int N = sizeof(A) - 1;
  stable_sort(A, A+N, lt_nocase);
  cout << A << endl;
  // The printed result is "AaBbCcdDeEfF".
}
```

Suppose that a vector contains a list of items, each of which has an associated priority. We want to sort the items by priority, but in cases of equal priority the items that were inserted earlier should not lose their positions. This example might represent jobs in a batch queue, or messages passed to a windowing system.

```
class job {
public:
  enum priority_code {standby, normal, high, urgent};
  job(string id, priority_code p = normal) : nam(id), pri(p) {}

  string name() const { return nam; }
  priority_code priority() const { return pri; }

private:
  string nam;
  priority_code pri;
};

ostream& operator<<(ostream& os, const job& j) {
  os << j.name() << " (" << j.priority() << ")";
  return os;
}
```

```
bool operator<(const job& j1, const job& j2) {
  return j1.priority() > j2.priority();
}

int main() {
  vector<job> jobs;

  jobs.push_back(job("Long computation", job::standby));
  jobs.push_back(job("System reboot", job::urgent));
  jobs.push_back(job("Print"));
  jobs.push_back(job("Another long computation", job::standby));
  jobs.push_back(job("Copy file"));

  stable_sort(jobs.begin(), jobs.end());
  copy(jobs.begin(), jobs.end(), ostream_iterator<job>(cout, "\n"));
}
```

13.1.3 partial_sort

① template <class RandomAccessIterator>
  void partial_sort(RandomAccessIterator first,
                    RandomAccessIterator middle,
                    RandomAccessIterator last);

② template <class RandomAccessIterator, class StrictWeakOrdering>
  void partial_sort(RandomAccessIterator first,
                    RandomAccessIterator middle,
                    RandomAccessIterator last,
                    StrictWeakOrdering comp);

The algorithm partial_sort rearranges the elements in the range [first, last) so that the smallest middle − first of them are sorted in ascending order.

The postcondition of partial_sort is that the smallest middle − first elements from the input range will be contained, sorted in ascending order, in the subrange [first, middle). The remaining last − middle elements from the input range will be contained, in an unspecified order, in the range [middle, last).

Note that if you call sort, it is also guaranteed that the smallest N elements will be contained, sorted in ascending order, in the range [first, first + N). The only reason to prefer partial_sort to sort is efficiency. Picking out the smallest N elements is faster than sorting the entire range.

The two versions of partial_sort differ in how they define whether one element is less than another. Version 1 compares objects using operator<, and version 2 compares objects using the function object comp.

Formally, the postcondition for version 1 is as follows. If i and j are any two valid iterators in the range [first, middle) such that i precedes j, and if k is a valid iterator in the range [middle, last), then *j < *i and *k < *i will both be false. The corresponding postcondition for version 2 is that comp(*j, *i) and comp(*k, *i) are both false. Less formally, this postcondition means that the first middle − first elements are in ascending order and that none of the elements in [middle, last) is less than any of the elements in [first, middle).

Internally, partial_sort is implemented using *heapsort*. See Williams [Wil64] and Section 5.2.3 of Knuth [Knu98b].

Where Defined

In the HP implementation, partial_sort was declared in the header <algo.h>. According to the C++ standard, it is declared in the header <algorithm>.

Requirements on Types

For version 1:

- RandomAccessIterator is a model of Random Access Iterator.
- RandomAccessIterator is mutable.
- RandomAccessIterator's value type is Strict Weakly Comparable.

For version 2:

- RandomAccessIterator is a model of Random Access Iterator.
- RandomAccessIterator is mutable.
- StrictWeakOrdering is a model of Strict Weak Ordering.
- RandomAccessIterator's value type is convertible to StrictWeakOrdering's argument type.

Preconditions

- [first, middle) is a valid range.
- [middle, last) is a valid range.

It follows from these two conditions that [first, last) is a valid range.

Complexity

Approximately (last − first) log(middle − first) comparisons.

Example

Find the five smallest values in an array of integers. The five elements A[0] through A[4] are sorted in ascending order, but the remaining elements are not sorted.

```
int main()
{
    int A[] = {7, 2, 6, 11, 9, 3, 12, 10, 8, 4, 1, 5};
    const int N = sizeof(A) / sizeof(int);
```

```
        partial_sort(A, A + 5, A + N);
        copy(A, A + N, ostream_iterator<int>(cout, " "));
        cout << endl;
        // The printed result is "1 2 3 4 5 11 12 10 9 8 7 6".
    }
```

In general, the expression `partial_sort(first, middle, last)` takes the smallest `middle − first` elements from the range [first,last), puts them in the range [first,middle), and sorts [first,middle) in ascending order. There are two obvious special cases: `middle == first`, and `middle == last`.

If `middle == first`, then `partial_sort` does nothing useful. It puts the zero smallest elements into the (empty) range [first,first), and then puts the remaining elements (that is, all of them), in an unspecified order, into the range [first,last). All that `partial_sort(first, first, last)` guarantees is that it will rearrange [first,last) in some unspecified way.

The special case `middle == last` is more interesting. It takes the smallest `last − first` elements from the range [first,last), puts them in the range [first,last), and sorts [first,last) in ascending order. In other words, the expression

```
    partial_sort(first, last, last)
```

sorts the entire range [first,last).

```
    int main() {
        int A[] = {7, 2, 6, 11, 9, 3, 12, 10, 8, 4, 1, 5};
        const int N = sizeof(A) / sizeof(int);

        partial_sort(A, A, A + N);
        copy(A, A + N, ostream_iterator<int>(cout, " "));
        cout << endl;

        partial_sort(A, A + N, A + N);
        copy(A, A + N, ostream_iterator<int>(cout, " "));
        cout << endl;
        // The printed result is "1 2 3 4 5 6 7 8 9 10 11 12".
    }
```

Is there any reason you would ever want to use `partial_sort` this way? If you're using a version of the STL where sort (page 292) is implemented in terms of introsort, then no. If you're sorting a range of N elements, both sort and `partial_sort` are $\mathcal{O}(N \log N)$, but sort is usually at least twice as fast.

If you're using an older version of the STL, where sort is implemented in terms of quicksort, there are cases where you should consider using `partial_sort` instead of sort to sort an entire range. Quicksort is usually $\mathcal{O}(N \log N)$, but in rare cases it is $\mathcal{O}(N^2)$.

13.1.4 `partial_sort_copy`

① template <class InputIterator, class RandomAccessIterator>
RandomAccessIterator
partial_sort_copy(InputIterator first, InputIterator last,
                  RandomAccessIterator result_first,
                  RandomAccessIterator result_last);

② template <class InputIterator, class RandomAccessIterator,
            class StrictWeakOrdering>
RandomAccessIterator
partial_sort_copy(InputIterator first, InputIterator last,
                  RandomAccessIterator result_first,
                  RandomAccessIterator result_last,
                  StrictWeakOrdering comp);

As the name suggests, the algorithm `partial_sort_copy` is the copying version of `partial_sort`. It does not, however, obey the usual convention for the copying version of an STL algorithm. It is *not* directly analogous to copy followed by `partial_sort`. Rather, `partial_sort_copy` uses [result_first,result_last) much the same way that `partial_sort` uses the range [first,middle).

The algorithm `partial_sort_copy` copies the smallest N elements from the range [first,last) to the range [result_first,result_first $+N$), where N is the smaller of last − first and result_last − result_first. The elements that are copied to [result_first,result_first $+N$) are sorted in ascending order.

The return value is result_first + N.

The two versions of `partial_sort_copy` differ in how they define whether one element is less than another. Version 1 compares objects using `operator<`, and version 2 compares objects using a function object `comp`. That is, version 1 has the postcondition that is_sorted(result_first, result_last) is true, and version 2 has the postcondition that is_sorted(result_first, result_last, comp) is true.

Where Defined

In the HP implementation, `partial_sort_copy` was declared in the header <algo.h>. According to the C++ standard, it is declared in the header <algorithm>.

Requirements on Types

For version 1:

- `InputIterator` is a model of Input Iterator.
- `RandomAccessIterator` is a model of Random Access Iterator.
- `RandomAccessIterator` is mutable.
- The value types of `InputIterator` and `RandomAccessIterator` are the same.
- `RandomAccessIterator`'s value type is Strict Weakly Comparable.

For version 2:

- InputIterator is a model of Input Iterator.
- RandomAccessIterator is a model of Random Access Iterator.
- RandomAccessIterator is mutable.
- The value types of InputIterator and RandomAccessIterator are the same.
- StrictWeakOrdering is a model of Strict Weak Ordering.
- RandomAccessIterator's value type is convertible to StrictWeakOrdering's argument type.

Preconditions

- [first, last) is a valid range.
- [result_first, result_last) is a valid range.
- [first, last) and [result_first, result_last) do not overlap.

Complexity

Approximately $(\text{last} - \text{first}) \log(N)$ comparisons, where N is the smaller of $\text{last} - \text{first}$ and result_last − result_first.

Example

Copy the smallest four values from an array of integers into a vector. We can't use partial_sort_copy to copy the result directly to the standard output because partial_sort_copy requires its output range to consist of Random Access Iterators.

```
int main()
{
  int A[] = {7, 2, 6, 11, 9, 3, 12, 10, 8, 4, 1, 5};
  const int N = sizeof(A) / sizeof(int);

  vector<int> V(4);
  partial_sort_copy(A, A + N, V.begin(), V.end());
  copy(V.begin(), V.end(), ostream_iterator<int>(cout, " "));
  cout << endl;
  // The printed result is "1 2 3 4".
}
```

13.1.5 nth_element

① template <class RandomAccessIterator>
void nth_element(RandomAccessIterator first, RandomAccessIterator nth,
                 RandomAccessIterator last);

```
② template <class RandomAccessIterator, class StrictWeakOrdering>
  void nth_element(RandomAccessIterator first, RandomAccessIterator nth,
                   RandomAccessIterator last, StrictWeakOrdering comp);
```

The algorithm nth_element is similar to partial_sort (page 297), in that it partially orders a range of elements: it arranges the range [first, last) such that the element pointed to by the iterator nth is the same as the element that would have been in that position if the entire range [first, last) had been sorted. Additionally, the iterator nth is used as a partition. It is guaranteed that none of the elements in the range [nth, last) is less than any of the elements in the range [first, nth).

This differs from partial_sort in that neither the range [nth, last) nor the range [nth, last) is guaranteed to be sorted. It is guaranteed only that the elements in [first, nth) are less than (or, more precisely, not greater than) the elements in [nth, last). In that sense, nth_element is more similar to partition (page 273) than to sort or partial_sort.

Since nth_element makes fewer guarantees than partial_sort, it is, reasonably enough, faster. That's the main reason to use nth_element instead of partial_sort.

The two versions of nth_element differ in how they define whether one element is less than another. Version 1 compares objects using operator<, and version 2 compares objects using a function object comp.

Formally, the postconditions for version 1 are that there exists no iterator i in the range [first, nth) such that *nth < *i, and that there exists no iterator j in the range [nth + 1, last) such that *j < *nth.

Similarly, the postconditions for version 2 are that there exists no iterator i in the range [first, nth) such that comp(*nth, *i) is true and that there exists no iterator j in the range [nth + 1, last) such that comp(*j, *nth) is true.

Where Defined

In the HP implementation, nth_element was declared in the header <algo.h>. According to the C++ standard, it is declared in the header <algorithm>.

Requirements on Types

For version 1:

- RandomAccessIterator is a model of Random Access Iterator.
- RandomAccessIterator is mutable.
- RandomAccessIterator's value type is Strict Weakly Comparable.

For version 2:

- RandomAccessIterator is a model of Random Access Iterator.
- RandomAccessIterator is mutable.
- StrictWeakOrdering is a model of Strict Weak Ordering.

- RandomAccessIterator's value type is convertible to StrictWeakOrdering's argument type.

Preconditions

- [first,nth) is a valid range.
- [nth,last) is a valid range.

It follows from these two preconditions that [first,last) is a valid range.

Complexity

On average, linear in last − first.

Note that this is significantly less than the runtime complexity of partial_sort. Unless partial_sort's additional guarantees are important for your application, you should always use nth_element instead.

Example

Given an array A of 12 integers, reorder the array such that:

- The element A[6] has the same value that it would have had if the entire array had been sorted.
- The elements in the positions A[0] through A[5] are less than the elements in the positions A[6] through A[11].

```
int main {
  int A[] = {7, 2, 6, 11, 9, 3, 12, 10, 8, 4, 1, 5};
  const int N = sizeof(A) / sizeof(int);

  nth_element(A, A + 6, A + N);
  copy(A, A + N, ostream_iterator<int>(cout, " "));
  cout << endl;
}
```

The printed result may be

    5 2 6 1 4 3 7 8 9 10 11 12

or any of several other possibilities. What is guaranteed is that the array has been divided into two pieces and that none of the elements in the first piece are greater than any of the elements in the second piece. The internal ordering within the ranges [A,A + 6) and [A + 7,A + 12) is not important.

13.1.6 is_sorted

① template <class ForwardIterator>
  bool is_sorted(ForwardIterator first, ForwardIterator last)

② template <class ForwardIterator, class StrictWeakOrdering>
bool is_sorted(ForwardIterator first, ForwardIterator last,
               StrictWeakOrdering comp)

Rather than sorting a range, is_sorted tests whether a range is already sorted. It returns true if the range [first,last) is sorted in ascending order and false otherwise, and it does not modify its input range.

The is_sorted algorithm appears as the precondition, the postcondition, or both, for many of the algorithms in this chapter.

The two versions of is_sorted differ in how they define whether one element is less than another. Version 1 compares objects using operator<, and version 2 compares objects using the function object comp.

Formally, version 1 returns true if and only if, for every two iterators i and j in the range [first,last) such that i precedes j, *j < *i is false. Version 2 returns true if and only if, for every two such iterators, comp(*j, *i) is false.

If [first,last) is an empty range (that is, if first == last), both versions of is_sorted return true. An empty range is always (trivially) sorted.

Where Defined

The algorithm is_sorted is not present in the original HP implementation of the STL, or in the C++ standard. In the SGI implementation, it is declared in the header <algorithm>.

Requirements on Types

For version 1:

- ForwardIterator is a model of Forward Iterator.
- ForwardIterator's value type is a model of Strict Weakly Comparable.

For version 2:

- ForwardIterator is a model of Forward Iterator.
- StrictWeakOrdering is a model of Strict Weak Ordering.
- ForwardIterator's value type is convertible to StrictWeakOrdering's argument type.

Preconditions

- [first,last) is a valid range.

Complexity

Linear. For nonempty ranges, at most (last − first) − 1 comparisons.

Example

```
int main()
{
  int A[] = {1, 4, 2, 8, 5, 7};
  const int N = sizeof(A) / sizeof(int);

  assert(is_sorted(A, A));
  assert(is_sorted(A, A, greater<int>()));

  assert(!is_sorted(A, A + N));
  assert(!is_sorted(A, A + N, greater<int>()));

  sort(A, A + N);
  assert(is_sorted(A, A + N));
  assert(!is_sorted(A, A + N, greater<int>()));

  sort(A, A + N, greater<int>());
  assert(!is_sorted(A, A + N));
  assert(is_sorted(A, A + N, greater<int>()));
}
```

13.2 Operations on Sorted Ranges

One of the reasons the sorting algorithms in Section 13.1 are so important is that many other algorithms require sorted ranges as inputs. Sorting a range makes it easy to search for a particular value, to combine the range with other sorted ranges, and so on.

13.2.1 Binary Search

Everyone who has ever used a dictionary understands one important property of a sorted range: It is easy to find something in it. If a range of N elements is completely unordered, finding an element in it is a linear operation. As seen with find (page 199), you may have to examine every element in the range. If the range is sorted, finding an element in it is only a logarithmic operation. The *binary search* method works by successively dividing a sorted range in half.

The STL contains four different binary search algorithms because there are several different questions that you might want to answer by performing a binary search. The most basic (but not, in fact, the most useful) is simply whether a particular element is contained in the range. This corresponds to the algorithm binary_search.

More commonly, though, that's not enough information. If the element is already contained in the range, you probably want to know where it is, and if it's not already contained in the range, you probably want to know where it would have been if it had been there.

This is the general basis for the three algorithms lower_bound, upper_bound, and equal_range. The reason there are three algorithms instead of one is that the element you're looking for might appear more than once in the range. If you're looking for the number 17 and there are four copies of 17 in a row, which one should the algorithm give you—the first, the last, or the entire range of 17s? Those three choices correspond, respectively, to lower_bound, upper_bound, and equal_range. In most cases, lower_bound tends to be the most convenient.

13.2.1.1 binary_search

① template <class ForwardIterator, class StrictWeaklyComparable>
bool binary_search(ForwardIterator first, ForwardIterator last,
                   const StrictWeaklyComparable& value);

② template <class ForwardIterator, class T, class StrictWeakOrdering>
bool binary_search(ForwardIterator first, ForwardIterator last,
                   const T& value,
                   StrictWeakOrdering comp);

The algorithm binary_search is a version of binary search. It attempts to find the element value in a sorted range [first,last). It returns true if an element that is equivalent to value is present in [first,last) and false if no such element exists.

A simple Boolean result is probably not the information you need. The other algorithms in Section 13.2.1, lower_bound, upper_bound, and equal_range, are versions of binary search that provide additional information.

Version 1 uses operator< for comparison, and version 2 uses the function object comp.

Formally, version 1 returns true if and only if there exists an iterator i in the range [first,last) such that *i < value and value < *i are both false. Version 2 returns true if and only if there exists an iterator i in [first,last) such that comp(*i, value) and comp(value, *i) are both false.

Where Defined

In the HP implementation, binary_search was declared in the header <algo.h>. According to the C++ standard, it is declared in the header <algorithm>.

Requirements on Types

For version 1:

- ForwardIterator is a model of Forward Iterator.
- StrictWeaklyComparable is a model of Strict Weakly Comparable.
- ForwardIterator's value type is the same type as StrictWeaklyComparable.

For version 2:

- ForwardIterator is a model of Forward Iterator.
- StrictWeakOrdering is a model of Strict Weak Ordering.

- ForwardIterator's value type is the same type as T.
- ForwardIterator's value type is convertible to StrictWeakOrdering's argument type.

Preconditions

For version 1:

- [first, last) is a valid range.
- [first, last) is sorted in ascending order according to operator<. That is, is_sorted(first, last) is true.

For version 2:

- [first, last) is a valid range.
- [first, last) is sorted in ascending order according to the function object comp. That is, is_sorted(first, last, comp) is true.

Complexity

The number of comparisons is logarithmic: at most $\log(\text{last} - \text{first}) + 2$. If the type ForwardIterator is a Random Access Iterator, then the number of steps through the range is also logarithmic; otherwise, the number of steps is proportional to last − first.

The runtime complexity is different for Random Access Iterators than for other types of iterators because advance (page 183) is constant time for Random Access Iterators and linear time for Forward Iterators.

Example

Search for elements in a sorted array of integers.

```
int main() {
  int A[] = { 1, 2, 3, 3, 3, 5, 8 };
  const int N = sizeof(A) / sizeof(int);

  for (int i = 1; i <= 10; ++i) {
    cout << "Searching for " << i << ": "
         << (binary_search(A, A + N, i) ? "present" : "not present")
         << endl;
  }
}
```

The output is:

```
Searching for 1: present
Searching for 2: present
Searching for 3: present
Searching for 4: not present
```

```
Searching for 5: present
Searching for 6: not present
Searching for 7: not present
Searching for 8: present
Searching for 9: not present
Searching for 10: not present
```

13.2.1.2 lower_bound

① ```
template <class ForwardIterator, class StrictWeaklyComparable>
ForwardIterator
lower_bound(ForwardIterator first, ForwardIterator last,
            const StrictWeaklyComparable& value);
```

② ```
template <class ForwardIterator, class T, class StrictWeakOrdering>
ForwardIterator
lower_bound(ForwardIterator first, ForwardIterator last,
            const T& value, StrictWeakOrdering comp);
```

The algorithm lower_bound is a version of binary search: It attempts to find the element value in a sorted range [first,last). If an element equivalent to value is already present, lower_bound returns an iterator pointing to the first such element. If no such element is present, it returns the location where value would have been if it had been present; that is, it returns an iterator that points to the first element that is not less than value. (Or else last if value is greater than any of the elements in [first,last).) A slightly different way to look at lower_bound is that its return value is the first position where value could be inserted without violating the ordering.

Version 1 uses operator< for comparison, and version 2 uses the function object comp.

Formally, version 1 returns the furthermost iterator i in [first,last) such that, for every iterator j in [first,i), *j < value. Similarly, version 2 returns the furthermost iterator i in [first,last) such that, for every iterator j in [first,i), comp(*j, value) is true.

Where Defined

In the HP implementation, lower_bound was declared in the header <algo.h>. According to the C++ standard, it is declared in the header <algorithm>.

Requirements on Types

For version 1:

- ForwardIterator is a model of Forward Iterator.
- StrictWeaklyComparable is a model of Strict Weakly Comparable.
- ForwardIterator's value type is the same type as StrictWeaklyComparable.

For version 2:

- `ForwardIterator` is a model of **Forward Iterator**.
- `StrictWeakOrdering` is a model of **Strict Weak Ordering**.
- `ForwardIterator`'s value type is the same type as T.
- `ForwardIterator`'s value type is convertible to `StrictWeakOrdering`'s argument type.

Preconditions

For version 1:

- `[first,last)` is a valid range.
- `[first,last)` is sorted in ascending order according to `operator<`. That is, `is_sorted(first, last)` is true.

For version 2:

- `[first,last)` is a valid range.
- `[first,last)` is sorted in ascending order according to the function object comp. That is, `is_sorted(first, last, comp)` is true.

Complexity

The number of comparisons is logarithmic: at most $\log(\text{last} - \text{first}) + 1$. If the type `ForwardIterator` is a **Random Access Iterator** then the number of steps through the range is also logarithmic; otherwise, the number of steps is proportional to last − first.

The runtime complexity is different for **Random Access Iterators** than for other types of iterators because advance (page 183) is constant time for **Random Access Iterators** and linear time for **Forward Iterators**.

Example

```
int main()
{
  int A[] = { 1, 2, 3, 3, 3, 5, 8 };
  const int N = sizeof(A) / sizeof(int);

  for (int i = 1; i <= 10; ++i) {
    int* p = lower_bound(A, A + N, i);
    cout << "Searching for " << i << ".  ";
    cout << "Result: index = " << p - A << ", ";
    if (p != A + N)
      cout << "A[" << p - A << "] == " << *p << endl;
    else
```

```
        cout << "which is off-the-end." << endl;
    }
}
```

The output is:

```
Searching for 1.   Result: index = 0, A[0] == 1
Searching for 2.   Result: index = 1, A[1] == 2
Searching for 3.   Result: index = 2, A[2] == 3
Searching for 4.   Result: index = 5, A[5] == 5
Searching for 5.   Result: index = 5, A[5] == 5
Searching for 6.   Result: index = 6, A[6] == 8
Searching for 7.   Result: index = 6, A[6] == 8
Searching for 8.   Result: index = 6, A[6] == 8
Searching for 9.   Result: index = 7, which is off-the-end.
Searching for 10.  Result: index = 7, which is off-the-end.
```

The algorithm lower_bound is very similar to the C library function bsearch. One of the main differences is what happens when you search for a value that turns out not to be present: lower_bound returns the location where that value would have been if it had been present, but bsearch returns a null pointer as an indication of failure.

If the value val that you are searching for is not present, lower_bound will return either last or an iterator i such that val < *i. This means that it is trivial to write a wrapper for lower_bound that gives it a bsearch-like interface.

```
template <class ForwardIterator, class StrictWeaklyComparable>
ForwardIterator stl_bsearch(ForwardIterator first, ForwardIterator last,
                    const StrictWeaklyComparable& value) {
  ForwardIterator loc = lower_bound(first, last, value);
  return loc == last || value < *loc ? last : loc;
}

template <class ForwardIterator, class T, class StrictWeakOrdering>
ForwardIterator stl_bsearch(ForwardIterator first, ForwardIterator last,
                    const T& value,
                    StrictWeakOrdering comp) {
  ForwardIterator loc = lower_bound(first, last, value, comp);
  return loc == last || comp(value, *loc) ? last : loc;
}
```

13.2.1.3 upper_bound

① template <class ForwardIterator, class StrictWeaklyComparable>
ForwardIterator
upper_bound(ForwardIterator first, ForwardIterator last,
            const StrictWeaklyComparable& value);

② template <class ForwardIterator, class T, class StrictWeakOrdering>
ForwardIterator
upper_bound(ForwardIterator first, ForwardIterator last,
            const T& value, StrictWeakOrdering comp);

The algorithm upper_bound is a version of binary search. It attempts to find an element that is equivalent to value in a sorted range [first,last). Specifically, it returns the last position where value could be inserted without violating the ordering.

Because ranges are not symmetrical between the beginning and the end (a range [first,last) includes first but not last), upper_bound's return value has a very different meaning than lower_bound's. If you are searching for a value that is present in a range, lower_bound returns an iterator that points to that element. By contrast, upper_bound does not. It can't, since upper_bound returns the *last* position where value could be inserted without violating the ordering. If value is present, then it is the iterator *before* upper_bound's return value, not upper_bound's return value itself, that points to value.

The first version of upper_bound uses operator< for comparison, and the second uses the function object comp.

Formally, version 1 returns the furthermost iterator i in [first,last) such that for every iterator j in [first,i), value < *j is false. Similarly, version 2 returns the furthermost iterator i in [first,last) such that for every iterator j in [first,i), comp(value, *j) is false.

Where Defined

In the HP implementation, upper_bound was declared in the header <algo.h>. According to the C++ standard, it is declared in the header <algorithm>.

Requirements on Types

For version 1:

- ForwardIterator is a model of Forward Iterator.
- StrictWeaklyComparable is a model of Strict Weakly Comparable.
- ForwardIterator's value type is the same type as StrictWeaklyComparable.

For version 2:

- ForwardIterator is a model of Forward Iterator.
- StrictWeakOrdering is a model of Strict Weak Ordering.
- ForwardIterator's value type is the same type as T.
- ForwardIterator's value type is convertible to StrictWeakOrdering's argument type.

Preconditions

For version 1:

- [first, last) is a valid range.
- [first, last) is sorted in ascending order according to operator<. That is, is_sorted(first, last) is true.

For version 2:

- [first, last) is a valid range.
- [first, last) is sorted in ascending order according to the function object comp. That is, is_sorted(first, last, comp) is true.

Complexity

The number of comparisons is logarithmic: at most $\log(\text{last} - \text{first}) + 1$. If the type ForwardIterator is a **Random Access Iterator**, the number of steps through the range is also logarithmic; otherwise, the number of steps is proportional to last − first.

The runtime complexity is different for **Random Access Iterators** than for other types of iterators because advance (page 183) is constant time for **Random Access Iterators** and linear time for **Forward Iterators**.

Example

```
int main()
{
  int A[] = { 1, 2, 3, 3, 3, 5, 8 };
  const int N = sizeof(A) / sizeof(int);

  for (int i = 1; i <= 10; ++i) {
    int* p = upper_bound(A, A + N, i);
    cout << "Searching for " << i << ".  ";
    cout << "Result: index = " << p - A << ", ";
    if (p != A + N)
      cout << "A[" << p - A << "] == " << *p << endl;
    else
      cout << "which is off-the-end." << endl;
  }
}
```

The output is:

```
Searching for 1.  Result: index = 1, A[1] == 2
Searching for 2.  Result: index = 2, A[2] == 3
Searching for 3.  Result: index = 5, A[5] == 5
Searching for 4.  Result: index = 5, A[5] == 5
Searching for 5.  Result: index = 6, A[6] == 8
Searching for 6.  Result: index = 6, A[6] == 8
Searching for 7.  Result: index = 6, A[6] == 8
```

```
Searching for 8.   Result: index = 7, which is off-the-end.
Searching for 9.   Result: index = 7, which is off-the-end.
Searching for 10.  Result: index = 7, which is off-the-end.
```

13.2.1.4 equal_range

① template <class ForwardIterator, class StrictWeaklyComparable>
pair<ForwardIterator, ForwardIterator>
equal_range(ForwardIterator first, ForwardIterator last,
       const StrictWeaklyComparable& value);

② template <class ForwardIterator, class T, class StrictWeakOrdering>
pair<ForwardIterator, ForwardIterator>
equal_range(ForwardIterator first, ForwardIterator last,
       const T& value,
       StrictWeakOrdering comp);

The algorithm equal_range is a version of binary search. It attempts to find the element value in a sorted range [first,last).

The value returned by equal_range is essentially a combination of the values returned by lower_bound and upper_bound. It is a pair of iterators i and j such that i is the first position where value could be inserted without violating the ordering and j is the last position where value could be inserted without violating the ordering.

It follows that every element in the range [i,j) is equivalent to value and that [i,j) is the largest subrange of [first,last) with this property.

A slightly different way to think about equal_range is to consider the range of all elements in [first,last) that are equivalent to value. (Since [first,last) is sorted, we know that all of the elements that are equivalent to value must be contiguous.) The algorithm lower_bound returns the first iterator in that range, the algorithm upper_bound returns the past-the-end iterator, and the algorithm equal_range returns the beginning iterator and the past-the-end iterator as a pair.

This description makes sense even if [first,last) contains no elements that are equivalent to value. In that case, the range of elements equivalent to value is an empty range. There is only one position where value could be inserted without violating the range's ordering, so equal_range's return value is a pair both of whose elements are iterators pointing to that position.

Version 1 uses operator< for comparison, and version 2 uses the function object comp.

Formally, version 1 returns a pair of iterators [i,j), where i is the furthermost iterator in [first,last) such that, for every iterator k in [first,i), *k < value, and where j is the furthermost iterator in [first,last) such that, for every iterator k in [first,j), value < *k is false. For every iterator k in [i,j), both value < *k and *k < value are false.

Similarly, version 2 returns a pair of iterators [i,j), where i is the furthermost iterator in [first,last) such that, for every iterator k in [first,i), comp(*k, value) is true, and where j is the furthermost iterator in [first,last) such that, for every iterator k in [first,j), comp(value, *k) is false. For every iterator k in [i,j), both comp(value, *k) and comp(*k, value) are false.

Where Defined

In the HP implementation, equal_range was declared in the header <algo.h>. According to the C++ standard, it is declared in the header <algorithm>.

Requirements on Types

For version 1:

- ForwardIterator is a model of Forward Iterator.
- StrictWeaklyComparable is a model of Strict Weakly Comparable.
- ForwardIterator's value type is the same type as StrictWeaklyComparable.

For version 2:

- ForwardIterator is a model of Forward Iterator.
- StrictWeakOrdering is a model of Strict Weak Ordering.
- ForwardIterator's value type is the same type as T.
- ForwardIterator's value type is convertible to StrictWeakOrdering's argument type.

Preconditions

For version 1:

- [first,last) is a valid range.
- [first,last) is ordered in ascending order according to operator<. That is, is_sorted(first, last) is true.

For version 2:

- [first,last) is a valid range.
- [first,last) is sorted in ascending order according to the function object comp. That is, is_sorted(first, last, comp) is true.

Complexity

The number of comparisons is logarithmic. It is at most $2\log(\text{last} - \text{first}) + 1$. If the type ForwardIterator is a Random Access Iterator, then the number of steps through the range is also logarithmic. Otherwise, the number of steps is proportional to last − first.

The runtime complexity is different for Random Access Iterators than for other types of iterators because advance (page 183) is constant time for Random Access Iterators and linear time for Forward Iterators.

Example

```
int main()
{
  int A[] = { 1, 2, 3, 3, 3, 5, 8 };
  const int N = sizeof(A) / sizeof(int);

  for (int i = 2; i <= 5; ++i) {
    pair<int*, int*> result = equal_range(A, A + N, i);

    cout << endl;
    cout << "Searching for " << i << endl;

    cout << "  First position where " << i << " could be inserted: "
         << result.first - A << endl;
    cout << "  Last position where " << i << " could be inserted: "
         << result.second - A << endl;

    if (result.first < A + N)
      cout << "  *result.first = " << *result.first << endl;
    if (result.second < A + N)
      cout << "  *result.second = " << *result.second << endl;
  }
}
```

The output is:

```
Searching for 2
  First position where 2 could be inserted: 1
  Last position where 2 could be inserted: 2
  *result.first = 2
  *result.second = 3

Searching for 3
  First position where 3 could be inserted: 2
  Last position where 3 could be inserted: 5
  *result.first = 3
  *result.second = 5

Searching for 4
  First position where 4 could be inserted: 5
  Last position where 4 could be inserted: 5
  *result.first = 5
  *result.second = 5

Searching for 5
  First position where 5 could be inserted: 5
  Last position where 5 could be inserted: 6
  *result.first = 5
  *result.second = 8
```

13.2.2 Merging Two Sorted Ranges

13.2.2.1 merge

① template <class InputIterator1, class InputIterator2,
          class OutputIterator>
OutputIterator merge(InputIterator1 first1, InputIterator1 last1,
                    InputIterator2 first2, InputIterator2 last2,
                    OutputIterator result);

② template <class InputIterator1, class InputIterator2,
          class OutputIterator,
          class StrictWeakOrdering>
OutputIterator merge(InputIterator1 first1, InputIterator1 last1,
                    InputIterator2 first2, InputIterator2 last2,
                    OutputIterator result, StrictWeakOrdering comp);

The algorithm merge combines two sorted ranges into a single sorted range. It copies elements from [first1, last1) and [first2, last2) into [result, result + (last1 − first1) + (last2 − first2)) such that the resulting range is sorted in ascending order. The return value is result + (last1 − first1) + (last2 − first2).

This operation is stable, meaning both that the relative order of elements within each input range is preserved and that for equivalent elements in both input ranges the element from the first range precedes the element from the second.

The two versions of merge differ in how elements are compared. Version 1 uses operator<. That is, the input ranges and the output range are sorted in ascending order by operator<. Version 2 uses the function object comp. That is, the input ranges and the output range are sorted in ascending order by comp.

Note that merge and set_union (page 324) are very similar in that they both construct a sorted range by copying elements from two sorted input ranges. The difference is what happens when a particular value is contained in both input ranges: set_union eliminates duplicates, and merge does not. As a consequence, one of merge's postconditions is that the length of its output range is equal to the sum of the lengths of its input ranges. By contrast, set_union guarantees only that the length of its output range is *less than or equal to* the sum of the lengths of its input ranges.

Where Defined

In the HP implementation, merge was declared in the header <algo.h>. According to the C++ standard, it is declared in the header <algorithm>.

Requirements on Types

For version 1:

- InputIterator1 is a model of Input Iterator.
- InputIterator2 is a model of Input Iterator.

- InputIterator1's value type is the same type as InputIterator2's value type.
- InputIterator1's value type is Strict Weakly Comparable.
- InputIterator1's value type is convertible to a type in OutputIterator's set of value types.

For version 2:

- InputIterator1 is a model of Input Iterator.
- InputIterator2 is a model of Input Iterator.
- InputIterator1's value type is the same type as InputIterator2's value type.
- StrictWeakOrdering is a model of Strict Weak Ordering.
- InputIterator1's value type is convertible to StrictWeakOrdering's argument type.
- InputIterator1's value type is convertible to a type in OutputIterator's set of value types.

Preconditions

For version 1:

- [first1, last1) is a valid range.
- The range [first1, last1) is sorted in ascending order by operator<. That is, is_sorted(first1, last1) is true.
- [first2, last2) is a valid range.
- The range [first2, last2) is sorted in ascending order by operator<. That is, is_sorted(first2, last2) is true.
- There is enough space to hold all of the elements being copied. More formally, the requirement is that $[\text{result}, \text{result} + (\text{last1} - \text{first1}) + (\text{last2} - \text{first2}))$ is a valid range.
- The ranges [first1, last1) and $[\text{result}, \text{result} + (\text{last1} - \text{first1}) + (\text{last2} - \text{first2}))$ do not overlap.
- The ranges [first2, last2) and $[\text{result}, \text{result} + (\text{last1} - \text{first1}) + (\text{last2} - \text{first2}))$ do not overlap.

For version 2:

- [first1, last1) is a valid range.
- The range [first1, last1) is sorted in ascending order by the function object comp. That is, is_sorted(first1, last1, comp) is true.
- [first2, last2) is a valid range.
- The range [first2, last2) is sorted in ascending order by the function object comp. That is, is_sorted(first2, last2, comp) is true.

- There is enough space to hold all of the elements being copied. More formally, the requirement is that [result, result + (last1 − first1) + (last2 − first2)) is a valid range.

- The ranges [first1, last1) and [result, result + (last1 − first1) + (last2 − first2)) do not overlap.

- The ranges [first2, last2) and [result, result + (last1 − first1) + (last2 − first2)) do not overlap.

Complexity

Linear. For nonempty ranges, at most (last1 − first1) + (last2 − first2) − 1 comparisons.

Example

```
int main()
{
  int A1[] = { 1, 3, 5, 7 };
  int A2[] = { 2, 4, 6, 8 };
  const int N1 = sizeof(A1) / sizeof(int);
  const int N2 = sizeof(A2) / sizeof(int);

  merge(A1, A1 + N1, A2, A2 + N2,
        ostream_iterator<int>(cout, " "));
  cout << endl;
  // The output is "1 2 3 4 5 6 7 8"
}
```

13.2.2.2 inplace_merge

① template <class BidirectionalIterator>
   inline void inplace_merge(BidirectionalIterator first,
                             BidirectionalIterator middle,
                             BidirectionalIterator last);

② template <class BidirectionalIterator, class StrictWeakOrdering>
   inline void inplace_merge(BidirectionalIterator first,
                             BidirectionalIterator middle,
                             BidirectionalIterator last,
                             StrictWeakOrdering comp);

If the two consecutive ranges [first, middle) and [middle, last) are both sorted, inplace_merge combines them into a single sorted range. That is, it starts with a range [first, last) that consists of two pieces each of which is sorted in ascending order and rearranges it so that the entire range is sorted in ascending order.

Like merge, inplace_merge is stable. The relative order of elements within each input range is preserved, and for equivalent elements in both input ranges, the element from the first range precedes the element from the second.

The two versions of inplace_merge differ in how they define whether one element is less than another. Version 1 compares objects using operator<, and version 2 compares objects using the function object comp.

Where Defined

In the HP implementation, inplace_merge was declared in the header <algo.h>. According to the C++ standard, it is declared in the header <algorithm>.

Requirements on Types

For version 1:

- BidirectionalIterator is a model of Bidirectional Iterator.
- BidirectionalIterator is mutable.
- BidirectionalIterator's value type is a model of Strict Weakly Comparable.

For version 2:

- BidirectionalIterator is a model of Bidirectional Iterator.
- BidirectionalIterator is mutable.
- StrictWeakOrdering is a model of Strict Weak Ordering.
- BidirectionalIterator's value type is convertible to StrictWeakOrdering's argument type.

Preconditions

For version 1:

- [first,middle) is a valid range.
- [middle,last) is a valid range.
- The range [first,middle) is sorted in ascending order by operator<. That is, is_sorted(first, middle) is true.
- The range [middle,last) is sorted in ascending order by operator<. That is, is_sorted(middle, last) is true.

For version 2:

- [first,middle) is a valid range.
- [middle,last) is a valid range.
- The range [first,middle) is sorted in ascending order by the function object comp. That is, is_sorted(first, middle, comp) is true.
- The range [middle,last) is sorted in ascending order by the function object comp. That is, is_sorted(middle, last, comp) is true.

Complexity

The algorithm `inplace_merge` is an *adaptive* algorithm. It attempts to allocate a temporary memory buffer, and its runtime complexity depends on how much memory is available. For nonempty ranges the worst-case behavior (if no auxiliary memory is available) is $O(N \log N)$, where N is `last − first`, and the best case (if a large enough auxiliary memory buffer is available) is at most $N − 1$ comparisons.

Example

Merge a range consisting of two consecutive sorted subranges of integers.

```
int main()
{
   int A[] = { 1, 3, 5, 7, 2, 4, 6, 8 };

   inplace_merge(A, A + 4, A + 8);
   copy(A, A + 8, ostream_iterator<int>(cout, " "));
   // The output is "1 2 3 4 5 6 7 8".
}
```

The fact that there is an efficient way of merging two consecutive sorted subranges suggests a "divide and conquer" algorithm for sorting a range: divide the range in half, sort each half, and then use `inplace_merge` to form a single sorted range.

```
template <class BidirectionalIter>
void mergesort(BidirectionalIter first, BidirectionalIter last) {
   typename iterator_traits<BidirectionalIter>::difference_type n
     = distance(first, last);
   if (n == 0 || n == 1)
     return;
   else {
     BidirectionalIter mid = first + n / 2;
     mergesort(first, mid);
     mergesort(mid, last);
     inplace_merge(first, mid, last);
   }
}
```

This is the *merge sort* algorithm. In fact, `stable_sort` (page 294) is implemented exactly this way (with some minor modifications for increased efficiency).

13.2.3   Set Operations on Sorted Ranges

One of the fundamental concepts of mathematics is the *set*, an unordered collection of elements. The basic operations of set theory include union, intersection, and set difference.

If sets are unordered, what are set operations doing in a chapter about sorted ranges? The answer lies in the distinction between *sets* in a purely abstract mathematical sense, and *sets* as represented in a computer program. In abstract mathematics, sets are unordered. The set $\{1, 2, 3\}$, for example, is the same as the set $\{3, 2, 1\}$. In a computer program, however, we have to choose some way to represent that set as a data structure, some representation that makes it easy to perform operations like union and intersection.

One convenient representation is as a sorted range of elements. It turns out that all of the basic operations from set theory can be performed efficiently on sorted ranges and that the ranges that result from those operations are naturally sorted. The algorithms in this section implement set operations as operations on sorted ranges.

In addition to these algorithms, the STL includes a container class called set (page 461). As the name suggests, a set is a convenient way of representing a collection of elements that you intend to use with the set algorithms in this section. Each value appears in a set at most once, and a set's members always form a sorted range.

Because these algorithms operate on sets represented as sorted ranges rather than on sets in the abstract mathematical definition, they generalize mathematical set operations in one important way: A particular value might appear more than once in a sorted range. Instead of imposing the precondition that every element appear at most once in each input range, these algorithms generalize mathematical set operations so that they are well-defined for input ranges with duplicated values. These generalized operations still satisfy the identities of ordinary set operations, and when the input ranges contain no duplicated values, these algorithms behave according to the usual mathematical definitions.

13.2.3.1 includes

① ```
template <class InputIterator1, class InputIterator2>
bool includes(InputIterator1 first1, InputIterator1 last1,
              InputIterator2 first2, InputIterator2 last2);
```

② ```
template <class InputIterator1, class InputIterator2,
          class StrictWeakOrdering>
bool includes(InputIterator1 first1, InputIterator1 last1,
              InputIterator2 first2, InputIterator2 last2,
              StrictWeakOrdering comp);
```

The algorithm includes tests whether one set is a subset of another, where both sets are represented as sorted ranges. That is, it returns true if and only if, for every element in [first2, last2), an equivalent element is also present in [first1, last1).

Like all of the STL set algorithms, includes generalizes the mathematical definition of set operations. There is no requirement that every element in [first1, last1) or [first2, last2) be unique. In this case, the definition of subset inclusion is generalized so that, for every element in [first2,last2), a distinct equivalent element must also be present in [first1,last1). That is, if some element appears n times in [first2,last2) and m times in [first1,last1), includes will return false if $m < n$.

The two versions of includes differ in how they define whether one element is less than another. Version 1 compares objects using operator<, and version 2 compares objects using the function object comp.

Where Defined

In the HP implementation, includes was declared in the header <algo.h>. According to the C++ standard, it is declared in the header <algorithm>.

Requirements on Types

For version 1:

- InputIterator1 is a model of Input Iterator.
- InputIterator2 is a model of Input Iterator.
- InputIterator1 and InputIterator2 have the same value type.
- InputIterator's value type is a model of StrictWeaklyComparable.

For version 2:

- InputIterator1 is a model of Input Iterator.
- InputIterator2 is a model of Input Iterator.
- InputIterator1 and InputIterator2 have the same value type.
- StrictWeakOrdering is a model of Strict Weak Ordering.
- InputIterator1's value type is convertible to StrictWeakOrdering's argument type.

Preconditions

For version 1:

- [first1,last1) is a valid range.
- [first2,last2) is a valid range.
- [first1,last1) is ordered in ascending order according to operator<. That is, is_sorted(first1, last1) is true.
- [first2,last2) is ordered in ascending order according to operator<. That is, is_sorted(first2, last2) is true.

For version 2:

- [first1,last1) is a valid range.
- [first2,last2) is a valid range.

- [first1,last1) is ordered in ascending order according to comp. That is,
    ```
    is_sorted(first1, last1, comp)
    ```
  is true.
- [first2,last2) is ordered in ascending order according to comp. That is,
    ```
    is_sorted(first2, last2, comp)
    ```
  is true.

Complexity

Linear. Zero comparisons if either [first1,last1) or [first2,last2) is an empty range. Otherwise, at most $2((last1 - first1) + (last2 - first2)) - 1$ comparisons.

Example

```
int main()
{
  int A1[] = { 1, 2, 3, 4, 5, 6, 7 };
  int A2[] = { 1, 4, 7 };
  int A3[] = { 2, 7, 9 };
  int A4[] = { 1, 1, 2, 3, 5, 8, 13, 21 };
  int A5[] = { 1, 2, 13, 13 };
  int A6[] = { 1, 1, 3, 21 };

  const int N1 = sizeof(A1) / sizeof(int);
  const int N2 = sizeof(A2) / sizeof(int);
  const int N3 = sizeof(A3) / sizeof(int);
  const int N4 = sizeof(A4) / sizeof(int);
  const int N5 = sizeof(A5) / sizeof(int);
  const int N6 = sizeof(A6) / sizeof(int);

  cout << "A2 contained in A1: "
       << (includes(A1, A1 + N1, A2, A2 + N2) ? "true" : "false")
       << endl;
  cout << "A3 contained in A1: "
       << (includes(A1, A1 + N2, A3, A3 + N3) ? "true" : "false")
       << endl;
  cout << "A5 contained in A4: "
       << (includes(A4, A4 + N4, A5, A5 + N5) ? "true" : "false")
       << endl;
  cout << "A6 contained in A4: "
       << (includes(A4, A4 + N4, A6, A6 + N6) ? "true" : "false")
       << endl;
}
```

The output is:

```
A2 contained in A1: true
A3 contained in A1: false
A5 contained in A4: false
A6 contained in A4: true
```

13.2.3.2 `set_union`

① ```
template <class InputIterator1, class InputIterator2,
          class OutputIterator>
OutputIterator set_union(InputIterator1 first1, InputIterator1 last1,
                         InputIterator2 first2, InputIterator2 last2,
                         OutputIterator result);
```

② ```
template <class InputIterator1, class InputIterator2,
          class OutputIterator,
          class StrictWeakOrdering>
OutputIterator set_union(InputIterator1 first1, InputIterator1 last1,
                         InputIterator2 first2, InputIterator2 last2,
                         OutputIterator result,
                         StrictWeakOrdering comp);
```

The algorithm `set_union` constructs the union of two sets—that is, it constructs the set $S_1 \cup S_2$ consisting of every element that is present in S_1, or in S_2, or in both. Both S_1 and S_2 and their union are represented as sorted ranges. The return value is the end of the output range.

Like all of the STL set algorithms, `set_union` generalizes the mathematical definition of set operations. There is no requirement that every element in input ranges [first1, last1) or [first2, last2) be unique. In this case, the definition of set union is generalized so that if a value appears n times in [first1, last1) and the same value appears m times in [first2, last2), it will appear $\max(m, n)$ times in the output range. (The ordinary definition of union is simply the case where $n \le 1$ and $m \le 1$.) This operation is stable, meaning both that the relative order of elements within each input range is preserved and that if an element is present in both input ranges it is copied from the first range rather than the second.

It is slightly imprecise to talk about a value appearing n times in [first1, last1) and m times in [first2, last2). A more precise formulation is that [first1, last1) contains a range of n elements that are equivalent to each other, and [first2, last2) contains m elements from the same equivalence class. The output range will contain $\max(n, m)$ values from that equivalence class; n of the elements in the output range will be copied from [first1, last1), and the other $\max(n - m, 0)$ will be copied from [first2, last2).

The two versions of `set_union` differ in how they define whether one element is less than another. Version 1 compares objects using `operator<`, and version 2 compares objects using a function object `comp`.

Where Defined

In the HP implementation, `set_union` was declared in the header `<algo.h>`. According to the C++ standard, it is declared in the header `<algorithm>`.

Requirements on Types

For version 1:

- InputIterator1 is a model of Input Iterator.
- InputIterator2 is a model of Input Iterator.
- OutputIterator is a model of Output Iterator.
- InputIterator1 and InputIterator2 have the same value type.
- InputIterator's value type is a model of Strict Weakly Comparable.
- InputIterator's value type is convertible to a type in OutputIterator's set of value types.

For version 2:

- InputIterator1 is a model of Input Iterator.
- InputIterator2 is a model of Input Iterator.
- OutputIterator is a model of Output Iterator.
- StrictWeakOrdering is a model of Strict Weak Ordering.
- InputIterator1 and InputIterator2 have the same value type.
- InputIterator1's value type is convertible to StrictWeakOrdering's argument type.
- InputIterator's value type is convertible to a type in OutputIterator's set of value types.

Preconditions

For version 1:

- [first1, last1) is a valid range.
- [first2, last2) is a valid range.
- [first1, last1) is ordered in ascending order according to operator<. That is, is_sorted(first1, last1) is true.
- [first2, last2) is ordered in ascending order according to operator<. That is, is_sorted(first2, last2) is true.
- There is enough space to hold all of the elements being copied. More formally, the requirement is that [result, result + n) is a valid range, where n is the number of elements in the union of the two input ranges.
- [first1, last1) and [result, result + n) do not overlap.
- [first2, last2) and [result, result + n) do not overlap.

For version 2:

- [first1, last1) is a valid range.
- [first2, last2) is a valid range.

- [first1, last1) is ordered in ascending order according to comp. That is,

  ```
  is_sorted(first1, last1, comp)
  ```
  is true.

- [first2, last2) is ordered in ascending order according to comp. That is,

  ```
  is_sorted(first2, last2, comp)
  ```
  is true.

- There is enough space to hold all of the elements being copied. More formally, the requirement is that [result, result + n) is a valid range, where n is the number of elements in the union of the two input ranges.

- [first1, last1) and [result, result + n) do not overlap.

- [first2, last2) and [result, result + n) do not overlap.

Complexity

Linear. For nonempty ranges, at most $2((last1 - first1) + (last2 - first2)) - 1$ comparisons.

Example

```cpp
inline bool lt_nocase(char c1, char c2) {
  return tolower(c1) < tolower(c2);
}

int main()
{
  int A1[] = {1, 3, 5, 7, 9, 11};
  int A2[] = {1, 1, 2, 3, 5, 8, 13};
  char A3[] = {'a', 'b', 'B', 'B', 'f', 'H'};
  char A4[] = {'A', 'B', 'b', 'C', 'D', 'F', 'F', 'h', 'h'};

  const int N1 = sizeof(A1) / sizeof(int);
  const int N2 = sizeof(A2) / sizeof(int);
  const int N3 = sizeof(A3);
  const int N4 = sizeof(A4);

  cout << "Union of A1 and A2: ";
  set_union(A1, A1 + N1, A2, A2 + N2,
            ostream_iterator<int>(cout, " "));
  cout << endl
       << "Union of A3 and A4: ";
  set_union(A3, A3 + N3, A4, A4 + N4,
            ostream_iterator<char>(cout, " "),
            lt_nocase);
  cout << endl;
}
```

The output is:

```
Union of A1 and A2: 1 1 2 3 5 7 8 9 11 13
Union of A3 and A4: a b B B C D f F H h
```

13.2.3.3 set_intersection

① template <class InputIterator1, class InputIterator2,
            class OutputIterator>
OutputIterator
set_intersection(InputIterator1 first1, InputIterator1 last1,
                 InputIterator2 first2, InputIterator2 last2,
                 OutputIterator result);

② template <class InputIterator1, class InputIterator2,
            class OutputIterator,
            class StrictWeakOrdering>
OutputIterator
set_intersection(InputIterator1 first1, InputIterator1 last1,
                 InputIterator2 first2, InputIterator2 last2,
                 OutputIterator result,
                 StrictWeakOrdering comp);

The algorithm set_intersection constructs the intersection of two sets. That is, it constructs the set $S_1 \cap S_2$ consisting of all of the elements that are present both in S_1 and in S_2. Both S_1 and S_2 and their intersection are represented as sorted ranges. The return value is the end of the output range.

Like all of the STL set algorithms, set_intersection generalizes the mathematical definition of set operations. There is no requirement that every element in the [first1,last1) or [first2,last2) be unique. The definition of set intersection is generalized so that if a value appears n times in [first1,last1) and the same value appears m times in [first2,last2), then it will appear $\min(n, m)$ times in the output range. (The definition from ordinary set theory is simply the case where $n \leq 1$ and $m \leq 1$.) This operation is stable, meaning both that elements are copied from the first range rather than the second, and that the relative order of elements in the output range is the same as in the first input range.

It is slightly imprecise to talk about a value appearing n times in [first1,last1) and m times in [first2,last2). A more precise formulation is that [first1,last1) contains a range of n elements that are equivalent to each other, and [first2,last2) will contain m elements from the same equivalence class. The output range contains $\min(n, m)$ values from that equivalence class, all copied from [first1,last1).

The two versions of set_intersection differ in how they define whether one element is less than another. Version 1 compares objects using operator<, and version 2 compares objects using a function object comp.

Where Defined

In the HP implementation, set_intersection was declared in the header <algo.h>. According to the C++ standard, it is declared in the header <algorithm>.

Requirements on Types

For version 1:

- `InputIterator1` is a model of Input Iterator.
- `InputIterator2` is a model of Input Iterator.
- `OutputIterator` is a model of Output Iterator.
- `InputIterator1` and `InputIterator2` have the same value type.
- `InputIterator`'s value type is a model of Strict Weakly Comparable.
- `InputIterator`'s value type is convertible to a type in `OutputIterator`'s set of value types.

For version 2:

- `InputIterator1` is a model of Input Iterator.
- `InputIterator2` is a model of Input Iterator.
- `OutputIterator` is a model of Output Iterator.
- `StrictWeakOrdering` is a model of Strict Weak Ordering.
- `InputIterator1` and `InputIterator2` have the same value type.
- `InputIterator1`'s value type is convertible to `StrictWeakOrdering`'s argument type.
- `InputIterator`'s value type is convertible to a type in `OutputIterator`'s set of value types.

Preconditions

For version 1:

- `[first1,last1)` is a valid range.
- `[first2,last2)` is a valid range.
- `[first1,last1)` is ordered in ascending order according to `operator<`. That is, `is_sorted(first1, last1)` is true.
- `[first2,last2)` is ordered in ascending order according to `operator<`. That is, `is_sorted(first2, last2)` is true.
- There is enough space to hold all of the elements being copied. More formally, the requirement is that `[result,result + n)` is a valid range, where n is the number of elements in the intersection of the two input ranges.
- `[first1,last1)` and `[result,result + n)` do not overlap.
- `[first2,last2)` and `[result,result + n)` do not overlap.

For version 2:

- `[first1,last1)` is a valid range.
- `[first2,last2)` is a valid range.

- [first1, last1) is ordered in ascending order according to comp. That is,
    is_sorted(first1, last1, comp)
  is true.
- [first2, last2) is ordered in ascending order according to comp. That is,
    is_sorted(first2, last2, comp)
  is true.
- There is enough space to hold all of the elements being copied. More formally, the requirement is that [result, result + n) is a valid range, where n is the number of elements in the intersection of the two input ranges.
- [first1, last1) and [result, result + n) do not overlap.
- [first2, last2) and [result, result + n) do not overlap.

Complexity

Linear. Zero comparisons if either [first1, last1) or [first2, last2) is empty. Otherwise, at most $2((last1 - first1) + (last2 - first2)) - 1$ comparisons.

Example

```
inline bool lt_nocase(char c1, char c2) {
  return tolower(c1) < tolower(c2);
}

int main()
{
  int A1[] = {1, 3, 5, 7, 9, 11};
  int A2[] = {1, 1, 2, 3, 5, 8, 13};
  char A3[] = {'a', 'b', 'b', 'B', 'B', 'f', 'h', 'H'};
  char A4[] = {'A', 'B', 'B', 'C', 'D', 'F', 'F', 'H' };

  const int N1 = sizeof(A1) / sizeof(int);
  const int N2 = sizeof(A2) / sizeof(int);
  const int N3 = sizeof(A3);
  const int N4 = sizeof(A4);

  cout << "Intersection of A1 and A2: ";
  set_intersection(A1, A1 + N1, A2, A2 + N2,
                   ostream_iterator<int>(cout, " "));
  cout << endl
       << "Intersection of A3 and A4: ";
  set_intersection(A3, A3 + N3, A4, A4 + N4,
                   ostream_iterator<char>(cout, " "),
                   lt_nocase);
  cout << endl;
}
```

The output is:

```
Intersection of A1 and A2: 1 3 5
Intersection of A3 and A4: a b b f h
```

13.2.3.4 set_difference

① template <class InputIterator1, class InputIterator2,
          class OutputIterator>
OutputIterator
set_difference(InputIterator1 first1, InputIterator1 last1,
               InputIterator2 first2, InputIterator2 last2,
               OutputIterator result);

② template <class InputIterator1, class InputIterator2,
          class OutputIterator,
          class StrictWeakOrdering>
OutputIterator
set_difference(InputIterator1 first1, InputIterator1 last1,
               InputIterator2 first2, InputIterator2 last2,
               OutputIterator result,
               StrictWeakOrdering comp);

The algorithm set_difference constructs the difference of two sets. That is, it constructs the set $S_1 - S_2$ consisting of all of the elements that are present in S_1 but not in S_2. Both S_1 and S_2 and their difference are represented as sorted ranges. The return value is the end of the output range.

Like all of the STL set algorithms, set_difference generalizes the mathematical definition of set operations. There is no requirement that every element in the input ranges [first1, last1) or [first2, last2) be unique. The definition of set difference is generalized so that if a value appears n times in [first1, last1) and the same value appears m times in [first2, last2), then it will appear $\max(n - m, 0)$ times in the output range. This operation is stable, meaning both that elements are copied from the first range rather than the second and that the relative order of elements in the output range is the same as in the first input range. (The definition of this operation in ordinary set theory is simply the case where $n \leq 1$ and $m \leq 1$.)

It is slightly imprecise to talk about a value appearing n times in [first1, last1) and m times in [first2, last2). A more precise formulation is that [first1, last1) contains a range of n elements that are equivalent to each other, and [first2, last2) contains m elements from the same equivalence class. The output range will contain $\max(n - m, 0)$ values from that equivalence class, all copied from [first1, last1.

The two versions of set_difference differ in how they define whether one element is less than another. Version 1 compares objects using operator<, and version 2 compares objects using a function object comp.

Where Defined

In the HP implementation, `set_difference` was declared in the header `<algo.h>`. According to the C++ standard, it is declared in the header `<algorithm>`.

Requirements on Types

For version 1:

- `InputIterator1` is a model of Input Iterator.
- `InputIterator2` is a model of Input Iterator.
- `OutputIterator` is a model of Output Iterator.
- `InputIterator1` and `InputIterator2` have the same value type.
- `InputIterator`'s value type is a model of Strict Weakly Comparable.
- `InputIterator`'s value type is convertible to a type in `OutputIterator`'s set of value types.

For version 2:

- `InputIterator1` is a model of Input Iterator.
- `InputIterator2` is a model of Input Iterator.
- `OutputIterator` is a model of Output Iterator.
- `StrictWeakOrdering` is a model of Strict Weak Ordering.
- `InputIterator1` and `InputIterator2` have the same value type.
- `InputIterator1`'s value type is convertible to `StrictWeakOrdering`'s argument type.
- `InputIterator`'s value type is convertible to a type in `OutputIterator`'s set of value types.

Preconditions

For version 1:

- `[first1,last1)` is a valid range.
- `[first2,last2)` is a valid range.
- `[first1,last1)` is ordered in ascending order according to `operator<`. That is, `is_sorted(first1, last1, comp)` is true.
- `[first2,last2)` is ordered in ascending order according to `operator<`. That is, `is_sorted(first2, last2, comp)` is true.
- There is enough space to hold all of the elements being copied. More formally, the requirement is that $[result, result + n)$ is a valid range, where n is the number of elements in the difference of the two input ranges.
- `[first1,last1)` and $[result, result + n)$ do not overlap.
- `[first2,last2)` and $[result, result + n)$ do not overlap.

For version 2:

- [first1,last1) is a valid range.
- [first2,last2) is a valid range.
- [first1,last1) is ordered in ascending order according to comp. That is,
      is_sorted(first1, last1, comp)
  is true.
- [first2,last2) is ordered in ascending order according to comp. That is,
      is_sorted(first2, last2, comp)
  is true.
- There is enough space to hold all of the elements being copied. More formally, the requirement is that [result,result + n) is a valid range, where n is the number of elements in the difference of the two input ranges.
- [first1,last1) and [result,result + n) do not overlap.
- [first2,last2) and [result,result + n) do not overlap.

Complexity

Linear. For nonempty ranges, at most $2((last1 - first1) + (last2 - first2)) - 1$ comparisons.

Example

```
inline bool lt_nocase(char c1, char c2) {
  return tolower(c1) < tolower(c2);
}

int main()
{
  int A1[] = {1, 3, 5, 7, 9, 11};
  int A2[] = {1, 1, 2, 3, 5, 8, 13};
  char A3[] = {'a', 'b', 'b', 'B', 'B', 'f', 'g', 'h', 'H'};
  char A4[] = {'A', 'B', 'B', 'C', 'D', 'F', 'F', 'H' };

  const int N1 = sizeof(A1) / sizeof(int);
  const int N2 = sizeof(A2) / sizeof(int);
  const int N3 = sizeof(A3);
  const int N4 = sizeof(A4);

  cout << "Difference of A1 and A2: ";
  set_difference(A1, A1 + N1, A2, A2 + N2,
                 ostream_iterator<int>(cout, " "));
  cout << endl
       << "Difference of A3 and A4: ";
  set_difference(A3, A3 + N3, A4, A4 + N4,
                 ostream_iterator<char>(cout, " "),
                 lt_nocase);
```

```
        cout << endl;
    }
```

The output is:

```
    Difference of A1 and A2: 7 9 11
    Difference of A3 and A4: B B g H
```

13.2.3.5 set_symmetric_difference

① template <class InputIterator1, class InputIterator2,
          class OutputIterator>
OutputIterator
set_symmetric_difference(InputIterator1 first1, InputIterator1 last1,
                  InputIterator2 first2, InputIterator2 last2,
                  OutputIterator result);

② template <class InputIterator1, class InputIterator2,
          class OutputIterator,
          class StrictWeakOrdering>
OutputIterator
set_symmetric_difference(InputIterator1 first1, InputIterator1 last1,
                  InputIterator2 first2, InputIterator2 last2,
                  OutputIterator result,
                  StrictWeakOrdering comp);

The algorithm set_symmetric_difference constructs the symmetric difference of two sets S_1 and S_2. That is, it constructs a set consisting of all elements in S_1 that are not present in S_2 and all elements in S_2 that are not present in S_1. (Mathematically, this can be written $(S_1 - S_2) \cup (S_2 - S_1)$.) Both S_1 and S_2 and their symmetric difference are represented as sorted ranges. The return value is the end of the output range.

Like all of the STL set algorithms, set_symmetric_difference generalizes the mathematical definition of set operations. There is no requirement that every element in [first1, last1) or [first2, last2) be unique. In this case, the definition is generalized so that if a value appears n times in [first1, last1) and the same value appears m times in [first2, last2), then it will appear $|n - m|$ times in the output range. (The definition from ordinary set theory is simply the case where $n \leq 1$ and $m \leq 1$.) This operation is stable, meaning that the relative order of elements within each input range is preserved.

It is slightly imprecise to talk about a value appearing n times in [first1, last1) and m times in [first2, last2). A more precise formulation is that [first1, last1) contains a range of n elements that are equivalent to each other, and [first2, last2) contains m elements in the same equivalence class. The output range contains $|n-m|$ values from that equivalence class; if $n > m$ then the output range contains the last

$n - m$ of these elements from the input range [first1,last1), and if $n < m$ then the output range contains the last $m - n$ of these elements from the input range [first2,last2).

The two versions of set_symmetric_difference differ in how they define whether one element is less than another. Version 1 compares objects using operator<, and version 2 compares objects using a function object comp.

Where Defined

In the HP implementation, set_symmetric_difference was declared in the header <algo.h>. According to the C++ standard, it is declared in the header <algorithm>.

Requirements on Types

For version 1:

- InputIterator1 is a model of Input Iterator.
- InputIterator2 is a model of Input Iterator.
- OutputIterator is a model of Output Iterator.
- InputIterator1 and InputIterator2 have the same value type.
- InputIterator's value type is a model of Strict Weakly Comparable.
- InputIterator's value type is convertible to a type in OutputIterator's set of value types.

For version 2:

- InputIterator1 is a model of Input Iterator.
- InputIterator2 is a model of Input Iterator.
- OutputIterator is a model of Output Iterator.
- StrictWeakOrdering is a model of Strict Weak Ordering.
- InputIterator1 and InputIterator2 have the same value type.
- InputIterator1's value type is convertible to StrictWeakOrdering's argument type.
- InputIterator's value type is convertible to a type in OutputIterator's set of value types.

Preconditions

For version 1:

- [first1,last1) is a valid range.
- [first2,last2) is a valid range.
- [first1,last1) is ordered in ascending order according to operator<. That is, is_sorted(first1, last1) is true.

- [first2, last2) is ordered in ascending order according to operator<. That is, is_sorted(first2, last2) is true.
- There is enough space to hold all of the elements being copied. More formally, the requirement is that [result, result + n) is a valid range, where n is the number of elements in the symmetric difference of the two input ranges.
- [first1, last1) and [result, result + n) do not overlap.
- [first2, last2) and [result, result + n) do not overlap.

For version 2:

- [first1, last1) is a valid range.
- [first2, last2) is a valid range.
- [first1, last1) is ordered in ascending order according to comp. That is,
     is_sorted(first1, last1, comp)
  is true.
- [first2, last2) is ordered in ascending order according to comp. That is,
     is_sorted(first2, last2, comp)
  is true.
- There is enough space to hold all of the elements being copied. More formally, the requirement is that [result, result + n) is a valid range, where n is the number of elements in the symmetric difference of the two input ranges.
- [first1, last1) and [result, result + n) do not overlap.
- [first2, last2) and [result, result + n) do not overlap.

Complexity

Linear. For nonempty ranges, at most $2((last1 - first1) + (last2 - first2)) - 1$ comparisons.

Example

```
inline bool lt_nocase(char c1, char c2) {
   return tolower(c1) < tolower(c2);
}

int main()
{
  int A1[] = {1, 3, 5, 7, 9, 11};
  int A2[] = {1, 1, 2, 3, 5, 8, 13};
  char A3[] = {'a', 'b', 'b', 'B', 'B', 'f', 'g', 'h', 'H'};
  char A4[] = {'A', 'B', 'B', 'C', 'D', 'F', 'F', 'H' };

  const int N1 = sizeof(A1) / sizeof(int);
  const int N2 = sizeof(A2) / sizeof(int);
  const int N3 = sizeof(A3);
  const int N4 = sizeof(A4);
```

```
    cout << "Symmetric difference of A1 and A2: ";
    set_symmetric_difference(A1, A1 + N1, A2, A2 + N2,
                          ostream_iterator<int>(cout, " "));
    cout << endl
         << "Symmetric difference of A3 and A4: ";
    set_symmetric_difference(A3, A3 + N3, A4, A4 + N4,
                          ostream_iterator<char>(cout, " "),
                          lt_nocase);
    cout << endl;
}
```

The output is:

```
Symmetric difference of A1 and A2: 1 2 7 8 9 11 13
Symmetric difference of A3 and A4: B B C D F g H
```

13.3   Heap Operations

Heaps are not sorted ranges. The elements in a heap aren't arranged in ascending order but rather are arranged in a more complicated way. (Internally, a heap is a tree represented as a sequential range. The tree is constructed so that each node is less than or equal to its parent node.)

Heaps are closely related to sorted ranges for three reasons. First, a heap, like a sorted range, provides efficient access to its largest element. If [first, last) is a heap, then *first is the largest element in the heap. Second, it is possible to add an element to a heap (using push_heap), or to remove an element from a heap (using pop_heap), in logarithmic time. Third, there is a simple and efficient algorithm, sort_heap, that turns a heap into a sorted range.

Heaps are a convenient way to represent priority queues, where elements are inserted in an arbitrary order but removed in order from largest to smallest. The STL container adaptor priority_queue, for example, is implemented using a heap.

13.3.1   make_heap

① template <class RandomAccessIterator>
  void make_heap(RandomAccessIterator first, RandomAccessIterator last);

② template <class RandomAccessIterator, class StrictWeakOrdering>
  void make_heap(RandomAccessIterator first, RandomAccessIterator last,
              StrictWeakOrdering comp);

The algorithm make_heap turns an arbitrary range [first, last) into a heap.

The two versions of make_heap differ in how they define whether one element is less than another. Version 1 compares objects using operator<, and version 2 compares objects using a function object comp.

In version 1 the postcondition is that `is_heap(first, last)` is true, and in version 2 the postcondition is that `is_heap(first, last, comp)` is true.

Where Defined

In the HP implementation, `make_heap` was declared in the header `<algo.h>`. According to the C++ standard, it is declared in the header `<algorithm>`.

Requirements on Types

For version 1:

- `RandomAccessIterator` is a model of Random Access Iterator.
- `RandomAccessIterator` is mutable.
- `RandomAccessIterator`'s value type is a model of Strict Weakly Comparable.

For version 2:

- `RandomAccessIterator` is a model of Random Access Iterator.
- `RandomAccessIterator` is mutable.
- `StrictWeakOrdering` is a model of Strict Weak Ordering.
- `RandomAccessIterator`'s value type is convertible to `StrictWeakOrdering`'s argument type.

Preconditions

- `[first,last)` is a valid range.

Complexity

Linear. At most $3(\text{last} - \text{first})$ comparisons.

Example

```
int main()
{
  int A[] = {1, 4, 2, 8, 5, 7};
  const int N = sizeof(A) / sizeof(int);

  make_heap(A, A+N);
  assert(is_heap(A, A+N));
  copy(A, A+N, ostream_iterator<int>(cout, " "));
  cout << endl;

  sort_heap(A, A+N);
  assert(is_sorted(A, A+N));
  copy(A, A+N, ostream_iterator<int>(cout, " "));
  cout << endl;
}
```

13.3.2 push_heap

① template <class RandomAccessIterator>
  void push_heap(RandomAccessIterator first, RandomAccessIterator last);

② template <class RandomAccessIterator, class StrictWeakOrdering>
  void push_heap(RandomAccessIterator first, RandomAccessIterator last,
               StrictWeakOrdering comp);

The algorithm push_heap adds an element to a heap. The interface is slightly peculiar. The heap to which the element will be added is the range [first, last − 1), and the element to be added is *(last − 1).

The two versions of push_heap differ in how they define whether one element is less than another. Version 1 compares objects using operator<, and version 2 compares objects using a function object comp.

Version 1 has the postcondition that is_heap(first, last) is true, and version 2 has the postcondition that is_heap(first, last, comp) is true.

Where Defined

In the HP implementation, push_heap was declared in the header <algo.h>. According to the C++ standard, it is declared in the header <algorithm>.

Requirements on Types

For version 1:

- RandomAccessIterator is a model of **Random Access Iterator**.
- RandomAccessIterator is mutable.
- RandomAccessIterator's value type is a model of **Strict Weakly Comparable**.

For version 2:

- RandomAccessIterator is a model of **Random Access Iterator**.
- RandomAccessIterator is mutable.
- StrictWeakOrdering is a model of **Strict Weak Ordering**.
- RandomAccessIterator's value type is convertible to StrictWeakOrdering's argument type.

Preconditions

For version 1:

- [first, last) is a valid range.
- [first, last − 1) is a valid range. That is, [first, last) is nonempty.
- [first, last − 1) is a heap. That is, is_heap(first, last - 1) is true.

For version 2:

- [first, last) is a valid range.
- [first, last − 1) is a valid range. That is, [first, last) is nonempty.
- [first, last − 1) is a heap. That is, is_heap(first, last - 1, comp) is true.

Complexity

Logarithmic. At most log(last − first) comparisons.

Example

```
int main()
{
  int A[10] = {0, 1, 2, 3, 4, 5, 6, 7, 8, 9 };

  make_heap(A, A + 9);
  cout << "[A, A + 9)  = ";
  copy(A, A + 9, ostream_iterator<int>(cout, " "));
  cout << endl;

  push_heap(A, A + 10);
  cout << "[A, A + 10) = ";
  copy(A, A + 10, ostream_iterator<int>(cout, " "));
  cout << endl;
}
```

The output is:

```
[A, A + 9)  = 8 7 6 3 4 5 2 1 0
[A, A + 10) = 9 8 6 3 7 5 2 1 0 4
```

13.3.3 pop_heap

① template <class RandomAccessIterator>
  void pop_heap(RandomAccessIterator first, RandomAccessIterator last);

② template <class RandomAccessIterator, class StrictWeakOrdering>
  void pop_heap(RandomAccessIterator first, RandomAccessIterator last,
                StrictWeakOrdering comp);

The algorithm pop_heap removes the largest element (that is, *first) from the heap [first, last). The two versions of pop_heap differ in how they define whether one element is less than another. Version 1 compares objects using operator<, and version 2 compares objects using a function object comp.

Both versions of pop_heap have the postcondition that *(last − 1) is the element that was removed from the heap. Additionally, version 1 has the postcondition that is_heap(first, last − 1) is true, and version 2 has the postcondition that is_heap(first, last − 1, comp) is true.

Where Defined

In the HP implementation, pop_heap was declared in the header <algo.h>. According to the C++ standard, it is declared in the header <algorithm>.

Requirements on Types

For version 1:

- RandomAccessIterator is a model of Random Access Iterator.
- RandomAccessIterator is mutable.
- RandomAccessIterator's value type is a model of Strict Weakly Comparable.

For version 2:

- RandomAccessIterator is a model of Random Access Iterator.
- RandomAccessIterator is mutable.
- StrictWeakOrdering is a model of Strict Weak Ordering.
- RandomAccessIterator's value type is convertible to StrictWeakOrdering's argument type.

Preconditions

For version 1:

- [first,last) is a valid range.
- [first,last − 1) is a valid range. That is, [first,last) is nonempty.
- [first,last) is a heap. That is, is_heap(first, last) is true.

For version 2:

- [first,last) is a valid range.
- [first,last − 1) is a valid range. That is, [first,last) is nonempty.
- [first,last) is a heap. That is, is_heap(first, last, comp) is true.

Complexity

Logarithmic. At most $2 \log(\text{last} - \text{first})$ comparisons.

Example

Remove the largest element from a heap.

```
int main()
{
  int A[] = {1, 2, 3, 4, 5, 6};
  const int N = sizeof(A) / sizeof(int);

  make_heap(A, A+N);
  cout << "Before pop: ";
  copy(A, A+N, ostream_iterator<int>(cout, " "));

  pop_heap(A, A+N);
  cout << endl << "After pop: ";
  copy(A, A+N-1, ostream_iterator<int>(cout, " "));
  cout << endl << "A[N-1] = " << A[N-1] << endl;
}
```

The output is:

```
Before pop: 6 5 3 4 2 1
After pop: 5 4 3 1 2
A[N-1] = 6
```

When you call pop_heap it removes the largest element from a heap, and then shrinks the heap. This means that if you keep calling pop_heap again and again until only a single element is left in the heap, you will end up with a sorted range where the heap used to be.

```
int main()
{
  int A[] = {1, 2, 3, 4, 5, 6};
  const int N = sizeof(A) / sizeof(int);

  make_heap(A, A+N);
  int n = N;

  while (n > 1) {
    copy(A, A + N, ostream_iterator<int>(cout, " "));
    cout << endl;
    pop_heap(A, A + n);
    --n;
  }

  copy(A, A + N, ostream_iterator<int>(cout, " "));
  cout << endl;
}
```

This is exactly how sort_heap is implemented.

13.3.4 `sort_heap`

① `template <class RandomAccessIterator>`
`void sort_heap(RandomAccessIterator first, RandomAccessIterator last);`

② `template <class RandomAccessIterator, class StrictWeakOrdering>`
`void sort_heap(RandomAccessIterator first, RandomAccessIterator last,`
`                StrictWeakOrdering comp);`

The algorithm `sort_heap` turns a heap [first,last) into a sorted range. Note that this is not a stable sort: It does not necessarily preserve the relative order of equivalent elements. (See page 294 for a discussion of stability.)

The two versions of `sort_heap` differ in how they define whether one element is less than another. Version 1 compares objects using `operator<`, and version 2 compares objects using a function object `comp`.

Where Defined

In the HP implementation, `sort_heap` was declared in the header `<algo.h>`. According to the C++ standard, it is declared in the header `<algorithm>`.

Requirements on Types

For version 1:

- `RandomAccessIterator` is a model of **Random Access Iterator**.
- `RandomAccessIterator` is mutable.
- `RandomAccessIterator`'s value type is a model of **Strict Weakly Comparable**.

For version 2:

- `RandomAccessIterator` is a model of **Random Access Iterator**.
- `RandomAccessIterator` is mutable.
- `StrictWeakOrdering` is a model of **Strict Weak Ordering**.
- `RandomAccessIterator`'s value type is convertible to `StrictWeakOrdering`'s argument type.

Preconditions

For version 1:

- [first,last) is a valid range.
- [first,last) is a heap. That is, is_heap(first, last) is true.

For version 2:

- [first,last) is a valid range.
- [first,last) is a heap. That is, is_heap(first, last, comp) is true.

Complexity

At most $N \log N$ comparisons, where N is last − first.

Example

```
int main()
{
  int A[] = {1, 4, 2, 8, 5, 7};
  const int N = sizeof(A) / sizeof(int);

  make_heap(A, A+N);
  copy(A, A+N, ostream_iterator<int>(cout, " "));
  cout << endl;

  sort_heap(A, A+N);
  copy(A, A+N, ostream_iterator<int>(cout, " "));
  cout << endl;
}
```

13.3.5 is_heap

① template <class RandomAccessIterator>
  bool is_heap(RandomAccessIterator first, RandomAccessIterator last);

② template <class RandomAccessIterator, class StrictWeakOrdering>
  bool is_heap(RandomAccessIterator first, RandomAccessIterator last,
               StrictWeakOrdering comp)

The algorithm is_heap returns true if the range [first,last) is a heap and false otherwise. The two versions differ in how they define whether one element is less than another. Version 1 compares objects using operator<, and version 2 compares objects using a function object comp.

Where Defined

The algorithm is_heap was not present in the original HP implementation of the STL, nor is it present in the C++ standard. In the SGI implementation, it is declared in the header <algorithm>.

Requirements on Types

For version 1:

- RandomAccessIterator is a model of Random Access Iterator.
- RandomAccessIterator's value type is a model of Strict Weakly Comparable.

For version 2:

- RandomAccessIterator is a model of Random Access Iterator.
- StrictWeakOrdering is a model of Strict Weak Ordering.
- RandomAccessIterator's value type is convertible to StrictWeakOrdering's argument type.

Preconditions

- [first, last) is a valid range.

Complexity

Linear. For nonempty ranges, at most (last − first) − 1 comparisons.

Example

```
int main()
{
  int A[] = {1, 2, 3, 4, 5, 6, 7};
  const int N = sizeof(A) / sizeof(int);

  assert(!is_heap(A, A+N));
  make_heap(A, A+N);
  assert(is_heap(A, A+N));
}
```

Chapter 14

Iterator Classes

Every STL container has nested iterator classes. (That's part of what it means to be a container.) Additionally, the STL includes several standalone iterator classes. Most of them are iterator adaptors.

The C++ standard calls for all of the standard iterator classes to inherit from the base class `iterator` (page 185), and this book follows the standard in that respect. You should remember that this is purely an implementation detail. All that really matters is for the iterator classes to contain the nested types that `iterator_traits` (page 177) requires, and inheriting from `iterator` is only one possible way to define those `typedefs`. It isn't even necessarily the easiest way. Inheriting type declarations from template base classes has some complicated technical restrictions, and it is often easier to provide the nested `typedefs` explicitly.

14.1 Insert Iterators

14.1.1 `front_insert_iterator`

`front_insert_iterator<FrontInsertionSequence>`

The class `front_insert_iterator` is an iterator adaptor that functions as an Output Iterator. Assignment through a `front_insert_iterator` inserts an object before the first element of a Front Insertion Sequence (page 141).

Note that a Front Insertion Sequence has iterators already. It's a Container, after all, and all Containers define their own iterators. Why, then, do we need yet another kind of iterator for Front Insertion Sequence?

We need it because its behavior is very different from that of the sequence's own iterators. If Seq is a Front Insertion Sequence, then `Seq::iterator` has overwrite semantics while `front_insert_iterator<Seq>` has insert semantics. If i is a valid `Seq::iterator` that points into a sequence S, it points to a particular element in S. The expression `*i = t` replaces that element with t and does not change S's total number of elements. But if ii is a valid `front_insert_iterator<Seq>`, then writing

345

*ii = t is equivalent to writing seq.push_front(t). It adds a new element to S, rather than overwriting any of S's existing elements.

Example

```
int main()
{
  list<int> L;

  L.push_front(3);
  front_insert_iterator<list<int> > ii(L);
  *ii++ = 0;
  *ii++ = 1;
  *ii++ = 2;
  copy(L.begin(), L.end(), ostream_iterator<int>(cout, " "));
  // The values that are printed are 2 1 0 3
}
```

Note that in the preceding example the elements appeared in L in the reverse of the order in which they were added. This is general. Each assignment through ii added a new element to the *beginning* of L. This suggests an easy way of creating a new Sequence that is the reverse of an existing Sequence: Copy all of the existing Sequence's elements into a front_insert_iterator.

```
int main()
{
  vector<int> V(100);
  for (int i = 0; i < 100; ++i)
    V[i] = i;

  list<int> L;
  copy(V.begin(), V.end(), front_inserter(L));
  // L now contains V's elements in reverse order.
}
```

In this last example, instead of explicitly writing front_insert_iterator's constructor, we used the helper function front_inserter. Using this helper function is almost always more convenient. It eliminates the need to write the exact type of the front_insert_iterator. Since we're passing the iterator to a generic algorithm rather than creating it on the stack, we need never mention its type explicitly.

Where Defined

In the HP implementation, front_insert_iterator was defined in <iterator.h>. According to the C++ standard, it is declared in <iterator>.

Template Parameters

FrontInsertionSequence   The type of Front Insertion Sequence into which values will be inserted.

Model Of

Output Iterator (page 96).

Type Requirements

- The template parameter FrontInsertionSequence must be a Front Insertion Sequence.

Public Base Classes

iterator<output_iterator_tag, void, void, void, void>

Members

Some of front_insert_iterator's members are not defined in the Output Iterator requirements but are specific to front_insert_iterator. These special members are flagged with the symbol ✳.

✳ **front_insert_iterator::front_insert_iterator(FrontInsertionSequence& S)**
The constructor. Creates a front_insert_iterator that inserts elements before the first element of S.

front_insert_iterator::front_insert_iterator(const front_insert_iterator&)
The copy constructor.
(Described in Assignable.)

front_insert_iterator::~front_insert_iterator()
The destructor.
(Described in Assignable.)

front_insert_iterator&
front_insert_iterator::operator= (const front_insert_iterator&)
The assignment operator
(Described in Assignable.)

front_insert_iterator& front_insert_iterator::operator* ()
Used to implement the Output Iterator expression *i = x.

front_insert_iterator&
front_insert_iterator::operator= (
    const typename FrontInsertionSequence::value_type&)
Used to implement the Output Iterator expression *i = x.

front_insert_iterator& front_insert_iterator::operator++()
Preincrement.
(Described in Output Iterator.)

front_insert_iterator front_insert_iterator::operator++(int)
Postincrement.
(Described in Output Iterator.)

front_insert_iterator::iterator_category
Tag type representing the iterator's category: output_iterator_tag.
(Described in Output Iterator.)

✳ `template <class FrontInsertionSequence>`
  `front_insert_iterator<FrontInsertionSequence>`
  `front_inserter(FrontInsertionSequence& S)`
  Equivalent to `front_insert_iterator<FrontInsertionSequence>(S)`. This helper function exists mainly for the sake of convenience. It is a nonmember function, so the template parameters may be inferred and the type of the `front_insert_iterator` need not be declared explicitly.

Note that the Output Iterator definition requires only that `*ii = t` be a valid expression. It says nothing about `operator*` or `operator=` on their own. The most obvious implementation is for `operator*` to return some proxy object, where the proxy object has some appropriate `operator=`, and in this case the proxy object is just the `front_insert_iterator` itself. That's just an implementation detail, and you should not rely on it. You should always write `*ii = t`, as described in the Output Iterator requirements.

14.1.2 `back_insert_iterator`

`back_insert_iterator<BackInsertionSequence>`

The class `back_insert_iterator` is an iterator adaptor that functions as an Output Iterator: assignment through a `back_insert_iterator` inserts an object after the last element of a Back Insertion Sequence (page 143).

The reason `back_insert_iterator` exists, when every Back Insertion Sequence has iterators already, is that `back_insert_iterator` provides insert rather than overwrite semantics. If i is a valid `Seq::iterator` that points into a sequence S, it points to a particular element in S. The expression `*i = t` replaces that element with t and does not change S's total number of elements. If ii is a `back_insert_iterator<Seq>`, writing `*ii = t` is equivalent to writing `seq.push_back(t)`. It adds a new element to S, rather than overwriting any of S's existing elements.

Example

```
int main()
{
  list<int> L;
  L.push_front(3);
  back_insert_iterator<list<int> > ii(L);
  *ii++ = 0;
  *ii++ = 1;
  *ii++ = 2;
  copy(L.begin(), L.end(), ostream_iterator<int>(cout, " "));
  // The values that are printed are 3 0 1 2
}
```

Note how this differs from the corresponding example in `front_insert_iterator` (page 345). In this example, the elements appear in L in the same order as the order in which they were added. This is general. Each assignment added a new element to the *end* of L. This means that copying a range through a `back_insert_iterator` is a way of creating a Sequence that's a copy of another Sequence.

```
int main()
{
  list<int> L;
  for (int i = 0; i < 100; ++i)
    L.push_back(i);

  vector<int> v1(L.begin(), L.end());
  vector<int> v2;
  copy(L.begin(), L.end(), back_inserter(v2));

  assert(v1 == v2);
}
```

These two versions are roughly equivalent, but the first is probably faster. Using vector's constructor inserts all of the elements at once, but using copy inserts them one at a time. If your compiler doesn't yet support member templates, you won't be able to use the first version at all—not for fully general ranges of iterators, in any case. You can use copy and `back_insert_iterator` in the meantime since it does not rely on member templates.

Where Defined

In the HP implementation, `back_insert_iterator` was defined in `<iterator.h>`. According to the C++ standard, it is declared in `<iterator>`.

Template Parameters

`BackInsertionSequence`   The type of Back Insertion Sequence into which values will be inserted.

Model Of

Output Iterator (page 96).

Type Requirements

- The template parameter `BackInsertionSequence` must be a Back Insertion Sequence.

Public Base Classes

`iterator<output_iterator_tag, void, void, void, void>`

Members

Some of back_insert_iterator's members are not defined in the Output Iterator requirements but are specific to back_insert_iterator. These special members are flagged with the symbol ✳.

✳ **back_insert_iterator::back_insert_iterator(BackInsertionSequence& S)**
The constructor. Creates a back_insert_iterator that inserts elements after the last element of S.

back_insert_iterator::back_insert_iterator(const back_insert_iterator&)
The copy constructor.
(Described in Assignable.)

back_insert_iterator::~back_insert_iterator()
The destructor.
(Described in Assignable.)

back_insert_iterator&
back_insert_iterator::operator= (const back_insert_iterator&)
The assignment operator
(Described in Assignable.)

back_insert_iterator& back_insert_iterator::operator* ()
Used to implement the Output Iterator expression *i = x.

back_insert_iterator&
back_insert_iterator::operator= (
    const typename BackInsertionSequence::value_type&)
Used to implement the Output Iterator expression *i = x.

back_insert_iterator& back_insert_iterator::operator++()
Preincrement.
(Described in Output Iterator.)

back_insert_iterator back_insert_iterator::operator++(int)
Postincrement.
(Described in Output Iterator.)

back_insert_iterator::iterator_category
Tag type representing the iterator's category: output_iterator_tag.
(Described in Output Iterator.)

✳ **template <class BackInsertionSequence>**
back_insert_iterator<BackInsertionSequence>
back_inserter(BackInsertionSequence& S)
Equivalent to back_insert_iterator<BackInsertionSequence>(S). This helper function exists mainly for the sake of convenience: it is a nonmember function, so the template parameters may be inferred and the type of the back_insert_iterator need not be declared explicitly.

Note that the Output Iterator definition requires only that *ii = t be a valid expression. It says nothing about operator* or operator= on their own. The most obvious implementation is for operator* to return some proxy object, where the proxy object has some appropriate operator=. In this case the proxy object is just the back_insert_iterator itself. That's just an implementation detail, and you should not rely on it. You should always write *ii = t, as described in the Output Iterator requirements.

14.1.3 `insert_iterator`

`insert_iterator<Container>`

The class `insert_iterator` is an iterator adaptor that functions as an Output Iterator. Assignment through an `insert_iterator` inserts an object into a Container. If ii is an `insert_iterator`, ii keeps track of a Container c and an insertion point p. The expression *ii = t performs the insertion c.insert(p, t).

The reason `insert_iterator` exists, when every Container has iterators already, is that `insert_iterator` provides insert rather than overwrite semantics. If i is a valid C::iterator that points into a container c, it points to a particular element in c. The expression *i = t replaces that element with t and does not change C's total number of elements. If ii is a valid insert_iterator<C>, then writing *ii = t is equivalent to writing c.insert(p, t). It adds a new element to S rather than overwriting any of S's existing elements.

You can use an `insert_iterator` with any kind of Container for which the expression C.insert(p, t) is defined. Two different Container concepts define that expression: Sequence (page 136) and Sorted Associative Container (page 156). Both concepts define insertion into a container by means of the expression c.insert(p, x), but the semantics of that expression is very different in the two cases.

For a Sequence S, the expression S.insert(p, x) means to insert the value x immediately before the iterator p. That is, the two-argument version of insert allows you to control the location at which the new element will be inserted. For a Sorted Associative Container, no such control is possible. The elements in a Sorted Associative Container always appear in ascending order of keys. Sorted Associative Containers define the two-argument version of insert as an optimization. The first argument is only a hint. It points to the location where the search begins.

If you assign through an `insert_iterator` several times, you will be inserting several elements into the underlying container. In the case of a Sequence, they will appear at a particular location in the underlying sequence in the order in which they were inserted. One of the arguments to `insert_iterator`'s constructor is an iterator p, and the new range will be inserted immediately before p.

In the case of a Sorted Associative Container, by contrast, the iterator that you pass to `insert_iterator`'s constructor is almost irrelevant. The new elements will not necessarily form a contiguous range. They will appear in the appropriate location in the container in ascending order by key. The order in which they are inserted only affects efficiency; inserting an already-sorted range into a Sorted Associative Container is an $\mathcal{O}(N)$ operation.

Example

Insert a range of elements into a `list`.

```
int main()
{
  list<int> L;
  L.push_front(3);
  insert_iterator<list<int> > ii(L, L.begin());
  *ii++ = 0;
  *ii++ = 1;
  *ii++ = 2;
  copy(L.begin(), L.end(), ostream_iterator<int>(cout, " "));
  // The values that are printed are 0 1 2 3.
}
```

Merge two sorted lists, inserting the resulting range into a set. Note that a set never contains duplicate elements.

```
int main()
{
  const int N = 6;

  int A1[N] = {1, 3, 5, 7, 9, 11};
  int A2[N] = {1, 2, 3, 4, 5, 6};
  set<int> result;

  merge(A1, A1 + N, A2, A2 + N,
        inserter(result, result.begin()));

  copy(result.begin(), result.end(), ostream_iterator<int>(cout, " "));
  cout << endl;

  // The output is "1 2 3 4 5 6 7 9 11".
}
```

Where Defined

In the HP implementation, insert_iterator was defined in <iterator.h>. According to the C++ standard, it is declared in <iterator>.

Template Parameters

Container The type of Container into which values will be inserted.

Model Of

Output Iterator (page 96).

Type Requirements

- The template parameter Container is a model of Container.
- Container is variable-sized, as described in the Container requirements.

- Container has a two-argument insert member function. Specifically, if c is an object of type `Container`, p is an object of type `Container::iterator` and v is an object of type `Container::value_type`, then `c.insert(p, v)` is a valid expression and its return type is `Container::iterator`.

Public Base Classes

`iterator<output_iterator_tag, void, void, void, void>`

Members

Some of `insert_iterator`'s members are not defined in the Output Iterator requirements but are specific to `insert_iterator`. These special members are flagged with the symbol ✳.

✳ **`insert_iterator::insert_iterator(Container& c, Container::iterator i)`**
Constructs an `insert_iterator` that inserts objects in c. If c is a Sequence, then each object will be inserted immediately before the element pointed to by i. If c is a Sorted Associative Container, the first insertion will use i as a hint for beginning the search. The iterator i must be a valid iterator (dereferenceable or past the end) in c.

`insert_iterator::insert_iterator(const insert_iterator&)`
The copy constructor.
(Described in Assignable.)

`insert_iterator::~insert_iterator()`
The destructor.
(Described in Assignable.)

`insert_iterator& insert_iterator::operator=(const insert_iterator&)`
The assignment operator.
(Described in Assignable.)

`insert_iterator& insert_iterator::operator* ()`
Used to implement the Output Iterator expression `*i = x`.

`insert_iterator&`
`insert_iterator::operator= (const typename Container::value_type&)`
Used to implement the Output Iterator expression `*i = x`.

`insert_iterator& insert_iterator::operator++()`
Preincrement.
(Described in Output Iterator.)

`insert_iterator insert_iterator::operator++(int)`
Postincrement.
(Described in Output Iterator.)

`insert_iterator::iterator_category`
Tag type representing the iterator's category: `output_iterator_tag`.
(Described in Output Iterator.)

✳ **`template <class Container, class Iterator>`**
`insert_iterator<Container> inserter(Container& c, Iterator p)`
Equivalent to `insert_iterator<Container>(c, i)`. (Which implies that i must be a type that is convertible to `Container::iterator`.) This helper function exists mainly for the

sake of convenience: it is a nonmember function, so the template parameters may be inferred and the type of the insert_iterator need not be declared explicitly.

Note that the Output Iterator definition requires only that *ii = t be a valid expression. It says nothing about operator* or operator= on their own. The most obvious implementation is for operator* to return some proxy object, where the proxy object has some appropriate operator=. In this case the proxy object is just the front_insert_iterator itself. That's just an implementation detail, though, and you should not rely on it. You should always write *ii = t, as described in the Output Iterator requirements.

14.2   Stream Iterators

Most of the predefined iterators in the STL iterate over elements in a container, but this is by no means required. The iterator concepts are very general. They can represent iteration through any ordered values, not just values that happen to be stored in a container. An example of this generality is the STL's stream iterators, which perform input and output using C++'s stream I/O library.

14.2.1   istream_iterator

istream_iterator<T, charT, traits, Distance>

An istream_iterator is an Input Iterator that performs formatted input of objects of type T from a particular basic_istream. When end of stream is reached the istream_iterator takes on a special end of stream value, which is a past-the-end iterator. All of the restrictions of an Input Iterator must be obeyed, including the restrictions on the ordering of operator* and operator++ operations.

   The definition of istream_iterator has been changed from that in the original HP STL because C++ now has more general stream I/O facilities than it once did. You have no reason to care about this extra complexity unless you want to use it. The new template parameters have defaults, and an istream_iterator<int> still has the same behavior it always did.

   In the original version of C++ stream I/O, istream was a class that read char from some input device. In the C++ standard, however, istream is not a class but rather a typedef. It is an alias for basic_istream<char, char_traits<char> >, where the class basic_istream is a template that performs formatted input using generalized characters. The difference between istream_iterator in the HP STL and in the standard, then, is the addition of the template parameters charT and traits. An iterator of type istream_iterator<T, charT, traits, Distance> reads values from a basic_istream<charT, traits>.

   As of 1998, not all C++ implementations provide the new templatized version of stream I/O. For maximum portability it is best to restrict yourself to the defaults. If you use an istream_iterator<T>, you can be sure that it will behave correctly regardless of whether you're using the new or the old version of stream I/O.

Example

```
int main()
{
  vector<int> V;
  copy(istream_iterator<int>(cin), istream_iterator<int>(),
       back_inserter(V));
}
```

Where Defined

In the HP implementation, istream_iterator was defined in <iterator.h>. According to the C++ standard, it is declared in <iterator>.

Template Parameters

T	The istream_iterator's value type. The iterator's operator* has the return type const T&.
charT	The input stream's character type. **Default:** char
traits	The input stream's character traits class. **Default:** char_traits<charT>
Distance	The iterator's difference type. **Default:** ptrdiff_t

Model Of

Input Iterator (page 94).

Type Requirements

- The value type T is a model of Default Constructible.

- The value type T is a type such that, for an object t of type T and a stream i of type basic_istream<charT, traits>, the expression i >> t is well-defined.

- The types charT and traits satisfy the requirements for a stream's character and character traits type.[1]

- The type Distance is, as described in the Input Iterator requirements, a signed integral type.

Public Base Classes

iterator<input_iterator_tag, T, Distance, const T*, const T&>

---

1. Character and character trait types are part of the C++ I/O library rather than the STL, so this book does not address the requirements for those types.

Members

Some of `istream_iterator`'s members are not defined in the Input Iterator requirements but are specific to `istream_iterator`. These special members are flagged with the symbol ✳.

✳ **`istream_iterator::char_type`**
The iterator's character type: `charT`

✳ **`istream_iterator::traits_type`**
The iterator's character traits type: `traits`

✳ **`istream_iterator::istream_type`**
The iterator's stream type: `basic_istream<charT, traits>`

`istream_iterator::iterator_category`
The iterator's category: `input_iterator_tag`
(Described in Input Iterator.)

`istream_iterator::value_type`
The iterator's value type: `T`
(Described in Input Iterator.)

`istream_iterator::difference_type`
The iterator's difference type: `Distance`
(Described in Input Iterator.)

`istream_iterator::pointer`
The iterator's pointer type: `const T*`
(Described in Input Iterator.)

`istream_iterator::reference`
The iterator's reference type: `const T&`
(Described in Input Iterator.)

✳ **`istream_iterator::istream_iterator(istream_type& s)`**
The constructor. Creates an `istream_iterator` that reads values from the input stream `s`. When `s` reaches end of stream, this iterator will compare equal to an end-of-stream iterator created using the default constructor.

✳ **`istream_iterator::istream_iterator()`**
The default constructor. Constructs an end-of-stream iterator. It is a past-the-end iterator, and it is useful when constructing a "range."

`istream_iterator::istream_iterator(const istream_iterator&)`
The copy constructor.
(Described in Input Iterator.)

`istream_iterator& istream_iterator::operator=(const istream_iterator&)`
The assignment operator.
(Described in Input Iterator.)

`const T& istream_iterator::operator*() const`
Returns the next object in the stream.
(Described in Input Iterator.)

`const T* istream_iterator::operator->() const`
`i->m` is equivalent to `(*i).m`.
(Described in Input Iterator.)

```
istream_iterator& istream_iterator::operator++()
```
Preincrement.
(Described in Input Iterator.)

```
istream_iterator istream_iterator::operator++(int)
```
Postincrement.
(Described in Input Iterator.)

```
bool operator==(const istream_iterator&, const istream_iterator&)
```
The equality operator.
(Described in Input Iterator.)

14.2.2 `ostream_iterator`

`ostream_iterator<T, charT, traits>`

An `ostream_iterator` is an Output Iterator that performs formatted output of objects of type `T` to a particular `basic_ostream`. All of the restrictions of an Output Iterator must be obeyed, including the restrictions on the ordering of `operator*` and `operator++` operations.

The definition of `ostream_iterator` has been changed from that in the original HP STL, for the same reason as `istream_iterator`: C++'s stream I/O library has been generalized. As with `istream_iterator`, you have no reason to care about this extra complexity unless you want to use it. The extra template parameters have defaults, and `ostream_iterator<int>` still works the same way it always did.

In the new version of stream I/O, `ostream` is not a type but a `typedef`. It is an alias for `basic_ostream<char, char_traits<char> >`. Correspondingly, the new version of `ostream_iterator` has extra template parameters that are forwarded as template parameters to `basic_ostream`.

As of 1998, not all C++ implementations provide the new templatized version of stream I/O. For maximum portability, it is best to restrict yourself to the defaults. If you use an `ostream_iterator<T>`, you can be sure that it will behave correctly regardless of whether you're using the new or the old version of stream I/O.

Example

Copy the elements of a `vector` to the standard output in reverse order, one per line. In this example we use the version of `ostream_iterator`'s constructor that takes two parameters. The second parameter is a string that is printed after each element.

```
int main()
{
  vector<int> V;
  for (int i = 0; i < 20; ++i)
    V.push_back(i);
  reverse_copy(V.begin(), V.end(), ostream_iterator<int>(cout, "\n"));
}
```

Where Defined

In the HP implementation, `ostream_iterator` was defined in `<iterator.h>`. According to the C++ standard, it is declared in `<iterator>`.

Template Parameters

T   The type of value that will be written to the output stream. The set of value types of an `ostream_iterator` consists of a single type, T.

charT   The output stream's character type.
          Default: char

traits   The output stream's character traits class.
          Default: char_traits<charT>

Model Of

Output Iterator (page 96).

Type Requirements

- The type T is a type such that, for a value t of type T and an output stream out of type basic_ostream<charT, traits>, the expression out << t is well-defined.

- The types charT and traits satisfy the requirements for a stream's character and character traits type.[2]

Public Base Classes

`iterator<output_iterator_tag, void, void, void, void>`

Members

Some of `ostream_iterator`'s members are not defined in the Output Iterator requirements but are specific to `ostream_iterator`. These special members are flagged with the symbol ✳.

✳ **ostream_iterator::char_type**
The iterator's character type: charT

✳ **ostream_iterator::traits_type**
The iterator's character traits type: traits

✳ **ostream_iterator::ostream_type**
The iterator's stream type: basic_ostream<charT, traits>

---

2. Character and character trait types are part of the C++ I/O library rather than the STL, so this book does not address the requirements for those types.

`ostream_iterator::iterator_category`
The iterator's category: `output_iterator_tag`
(Described in Output Iterator.)

✴ `ostream_iterator::ostream_iterator(ostream_type& s)`
The constructor. Creates an `ostream_iterator` such that assignment of t through it is equivalent to s << t.

✴ `ostream_iterator::ostream_iterator(ostream_type& s, const charT* delim)`
Constructor with delimiter. Creates an `ostream_iterator` such that assignment of t through it is equivalent to s << t << delim.

`ostream_iterator::ostream_iterator(const ostream_iterator&)`
The copy constructor.
(Described in Output Iterator.)

`ostream_iterator& ostream_iterator::operator=(const ostream_iterator&)`
The assignment operator.
(Described in Output Iterator.)

`ostream_iterator& ostream_iterator::operator=(const T&)`
Used to implement the Output Iterator expression *i = t.

`ostream_iterator& ostream_iterator::operator*()`
Used to implement the Output Iterator expression *i = t.

`ostream_iterator& ostream_iterator::operator++()`
Preincrement.
(Described in Output Iterator.)

`ostream_iterator ostream_iterator::operator++(int)`
Postincrement.
(Described in Output Iterator.)

Note that the Output Iterator definition requires only that *ii = t be a valid expression. It says nothing about `operator*` or `operator=` on their own. The most obvious implementation is for `operator*` to return some proxy object, where the proxy object has some appropriate `operator=`. In this case the proxy object is just the `ostream_iterator` itself. That's an implementation detail, and you should not rely on it. You should always write *ii = t, as described in the Output Iterator requirements.

14.2.3 `istreambuf_iterator`

`istreambuf_iterator<charT, traits>`

The `istreambuf_iterator` class is very much like `istream_iterator` except that instead of performing general formatted input of arbitrary types, it reads single characters from an input stream. It is an Input Iterator, and as with `istream_iterator`, an `istreambuf_iterator` takes on a special past-the-end value when it encounters end of stream.

Example

Read all of the remaining characters in the standard input stream into a buffer.

```
int main()
{
  istreambuf_iterator<char> first(cin);
  istreambuf_iterator<char> end_of_stream;
  vector<char> buffer(first, end_of_stream);
  ...
};
```

Where Defined

The HP implementation did not include `istreambuf_iterator`. According to the C++ standard, it is declared in `<iterator>`.

Template Parameters

charT   The `istreambuf_iterator`'s value type. The iterator reads characters of type charT.

traits The input stream's character traits class.
        Default: `char_traits<charT>`

Model Of

Input Iterator (page 94).

Type Requirements

- The types charT and traits satisfy the requirements for a stream's character and character traits type.[3]

Public Base Classes

`iterator<input_iterator_tag, charT, traits::off_type, charT*, charT&>`

Members

Some of `istreambuf_iterator`'s members are not defined in the Input Iterator requirements but are specific to `istreambuf_iterator`. These special members are flagged with the symbol *.

* **`istreambuf_iterator::char_type`**
  Equivalent to charT

* **`istreambuf_iterator::traits_type`**
  Equivalent to traits

* **`istreambuf_iterator::int_type`**
  Equivalent to traits::int_type

---

3. Character and character trait types are part of the C++ I/O library rather than the STL, so this book does not address the requirements for those types.

✳ `istreambuf_iterator::streambuf_type`
Equivalent to `basic_streambuf<charT, traits>`

✳ `istreambuf_iterator::istream_type`
Equivalent to `basic_istream<charT, traits>`

`istreambuf_iterator::iterator_category`
The iterator's category: `input_iterator_tag`
(Described in Input Iterator.)

`istreambuf_iterator::value_type`
The iterator's value type: `charT`
(Described in Input Iterator.)

`istreambuf_iterator::difference_type`
The iterator's difference type: `traits::off_type`
(Described in Input Iterator.)

`istreambuf_iterator::pointer`
The iterator's pointer type: `charT*`
(Described in Input Iterator.)

`istreambuf_iterator::reference`
The iterator's reference type: `charT&`
(Described in Input Iterator.)

✳ `istreambuf_iterator::istreambuf_iterator(istream_type& s)`
The constructor. Creates an `istreambuf_iterator` that reads values from the input stream s. When s reaches end of stream, this iterator will compare equal to an end-of-stream iterator created using the default constructor.

✳ `istreambuf_iterator::istreambuf_iterator(streambuf_type* s)`
The constructor. Creates an `istreambuf_iterator` that reads values from the streambuf `*s`. When that streambuf reaches end of stream, this iterator will compare equal to an end-of-stream iterator created using the default constructor. If s is a null pointer, this constructor is equivalent to the default constructor.

✳ `istreambuf_iterator::istreambuf_iterator()`
The default constructor. Constructs an end-of-stream iterator. It is a past-the-end iterator, and it is useful when constructing a "range."

`charT istreambuf_iterator::operator*() const`
Returns the next character in the stream.
(Described in Input Iterator.)

`istreambuf_iterator& istreambuf_iterator::operator++()`
Preincrement.
(Described in Input Iterator.)

`istreambuf_iterator istreambuf_iterator::operator++(int)`
Postincrement. Note that implementing the postincrement operator is slightly tricky because it must "increment" the streambuf (that is, move to the next character) while returning an iterator that continues to point to the current character. Typically, the postincrement operator returns a proxy class that's convertible to an `istreambuf_iterator`.
(Described in Input Iterator.)

`bool operator==(const istreambuf_iterator&, const istreambuf_iterator&)`
The equality operator.
(Described in Input Iterator.)

✳ `bool istreambuf_iterator::equal(const istreambuf_iterator&) const`
The expression `i.equal(j)` is equivalent to `i == j`.

14.2.4 ostreambuf_iterator

`ostreambuf_iterator<charT, traits>`

The `ostreambuf_iterator` class is an Output Iterator that writes characters to an output stream. It is very much like `ostream_iterator`, except that instead of performing general formatted output of arbitrary types, it writes single characters using the streambuf class's `sputc` member function.

Example

Use `ostreambuf_iterator` to write a string to the standard output.

```
int main()
{
  string s = "This is a test.\n";
  copy(s.begin(), s.end(), ostreambuf_iterator<char>(cout));
}
```

Where Defined

The HP implementation did not include `ostreambuf_iterator`. According to the C++ standard, it is declared in `<iterator>`.

Template Parameters

charT   The `ostreambuf_iterator`'s value type. The iterator writes characters of type charT.

traits   The output stream's character traits class.
        Default: `char_traits<charT>`.

Model Of

Output Iterator (page 96).

Type Requirements

- The types charT and traits satisfy the requirements for a stream's character and character traits type.[4]

Public Base Classes

`iterator<output_iterator_tag, void, void, void, void>`

---

4. Character and character trait types are part of the C++ I/O library rather than the STL, so this book does not address the requirements for those types.

Members

Some of `ostreambuf_iterator`'s members are not defined in the Output Iterator requirements but are specific to `ostreambuf_iterator`. These special members are flagged with the symbol ✳.

✳ **`ostreambuf_iterator::char_type`**
Equivalent to `charT`

✳ **`ostreambuf_iterator::traits_type`**
Equivalent to `traits`

✳ **`ostreambuf_iterator::streambuf_type`**
Equivalent to `basic_streambuf<charT, traits>`

✳ **`ostreambuf_iterator::ostream_type`**
Equivalent to `basic_ostream<charT, traits>`

✳ **`ostreambuf_iterator::ostreambuf_iterator(ostream_type& s)`**
The constructor. Creates an `ostreambuf_iterator` such that assignment of c through it is equivalent to `s.rdbuf()->sputc(c)`.

`ostream_iterator::iterator_category`
The iterator's category: `output_iterator_tag`
(Described in Output Iterator.)

✳ **`ostreambuf_iterator::ostreambuf_iterator(streambuf_type* s)`**
The constructor. Creates an `ostreambuf_iterator` such that assignment of c through it is equivalent to `s->sputc(c)`.

`ostreambuf_iterator& ostreambuf_iterator::operator=(const CharT&)`
Used to implement the Output Iterator expression `*i = c`. If i is an iterator of type `ostreambuf_iterator` then the expression `*i = c` is equivalent to `s->sputc(c)`, where s is i's streambuf.

`ostreambuf_iterator& ostreambuf_iterator::operator*()`
Used to implement the Output Iterator expression `*i = c`.

`ostreambuf_iterator& ostreambuf_iterator::operator++()`
Preincrement.
(Described in Output Iterator.)

`ostreambuf_iterator ostreambuf_iterator::operator++(int)`
Postincrement.
(Described in Output Iterator.)

✳ **`bool ostreambuf_iterator::failed() const`**
Returns `true` if and only if one of the previous calls to `sputc` returned `eof`.

14.3 `reverse_iterator`

`reverse_iterator<Iterator>`

The class `reverse_iterator` is an iterator adaptor that enables backward traversal of a range. Applying `operator++` to an object of class `reverse_iterator<Iter>` is the same as applying `operator--` to an object of class `Iter`, and vice versa. Given a

range [f,1), the range [reverse_iterator<Iter>(1), reverse_iterator<Iter>(f))
contains exactly the same elements but in the opposite order.

This property has an important consequence. The roles of f and 1 have been
reversed: 1 represents the end of the range, but reverse_iterator(1) represents
the beginning of the reversed range. The beginning and end of a range, though, are
not symmetrical, since f is the first iterator in the range [f,1), and 1 is *one past* the
last iterator in the range.

This means that reverse_iterator(1) can't point to the same element as 1 does.
(For that matter, 1 might not point to any element at all; it might be a past-the-end
iterator.) Instead, reverse_iterator(1) must point to the element *(1 − 1). The
fundamental identity of reverse iterators is:

&*(reverse_iterator(i)) == &*(i − 1)

A reverse_iterator<Iter> maintains the value of its underlying iterator of type
Iter, and you can access that underlying iterator with the base() member function.
Thus an equivalent way of writing the fundamental identity of reverse iterators is
&*ri == &*(ri.base() − 1).

The original HP STL had two different classes: reverse_iterator, which could
only be used with Random Access Iterators, and reverse_bidirectional_iterator,
which could be used with other Bidirectional Iterators. The reason for that distinction
was purely technical,[5] and reverse_bidirectional_iterator is now completely unnecessary. Some implementations still provide it for backward compatibility, but it
has been removed from the C++ standard.

Example

```
int main() {
  const int N = 10;
  int A[N] = {2, 5, 7, 8, 1, 5, 3, 6, 9, 1};

  list<int> L(A, A+N);

  // Print L's elements in forward order.
  copy(L.begin(), L.end(), ostream_iterator<int>(cout, " "));
  cout << endl;

  // Print L's elements in reverse order.
  copy(reverse_iterator<list<int>::iterator>(L.end()),
       reverse_iterator<list<int>::iterator>(L.begin()),
       ostream_iterator<int>(cout, " "));
  cout << endl;

  // Find the first occurrence of the number '5'.
  list<int>::iterator i1 = find(L.begin(), L.end(), 5);

  // Find the last occurrence of the number '5'.
```

---

5. The original HP STL did not have iterator_traits (page 177).

```
    list<int>::iterator i2 =
      (find(reverse_iterator<list<int>::iterator>(L.end()),
            reverse_iterator<list<int>::iterator>(L.begin()),
            5)).base();
    --i2;
    assert(*i1 == 5 && *i2 == 5 && distance(i1, i2) == 4);
}
```

In practice, incidentally, you would never write code like this to iterate backward through a `list`. Like all other Reversible Containers, `list` contains member functions and nested types that make it easier to use reverse iterators. In practice, you would write

```
    list<int>::reverse_iterator ri = L.rbegin();
```
rather than
```
    reverse_iterator<list<int>::iterator> ri(L.rbegin());
```

If you are defining a Reversible Container, you must provide those typedefs and member functions for your container, and you will probably use a code fragment that looks something like this:

```
    typedef std::reverse_iterator<iterator> reverse_iterator;
    typedef std::reverse_iterator<const_iterator>
            const_reverse_iterator;

    reverse_iterator rbegin() { return reverse_iterator(end()); }
    reverse_iterator rend() { return reverse_iterator(begin()); }

    const_reverse_iterator rbegin() const
      { return const_reverse_iterator(end()); }
    const_reverse_iterator rend() const
      { return const_reverse_iterator(begin()); }
```

Where Defined

In the HP implementation, `reverse_iterator` was defined in `<iterator.h>`. According to the C++ standard, it is declared in `<iterator>`.

Template Parameters

`Iterator`   The reverse iterator's base iterator type, a Bidirectional Iterator.

Model Of

Bidirectional Iterator (page 102). If `Iterator` is a model of Random Access Iterator (page 103), then `reverse_iterator<Iterator>` is also a model of Random Access Iterator.

Type Requirements

- The template parameter `Iterator` is a model of Bidirectional Iterator. Note that some of `reverse_iterator`'s member functions are only usable if `Iterator` is also a model of Random Access Iterator.

Public Base Classes

```
iterator<typename iterator_traits<Iterator>::iterator_category,
         typename iterator_traits<Iterator>::value_type,
         typename iterator_traits<Iterator>::difference_type,
         typename iterator_traits<Iterator>::pointer,
         typename iterator_traits<Iterator>::reference>
```

Members

Some of `reverse_iterator`'s members are not defined in the Bidirectional Iterator or Random Access Iterator requirements but are specific to `reverse_iterator`. These special members are flagged with the symbol ✳.

> **`reverse_iterator::iterator_category`**
> The reverse iterator's category tag: the same as `Iterator`'s category tag.
> (Described in Input Iterator.)

> **`reverse_iterator::value_type`**
> The reverse iterator's value type: the same as `Iterator`'s value type.
> (Described in Input Iterator.)

> **`reverse_iterator::difference_type`**
> The reverse iterator's difference type: the same as `Iterator`'s difference type.
> (Described in Input Iterator.)

> **`reverse_iterator::pointer`**
> The reverse iterator's pointer type: the same as `Iterator`'s pointer type.
> (Described in Input Iterator.)

> **`reverse_iterator::reference`**
> The reverse iterator's reference type: the same as `Iterator`'s reference type.
> (Described in Input Iterator.)

✳ **`reverse_iterator::iterator_type`**
The same as `Iterator`.

✳ **`explicit reverse_iterator::reverse_iterator(Iterator i)`**
The constructor. Constructs a `reverse_iterator` whose underlying iterator is `i`.

> **`reverse_iterator::reverse_iterator()`**
> The default constructor.
> (Described in Input Iterator.)

> **`reverse_iterator::reverse_iterator(const reverse_iterator&)`**
> The copy constructor.
> (Described in Input Iterator.)

✳ **`template <class I>`**
`reverse_iterator::reverse_iterator(const reverse_iterator<I>& i)`
Generalized copy constructor. Constructs a `reverse_iterator` whose underlying iterator is `i.base()`.

The effect of this constructor is that the type `reverse_iterator<X>` is convertible to the type `reverse_iterator<Y>` if and only if X is convertible to Y. The main reason it exists is so that a Reversible Container's `reverse_iterator` type is convertible to its `const_reverse_iterator` type, just as every Container's `iterator` type is convertible to its `const_iterator` type.

`reverse_iterator& reverse_iterator::operator=(const reverse_iterator&)`
The assignment operator.
(Described in Input Iterator.)

＊ `Iterator reverse_iterator::base() const`
Returns the underlying iterator.

`reference reverse_iterator::operator*() const`
Returns the element that the iterator points to.
(Described in Forward Iterator.)

`reverse_iterator& reverse_iterator::operator++()`
Preincrement.
(Described in Forward Iterator.)

`reverse_iterator reverse_iterator::operator++(int)`
Postincrement.
(Described in Forward Iterator.)

`reverse_iterator& reverse_iterator::operator--()`
Predecrement.
(Described in Bidirectional Iterator.)

`reverse_iterator reverse_iterator::operator--(int)`
Postdecrement.
(Described in Bidirectional Iterator.)

`reverse_iterator reverse_iterator::operator+(difference_type)`
Iterator addition. This member function may only be used if `Iterator` is a model of Random Access Iterator.
(Described in Random Access Iterator.)

`reverse_iterator& reverse_iterator::operator+=(difference_type)`
Iterator addition. This member function may only be used if `Iterator` is a model of Random Access Iterator.
(Described in Random Access Iterator.)

`reverse_iterator reverse_iterator::operator-(difference_type)`
Iterator subtraction. This member function may only be used if `Iterator` is a model of Random Access Iterator.
(Described in Random Access Iterator.)

`reverse_iterator& reverse_iterator::operator-=(difference_type)`
Iterator subtraction. This member function may only be used if `Iterator` is a model of Random Access Iterator.
(Described in Random Access Iterator.)

`reference& reverse_iterator::operator[](difference_type) const`
Element access. This member function may only be used if `Iterator` is a model of Random Access Iterator.
(Described in Random Access Iterator.)

```
reverse_iterator operator+(difference_type, reverse_iterator)
```
Iterator addition. This member function may only be used if `Iterator` is a model of
Random Access Iterator.
(Described in Random Access Iterator.)

```
difference_type operator-(const reverse_iterator&,
                          const reverse_iterator&)
```
Returns the difference of two iterators. This function may only be used if `Iterator` is a
model of Random Access Iterator.
(Described in Random Access Iterator.)

```
bool operator==(const reverse_iterator&, const reverse_iterator&)
```
The equality operator.
(Described in Input Iterator.)

```
bool operator<(const reverse_iterator&, const reverse_iterator&)
```
Returns `true` if and only if the first argument precedes the second. This function may
only be used if `Iterator` is a model of Random Access Iterator.
(Described in Random Access Iterator.)

14.4   raw_storage_iterator

```
raw_storage_iterator<ForwardIterator, T>
```

The `raw_storage_iterator` class is an adaptor that makes it possible to combine
STL algorithms with low-level memory manipulation. You can use it when you need
to separate memory allocation and object construction.

If `i` is an iterator that points to a region of uninitialized memory, you can use
construct (page 189), or the placement form of operator new, to create an object
in the location that i points to. The `raw_storage_iterator` adaptor is an Output
Iterator that makes this procedure more convenient. It constructs objects in memory
that's pointed to by iterators of type `ForwardIterator`.

A raw_storage_iterator<Iter> r refers to the same memory location that some
underlying iterator i of type Iter does. The expression *r = x is equivalent to
construct(&*i, x).

You should never use the `raw_storage_iterator` adaptor unless you are writing
a container or an adaptive algorithm. In fact, you probably shouldn't use it at all. The
`raw_storage_iterator` adaptor provides a different interface for construct, and it
is almost always better to use construct (or one of the algorithms that initializes all
of the elements in a range) directly.

It is possible to write exception-safe code using `raw_storage_iterator`, but it
isn't easy. If you are concerned about exception safety, it is much easier to use the
algorithms uninitialized_copy (page 192), uninitialized_fill (page 194), and
uninitialized_fill_n (page 195).

Example

```
class Int {
public:
  Int(int x) : val(x) {}      // Int has no default constructor.
  int get() { return val; }
```

```
private:
  int val;
};

int main()
{
  int A1[] = {1, 2, 3, 4, 5, 6, 7};
  const int N = sizeof(A1) / sizeof(int);

  Int* A2 = (Int*) malloc(N * sizeof(Int));
  transform(A1, A1 + N,
            raw_storage_iterator<Int*, int>(A2),
            negate<int>());
}
```

Where Defined

In the HP implementation, raw_storage_iterator was defined in <iterator.h>. According to the C++ standard, it is declared in <memory>.

Template Parameters

ForwardIterator   The type of the raw_storage_iterator's underlying iterator.

T   The type that will be used as the argument to the constructor.

Type Requirements

- ForwardIterator is a model of Forward Iterator.
- ForwardIterator is mutable.
- ForwardIterator's value type has a constructor that takes a single argument of type T.

Public Base Classes

iterator<output_iterator_tag, void, void, void, void>

Members

Some of raw_storage_iterator's members are not defined in the Output Iterator requirements but are specific to raw_storage_iterator. These special members are flagged with the symbol *.

* **raw_storage_iterator::raw_storage_iterator(ForwardIterator i)**
  The constructor. Creates a raw_storage_iterator whose underlying iterator is i.

  raw_storage_iterator::raw_storage_iterator(const raw_storage_iterator&)
  The copy constructor.
  (Described in Output Iterator.)

```
raw_storage_iterator&
raw_storage_iterator::operator=(const raw_storage_iterator&)
```
The assignment operator.
(Described in Output Iterator.)

```
raw_storage_iterator& raw_storage_iterator::operator*()
```
Used to implement the Output Iterator expression *i = t.
(Described in Output Iterator.)

```
raw_storage_iterator& raw_storage_iterator::operator=(const T& val)
```
Used to implement the Output Iterator expression *i = t. Constructs an object at the location pointed to by the iterator, using val as the constructor's argument. The type of the new object is ForwardIterator's value type.

```
raw_storage_iterator& raw_storage_iterator::operator++()
```
Preincrement.
(Described in Output Iterator.)

```
raw_storage_iterator raw_storage_iterator::operator++(int)
```
Postincrement.
(Described in Output Iterator.)

```
raw_storage_iterator::iterator_category
```
Tag type representing the iterator's category: output_iterator_tag.
(Described in Output Iterator.)

Note that the Output Iterator definition requires only that *i = t be a valid expression; it says nothing about operator* or operator= on their own. The most obvious implementation is for operator* to return some proxy object, where the proxy object has some appropriate operator=. In this case, the proxy object is just the raw_storage_iterator itself. That's an implementation detail, and you should not rely on it. You should always write *i = t, as described in the Output Iterator requirements.

Chapter 15

Function Object Classes

As discussed in Chapter 8, many of the STL's algorithms use *function objects* as a means of parameterizing behavior. The STL also includes a large collection of predefined function objects that perform basic arithmetic and logical operations.

All of the STL's predefined function objects are models of Adaptable Unary Function (page 114) or Adaptable Binary Function (page 115), meaning that they have nested type declarations specifying their argument type(s) and return type. If you are implementing a function object, one way to provide those nested types—not the only way, and not necessarily the preferred way—is to inherit from one of the empty base classes unary_function (below) and binary_function (page 372). You may sometimes find it easier to put in the typedefs directly because the C++ language places complicated technical restrictions on inheriting type declarations from a template base class.

The C++ standard calls for all of the standard function object classes to inherit from unary_function or binary_function, and this book follows the standard in that respect, but you should remember that this is purely an implementation detail. All that really matters is for the function objects to have the nested types that are required by the concepts Adaptable Unary Function and Adaptable Binary Function.

15.1 Function Object Base Classes

15.1.1 unary_function

unary_function<Arg, Result>

The unary_function class is an empty base class. It contains no member functions or member variables, only type information. It exists only to make it more convenient to define types that are models of the concept Adaptable Unary Function (page 114). Any model of Adaptable Unary Function must contain nested type declarations, and one of the ways to define those typedefs is to inherit from the base class unary_function.

Example

```
struct sine : public unary_function<double, double> {
  double operator()(double x) const { return sin(x); }
};
```

Where Defined

In the HP implementation, unary_function was defined in the header <function.h>. According to the C++ standard, it is declared in the header <functional>.

Template Parameters

Arg   The function object's argument type.

Result   The function object's result type.

Model Of

Assignable (page 83), Default Constructible (page 84).

Public Base Classes

None.

Members

All of unary_function's members are nested types:

unary_function::argument_type
The function object's argument type. This is a typedef for the template parameter Arg.

unary_function::result_type
The function object's result type. This is a typedef for the template parameter Result.

15.1.2   binary_function

binary_function<Arg1, Arg2, Result>

The binary_function class is an empty base class. It contains no member functions or member variables, only type information. The only reason it exists is to make it more convenient to define types that are models of the concept Adaptable Binary Function. Any model of Adaptable Binary Function must contain nested type declarations, and one way to define those typedefs is to inherit from the base class binary_function.

Example

```
struct exponentiate : public binary_function<double, double, double>
{
  double operator()(double x, double y) const { return pow(x, y); }
};
```

Where Defined

In the HP implementation, `binary_function` was defined in `<function.h>`. According to the C++ standard, it is declared in `<functional>`.

Template Parameters

Arg1   The function object's first argument type.

Arg2   The function object's second argument type.

Result   The function object's result type.

Model Of

Assignable (page 83), Default Constructible (page 84).

Public Base Classes

None.

Members

All of `binary_function`'s members are nested types:

> `binary_function::first_argument_type`
> The function object's first argument type. This is a `typedef` for the template parameter `Arg1`.
>
> `binary_function::second_argument_type`
> The function object's second argument type. This is a `typedef` for the template parameter `Arg2`.
>
> `binary_function::result_type`
> The function object's result type. This is a `typedef` for the template parameter `Result`.

15.2   Arithmetic Operations

15.2.1   plus

plus<T>

The class plus<T> is an **Adaptable Binary Function**. If f is an object of class plus<T> and x and y are values of type T, then f(x,y) returns x + y.

Example

Each element in v3 will be the sum of the corresponding elements in v1 and v2.

```
int main()
{
  const int N = 1000;
  vector<double> v1(N);
  vector<double> v2(N);
  vector<double> v3(N);

  generate(v1.begin(), v1.end(), rand);
  fill(v2.begin(), v2.end(), -RAND_MAX / 2.);

  transform(v1.begin(), v1.end(), v2.begin(), v3.begin(),
            plus<double>());

  for (int i = 0; i < N; ++i)
    assert(v3[i] == v1[i] + v2[i]);
}
```

Where Defined

In the HP implementation, plus was defined in the header <function.h>. According to the C++ standard, it is declared in the header <functional>.

Template Parameters

T   The function object's argument type and result type.

Model Of

Adaptable Binary Function (page 115), Default Constructible (page 84).

Type Requirements

- T is Assignable.
- T is a numeric type. If x and y are value of type T, then x + y is defined and has a return type that is convertible to T.

Public Base Classes

binary_function<T, T, T>

Members

plus::first_argument_type
The type of the first argument: T
(Described in Adaptable Binary Function.)

plus::second_argument_type
The type of the second argument: T
(Described in Adaptable Binary Function.)

plus::result_type
The type of the result: T
(Described in Adaptable Binary Function.)

T plus::operator()(const T& x, const T& y) const
Function call operator. The result is x + y.
(Described in Adaptable Binary Function.)

plus::plus()
The default constructor.
(Described in Default Constructible.)

15.2.2 minus

minus<T>

The class minus<T> is an **Adaptable Binary Function**. If f is an object of class minus<T> and x and y are values of type T, then f(x,y) returns x − y.

Example

Construct a vector v3 each element of which is the difference of the corresponding elements in v1 and v2.

```
int main()
{
  const int N = 1000;
  vector<double> v1(N);
  vector<double> v2(N);
  vector<double> v3(N);

  generate(v1.begin(), v1.end(), rand);
  fill(v2.begin(), v2.end(), RAND_MAX / 2.);

  transform(v1.begin(), v1.end(), v2.begin(), v3.begin(),
            minus<double>());

  for (int i = 0; i < N; ++i)
    assert(v3[i] == v1[i] - v2[i]);
}
```

Where Defined

In the HP implementation, minus was defined in the header <function.h>. According to the C++ standard, it is declared in the header <functional>.

Template Parameters

T   The function object's argument type and result type.

Model Of

Adaptable Binary Function (page 115), Default Constructible (page 84).

Type Requirements

- T is Assignable.
- T is a numeric type. If x and y are value of type T, then x − y is defined and has a return type that is convertible to T.

Public Base Classes

`binary_function<T, T, T>`

Members

`minus::first_argument_type`
The type of the first argument: T
(Described in Adaptable Binary Function.)

`minus::second_argument_type`
The type of the second argument: T
(Described in Adaptable Binary Function.)

`minus::result_type`
The type of the result: T
(Described in Adaptable Binary Function.)

`T minus::operator()(const T& x, const T& y) const`
Function call operator. The result is x − y.
(Described in Adaptable Binary Function.)

`minus::minus()`
The default constructor.
(Described in Default Constructible.)

15.2.3 `multiplies`

`multiplies<T>`

The class `multiplies<T>` is an Adaptable Binary Function.[1] If f is an object of class `multiplies<T>` and x and y are values of type T, then f(x,y) returns x * y.

Example

Fill a table with the values 1! through 20!.

---

1. In the HP STL this function object was called `times`. The name was changed to `multiplies` in the C++ standard because the name `times` conflicted with a function in the UNIX header `<sys/times.h>`.

```
int main() {
  const int N = 20;
  vector<double> V(N);
  for (int i = 0; i < N; ++i)
    V[i] = i + 1;

  partial_sum(V.begin(), V.end(), V.begin(), multiplies<double>());
  copy(V.begin(), V.end(), ostream_iterator<double>(cout, "\n"));
}
```

Where Defined

In the HP implementation, multiplies was defined in the header <function.h>. According to the C++ standard, it is declared in the header <functional>.

Template Parameters

T   The function object's argument type and result type.

Model Of

Adaptable Binary Function (page 115), Default Constructible (page 84).

Type Requirements

- T is Assignable.
- T is a numeric type: if x and y are value of type T, then x * y is defined and has a return type that is convertible to T.

Public Base Classes

binary_function<T, T, T>

Members

multiplies::first_argument_type
The type of the first argument: T
(Described in Adaptable Binary Function.)

multiplies::second_argument_type
The type of the second argument: T
(Described in Adaptable Binary Function.)

multiplies::result_type
The type of the result: T
(Described in Adaptable Binary Function.)

T multiplies::operator()(const T& x, const T& y) const
Function call operator. The result is x * y.
(Described in Adaptable Binary Function.)

multiplies::multiplies()
The default constructor.
(Described in Default Constructible.)

15.2.4 divides

divides<T>

The class divides<T> is an Adaptable Binary Function. If f is an object of class divides<T> and x and y are values of type T, then f(x,y) returns x / y.

Example

Divide every element in a vector by a constant value.

```
int main()
{
  const int N = 1000;
  vector<double> v(N);

  generate(v.begin(), v.end(), rand);
  transform(v.begin(), v.end(), v.begin(),
            bind2nd(divides<double>(), double(RAND_MAX)));

  for (int i = 0; i < N; ++i)
    assert(0 <= v[i] && v[i] <= 1.);
}
```

Where Defined

In the HP implementation, divides was defined in the header <function.h>. According to the C++ standard, it is declared in the header <functional>.

Template Parameters

T   The function object's argument type and result type.

Model Of

Adaptable Binary Function (page 115), Default Constructible (page 84).

Type Requirements

- T is Assignable.
- T is a numeric type. If x and y are value of type T, then x / y is defined and has a return type that is convertible to T.

Public Base Classes

binary_function<T, T, T>

Members

divides::first_argument_type
The type of the first argument: T
(Described in Adaptable Binary Function.)

divides::second_argument_type
The type of the second argument: T
(Described in Adaptable Binary Function.)

divides::result_type
The type of the result: T
(Described in Adaptable Binary Function.)

T divides::operator()(const T& x, const T& y) const
Function call operator. The result is x / y.
(Described in Adaptable Binary Function.)

divides::divides()
The default constructor.
(Described in Default Constructible.)

15.2.5 modulus

modulus<T>

The class modulus<T> is an Adaptable Binary Function. If f is an object of class modulus<T> and x and y are values of type T, then f(x,y) returns x % y.

Example

Replace every element in a vector with the last digit of that element.

```
int main()
{
  const int N = 1000;
  vector<int> v(N);

  generate(v.begin(), v.end(), rand);
  transform(v.begin(), v.end(), v.begin(),
          bind2nd(modulus<int>(), 10));

  for (int i = 0; i < N; ++i)
    assert(0 <= v[i] && v[i] < 10);
}
```

Where Defined

In the HP implementation, modulus was defined in the header <function.h>. According to the C++ standard, it is declared in the header <functional>.

Template Parameters

T   The function object's argument type and result type.

Model Of

Adaptable Binary Function (page 115), Default Constructible (page 84).

Type Requirements

- T is Assignable.
- T is an integral type. If x and y are value of type T, then x % y is defined and has a return type that is convertible to T.

Public Base Classes

binary_function<T, T, T>

Members

modulus::first_argument_type
The type of the first argument: T
(Described in Adaptable Binary Function.)

modulus::second_argument_type
The type of the second argument: T
(Described in Adaptable Binary Function.)

modulus::result_type
The type of the result: T
(Described in Adaptable Binary Function.)

T modulus::operator()(const T& x, const T& y) const
Function call operator. The result is x % y.
(Described in Adaptable Binary Function.)

modulus::modulus()
The default constructor.
(Described in Default Constructible.)

15.2.6 negate

negate<T>

The class negate<T> is an Adaptable Unary Function, a function object that takes a single argument. If f is an object of class negate<T> and x is a value of type T, then f(x) returns -x.

Example

Construct a vector v2 each of element of which is the negative (additive inverse) of the corresponding element in v1.

```
int main()
{
  const int N = 1000;
```

```
    vector<int> v1(N);
    vector<int> v2(N);

    generate(v1.begin(), v1.end(), rand);

    transform(v1.begin(), v1.end(), v2.begin(),
              negate<int>());

    for (int i = 0; i < N; ++i)
      assert(v1[i] + v2[i] == 0);
}
```

Where Defined

In the HP implementation, negate was defined in the header <function.h>. According to the C++ standard, it is declared in the header <functional>.

Template Parameters

T   The function object's argument type and result type.

Model Of

Adaptable Unary Function (page 114), Default Constructible (page 84).

Type Requirements

- T is Assignable.
- T is a numeric type. If x is a value of type T, then -x is defined and has a return type that is convertible to T.

Public Base Classes

unary_function<T, T>

Members

negate::argument_type
The type of the argument: T
(Described in Adaptable Unary Function.)

negate::result_type
The type of the result: T
(Described in Adaptable Unary Function.)

T negate::operator()(const T& x) const
Function call operator. The result is -x.
(Described in Adaptable Unary Function.)

negate::negate()
The default constructor.
(Described in Default Constructible.)

15.3 Comparisons

15.3.1 equal_to

equal_to<T>

The class equal_to<T> is an **Adaptable Binary Predicate**, which means it is a function object that tests the truth or falsehood of some condition. If f is an object of class equal_to<T> and x and y are values of type T, then f(x,y) returns true if and only if x == y.

Example

Rearrange an array such that all of the elements that are equal to zero precede all nonzero elements.

```
int main()
{
  const int N = 10;
  int A[N] = {1, 3, 0, 2, 5, 9, 0, 0, 6, 0};

  partition(A, A+N, bind2nd(equal_to<int>(), 0));
  copy(A, A+N, ostream_iterator<int>(cout, " "));
  cout << endl;
}
```

Where Defined

In the HP implementation, equal_to was defined in the header <function.h>. According to the C++ standard, it is declared in the header <functional>.

Template Parameters

T   The type of equal_to's arguments.

Model Of

Adaptable Binary Predicate (page 119), Default Constructible (page 84).

Type Requirements

- T is a model of Equality Comparable.

Public Base Classes

binary_function<T, T, bool>

Members

equal_to::first_argument_type
The type of the first argument: T
(Described in Adaptable Binary Predicate.)

equal_to::second_argument_type
The type of the second argument: T
(Described in Adaptable Binary Predicate.)

equal_to::result_type
The type of the result: bool
(Described in Adaptable Binary Predicate.)

bool equal_to::operator()(const T& x, const T& y) const
Function call operator. The return value is x == y.
(Described in Binary Predicate.)

equal_to::equal_to()
The default constructor.
(Described in Default Constructible.)

15.3.2 not_equal_to

not_equal_to<T>

The class not_equal_to<T> is an **Adaptable Binary Predicate**, which means it is a function object that tests the truth or falsehood of some condition. If f is an object of class not_equal_to<T> and x and y are values of type T, then f(x,y) returns true if and only if x != y.

Example

Finds the first nonzero element in a list.

```
int main()
{
  const int N = 9;
  int A[N] = {0, 0, 0, 0, 1, 2, 4, 8, 0};
  list<int> L(A, A+N);

  list<int>::iterator i = find_if(L.begin(), L.end(),
                          bind2nd(not_equal_to<int>(), 0));
  cout << "Elements after initial zeros (if any): ";
  copy(i, L.end(), ostream_iterator<int>(cout, " "));
  cout << endl;
}
```

Where Defined

In the HP implementation, not_equal_to was defined in the header <function.h>.
According to the C++ standard, it is declared in the header <functional>.

Template Parameters

T   The type of not_equal_to's arguments.

Model Of

Adaptable Binary Predicate (page 119), Default Constructible (page 84).

Type Requirements

- T is a model of Equality Comparable.

Public Base Classes

binary_function<T, T, bool>

Members

not_equal_to::first_argument_type
The type of the first argument: T
(Described in Adaptable Binary Predicate.)

not_equal_to::second_argument_type
The type of the second argument: T
(Described in Adaptable Binary Predicate.)

not_equal_to::result_type
The type of the result: bool
(Described in Adaptable Binary Predicate.)

bool not_equal_to::operator()(const T& x, const T& y) const
Function call operator. The return value is x != y.
(Described in Binary Predicate.)

not_equal_to::not_equal_to()
The default constructor.
(Described in Default Constructible.)

15.3.3   less

less<T>

The class less<T> is an Adaptable Binary Predicate, which means it is a function object that tests the truth or falsehood of some condition. If f is an object of class less<T> and x and y are values of type T, then f(x,y) returns true if and only if x < y.

Many STL classes and algorithms, such as sort, set, and map, require comparison functions. Typically, the default is less.

Example

Rearrange an array such that the negative numbers precede the nonnegative ones.

```
int main()
{
  const int N = 10;
  int A[N] = {1, -3, -7, 2, 5, -9, -2, 1, 6, -8};

  partition(A, A+N, bind2nd(less<int>(), 0));
  copy(A, A+N, ostream_iterator<int>(cout, " "));
  cout << endl;
}
```

Where Defined

In the HP implementation, less was defined in the header <function.h>. According to the C++ standard, it is declared in the header <functional>.

Template Parameters

T   The type of less's arguments.

Model Of

Adaptable Binary Predicate (page 119), Default Constructible (page 84). Additionally, less<T> is a model of Strict Weak Ordering (page 119) if and only if T is a model of Strict Weakly Comparable (page 88).

Type Requirements

- T is a model of LessThan Comparable.

Public Base Classes

binary_function<T, T, bool>

Members

less::first_argument_type
The type of the first argument: T
(Described in Adaptable Binary Predicate.)

less::second_argument_type
The type of the second argument: T
(Described in Adaptable Binary Predicate.)

less::result_type
The type of the result: bool
(Described in Adaptable Binary Predicate.)

```
bool less::operator()(const T& x, const T& y) const
```
Function call operator. The return value is x < y.
(Described in Binary Predicate.)

```
less::less()
```
The default constructor.
(Described in Default Constructible.)

15.3.4 greater

greater<T>

The class greater<T> is an **Adaptable Binary Predicate**, which means it is a function object that tests the truth or falsehood of some condition. If f is an object of class greater<T> and x and y are values of type T, then f(x,y) returns true if and only if x > y.

Example

Sort a vector in descending order rather than ascending order.

```
int main()
{
  const int N = 10;
  int A[N] = {1, -3, -7, 2, 5, -9, -2, 1, 6, -8};
  vector<int> V(A, A+N);

  sort(V.begin(), V.end(), greater<int>());
  copy(V.begin(), V.end(), ostream_iterator<int>(cout, " "));
  cout << endl;
}
```

Where Defined

In the HP implementation, greater was defined in the header <function.h>. According to the C++ standard, it is declared in the header <functional>.

Template Parameters

T   The type of greater's arguments.

Model of

Adaptable Binary Predicate (page 119), Default Constructible (page 84). Additionally, greater<T> is a model of Strict Weak Ordering (page 119) if and only if T is a model of Strict Weakly Comparable (page 88).

Type Requirements

- T is a model of LessThan Comparable.

Public Base Classes

binary_function<T, T, bool>

Members

greater::**first_argument_type**
The type of the first argument: T
(Described in Adaptable Binary Predicate.)

greater::**second_argument_type**
The type of the second argument: T
(Described in Adaptable Binary Predicate.)

greater::**result_type**
The type of the result: bool
(Described in Adaptable Binary Predicate.)

bool greater::operator()(const T& x, const T& y) const
Function call operator. The return value is x > y.
(Described in Binary Predicate.)

greater::**greater()**
The default constructor.
(Described in Default Constructible.)

15.3.5 less_equal

less_equal<T>

The class less_equal<T> is an **Adaptable Binary Predicate**, which means it is a function object that tests the truth or falsehood of some condition. If f is an object of class less_equal<T> and x and y are values of type T, then f(x,y) returns true if and only if x <= y.

Example

Create a list consisting of the positive numbers from a range.

```
int main()
{
  const int N = 10;
  int A[N] = {3, -7, 0, 6, 5, -1, -3, 0, 4, -2};

  list<int> L;
  remove_copy_if(A, A+N, back_inserter(L),
                 bind2nd(less_equal<int>(), 0));

  cout << "Elements in list: ";
  copy(L.begin(), L.end(), ostream_iterator<int>(cout, " "));
  cout << endl;
}
```

Where Defined

In the HP implementation, `less_equal` was defined in the header `<function.h>`. According to the C++ standard, it is declared in the header `<functional>`.

Template Parameters

T   The type of `less_equal`'s arguments.

Model Of

Adaptable Binary Predicate (page 119), Default Constructible (page 84).

Note that `less_equal` is not a model of Strict Weak Ordering. For example, you can't use `less_equal` as sort's comparison function. It isn't even a partial ordering, let alone a strict weak ordering. For a partial ordering, `f(x, x)` must always be `false`.

Type Requirements

- T is a model of LessThan Comparable.

Public Base Classes

`binary_function<T, T, bool>`

Members

`less_equal::first_argument_type`
The type of the first argument: T
(Described in Adaptable Binary Predicate.)

`less_equal::second_argument_type`
The type of the second argument: T
(Described in Adaptable Binary Predicate.)

`less_equal::result_type`
The type of the result: `bool`
(Described in Adaptable Binary Predicate.)

`bool less_equal::operator()(const T& x, const T& y) const`
Function call operator. The return value is `x <= y`.
(Described in Binary Predicate.)

`less_equal::less_equal()`
The default constructor.
(Described in Default Constructible.)

15.3.6 `greater_equal`

`greater_equal<T>`

The class `greater_equal<T>` is an Adaptable Binary Predicate, which means it is a function object that tests the truth or falsehood of some condition. If `f` is an object of class greater_equal<T> and x and y are values of type T, then f(x,y) returns true if and only if x >= y.

Example

Find the first non-negative number in a vector.

```
int main()
{
  const int N = 10;
  int A[N] = {-4, -3, 0, -6, 5, -1, -3, 0, 4, -2};
  vector<int> v(A, A+N);

  vector<int>::iterator i = find_if(v.begin(), v.end(),
                                bind2nd(greater_equal<int>(), 0));

  assert(i == v.end() || *i >= 0);
}
```

Where Defined

In the HP implementation, greater_equal was defined in the header <function.h>. According to the C++ standard, it is declared in the header <functional>.

Template Parameters

T   The type of greater_equal's arguments.

Model Of

Adaptable Binary Predicate (page 119), Default Constructible (page 84).

Note that greater_equal is not a model of Strict Weak Ordering. It isn't even a partial ordering, let alone a strict weak ordering. For a partial ordering, f(x, x) must always be false.

Type Requirements

• T is a model of LessThan Comparable.

Public Base Classes

binary_function<T, T, bool>

Members

greater_equal::first_argument_type
The type of the first argument: T
(Described in Adaptable Binary Predicate.)

greater_equal::second_argument_type
The type of the second argument: T
(Described in Adaptable Binary Predicate.)

greater_equal::result_type
The type of the result: bool
(Described in Adaptable Binary Predicate.)

bool greater_equal::operator()(const T& x, const T& y) const
Function call operator. The return value is x >= y.
(Described in Binary Predicate.)

greater_equal::greater_equal()
The default constructor.
(Described in Default Constructible.)

15.4   Logical Operations

The logical function objects are very much like the arithmetic function objects; they perform operations like x || y and x && y.

The classes logical_and and logical_or are not very useful by themselves. They are mainly useful because, when combined with the function object adaptor binary_compose (page 433), they perform logical operations on other function objects.

15.4.1   logical_and

logical_and<T>

The class logical_and<T> is an **Adaptable Binary Predicate**, which means it is a function object that tests the truth or falsehood of some condition. If f is an object of class logical_and<T> and x and y are values of type T (where T is convertible to bool) then f(x,y) is true if and only if x and y are both true.

Example

Finds the first element in a list that lies in the range 0...10.

```
int main()
{
  list<int> L;
  generate_n(back_inserter(L), 10000, rand);

  list<int>::iterator i =
    find_if(L.begin(), L.end(),
            compose2(logical_and<bool>(),
                     bind2nd(greater_equal<int>(), 1),
                     bind2nd(less_equal<int>(), 10)));
  assert(i == L.end() || (*i >= 1 && *i <= 10));
}
```

Where Defined

In the HP implementation, logical_and was defined in the header <function.h>. According to the C++ standard, it is declared in the header <functional>.

Template Parameters

T   The type of logical_and's arguments.

Model Of

Adaptable Binary Predicate (page 119), Default Constructible (page 84).

Type Requirements

- T is convertible to bool.

Public Base Classes

binary_function<T, T, bool>

Members

logical_and::first_argument_type
The type of the first argument: T
(Described in Adaptable Binary Predicate.)

logical_and::second_argument_type
The type of the second argument: T
(Described in Adaptable Binary Predicate.)

logical_and::result_type
The type of the result: bool
(Described in Adaptable Binary Predicate.)

bool logical_and::operator()(const T& x, const T& y) const
Function call operator. The return value is x && y.
(Described in Binary Predicate.)

logical_and::logical_and()
The default constructor.
(Described in Default Constructible.)

15.4.2 logical_or

logical_or<T>

The class logical_or<T> is an **Adaptable Binary Predicate**, which means it is a function object that tests the truth or falsehood of some condition. If f is an object of class logical_or<T> and x and y are values of type T (where T is convertible to bool) then f(x,y) is true if either x or y is true.

Example

Finds the first instance of either ' ' or '\n' in a string.

```
int main()
{
  char str[] = "The first line\nThe second line";
  int len = strlen(str);

  const char* wptr = find_if(str, str + len,
                       compose2(logical_or<bool>(),
                                bind2nd(equal_to<char>(), ' '),
                                bind2nd(equal_to<char>(), '\n')));
  assert(wptr == str + len || *wptr == ' ' || *wptr == '\n');
}
```

Where Defined

In the HP implementation, logical_or was defined in the header <function.h>. According to the C++ standard, it is declared in the header <functional>.

Template Parameters

T   The type of logical_or's arguments.

Model Of

Adaptable Binary Predicate (page 119), Default Constructible (page 84).

Type Requirements

- T is convertible to bool.

Public Base Classes

binary_function<T, T, bool>

Members

logical_or::first_argument_type
The type of the first argument: T
(Described in Adaptable Binary Predicate.)

logical_or::second_argument_type
The type of the second argument: T
(Described in Adaptable Binary Predicate.)

logical_or::result_type
The type of the result: bool
(Described in Adaptable Binary Predicate.)

```
bool logical_or::operator()(const T& x, const T& y) const
```
Function call operator. The return value is x || y.
(Described in Binary Predicate.)

```
logical_or::logical_or()
```
The default constructor.
(Described in Default Constructible.)

15.4.3 logical_not

```
logical_not<T>
```

The class logical_not<T> is an Adaptable Predicate, which means it is a function object that takes a single argument and tests the truth or falsehood of some condition. If f is an object of class logical_not<T> and x is a value of type T (where T is convertible to bool) then f(x) is true if and only if x is false.

Example

Transform a bit vector into its logical complement.

```
int main()
{
  const int N = 1000;

  vector<bool> v1;
  for (int i = 0; i < N; ++i)
    v1.push_back(rand() > (RAND_MAX / 2));

  vector<bool> v2;
  transform(v1.begin(), v1.end(), back_inserter(v2),
            logical_not<bool>());

  for (int i = 0; i < N; ++i)
    assert(v1[i] == !v2[i]);
}
```

Where Defined

In the HP implementation, logical_not was defined in the header <function.h>. According to the C++ standard, it is declared in the header <functional>.

Template Parameters

T   The type of logical_not's argument.

Model Of

Adaptable Unary Predicate (page 118), Default Constructible (page 84).

Type Requirements

- T is convertible to bool.

Public Base Classes

unary_function<T, bool>

Members

logical_not::argument_type
The type of the argument: T
(Described in Adaptable Predicate.)

logical_not::result_type
The type of the result: bool
(Described in Adaptable Predicate.)

bool logical_not::operator()(const T& x) const
Function call operator. The return value is !x.
(Described in Binary Predicate.)

logical_not::logical_not()
The default constructor.
(Described in Default Constructible.)

15.5   Identity and Projection

All of the function objects in this section are, in some sense, ones that return their arguments unchanged. The basic identity function object is identity, and the others are generalizations of it.

The C++ standard does not include any of the identity and projection operations, but they are commonly available as extensions.

15.5.1   identity

identity<T>

The class identity is a Unary Function that represents the identity function. It takes a single argument x, and returns x unchanged.

Example

```
int main()
{
  int x = 137;
  identity<int> id;
  assert(x == id(x));
}
```

Where Defined

In the original HP STL, identity was defined in the header <projectn.h>, and in the SGI STL it is defined in the header <functional>. It is not present in the C++ standard.

Template Parameters

T   The function object's argument type, and its return type.[2]

Model Of

Adaptable Unary Function (page 114), Default Constructible (page 84).

Public Base Classes

unary_function<T, T>

Members

identity::argument_type
The type of the argument: T
(Described in Adaptable Unary Function.)

identity::result_type
The type of the result: T
(Described in Adaptable Unary Function.)

const T& identity::operator()(const T& x) const
Function call operator. The return value is x.
(Described in Adaptable Unary Function.)

identity::identity()
The default constructor.
(Described in Default Constructible.)

15.5.2 project1st

project1st<Arg1, Arg2>

The class project1st is a function object that takes two arguments and returns the first; the second argument is ignored. It is essentially a generalization of identity to the case of a Binary Function.

Example

```
int main()
{
  vector<int> v1(10, 137);
  vector<char*> v2(10, (char*) 0);
```

---

2. It is essential that the argument and return types are the same. Generalizing identity so they could differ would not work, because identity returns a const reference to its argument rather than a copy of its argument. If identity performed type conversions, the return value would be a dangling reference.

```
    vector<int> result(10);

    transform(v1.begin(), v1.end(), v2.begin(), result.begin(),
             project1st<int, char*>());
    assert(equal(v1.begin(), v1.end(), result.begin()));
  }
```

Where Defined

The project1st class was not present in the original HP implementation, nor is it present in the C++ standard. In the SGI implementation it is defined in the header <functional>.

Template Parameters

Arg1   project1st's first argument type, and its result type.

Arg2   project1st's second argument type.

Model Of

Adaptable Binary Function (page 115), Default Constructible (page 84).

Type Requirements

   • Arg1 is a model of Assignable.

Public Base Classes

binary_function<Arg1, Arg2, Arg1>

Members

project1st::first_argument_type
The type of the first argument: Arg1
(Described in Adaptable Binary Function.)

project1st::second_argument_type
The type of the second argument: Arg2
(Described in Adaptable Binary Function.)

project1st::result_type
The type of the result: Arg1
(Described in Adaptable Binary Function.)

Arg1 project1st::operator()(const Arg1& x, const Arg2& y) const
Function call operator. The return value is x.
(Described in Adaptable Binary Function.)

project1st::project1st()
The default constructor.
(Described in Default Constructible.)

15.5.3 project2nd

project2nd<Arg1, Arg2>

The class project2nd is a function object that takes two arguments and returns the second; the first argument is ignored. It is essentially a generalization of identity to the case of a Binary Function.

Example

```
int main()
{
  vector<char*> v1(10, (char*) 0);
  vector<int> v2(10, 137);
  vector<int> result(10);

  transform(v1.begin(), v1.end(), v2.begin(), result.begin(),
            project2nd<char*, int>());
  assert(equal(v2.begin(), v2.end(), result.begin()));
}
```

Where Defined

The project2nd class was not present in the original HP implementation, nor is it present in the C++ standard. In the SGI implementation it is defined in the header <functional>.

Template Parameters

Arg1   project2nd's first argument type.

Arg2   project2nd's second argument type, and its result type.

Model Of

Adaptable Binary Function (page 115), Default Constructible (page 84).

Type Requirements

- Arg2 is a model of Assignable.

Public Base Classes

binary_function<Arg1, Arg2, Arg2>

Members

project2nd::first_argument_type
The type of the first argument: Arg1
(Described in Adaptable Binary Function.)

project2nd::second_argument_type
The type of the second argument: Arg2
(Described in Adaptable Binary Function.)

project2nd::result_type
The type of the result: Arg2
(Described in Adaptable Binary Function.)

Arg1 project2nd::operator()(const Arg1& x, const Arg2& y) const
Function call operator. The return value is y.
(Described in Adaptable Binary Function.)

project2nd::project2nd()
The default constructor.
(Described in Default Constructible.)

15.5.4 select1st

select1st<Pair>

The class select1st is a function object that takes a single argument, a pair (or at
least a class with the same interface as pair), and returns the pair's first element.

Example

The elements of a map are pairs, so we can use select1st to extract and print all of
a map's keys.

```
int main()
{
  map<int, double> M;
  M[1] = 0.3;
  M[47] = 0.8;
  M[33] = 0.1;

  transform(M.begin(), M.end(), ostream_iterator<int>(cout, " "),
          select1st<map<int, double>::value_type>());
  cout << endl;
  // The output is  1 33 47.
}
```

Where Defined

In the original HP STL select1st was defined in the header <projectn.h>, and in
the SGI STL it is defined in the header <functional>. It is not present in the C++
standard.

Template Parameters

Pair   The function object's argument type.

Model Of

Adaptable Unary Function (page 114), Default Constructible (page 84).

Type Requirements

- Pair has a public member variable, `Pair::first`, of type `Pair::first_type`.

Public Base Classes

`unary_function<Pair, typename Pair::first_type>`

Members

`select1st::argument_type`
The argument type: `Pair`
(Described in Adaptable Unary Function.)

`select1st::result_type`
The result type: `typename Pair::first_type`
(Described in Adaptable Unary Function.)

`const typename Pair::first_type&`
`select1st::operator()(const Pair& p) const`
Function call operator. The return value is `p.first`.
(Described in Adaptable Unary Function.)

`select1st::select1st()`
The default constructor.
(Described in Default Constructible.)

15.5.5 select2nd

`select2nd<Pair>`

The class `select2nd` is a function object that takes a single argument, a `pair` (or at least a class with the same interface as `pair`), and returns the `pair`'s second element.

Example

The elements of a `map` are `pairs`, so we can use `select2nd` to extract and print all of a map's values.

```
int main()
{
  map<int, double> M;
  M[1] = 0.3;
  M[47] = 0.8;
  M[33] = 0.1;

  transform(M.begin(), M.end(), ostream_iterator<double>(cout, " "),
            select2nd<map<int, double>::value_type>());
  cout << endl;
  // The output is  0.3 0.1 0.8
}
```

Where Defined

In the original HP STL select2nd was defined in the header <projectn.h>, and in
the SGI STL it is defined in the header <functional>. It is not present in the C++
standard.

Template Parameters

Pair   The function object's argument type.

Model Of

Adaptable Unary Function (page 114), Default Constructible (page 84).

Type Requirements

   • Pair has a public member variable, Pair::second, of type Pair::second_type.

Public Base Classes

unary_function<Pair, typename Pair::second_type>

Members

   select2nd::argument_type
   The argument type: Pair
   (Described in Adaptable Unary Function.)

   select2nd::result_type
   The result type: typename Pair::second_type
   (Described in Adaptable Unary Function.)

   const typename Pair::second_type&
   select2nd::operator()(const Pair& p) const
   Function call operator. The return value is p.second.
   (Described in Adaptable Unary Function.)

   select2nd::select2nd()
   The default constructor.
   (Described in Default Constructible.)

15.6   Specialized Function Objects

15.6.1   hash

hash<T>

The class hash<T> is a Hash Function. It is used as the default hash function by all
of the Hashed Associative Containers that are included in the STL.

The template hash<T> is only defined for template arguments of type char*, const char*, string, and the built-in integral types.[3] If you need a Hash Function with a different argument type, you must either provide your own template specialization or else write a new Hash Function class.

Example

```
int main()
{
  hash<const char*> H;
  cout << "foo -> " << H("foo") << endl;
  cout << "bar -> " << H("bar") << endl;
}
```

Where Defined

The hash class was not present in the original HP implementation, nor is it present in the C++ standard. It is, however, a common extension. In the SGI implementation it is declared in the headers <hash_set> and <hash_map>.

Template Parameters

T   The argument type. That is, the type of value that is being hashed.

Model Of

Hash Function (page 123).

Type Requirements

T must be a type for which a specialization of hash has been defined. The STL defines the following specializations:

- char*
- const char*
- string
- char
- signed char
- unsigned char
- short
- unsigned short
- int

---

3. The actual template hash<T> is an empty class. The member function operator() is defined only in the various specializations.

- unsigned int
- long
- unsigned long

Public Base Classes

None.

Members

```
size_t hash::operator()(const T& x) const
```
Returns x's hash value.
(Described in Hash Function.)

15.6.2 subtractive_rng

subtractive_rng

The class subtractive_rng is a Random Number Generator that uses the subtractive method for generating pseudo-random numbers.[4] It is a Unary Function. It takes a single argument N of type unsigned int and returns an unsigned int that is less than N. Successive calls to the same subtractive_rng object yield a pseudo-random sequence.

Note that the sequence produced by a subtractive_rng is completely deterministic, and also that the sequences produced by two different subtractive_rng objects are independent of each other. That is, if R1 is a subtractive_rng, the value returned when R1 is called depends only on R1's seed and on the number of previous calls of R1. Calls to other subtractive_rng objects are irrelevant. In implementation terms, this is because the class subtractive_rng contains no static member variables.

Example

```
int main()
{
  subtractive_rng R;
  for (int i = 0; i < 20; ++i)
    cout << R(5) << ' ';
  cout << endl;
}
// The output is    3 2 3 2 4 3 1 1 2 2 0 3 4 4 4 4 2 1 0 0
```

Where Defined

The class subtractive_rng is not part of the C++ standard. In the SGI STL it is defined in the header <functional>.

---

4. See Section 3.6 of Knuth [Knu98a] for a FORTRAN implementation of the subtractive method and Section 3.2.2 for an analysis of this class of algorithms.

Template Parameters

None.

Model Of

Random Number Generator (page 122), Adaptable Unary Function (page 114).

Public Base Classes

`unary_function<unsigned int, unsigned int>`

Members

Some of `subtractive_rng`'s members are not defined in the Random Number Generator or Adaptable Unary Function requirements but are specific to `subtractive_rng`. These special members are flagged with the symbol ✳.

> `subtractive_rng::argument_type`
> The argument type: `unsigned int`
> (Described in Adaptable Unary Function.)
>
> `subtractive_rng::result_type`
> The result type: `unsigned int`
> (Described in Adaptable Unary Function.)

✳ `subtractive_rng::subtractive_rng(unsigned int seed)`
  The constructor. Creates a `subtractive_rng`, initializing its internal state using the value seed.

✳ `subtractive_rng::subtractive_rng()`
  The default constructor. Creates a `subtractive_rng`, initializing its internal state using a default seed.

  `unsigned int subtractive_rng::operator()(unsigned int n)`
  Function call. Returns a pseudo-random number in the range $[0, N)$.

✳ `void subtractive_rng::initialize(unsigned int seed)`
  Reinitialize the random number generator so that it will have the same internal state as if it had just been constructed using the value seed.

15.7 Member Function Adaptors

The member function adaptors are a family of small classes that allow you to call member functions as function objects. Each takes an argument of type X* or X&, and calls one of X's member functions through that argument. If the member function is virtual, this will be a polymorphic function call. The member function adaptors are therefore a link between object-oriented programming and generic programming.

The number of member function adaptors may seem daunting, but they fall into a simple pattern with systematic names. There are $2^3 = 8$ adaptors as a result of three different distinctions:

1. Does the adaptor take an argument of type X* or of type X&? In the latter case, the adaptor has _ref appended to its name.

2. Does the adaptor encapsulate a member function that takes no arguments, or does it encapsulate a member function that takes a single argument? In the latter case, the adaptor has 1 appended to its name.

3. Does the adaptor encapsulate a non-const member function, or a const member function? (The C++ type declaration syntax doesn't make it possible to handle both with a single class.) In the latter case, the adaptor's name begins with const_.

Much of this complexity is invisible in normal use. The usual way to construct a function object adaptor is to use a helper function, rather than calling its constructor directly. Since the helper functions are overloaded, there are only two names to remember: mem_fun and mem_fun_ref.

15.7.1 mem_fun_t

mem_fun_t<R, X>

The class mem_fun_t is an adaptor for member functions. If X is some class with a member function R X::f() (that is, a member function that takes no arguments and that returns a value of type R[5]), then a mem_fun_t<R, X> is a function object adaptor that makes it possible to call f() as if it were an ordinary function instead of a member function.

The constructor takes a pointer to one of X's member functions. Then, like all function objects, mem_fun_t has an operator() that allows the mem_fun_t to be invoked with ordinary function call syntax. In this case, mem_fun_t's operator() takes an argument of type X*.

If F is a mem_fun_t that was constructed to use the member function X::f and if x is a pointer of type X*, then the expression F(x) is equivalent to the expression x->f(). The difference is syntactic: F supports the interface of an Adaptable Unary Function.

As with many other adaptors, it is usually inconvenient to use mem_fun_t's constructor directly. It is usually better to use the helper function mem_fun instead.

Example

```
struct B {
  virtual void print() = 0;
};

struct D1 : public B {
  void print() { cout << "I'm a D1" << endl; }
};
```

---

5. The type R is permitted to be void.

```
struct D2 : public B {
  void print() { cout << "I'm a D2" << endl; }
};

int main()
{
  vector<B*> V;

  V.push_back(new D1);
  V.push_back(new D2);
  V.push_back(new D2);
  V.push_back(new D1);

  for_each(V.begin(), V.end(), mem_fun(&B::print));
}
```

Where Defined

The class mem_fun_t was not part of the HP implementation. According to the C++ standard it is declared in the header <functional>.

Template Parameters

R   The member function's return type.

X   The class whose member function the mem_fun_t invokes.

Model Of

Adaptable Unary Function (page 114).

Type Requirements

- R is Assignable or void.
- X is a class with at least one non-const member function that takes no arguments and that returns a value of type R.

Public Base Classes

unary_function<X*, R>

Members

Some of mem_fun_t's members are not defined in the Adaptable Unary Function requirements but are specific to mem_fun_t. These special members are flagged with the symbol ∗.

`mem_fun_t::argument_type`
The argument type: X*
(Described in Adaptable Unary Function.)

`mem_fun_t::result_type`
The result type: R
(Described in Adaptable Unary Function.)

`R mem_fun_t::operator(X* x) const`
Function call operator. Invokes x->f(), where f is the member function that was passed
to the constructor.
(Described in Adaptable Unary Function.)

✳ `explicit mem_fun_t::mem_fun_t(R (X::*f)())`
The constructor. Creates a mem_fun_t that calls the member function f.

✳ `template <class R, class X>`
`mem_fun_t<R, X> mem_fun(R (X::*f)())`
Helper function to create a mem_fun_t. If f is of type R (X::*) then mem_fun(f) is the
same as mem_fun_t<R, X>(f).

15.7.2 mem_fun_ref_t

`mem_fun_ref_t<R, X>`

The class mem_fun_ref_t is an adaptor for member functions. If X is some class with
a member function R X::f() (that is, a member function that takes no arguments
and that returns a value of type R[6]), then a mem_fun_ref_t<R, X> is a function object
adaptor that makes it possible to call f() as if it were an ordinary function instead
of a member function.

The constructor takes a pointer to one of X's member functions. Then, like all
function objects, mem_fun_ref_t has an operator() that allows the mem_fun_ref_t
to be invoked with ordinary function call syntax. In this case, operator() takes an
argument of type X&.

If F is a mem_fun_ref_t that was constructed to use the member function X::f and
if x is an object of type X, then the expression F(x) is equivalent to the expression
x.f(). The difference is syntactic: F supports the interface of an Adaptable Unary
Function.

As with many other adaptors, it is usually inconvenient to use mem_fun_ref_t's
constructor directly. It is usually better to use the helper function mem_fun_ref instead.

Example

```
struct B {
  virtual void print() = 0;
};
```

---

6. The type R is permitted to be void.

```
struct D1 : public B {
  void print() { cout << "I'm a D1" << endl; }
};

struct D2 : public B {
  void print() { cout << "I'm a D2" << endl; }
};

int main()
{
  vector<D1> V;

  V.push_back(D1());
  V.push_back(D1());

  for_each(V.begin(), V.end(), mem_fun_ref(&B::print));
}
```

Where Defined

The class `mem_fun_ref_t` was not part of the HP implementation. According to the C++ standard it is declared in the header `<functional>`.

Template Parameters

R   The member function's return type.

X   The class whose member function the `mem_fun_ref_t` invokes.

Model Of

Adaptable Unary Function (page 114).

Type Requirements

- R is Assignable or void.
- X is a class with at least one non-const member function that takes no arguments and that returns a value of type R.

Public Base Classes

`unary_function<X, R>`

Members

Some of `mem_fun_ref_t`'s members are not defined in the Adaptable Unary Function requirements but are specific to `mem_fun_ref_t`. These special members are flagged with the symbol ∗.

`mem_fun_ref_t::argument_type`
The argument type: X
(Described in Adaptable Unary Function.)

`mem_fun_ref_t::result_type`
The result type: R
(Described in Adaptable Unary Function.)

`R mem_fun_ref_t::operator(X& x) const`
Function call operator. Invokes `x.f()`, where f is the member function that was passed
to the constructor.
(Described in Adaptable Unary Function.)

✳ `explicit mem_fun_ref_t::mem_fun_ref_t(R (X::*f)())`
The constructor. Creates a `mem_fun_ref_t` that calls the member function f.

✳ `template <class R, class X>`
`mem_fun_ref_t<R, X> mem_fun_ref(R (X::*f)())`
Helper function to create a `mem_fun_ref_t`. If f is of type `R (X::*)`, then `mem_fun_ref(f)`
is the same as `mem_fun_ref_t<R, X>(f)`.

15.7.3 mem_fun1_t

`mem_fun1_t<R, X, A>`

The class `mem_fun1_t` is an adaptor for member functions. If X is some class with a
member function `R X::f(A)` (that is, a member function that takes a single argument
of type A and that returns a value of type R^7), then a `mem_fun1_t<R, X, A>` is a
function object adaptor that makes it possible to call f as if it were an ordinary
function instead of a member function.

The constructor takes a pointer to one of X's member functions. Then, like all
function objects, `mem_fun1_t` has an `operator()` that allows the `mem_fun1_t` to be
invoked with ordinary function call syntax. In this case, `mem_fun1_t`'s `operator()`
takes two arguments. The first is of type X*, and the second is of type A.

If F is a `mem_fun1_t` that was constructed to use the member function `X::f` and
if x is a pointer of type X* and a is a value of type A, then the expression `F(x,a)`
is equivalent to the expression `x->f(a)`. The difference is syntactic: F supports the
interface of an Adaptable Binary Function.

As with many other adaptors, it is usually inconvenient to use `mem_fun1_t`'s constructor directly. It is usually better to use the helper function `mem_fun` instead.

Example

```
struct Operation {
  virtual double eval(double) = 0;
};

struct Square : public Operation {
  double eval(double x) { return x * x; }
};
```

---

7. The type R is permitted to be void.

```
struct Negate : public Operation {
  double eval(double x) { return -x; }
};

int main() {
  vector<Operation*> operations;
  vector<double> operands;

  operations.push_back(new Square);
  operations.push_back(new Square);
  operations.push_back(new Negate);
  operations.push_back(new Negate);
  operations.push_back(new Square);

  operands.push_back(1);
  operands.push_back(2);
  operands.push_back(3);
  operands.push_back(4);
  operands.push_back(5);

  transform(operations.begin(), operations.end(),
            operands.begin(),
            ostream_iterator<double>(cout, "\n"),
            mem_fun(&Operation::eval));
}
```

Where Defined

The class `mem_fun1_t` was not part of the HP implementation. According to the C++ standard it is declared in the header `<functional>`.

Template Parameters

R   The member function's return type.

X   The class whose member function the `mem_fun1_t` invokes.

A   The member function's argument type.

Model Of

Adaptable Binary Function (page 115).

Type Requirements

- R is Assignable or void.
- X is a class with at least one non-const member function that takes a single argument of type A and that returns a value of type R.
- A is Assignable.

Public Base Classes

```
binary_function<X*, A, R>
```

Members

Some of `mem_fun1_t`'s members are not defined in the Adaptable Binary Function requirements but are specific to `mem_fun1_t`. These special members are flagged with the symbol ✻.

> **mem_fun1_t::first_argument_type**
> The first argument type: X✻
> (Described in Adaptable Binary Function.)

> **mem_fun1_t::second_argument_type**
> The second argument type: A
> (Described in Adaptable Binary Function.)

> **mem_fun1_t::result_type**
> The result type: R
> (Described in Adaptable Binary Function.)

> **R mem_fun1_t::operator(X* x, A a) const**
> Function call operator. Invokes x->f(a), where f is the member function that was passed to the constructor.
> (Described in Adaptable Binary Function.)

✻ > **explicit mem_fun1_t::mem_fun1_t(R (X::*f)(A))**
> The constructor. Creates a `mem_fun1_t` that calls the member function f.

✻ > **template <class R, class X, class A>**
> **mem_fun1_t<R, X, A> mem_fun(R (X::*f)(A))**
> Helper function to create a `mem_fun1_t`. If f is of type R (X::*)(A) then mem_fun(f) is the same as `mem_fun1_t<R, X, A>(f)`.

15.7.4 mem_fun1_ref_t

```
mem_fun1_ref_t<R, X, A>
```

The class `mem_fun1_ref_t` is an adaptor for member functions. If X is a class with a member function R X::f(A) (that is, a member function that takes a single argument of type A and that returns a value of type R^{8}), then a `mem_fun1_ref_t<R, X, A>` is a function object adaptor that makes it possible to call f as if it were an ordinary function instead of a member function.

The constructor takes a pointer to one of X's member functions. Then, like all function objects, `mem_fun1_ref_t` has an `operator()` that allows the `mem_fun1_ref_t` to be invoked with ordinary function call syntax. In this case, `mem_fun1_ref_t`'s `operator()` takes two arguments. The first is of type X& and the second is of type A.

If F is a `mem_fun1_ref_t` that was constructed to use the member function X::f, and if x is an object of type X and a is a value of type A, then the expression F(x,a)

---

8. The type R is permitted to be void.

is equivalent to the expression x.f(a). The difference is syntactic: F supports the interface of an Adaptable Binary Function.

As with many other adaptors, it is usually inconvenient to use mem_fun1_ref_t's constructor directly. It is usually better to use the helper function mem_fun_ref instead.

Example

Given a vector of vectors, extract one element from each vector.

```
int main() {
   int A1[5] = {1, 2, 3, 4, 5};
   int A2[5] = {1, 1, 2, 3, 5};
   int A3[5] = {1, 4, 1, 5, 9};

   vector<vector<int> > V;
   V.push_back(vector<int>(A1, A1 + 5));
   V.push_back(vector<int>(A2, A2 + 5));
   V.push_back(vector<int>(A3, A3 + 5));

   int indices[3] = {0, 2, 4};

   int& (vector<int>::*extract)(vector<int>::size_type);
   extract = &vector<int>::operator[];
   transform(V.begin(), V.end(), indices,
             ostream_iterator<int>(cout, " "),
             mem_fun_ref(extract));
   cout << endl;
}
```

The output is:

```
1 2 9
```

Where Defined

The class mem_fun1_ref_t was not part of the HP implementation. According to the C++ standard, it is declared in the header <functional>.

Template Parameters

R   The member function's return type.

X   The class whose member function the mem_fun1_ref_t invokes.

A   The member function's argument type.

Model Of

Adaptable Binary Function (page 115).

Type Requirements

- R is Assignable or void.
- X is a class with at least one non-const member function that takes a single argument of type A and returns a value of type R.
- A is Assignable.

Public Base Classes

binary_function<X, A, R>

Members

Some of mem_fun1_ref_t's members are not defined in the Adaptable Binary Function requirements but are specific to mem_fun1_ref_t. These special members are flagged with the symbol ∗.

mem_fun1_ref_t::first_argument_type
The first argument type: X
(Described in Adaptable Binary Function.)

mem_fun1_ref_t::second_argument_type
The second argument type: A
(Described in Adaptable Binary Function.)

mem_fun1_ref_t::result_type
The result type: R
(Described in Adaptable Binary Function.)

R mem_fun1_ref_t::operator(X& x, A a) const
Function call operator. Invokes x.f(a), where f is the member function that was passed to the constructor.
(Described in Adaptable Binary Function.)

∗ explicit mem_fun1_ref_t::mem_fun1_ref_t(R (X::∗f)(A))
The constructor. Creates a mem_fun1_ref_t that calls the member function f.

∗ template <class R, class X, class A>
mem_fun1_ref_t<R, X, A> mem_fun_ref(R (X::∗f)(A))
Helper function to create a mem_fun1_ref_t. If f is a value of type R (X::∗)(A) then mem_fun_ref(f) is the same as mem_fun1_ref_t<R, X, A>(f).

15.7.5   const_mem_fun_t

const_mem_fun_t<R, X>

The class const_mem_fun_t is an adaptor for member functions. If X is some class with a member function
     R X::f() const
(that is, a const member function that takes no arguments and that returns a value

of type R[9]), then a const_mem_fun_t<R, X> is a function object adaptor that makes it possible to call f() as if it were an ordinary function instead of a member function.

The constructor takes a pointer to one of X's member functions. Then, like all function objects, const_mem_fun_t has an operator() that allows an object of type const_mem_fun_t to be invoked with ordinary function call syntax. In this case, const_mem_fun_t's operator() takes an argument of type const X*.

If F is a const_mem_fun_t that was constructed to use the member function X::f and if x is a pointer of type const X*, then the expression F(x) is equivalent to the expression x->f(). The difference is syntactic: F supports the interface of an Adaptable Unary Function.

As with many other adaptors, it is usually inconvenient to use const_mem_fun_t's constructor directly. It is usually better to use the helper function mem_fun instead.

Example

Given a vector of vectors, print the size of each element.

```
int main() {
  vector<vector<int>*> v;
  v.push_back(new vector<int>(5));
  v.push_back(new vector<int>(3));
  v.push_back(new vector<int>(4));

  transform(v.begin(), v.end(),
          ostream_iterator<int>(cout, " "),
          mem_fun(&vector<int>::size));
  cout << endl;
  // The output is "5 3 4"
}
```

Where Defined

The class const_mem_fun_t was not part of the HP implementation. According to the C++ standard it is declared in the header <functional>.

Template Parameters

R   The member function's return type.

X   The class whose member function the const_mem_fun_t invokes.

Model Of

Adaptable Unary Function (page 114).

---

9. The type R is permitted to be void.

Type Requirements

- R is Assignable or void.

- X is a class with at least one const member function that takes no arguments and that returns a value of type R.

Public Base Classes

unary_function<const X*, R>

Members

Some of const_mem_fun_t's members are not defined in the Adaptable Unary Function requirements but are specific to const_mem_fun_t. These special members are flagged with the symbol ✳.

> const_mem_fun_t::argument_type
> The argument type: const X*
> (Described in Adaptable Unary Function.)
>
> const_mem_fun_t::result_type
> The result type: R
> (Described in Adaptable Unary Function.)
>
> R const_mem_fun_t::operator(const X* x) const
> Function call operator. Invokes x->f(), where f is the member function that was passed to the constructor.
> (Described in Adaptable Unary Function.)

✳ **explicit const_mem_fun_t::const_mem_fun_t(R (X::*f)() const)**
   The constructor. Creates a const_mem_fun_t that calls the member function f.

✳ **template <class R, class X>**
   const_mem_fun_t<R, X> mem_fun(R (X::*f)() const)
   Helper function to create a const_mem_fun_t. If f is a value of type R (X::*) const, then mem_fun(f) is the same as const_mem_fun_t<R, X>(f).

15.7.6 const_mem_fun_ref_t

const_mem_fun_ref_t<R, X>

The class const_mem_fun_ref_t is an adaptor for member functions. If X is some class that has a member function
     R X::f() const
(that is, a const member function that takes no arguments and that returns a value of type R[10]), then an object of type const_mem_fun_ref_t<R, X> is a function object adaptor that makes it possible to call f() as if it were an ordinary function instead of a member function.

---

10. The type R is permitted to be void.

The const_mem_fun_ref_t<R, X>'s constructor takes a pointer to one of X's member functions. Then, like all function objects, the const_mem_fun_ref_t adaptor has an operator() that allows the const_mem_fun_ref_t to be invoked with ordinary function call syntax. In this case, const_mem_fun_ref_t's operator() takes an argument of type const X&.

If F is a const_mem_fun_ref_t that was constructed to use the member function X::f and if x is an object of type X, then the expression F(x) is equivalent to the expression x.f(). The difference is syntactic: F supports the interface of an Adaptable Unary Function.

As with many other function object adaptors, it is usually inconvenient to use const_mem_fun_ref_t's constructor directly. It is usually better to use the helper function mem_fun_ref instead.

Example

```
int main() {
  vector<vector<int> > v;
  v.push_back(vector<int>(2));
  v.push_back(vector<int>(7));
  v.push_back(vector<int>(3));

  transform(v.begin(), v.end(),
            ostream_iterator<int>(cout, " "),
            mem_fun_ref(&vector<int>::size));
  cout << endl;
  // The output is "2 7 3"
}
```

Where Defined

The class const_mem_fun_ref_t was not part of the HP implementation. According to the C++ standard it is declared in the header <functional>.

Template Parameters

R   The member function's return type.

X   The class whose member function the const_mem_fun_ref_t invokes.

Model Of

Adaptable Unary Function (page 114).

Type Requirements

* R is Assignable or void.
* X is a class with at least one const member function that takes no arguments and that returns a value of type R.

Public Base Classes

unary_function<X, R>

Members

Some of const_mem_fun_ref_t's members aren't defined by Adaptable Unary Function but are specific to const_mem_fun_ref_t. These special members are flagged with the symbol ✳.

> const_mem_fun_ref_t::argument_type
> The argument type: X
> (Described in Adaptable Unary Function.)

> const_mem_fun_ref_t::result_type
> The result type: R
> (Described in Adaptable Unary Function.)

> R const_mem_fun_ref_t::operator(const X& x) const
> Function call operator. Invokes x.f(), where f is the member function that was passed to the constructor.
> (Described in Adaptable Unary Function.)

✳ explicit const_mem_fun_ref_t::const_mem_fun_ref_t(R (X::*f)() const)
> The constructor. Creates a const_mem_fun_ref_t that calls the member function f.

✳ template <class R, class X>
const_mem_fun_ref_t<R, X> mem_fun_ref(R (X::*f)() const)
> Helper function to create a const_mem_fun_ref_t. If f is of type R (X::*) const, then mem_fun_ref(f) is the same as const_mem_fun_ref_t<R, X>(f).

15.7.7   const_mem_fun1_t

const_mem_fun1_t<R, X, A>

The class const_mem_fun1_t is an adaptor for member functions. If X is some class with a member function
    R X::f(A) const
(that is, a const member function that takes a single argument of type A and that returns a value of type R[11]), then a const_mem_fun1_t<R, X, A> is a function object adaptor that makes it possible to call f as if it were an ordinary function instead of a member function.

The constructor takes a pointer to one of X's member functions. Then, like all function objects, the const_mem_fun1_t adaptor has an operator() that allows the const_mem_fun1_t to be invoked with ordinary function call syntax. In this case, const_mem_fun1_t's operator() takes two arguments. The first is of type const X*, and the second is of type A.

If F is a const_mem_fun1_t that was constructed to use the member function X::f and if x is a pointer of type const X* and a is a value of type A, then the expression

---

11. The type R is permitted to be void.

F(x,a) is equivalent to the expression x->f(a). The difference is syntactic: F supports the interface of an Adaptable Binary Function.

As with many other function object adaptors, it is usually inconvenient to use const_mem_fun1_t's constructor directly. It is usually better to use the helper function mem_fun instead.

Example

```
struct B {
  virtual int f(int x) const = 0;
};

struct D : public B {
  int val;

  D(int x) : val(x) {}
  int f(int x) const { return val + x; }
};

int main() {
  vector<B*> v;
  v.push_back(new D(3));
  v.push_back(new D(4));
  v.push_back(new D(5));

  int A[3] = {7, 8, 9};
  transform(v.begin(), v.end(), A, ostream_iterator<int>(cout, " "),
            mem_fun(&B::f));
  cout << endl;
  // The output is "10 12 14"
}
```

Where Defined

The class const_mem_fun1_t was not part of the HP implementation. According to the C++ standard, it is declared in the header <functional>.

Template Parameters

R	The member function's return type.
X	The class whose member function the const_mem_fun1_t invokes.
A	The member function's argument type.

Model Of

Adaptable Binary Function (page 115).

Type Requirements

- R is Assignable or void.
- X is a class with at least one const member function that takes a single argument of type A and that returns a value of type R.
- A is Assignable.

Public Base Classes

binary_function<const X*, A, R>

Members

Some of const_mem_fun1_t's members are not defined in the Adaptable Binary Function requirements but are specific to const_mem_fun1_t. These special members are flagged with the symbol ✳.

const_mem_fun1_t::first_argument_type
The first argument type: const X*
(Described in Adaptable Binary Function.)

const_mem_fun1_t::second_argument_type
The second argument type: A
(Described in Adaptable Binary Function.)

const_mem_fun1_t::result_type
The result type: R
(Described in Adaptable Binary Function.)

R const_mem_fun1_t::operator(const X* x, A a) const
Function call operator. Invokes x->f(a), where f is the member function that was passed to the constructor.
(Described in Adaptable Binary Function.)

✳ **explicit const_mem_fun1_t::const_mem_fun1_t(R (X::*f)(A) const)**
The constructor. Creates a const_mem_fun1_t that calls the member function f.

✳ **template <class R, class X, class A>**
   const_mem_fun1_t<R, X, A> mem_fun(R (X::*f)(A) const)
Helper function to create a const_mem_fun1_t. If f is of type R (X::*)(A) const, then mem_fun(f) is the same as const_mem_fun1_t<R, X, A>(f).

15.7.8   const_mem_fun1_ref_t

const_mem_fun1_ref_t<R, X, A>

The class const_mem_fun1_ref_t is an adaptor for member functions. If X is some class with a member function

    R X::f(A) const

(that is, a const member function that takes a single argument of type A and that returns a value of type R[12]), then a const_mem_fun1_ref_t<R, X, A> is a function

---

12. The type R is permitted to be void.

object adaptor that makes it possible to call f as if it were an ordinary function instead of a member function.

The constructor takes a pointer to one of X's member functions. Then, like all function objects, the const_mem_fun1_ref_t adaptor has an operator() that allows the const_mem_fun1_ref_t to be invoked with ordinary function call syntax. In this case, const_mem_fun1_ref_t's operator() takes two arguments. The first is of type const X&, and the second is of type A.

If F is a const_mem_fun1_ref_t that was constructed to use the member function X::f and if x is an object of type X and a is a value of type A, then the expression F(x,a) is equivalent to the expression x.f(a). The difference is syntactic: F supports the interface of an Adaptable Binary Function.

As with many other function object adaptors, it is usually inconvenient to use const_mem_fun1_ref_t's constructor explicitly. It is usually better to use the helper function mem_fun_ref instead.

Example

```
struct B {
  virtual int f(int x) const = 0;
};

struct D : public B {
  int val;

  D(int x) : val(x) {}
  int f(int x) const { return val + x; }
};

int main() {
  vector<D> v;
  v.push_back(D(3));
  v.push_back(D(4));
  v.push_back(D(5));

  int A[3] = {7, 8, 9};
  transform(v.begin(), v.end(), A,
            ostream_iterator<int>(cout, " "),
            mem_fun_ref(&B::f));
  cout << endl;
  // The output is "10 12 14"
}
```

Where Defined

The class const_mem_fun1_ref_t was not part of the HP implementation. According to the C++ standard, it is declared in the header <functional>.

Template Parameters

R   The member function's return type.

X   The class whose member function the const_mem_fun1_ref_t invokes.

A   The member function's argument type.

Model Of

Adaptable Binary Function (page 115).

Type Requirements

- R is Assignable or void.
- X is a class with at least one const member function that takes a single argument of type A and that returns a value of type R.
- A is Assignable.

Public Base Classes

binary_function<X, A, R>.

Members

Some of const_mem_fun1_ref_t's members are not defined in the Adaptable Binary Function requirements but are specific to const_mem_fun1_ref_t. These special members are flagged with the symbol ∗.

> **const_mem_fun1_ref_t::first_argument_type**
> The first argument type: X
> (Described in Adaptable Binary Function.)
>
> **const_mem_fun1_ref_t::second_argument_type**
> The second argument type: A
> (Described in Adaptable Binary Function.)
>
> **const_mem_fun1_ref_t::result_type**
> The result type: R
> (Described in Adaptable Binary Function.)
>
> **R const_mem_fun1_ref_t::operator(const X& x, A a) const**
> Function call operator. Invokes x.f(a), where f is the member function that was passed to the constructor.
> (Described in Adaptable Binary Function.)

∗ **explicit const_mem_fun1_ref_t::const_mem_fun1_ref_t(R (X::*f)(A) const)**
   The constructor. Creates a const_mem_fun1_ref_t that calls the member function f.

∗ **template <class R, class X, class A>**
   const_mem_fun1_ref_t<R, X, A> mem_fun_ref(R (X::*f)(A) const)
   Helper function to create a const_mem_fun1_ref_t. If f is of type R (X::*)(A) const
   then mem_fun_ref(f) is the same as const_mem_fun1_ref_t<R, X, A>(f).

15.8 Other Adaptors

15.8.1 binder1st

binder1st<BinaryFun>

The class binder1st is a function object adaptor. It is used to transform an Adaptable Binary Function into an Adaptable Unary Function. If f is an object of class binder1st<BinaryFun>, then f(x) returns F(c, x), where F is an object of class BinaryFun and where c is a constant. Both F and c are passed as arguments to binder1st's constructor.

Intuitively, you can think of this operation as "binding" the first argument of a binary function to a constant, thus yielding a unary function.

The easiest way to create a binder1st is not to call the constructor explicitly but instead to use the helper function bind1st.

Example

Find the first nonzero element in a list.

```
int main()
{
  list<int> L;
  for (int i = 0; i < 20; ++i)
    L.push_back(rand() % 3);

  list<int>::iterator first_nonzero =
          find_if(L.begin(), L.end(),
                  bind1st(not_equal_to<int>(), 0));
  assert(first_nonzero == L.end() || *first_nonzero != 0);
}
```

Where Defined

In the HP implementation, binder1st was defined in the header <function.h>. According to the C++ standard, it is declared in the header <functional>.

Template Parameters

BinaryFun   The type of the binary function whose first argument is to be bound to a constant.

Model Of

Adaptable Unary Function (page 114).

Type Requirements

• BinaryFun must be a model of Adaptable Binary Function.

Public Base Classes

```
unary_function<typename BinaryFun::second_argument_type,
               typename BinaryFun::result_type>
```

Members

Some of binder1st's members are not defined in the Adaptable Unary Function requirements but are specific to binder1st. These special members are flagged with the symbol ✳.

    binder1st::argument_type
    The argument type: BinaryFun::second_argument_type
    (Described in Adaptable Unary Function.)

    binder1st::result_type
    The result type: BinaryFun::result_type
    (Described in Adaptable Unary Function.)

    result_type binder1st::operator()(const argument_type& x) const
    Function call operator. Returns F(c, x), where F and c are the arguments with which
    the binder1st object was constructed.
    (Described in Adaptable Unary Function.)

✳ **binder1st::binder1st(const BinaryFun& F,**
                    typename BinaryFun::first_argument_type c)
    The constructor. Creates a binder1st such that calling it with the argument x (where x
    is of type BinaryFun::second_argument_type) corresponds to the call F(c, x).

✳ **template <class BinaryFun, class T>**
    binder1st<BinaryFun> bind1st(const BinaryFun& F, const T& c)
    Helper function to create a binder1st object. If F is an object of type BinaryFun, then
    bind1st(F, c) is equivalent to binder1st<BinaryFun>(F, c) but is more convenient.
    The type T must be convertible to BinaryFun's first argument type.

15.8.2 binder2nd

binder2nd<BinaryFun>

The class binder2nd is a function object adaptor. It is used to transform an Adaptable Binary Function into an Adaptable Unary Function. If f is an object of class binder2nd<BinaryFun>, then f(x) returns F(x, c), where F is an object of class BinaryFun and where c is a constant. Both F and c are passed as arguments to binder2nd's constructor.

Intuitively, you can think of this operation as "binding" the second argument of a binary function to a constant, thus yielding a unary function.

The easiest way to create a binder2nd is not to call the constructor explicitly but instead to use the helper function bind2nd.

Example

Find the first positive number in a list.

```
int main()
{
  list<int> L;
  for (int i = 0; i < 20; ++i)
    L.push_back(rand() % 4 - 3);

  list<int>::iterator first_positive =
          find_if(L.begin(), L.end(),
                  bind2nd(greater<int>(), 0));

  assert(first_positive == L.end() || *first_positive > 0);
}
```

Where Defined

In the HP implementation, binder2nd was defined in the header <function.h>. According to the C++ standard, it is declared in the header <functional>.

Template Parameters

BinaryFun   The type of the binary function whose second argument is to be bound to a constant.

Model Of

Adaptable Unary Function (page 114).

Type Requirements

- BinaryFun must be a model of Adaptable Binary Function.

Public Base Classes

unary_function<typename BinaryFun::first_argument_type,
               typename BinaryFun::result_type>

Members

Some of binder2nd's members are not defined in the Adaptable Unary Function requirements but are specific to binder2nd. These special members are flagged with the symbol *.

binder2nd::argument_type
The argument type: BinaryFun::first_argument_type
(Described in Adaptable Unary Function.)

binder2nd::result_type
The result type: BinaryFun::result_type
(Described in Adaptable Unary Function.)

```
result_type binder2nd::operator()(const argument_type& x) const
```
Function call operator. Returns F(x, c), where F and c are the arguments with which the binder2nd object was constructed.
(Described in Adaptable Unary Function.)

* `binder2nd::binder2nd(const BinaryFun& F,`
  `                typename BinaryFun::second_argument_type c)`
  The constructor. Creates a binder2nd such that calling it with the argument x (where x is of type BinaryFun::first_argument_type) corresponds to the call F(x, c).

* `template <class BinaryFun, class T>`
  `binder2nd<BinaryFun>`
  `bind2nd(const BinaryFun& F, const T& c)`
  Helper function to create a binder2nd object. If F is an object of type BinaryFun, then bind2nd(F, c) is equivalent to binder2nd<BinaryFun>(F, c) but is more convenient. The type T must be convertible to BinaryFun's second argument type.

15.8.3   pointer_to_unary_function

`pointer_to_unary_function<Arg, Result>`

The class pointer_to_unary_function is a function object adaptor that allows a function pointer Result (*f)(Arg) to be treated as an Adaptable Unary Function. If F is a pointer_to_unary_function<Arg, Result> that was initialized with an underlying function pointer f of type Result (*)(Arg), then F(x) calls the function f(x). The difference between f and F is that pointer_to_unary_function is an Adaptable Unary Function; that is, it defines the nested types argument_type and result_type.

A function pointer of type Result (*)(Arg) is already a perfectly good Unary Function object in its own right and may be passed to any STL algorithm that expects a Unary Function as an argument. You only need pointer_to_unary_function when you are using an ordinary function pointer in a context that requires an Adaptable Unary Function (for example, as the argument of a function object adaptor).

Most of the time, you should not write pointer_to_unary_function's constructor directly. It is almost always easier to use the ptr_fun helper function.

Example

Replace the numbers in a range with their absolute values, using the standard library function fabs. There is no need to use the pointer_to_unary_function adaptor for this, because we can just pass fabs directly to transform:

```
transform(first, last, first, fabs);
```

By contrast, the following code fragment replaces all of the numbers in a range with the negative of their absolute values. We're composing fabs and negate, which requires fabs to be treated as an Adaptable Unary Function, so we do need to use pointer_to_unary_function:

```
transform(first, last, first, compose1(negate<double>, ptr_fun(fabs)));
```

Where Defined

In the HP implementation, the pointer_to_unary_function adaptor was defined in
<function.h>. According to the C++ standard, it is declared in <functional>.

Template Parameters

Arg   The function object's argument type.

Result   The function object's result type.

Model of

Adaptable Unary Function (page 114).

Type Requirements

- Arg is Assignable.
- Result is Assignable.

Public Base Classes

unary_function<Arg, Result>

Members

Some of pointer_to_unary_function's members are not defined in the Adaptable
Unary Function requirements but are specific to pointer_to_unary_function. These
special members are flagged with the symbol ✳.

pointer_to_unary_function::argument_type
The argument type: Arg
(Described in Adaptable Unary Function.)

pointer_to_unary_function::result_type
The result type: Result
(Described in Adaptable Unary Function.)

Result pointer_to_unary_function::operator()(Arg) const
Function call operator.
(Described in Adaptable Unary Function.)

✳ **pointer_to_unary_function::pointer_to_unary_function(Result (*f)(Arg))**
The constructor. Creates a pointer_to_unary_function whose underlying function
pointer is f.

pointer_to_unary_function::pointer_to_unary_function()
The default constructor. Creates a pointer_to_unary_function whose underlying function pointer is a null pointer.

* `template <class Arg, class Result>`
`  pointer_to_unary_function<Arg, Result> ptr_fun(Result (*x)(Arg))`
Helper function to create a `pointer_to_unary_function`. If f is of type `Result (*)(Arg)`
then the expression `ptr_fun(f)` is equivalent to but more convenient than the explicit
constructor call `pointer_to_unary_function<Arg,Result>(f)`.

15.8.4 `pointer_to_binary_function`

`pointer_to_binary_function<Arg1, Arg2, Result>`

The class `pointer_to_binary_function` is a function object adaptor that allows a
function pointer `Result (*f)(Arg1, Arg2)` to be treated as an **Adaptable Binary
Function**. If F is an object of class
        `pointer_to_binary_function<Arg1, Arg2, Result>`
with underlying function pointer f of type `Result (*)(Arg1, Arg2)`, then F(x, y)
calls the function f(x, y). The only important difference between f and F is that
`pointer_to_binary_function` is an **Adaptable Binary Function**; that is, it defines the
nested types `first_argument_type`, `second_argument_type`, and `result_type`.

A function pointer of type `Result (*)(Arg1, Arg2)` is already a perfectly good
Binary Function object in its own right, and may be passed to any STL algorithm that
expects a Binary Function as an argument. The only time you ever need to use the
`pointer_to_binary_function` class is when you need to use an ordinary function in
a context that requires an **Adaptable Binary Function** (for example, as the argument
of a function object adaptor).

Most of the time, you should not write `pointer_to_binary_function`'s constructor directly. It is almost always easier to use the `ptr_fun` helper function.

Example

The following code fragment finds the first string in a list that is equal to "OK".
It uses the standard library function `strcmp` as an argument to a function object
adaptor, so it must first use a `pointer_to_binary_function` adaptor to give `strcmp`
the Adaptable Binary Function interface.

```
list<char*>::iterator item =
            find_if(L.begin(), L.end(),
                    not1(binder2nd(ptr_fun(strcmp), "OK")));
```

Where Defined

In the HP implementation, the `pointer_to_binary_function` adaptor was defined in
`<function.h>`. According to the C++ standard, it is declared in `<functional>`.

Template Parameters

Arg1   The function object's first argument type.

Arg2   The function object's second argument type.

Result   The function object's result type.

Model Of

Adaptable Binary Function (page 115).

Type Requirements

- `Arg1` is Assignable.
- `Arg2` is Assignable.
- `Result` is Assignable.

Public Base Classes

`binary_function<Arg1, Arg2, Result>`

Members

Some of `pointer_to_binary_function`'s members are not defined in the Adaptable Binary Function requirements but are specific to `pointer_to_binary_function`. These special members are flagged with the symbol ✳.

> `pointer_to_binary_function::first_argument_type`
> The first argument type: `Arg1`
> (Described in Adaptable Binary Function.)
>
> `pointer_to_binary_function::second_argument_type`
> The first argument type: `Arg2`
> (Described in Adaptable Binary Function.)
>
> `pointer_to_binary_function::result_type`
> The result type: `Result`
> (Described in Adaptable Binary Function.)
>
> `Result`
> `pointer_to_binary_function::operator()(Arg1, Arg2) const`
> Function call operator.
> (Described in Adaptable Binary Function.)

✳ `pointer_to_binary_function`
    `::pointer_to_binary_function(Result (*f)(Arg1, Arg2))`
The constructor. Creates a `pointer_to_binary_function` whose underlying function pointer is f.

> `pointer_to_binary_function::pointer_to_binary_function()`
> The default constructor. Creates a `pointer_to_unary_function` whose underlying function pointer is a null pointer.

✳ `template <class Arg1, Arg2, class Result>`
`pointer_to_binary_function<Arg1, Arg2, Result>`
`ptr_fun(Result (*x)(Arg1, Arg2))`
Helper function to create a `pointer_to_binary_function` object. If f is a function pointer of type `Result (*)(Arg1, Arg2)`, then `ptr_fun(f)` is equivalent to
    `pointer_to_binary_function<Arg1,Arg2,Result>(f)`
but more convenient.

15.8.5 unary_negate

unary_negate<Predicate>

The class unary_negate is an Adaptable Predicate that represents the logical negation of some other Adaptable Predicate. If f is an object of type unary_negate<Predicate> and pred is the function object that it was constructed with, then f(x) returns !pred(x). (Strictly speaking, unary_negate is redundant. It can be constructed using the function object logical_not and the adaptor unary_compose.)

There is rarely any reason to write unary_negate's constructor directly. It is almost always easier to use the helper function not1 instead. For example, rather than writing unary_negate<Pred>(f), you should usually write not1(f).

Example

Finds the first element in a list that does not lie in the range 1 . . . 10.

```
int main()
{
  list<int> L;
  generate_n(back_inserter(L), 10000, rand);

  list<int>::iterator i =
    find_if(L.begin(), L.end(),
            not1(compose2(logical_and<bool>(),
                          bind2nd(greater_equal<int>(), 1),
                          bind2nd(less_equal<int>(), 10))));
  assert(i == L.end() || !(*i >= 1 && *i <= 10));
}
```

Where Defined

In the HP implementation, unary_negate was defined in the header <function.h>. According to the C++ standard, it is declared in the header <functional>.

Template Parameters

Predicate   The type of function object that this unary_negate is the logical negation of.

Model Of

Adaptable Predicate (page 118).

Type Requirements

- Predicate is a model of Adaptable Predicate.

Public Base Classes

unary_function<typename Predicate::argument_type, bool>

Members

Some of unary_negate's members are not defined in the Adaptable Predicate requirements but are specific to unary_negate. These special members are flagged with the symbol ∗.

> **unary_negate::argument_type**
> The type of the argument: Predicate::argument_type
> (Described in Adaptable Predicate.)
>
> **unary_negate::result_type**
> The type of the result: bool
> (Described in Adaptable Predicate.)
>
> **bool unary_negate::operator()(argument_type) const**
> Function call operator.
> (Described in Adaptable Predicate.)

∗ **unary_negate::unary_negate(const Predicate&)**
The constructor. Creates a unary_negate<Predicate> whose underlying predicate is p.

∗ **template <class Predicate>**
unary_negate<Predicate> not1(const Predicate& p)
Helper function to create a unary_negate. If p is of type Predicate, then not1(p) is equivalent to unary_negate<Predicate>(p) but more convenient.

15.8.6 binary_negate

binary_negate<BinaryPredicate>

The class binary_negate is an Adaptable Binary Predicate that represents the logical negation of some other Adaptable Binary Predicate. If f is an object of class binary_negate<BinaryPredicate> and pred is the function object that it was constructed with, then f(x,y) returns !pred(x,y).

There is rarely any reason to use binary_negate's constructor directly. It is almost always easier to use the helper function not2 instead. Rather than writing binary_negate<Pred>(f), you should usually write not2(f).

Example

Find the first character in a string that is neither ' ' nor '\n'.

```
char str[MAXLEN];
...
const char* wptr = find_if(str, str + MAXLEN,
                    compose2(not2(logical_or<bool>()),
                             bind2nd(equal_to<char>(), ' '),
                             bind2nd(equal_to<char>(), '\n')));
assert(wptr == str + MAXLEN || !(*wptr == ' ' || *wptr == '\n'));
```

Where Defined

In the HP implementation, `binary_negate` was defined in the header `<function.h>`. According to the C++ standard, it is declared in the header `<functional>`.

Template Parameters

`BinaryPredicate`   The type of function object that this `binary_negate` is the logical negation of.

Model Of

Adaptable Binary Predicate (page 119).

Type Requirements

- `BinaryPredicate` is a model of Adaptable Binary Predicate.

Public Base Classes

```
binary_function<typename BinaryPredicate::first_argument_type,
                typename BinaryPredicate::second_argument_type,
                bool>
```

Members

Some of `binary_negate`'s members are not defined in the Adaptable Binary Predicate requirements but are specific to `binary_negate`. These special members are flagged with the symbol ∗.

`binary_negate::first_argument_type`
The type of the first argument: `BinaryPredicate::first_argument_type`
(Described in Adaptable Binary Predicate.)

`binary_negate::second_argument_type`
The type of the second argument: `BinaryPredicate::second_argument_type`
(Described in Adaptable Binary Predicate.)

`binary_negate::result_type`
The type of the result: `bool`
(Described in Adaptable Binary Predicate.)

`bool binary_negate::operator()(first_argument_type,`
`                               second_argument_type) const`
Function call operator.
(Described in Adaptable Binary Predicate.)

∗ `binary_negate::binary_negate(const BinaryPredicate&)`
The constructor. Creates a `binary_negate<BinaryPredicate>` whose underlying predicate is p.

✳ `template <class BinaryPredicate>`
  `binary_negate<BinaryPredicate> not2(const BinaryPredicate& p)`
  Helper function to create a `binary_negate`. If `p` is of type `BinaryPredicate`, then the
  expression `not2(p)` is equivalent to but more convenient than the explicit constructor
  call `binary_negate<BinaryPredicate>(p)`.

15.8.7 unary_compose

`unary_compose<Function1,Function2>`

The class `unary_compose` is a function object adaptor. If `f` and `g` are both Adaptable Unary Functions and if `g`'s return type is convertible to `f`'s argument type, then
`unary_compose` can be used to create a function object `h` such that `h(x)` is the same
as `f(g(x))`.

   This operation is called function composition, hence the name `unary_compose`.
It is often represented in mathematics as the operation $f \circ g$, yielding a function
such that $(f \circ g)(x)$ is $f(g(x))$. Function composition is a very important concept
in algebra. It is also important as a method of building software components out of
other components because it makes it possible to construct arbitrarily complicated
function objects out of simple ones.

   As with other function object adaptors, the easiest way to create a `unary_compose`
is to use the helper function `compose1`. It is possible to call `unary_compose`'s constructor directly, but there is usually no reason to do so.

Example

Calculates the negative of the sines of the elements in a `vector`, where the elements
are angles measured in degrees. Since the C library function `sin` takes its arguments
in radians, this operation is the composition of three operations: negation, sine, and
the conversion of degrees to radians.

```
vector<double> angles;
vector<double> sines;
const double pi = 3.14159265358979323846;
...
assert(sines.size() >= angles.size());
transform(angles.begin(), angles.end(), sines.begin(),
          compose1(negate<double>(),
                   compose1(ptr_fun(sin),
                            bind2nd(multiplies<double>(), pi / 180.))));
```

Where Defined

In the original HP STL `unary_compose` was defined in the header `<function.h>`, and
in the SGI STL it is defined in the header `<functional>`. It is not present in the C++
standard, but it is a common extension.

Template Parameters

Function1   The type of the first operand in the function composition operation. That is, if the composition is written f ∘ g, then Function1 is the type of the function object f.

Function2   The type of the second operand in the function composition operation. That is, if the composition is written f ∘ g, then Function2 is the type of the function object g.

Model Of

Adaptable Unary Function (page 114).

Type Requirements

- Function1 is a model of Adaptable Unary Function.
- Function2 is a model of Adaptable Unary Function.
- Function2::result_type is convertible to Function1::argument_type.

Public Base Classes

```
unary_function<typename Function2::argument_type,
               typename Function1::result_type>
```

Members

Some of unary_compose's members are not defined in the Adaptable Unary Function requirements but are specific to unary_compose. These special members are flagged with the symbol *.

   unary_compose::argument_type
   The type of the function object's argument: Function2::argument_type
   (Described in Adaptable Unary Function.)

   unary_compose::result_type
   The type of the function object's return value: Function1::result_type
   (Described in Adaptable Unary Function.)

* **unary_compose(const Function1& f, const Function2& g)**
   The constructor. Constructs a unary_compose object that represents the function object f ∘ g.

* **template <class Function1, class Function2>**
   unary_compose<Function1, Function2>
   compose1(const Function1& op1, const Function2& op2);
   Helper function to create a unary_compose object. If f and g are function objects of classes Function1 and Function2, respectively, then compose1(f, g) is equivalent to unary_compose<Function1, Function2>(f, g) but is more convenient.

15.8.8 binary_compose

binary_compose<BinaryFunction,UnaryFunction1, UnaryFunction2>

The class binary_compose is a function object adaptor. If f is an Adaptable Binary
Function and g1 and g2 are both Adaptable Unary Functions and if g1's and g2's return
types are convertible to f's argument types, then binary_compose can be used to
create a function object h such that h(x) is the same as f(g1(x), g2(x)).

Example

Finds the first element in a list that lies in the range $1 \dots 10$.

```
list<int> L;
...
list<int>::iterator in_range =
    find_if(L.begin(), L.end(),
            compose2(logical_and<bool>(),
                    bind2nd(greater_equal<int>(), 1),
                    bind2nd(less_equal<int>(), 10)));
assert(in_range == L.end() || (*in_range >= 1 && *in_range <= 10));
```

Computes $\sin(x)/(x + DBL\_MIN)$ for each element of a range.

```
transform(first, last, first,
          compose2(divides<double>(),
                  ptr_fun(sin),
                  bind2nd(plus<double>(), DBL_MIN)));
```

Where Defined

In the original HP STL binary_compose was defined in the header <function.h>, and
in the SGI STL it is defined in the header <functional>. It is not present in the C++
standard, but it is a common extension.

Template Parameters

BinaryFunction   The type of the "outer" function in the function composition oper-
                  ation. That is, if the binary_compose adaptor represents a function object
                  h such that h(x) == f(g1(x), g2(x)), then BinaryFunction is the type
                  of f.

UnaryFunction1   The type of the first "inner" function in the function composition
                  operation. That is, if the binary_compose adaptor represents a function
                  object h such that h(x) == f(g1(x), g2(x)), then UnaryFunction1 is
                  the type of g1.

UnaryFunction2   The type of the second "inner" function in the function composi-
                  tion operation. That is, if the binary_compose adaptor represents a func-
                  tion object h such that h(x) == f(g1(x), g2(x)), then UnaryFunction2
                  is the type of g2.

Model Of

Adaptable Binary Function (page 115).

Type Requirements

- BinaryFunction is a model of **Adaptable Binary Function**.
- UnaryFunction1 and UnaryFunction2 are models of **Adaptable Unary Function**.
- The argument types of UnaryFunction1 and UnaryFunction2 are convertible to each other.
- The result types of UnaryFunction1 and UnaryFunction2 are convertible, respectively, to the first and second argument types of BinaryFunction.

Public Base Classes

unary_function<UnaryFunction1::argument_type,
                BinaryFunction::result_type>

Members

Some of binary_compose's members are not defined in the Adaptable Binary Function requirements but are specific to binary_compose. These special members are flagged with the symbol ✳.

binary_compose::argument_type
The type of the function object's argument: UnaryFunction1::argument_type
(Described in Adaptable Unary Function.)

binary_compose::result_type
The type of the function object's argument: BinaryFunction::argument_type
(Described in Adaptable Unary Function.)

✳ **binary_compose(const BinaryFunction& f,**
          const UnaryFunction1& g1, const UnaryFunction1& g2)
The constructor. Constructs a binary_compose object such that calling that object with the argument x returns f(g1(x), g2(x)).

✳ **template <class BinaryFunction,**
          class UnaryFunction1, class UnaryFunction2>
binary_compose<BinaryFunction, UnaryFunction1, UnaryFunction2>
compose2(const BinaryFunction&,
          const UnaryFunction1&, const UnaryFunction2&)
Helper function to create a binary_compose object. If f, g1, and g2 are values of, respectively, types BinaryFunction, UnaryFunction1, and UnaryFunction2, then the expression compose2(f, g1, g2) is equivalent to the explicit constructor call
    binary_compose<BinaryFunction,
                UnaryFunction1, UnaryFunction2>(f, g1, g2)
but is more convenient.

Chapter 16

Container Classes

All of the STL's predefined container classes are models of **Sequence** or **Associative Container**. All of them are templates and can be instantiated to contain any type of object. You can, for example, use a vector<int> much as you would use an ordinary C array, except that the vector class eliminates the chore of managing dynamic memory allocation by hand.

In addition to sequences and associative containers, the STL defines three container *adaptors*. The container adaptors are not themselves containers. They are not models of the concept **Container**, and they deliberately provide only limited functionality.

16.1 Sequences

The C++ standard defines three sequences: vector (a simple data structure that provides fast random access to its elements), deque (a more complicated data structure that allows efficient insertion and removal of elements at both ends of the container), and list (a doubly linked list class). Because vector is the simplest of the STL container classes, it is usually the best choice.

There is no singly linked list class in the standard, but singly linked lists classes are a common extension. This chapter includes a description of the class slist, a singly linked list class from SGI's implementation of the STL.

16.1.1 vector

vector<T, Allocator>

A vector is a **Sequence** that supports random access to elements, constant time insertion and removal of elements at the end, and linear time insertion and removal of elements at the beginning or in the middle. The number of elements in a vector may vary dynamically. Memory management is automatic.

The vector class is the simplest of the STL container classes, and in many cases, it is the most efficient. It usually is implemented so that its elements are arranged in a contiguous block of storage, which makes it possible for a vector's iterators to be ordinary pointers.

There is an important distinction between a vector's *size* (the number of elements it contains) and its *capacity* (the number of elements that it has allocated memory for). It's easiest to understand this distinction in terms of a typical implementation. A vector manages a block of memory and constructs its elements at the beginning of that block. A vector typically has three member variables, all of which are pointers: start, finish, and end_of_storage. The vector's elements are in the range [start, finish), while the range [finish, end_of_storage) consists of uninitialized storage. The vector's size is finish − start, while its capacity is end_of_storage − start. The capacity is, of course, always greater than or equal to the size.

The distinction between size and capacity becomes particularly significant when you are inserting an element into a vector. If a vector's size is equal to its capacity (that is, if the vector has no uninitialized storage available), the only way to insert a new element is to actually increase the amount of memory that the vector has allocated.[1] This means allocating a new, larger block of memory, copying the contents of the old block to the new, and then deallocating the old block.

Reallocation can be a slow operation, and it also invalidates all of the iterators that point into the vector. You can control when reallocations happen by using the special member function reserve, which increases a vector's capacity without changing the vector's size or the value of any of its elements.

A vector's iterators are invalidated when its memory is reallocated. Additionally, inserting or deleting an element in the middle of a vector invalidates all iterators that point to elements following the insertion or deletion point. What this means is that you can prevent a vector's iterators from being invalidated if you use the member function reserve to preallocate as much memory as the vector will ever use and if all insertions and deletions are at the end of the vector.

Example

Create an empty vector and then insert a single element into it.

```
int main()
{
  vector<int> v;
  v.insert(v.begin(), 3);
  assert(v.size() == 1 && v.capacity() >= 1 && v[0] == 3);
}
```

Read numbers from the standard input using a vector for temporary storage, and then print the median of those numbers. (The vector expands to as large a size

---

1. When vector performs an automatic reallocation, it usually increases its capacity by a factor of two. It is crucial that the amount of growth is proportional to the current capacity rather than a fixed constant. In the former case, inserting a series of elements into a vector is a linear-time operation, and in the latter case, it would be quadratic.

as necessary.) This example relies on an important fact about `vector`'s constructor: A `vector` can be constructed from a range of any sort of Input Iterators—in this case, a range of type `istream_iterator`. This example also relies on the fact that `vector` provides Random Access Iterators.

```
int main()
{
  istream_iterator<double> first(cin);
  istream_iterator<double> end_of_file;
  vector<double> buf(first, end_of_file);

  nth_element(buf.begin(), buf.begin() + buf.size() / 2, buf.end());
  cout << "Median: " << buf[buf.size() / 2] << endl;
}
```

You can use the member function `reserve` to increase a `vector`'s capacity, but there is no member function for shrinking the capacity. That's because it's easy to shrink a `vector`'s capacity without any special member functions. This example shows one way to do it.

```
template <class T, class Allocator>
void shrink_to_fit(vector<T, Allocator>& v)
{
  vector<T, Allocator> tmp(v.begin(), v.end());
  tmp.swap(v);
}
```

Where Defined

In the HP implementation, `vector` was defined in the header `<vector.h>`. According to the C++ standard, it is declared in the header `<vector>`.

Template Parameters

T   The `vector`'s value type: the type of object stored in the `vector`.

Allocator The `vector`'s allocator, used for all internal memory management.
           Default: `allocator<T>`

Model Of

Random Access Container (page 135), Back Insertion Sequence (page 143).

Type Requirements

- T is a model of Assignable.
- Allocator is a model of Allocator whose value type is T.

Public Base Classes

None.

Members

Some of vector's members are not defined in the Random Access Container and Back Insertion Sequence requirements but are specific to vector. These special members are flagged with the symbol ✳.

vector::value_type
The type of object, T, stored in the vector.
(Described in Container.)

vector::pointer
Pointer to T.
(Described in Container.)

vector::const_pointer
Pointer to const T.
(Described in Container.)

vector::reference
Reference to T.
(Described in Container.)

vector::const_reference
Reference to const T.
(Described in Container.)

vector::size_type
An unsigned integral type, usually size_t.
(Described in Container.)

vector::difference_type
A signed integral type, usually ptrdiff_t.
(Described in Container.)

vector::iterator
The vector's iterator type, a mutable Random Access Iterator.
(Described in Container.)

vector::const_iterator
The vector's constant iterator type, a constant Random Access Iterator.
(Described in Container.)

vector::reverse_iterator
Iterator used to iterate backward through a vector, a mutable Random Access Iterator.
(Described in Reversible Container.)

vector::const_reverse_iterator
Iterator used to iterate backward through a vector, a constant Random Access Iterator.
(Described in Reversible Container.)

vector::begin()
Returns an iterator pointing to the beginning of the vector.
(Described in Container.)

vector::end()
Returns an iterator pointing to the end of the vector.
(Described in Container.)

vector::begin() const
Returns a const_iterator pointing to the beginning of the vector.
(Described in Container.)

`vector::end() const`
Returns a `const_iterator` pointing to the end of the `vector`.
(Described in Container.)

`vector::rbegin()`
Returns a `reverse_iterator` pointing to the beginning of the reversed `vector`.
(Described in Reversible Container.)

`vector::rend()`
Returns a `reverse_iterator` pointing to the end of the reversed `vector`.
(Described in Reversible Container.)

`vector::rbegin() const`
Returns a `const_reverse_iterator` pointing to the beginning of the reversed `vector`.
(Described in Reversible Container.)

`vector::rend() const`
Returns a `const_reverse_iterator` pointing to the end of the reversed `vector`.
(Described in Reversible Container.)

`size_type vector::size() const`
Returns the number of elements in the `vector`.
(Described in Container.)

`size_type vector::max_size() const`
Returns the `vector`'s maximum possible size.
(Described in Container.)

✳ `size_type vector::capacity() const`
Returns the `vector`'s capacity, that is, the number of elements for which memory has
been allocated. The capacity is always greater than or equal to the size. (The `vector`'s
memory is automatically reallocated if more than `capacity()` − `size()` elements are
inserted. Reallocation does not increase the `vector`'s size, nor does it change the values
of any of the `vector`'s elements. It does, however, increase `capacity()`, and it invalidates
any iterators that point into the `vector`.)

`bool vector::empty() const`
Returns `true` if and only if the `vector`'s size is zero.
(Described in Container.)

`reference vector::operator[](size_type n)`
Returns the nth element.
(Described in Random Access Container.)

`const_reference vector::operator[](size_type n) const`
Returns the nth element.
(Described in Random Access Container.)

`explicit vector::vector(const Allocator& A = Allocator())`
Creates an empty `vector` using the specified allocator.
(Described in Sequence.)

`explicit vector::vector(size_type n, const T& x = T(),`
`                        const Allocator& A = Allocator())`
Creates a `vector` with n copies of x, using the specified allocator.
(Described in Sequence.)

`vector::vector(const vector& v)`
The copy constructor.
(Described in Container.)

```
template <class InputIterator>
vector::vector(InputIterator f, InputIterator l,
               const Allocator& A = Allocator())
```
Creates a vector with a copy of the range [f,l), using the specified allocator.
(Described in Sequence.)

`vector::~vector()`
The destructor.
(Described in Container.)

`vector& operator=(const vector&)`
The assignment operator.
(Described in Container.)

✳ `allocator_type vector::get_allocator() const`
Returns a copy of the allocator with which the vector was constructed.

`void vector::swap(vector&)`
Swaps the contents of two vectors.
(Described in Container.)

✳ `void vector::reserve(size_type n)`
Increases the vector's capacity. If n is less than or equal to capacity(), this call has
no effect. Otherwise it is a request for allocation of additional memory. If the request is
successful, capacity() will be increased to a value greater than or equal to n and any
iterators pointing into the vector will be invalidated. The vector's size and the values
of its elements are unchanged.

The main reason for using reserve() is efficiency. If you know the capacity to which a
vector will eventually grow, it is usually more efficient to allocate that memory all at
once than to rely on the automatic reallocation scheme. Using reserve() also lets you
control when iterators are invalidated.

`reference vector::front()`
Returns the first element.
(Described in Sequence.)

`const_reference vector::front() const`
Returns the first element.
(Described in Sequence.)

`reference vector::back()`
Returns the last element.
(Described in Back Insertion Sequence.)

`const_reference vector::back() const`
Returns the last element.
(Described in Back Insertion Sequence.)

`void vector::push_back(const T& x)`
Appends x to the vector.
(Described in Back Insertion Sequence.)

`void vector::pop_back()`
Removes the last element.
(Described in Back Insertion Sequence.)

`iterator vector::insert(iterator pos, const T& x)`

Inserts x before pos. All iterators that point into the vector may be invalidated.
(Described in Sequence.)

```
template <class InputIterator>
void vector::insert(iterator pos, InputIterator f, InputIterator l)
```
Inserts the range [f, l) before pos. All iterators that point into the vector may be invalidated.
(Described in Sequence.)

```
void vector::insert(iterator pos, size_type n, const T& x)
```
Inserts n copies of x before pos. All iterators that point into the vector may be invalidated.
(Described in Sequence.)

```
iterator vector::erase(iterator pos)
```
Deletes the element pointed to by pos. Any iterators following pos are invalidated.
(Described in Sequence.)

```
iterator vector::erase(iterator first, iterator last)
```
Deletes the elements in the range [first, last). Any iterators following that range are invalidated.
(Described in Sequence.)

```
void vector::clear()
```
Erases all of the vector's elements.
(Described in Sequence.)

```
void vector::resize(size_type n, const T& t = T())
```
Changes the vector's size to n.
(Described in Sequence.)

✳ ```
template <class InputIterator>
void vector::assign(InputIterator first, InputIterator last)
```
Equivalent to erasing all of the elements in *this and replacing them with the elements in the range [first, last).

✳ ```
void vector::assign(size_type n, const T& x)
```
Equivalent to erasing all of the elements in *this and replacing them with n copies of x.

```
bool operator==(const vector&, const vector&)
```
Tests two vectors for equality.
(Described in Forward Container.)

```
bool operator<(const vector&, const vector&)
```
Lexicographical comparison.
(Described in Forward Container.)

16.1.2 list

list<T, Allocator>

A list is a doubly linked list, where every element has a predecessor and a successor. That is, it is a Sequence that supports both forward and backward traversal, as well as (amortized) constant time insertion and removal of elements at the beginning, at the end, or in the middle. It has the important property that insertion and splicing do not invalidate iterators to list elements and that even deletion invalidates only iterators that point to the elements that are actually deleted. The ordering of iterators may be changed (that is, a list<T>::iterator might have a different predecessor or successor after a list operation than it did before), but the iterators themselves will never be invalidated or made to point to different elements unless that invalidation or mutation is explicit.

A comparison with vector is instructive. Suppose that i is a valid iterator of type vector<T>::iterator. If an element is inserted or removed in a position that precedes i, then either i will be made to point to a different element than it did before or it will be invalidated completely. Suppose, on the other hand, that i and j are both iterators into a vector, and that there exists some integer n such that i == j + n. In that case, even if elements are inserted into the vector and i and j are made to point to different elements, the relation between the two iterators will still hold. A list is exactly the opposite. Iterators aren't invalidated and aren't made to point to different elements, but for list iterators, the predecessor/successor relationship is not invariant.

Typically, list is implemented as a set of nodes, each of which contains one of the list's elements and also points to a predecessor and a successor node.

Singly linked lists, which support only forward traversal, are also sometimes useful. If you do not need backward traversal, slist (page 448) may be more efficient than list.

Example

Create two empty lists, add elements to them, sort each list, and merge the two into a single list.

```
int main()
{
    list<int> L1;
    L1.push_back(0);
    L1.push_front(1);
    L1.insert(++L1.begin(), 3);

    list<int> L2;
    L2.push_back(4);
    L2.push_front(2);

    L1.sort();
    L2.sort();
    L1.merge(L2);
    assert(L1.size() == 5);
    assert(L2.size() == 0);
    L1.reverse();
    copy(L1.begin(), L1.end(), ostream_iterator<int>(cout, " "));
    cout << endl;
}
```

The output is:

```
4 3 2 1 0
```

Where Defined

In the HP implementation, `list` was defined in the header `<list.h>`. According to the C++ standard, it is declared in the header `<list>`.

Template Parameters

T   The `list`'s value type: the type of object stored in the `list`.

Allocator The `list`'s allocator, used for all internal memory management.
             Default: `allocator<T>`

Model Of

Reversible Container (page 133), Front Insertion Sequence (page 141), Back Insertion Sequence (page 143).

Type Requirements

- T is a model of **Assignable**.
- `Allocator` is a model of **Allocator** whose value type is T.

Public Base Classes

None.

Members

Some of `list`'s members are not defined in the Reversible Container, Front Insertion Sequence, or Back Insertion Sequence requirements but are specific to `list`. These special members are flagged with the symbol ✳.

`list::value_type`
The type of object, T, stored in the `list`.
(Described in Container.)

`list::pointer`
Pointer to T.
(Described in Container.)

`list::const_pointer`
Pointer to const T.
(Described in Container.)

`list::reference`
Reference to T.
(Described in Container.)

`list::const_reference`
Reference to const T.
(Described in Container.)

`list::size_type`
An unsigned integral type, usually `size_t`.
(Described in Container.)

`list::difference_type`
A signed integral type, usually `ptrdiff_t`.
(Described in Container.)

`list::iterator`
The `list`'s iterator type, a mutable Bidirectional Iterator.
(Described in Container.)

`list::const_iterator`
The `list`'s constant iterator type, a constant Bidirectional Iterator.
(Described in Container.)

`list::reverse_iterator`
Iterator used to iterate backward through a `list`, a mutable Bidirectional Iterator.
(Described in Reversible Container.)

`list::const_reverse_iterator`
Iterator used to iterate backward through a `list`, a constant Bidirectional Iterator.
(Described in Reversible Container.)

`list::begin()`
Returns an `iterator` pointing to the beginning of the `list`.
(Described in Container.)

`list::end()`
Returns an `iterator` pointing to the end of the `list`.
(Described in Container.)

`list::begin() const`
Returns a `const_iterator` pointing to the beginning of the `list`.
(Described in Container.)

`list::end() const`
Returns a `const_iterator` pointing to the end of the `list`.
(Described in Container.)

`list::rbegin()`
Returns a `reverse_iterator` pointing to the beginning of the reversed `list`.
(Described in Reversible Container.)

`list::rend()`
Returns a `reverse_iterator` pointing to the end of the reversed `list`.
(Described in Reversible Container.)

`list::rbegin() const`
Returns a `const_reverse_iterator` pointing to the beginning of the reversed `list`.
(Described in Reversible Container.)

`list::rend() const`
Returns a `const_reverse_iterator` pointing to the end of the reversed `list`.
(Described in Reversible Container.)

`size_type list::size() const`
Returns the number of elements in the `list`. Note that size's runtime complexity is required only to be $\mathcal{O}(N)$. You should not assume that it is $\mathcal{O}(1)$.
(Described in Container.)

```
size_type list::max_size() const
```
Returns the list's maximum possible size.
(Described in Container.)

```
bool list::empty() const
```
Returns true if and only if the list's size is zero.
(Described in Container.)

```
explicit list::list(const Allocator& A = Allocator())
```
Creates an empty list, using the specified allocator.
(Described in Sequence.)

```
explicit list::list(size_type n, const T& x = T(),
                     const Allocator& A = Allocator())
```
Creates a list with n copies of x, using the specified allocator.
(Described in Sequence.)

```
list::list(const list& l)
```
The copy constructor.
(Described in Container.)

```
template <class InputIterator>
list::list(InputIterator f, InputIterator l,
           const Allocator& A = Allocator())
```
Creates a list with a copy of the range [f,l), using the specified allocator.
(Described in Sequence.)

```
list::~list()
```
The destructor.
(Described in Container.)

```
list& operator=(const list&)
```
The assignment operator.
(Described in Container.)

∗ `allocator_type list::get_allocator() const`
Returns a copy of the allocator with which the list was constructed.

```
void list::swap(list&)
```
Swaps the contents of two lists.
(Described in Container.)

```
reference list::front()
```
Returns the first element.
(Described in Sequence.)

```
const_reference list::front() const
```
Returns the first element.
(Described in Sequence.)

```
reference list::back()
```
Returns the last element.
(Described in Back Insertion Sequence.)

```
const_reference list::back() const
```
Returns the last element.
(Described in Back Insertion Sequence.)

```
void list::push_front(const T& t)
```
Inserts t at the beginning.
(Described in Front Insertion Sequence.)

void list::pop_front()
Removes the first element.
(Described in Front Insertion Sequence.)

void list::push_back(const T& t)
Inserts t at the end.
(Described in Front Insertion Sequence.)

void list::pop_back()
Removes the last element.
(Described in Front Insertion Sequence.)

iterator list::insert(iterator pos, const T& t)
Inserts x before pos. No iterators are invalidated.
(Described in Sequence.)

template <class InputIterator>
void list::insert(iterator pos, InputIterator f, InputIterator l)
Inserts the range [f,l) before pos. No iterators are invalidated.
(Described in Sequence.)

void list::insert(iterator pos, size_type n, const T& x)
Inserts n copies of x before pos. No iterators are invalidated.
(Described in Sequence.)

iterator list::erase(iterator pos)
Deletes the element pointed to by pos. No iterators other than pos are invalidated.
(Described in Sequence.)

iterator list::erase(iterator first, iterator last)
Deletes the elements in the range [first,last). No iterators are invalidated, except for
iterators pointing to the deleted elements themselves.
(Described in Sequence.)

void list::clear()
Erases all of the list's elements.
(Described in Sequence.)

void list::resize(size_type n, const T& t = T())
Changes the list's size to n.
(Described in Sequence.)

✳ **template <class InputIterator>**
void list::assign(InputIterator first, InputIterator last)
Equivalent to erasing all of the elements in *this and replacing them with the elements
in the range [first,last).

✳ **void list::assign(size_type n, const T& x)**
Equivalent to erasing all of the elements in *this and replacing them with n copies of x.

✳ **void list::splice(iterator pos, list& x)**
Removes all of x's elements and inserts them before pos. The iterator pos must be a valid
iterator in *this, and x must be a list that is distinct from *this. All iterators remain
valid, including those that point to elements of x. Complexity: $\mathcal{O}(1)$.

✳ **void list::splice(iterator pos, list& x, iterator i)**
Moves the element that i points to from x to *this, inserting it before pos. The iterator
pos must be a valid iterator in *this, and i must be a dereferenceable iterator in x. (The
lists *this and x are not required to be distinct.) All iterators remain valid, including

iterators that point to elements of x. If pos == i or pos == ++i, this function is a null operation. Complexity: $\mathcal{O}(1)$.

✳ **void list::splice(iterator pos, list& x, iterator f, iterator l)**
Moves the range [f,l) from x to *this, inserting it immediately before pos. The iterator pos must be a valid iterator in *this, and [first,last) must be a valid range in x. The lists *this and x are not required to be distinct, but pos may not be an iterator in the range [first,last). All iterators remain valid, including iterators that point to elements of x. Complexity: $\mathcal{O}(1)$.

✳ **void list::remove(const T& val)**
Removes all elements that compare equal to val. The relative order of elements that are not removed is unchanged, and iterators to elements that are not removed remain valid. This function is $\mathcal{O}(N)$. It performs exactly size() comparisons for equality.

✳ **template <class Predicate>**
void list::remove_if(Predicate p)
Removes all elements *i such that p(*i) is true. The relative order of elements that are not removed is unchanged, and iterators to elements that are not removed remain valid. This function is $\mathcal{O}(N)$. It performs exactly size() applications of p.

✳ **void list::unique()**
Removes all but the first element in every consecutive group of equal elements. The relative order of elements that are not removed is unchanged, and iterators pointing to elements that are not removed remain valid. This function is $\mathcal{O}(N)$. It performs exactly size() − 1 comparisons for equality.

✳ **template <class BinaryPredicate>**
void list::unique(BinaryPredicate p)
Removes all but the first element in every consecutive group of equivalent elements, where two elements *i and *j are considered equivalent if p(*i, *j) is true. The relative order of elements that are not removed is unchanged, and iterators pointing to elements that are not removed remain valid. This function is linear time. It performs exactly size() − 1 comparisons for equality.

✳ **void list::merge(list& x)**
Merges two sorted lists, removing all of x's elements and inserting them into *this. Both *this and x must be sorted according to operator<, and the two lists must be distinct. The merge is stable. If an element from *this is equivalent to one from x, then the element from *this will precede the one from x. All iterators pointing to elements in *this and x remain valid. This function is $\mathcal{O}(N)$: it performs at most size()+x.size()−1 comparisons.

✳ **template <class StrictWeakOrdering>**
void list::merge(list& x, StrictWeakOrdering Comp)
Merges two sorted lists, removing all of x's elements and inserting them into *this, where the ordering relation is defined by Comp. The comparison function Comp must be a Strict Weak Ordering whose argument type is T, and both *this and x must be sorted according to that ordering. The two lists x and *this must be distinct. The merge is stable. If an element from *this is equivalent to one from x, then the element from *this will precede the one from x. All iterators pointing to elements in *this and x remain valid. This function is $\mathcal{O}(N)$. It performs at most size() + x.size() − 1 applications of Comp.

✳ **void list::reverse()**
Reverses the order of elements in the list. All iterators remain valid and continue to point to the same elements. This function is linear time.

Note that there is a global algorithm reverse. If L is a list, then L.reverse() and reverse(L.begin(), L.end()) are both correct ways of reversing L. The difference is that L.reverse() preserves the value that each iterator into L points to but does not preserve the iterators' predecessor/successor relationships, while reverse(L.begin(), L.end()) does not preserve the value that each iterator points to but does preserve the iterators' predecessor/successor relationships. Additionally, the reverse algorithm uses T's assignment operator while the member function reverse does not.

✳ **void list::sort()**
Sorts *this according to operator<. The sort is stable. The relative order of equivalent elements is preserved. All iterators remain valid and continue to point to the same elements. The number of comparisons is approximately $N \log N$, where N is the list's size.

✳ **template <class StrictWeakOrdering>**
void list::sort(StrictWeakOrdering Comp)
Sorts *this according to the Strict Weak Ordering Comp. The sort is stable. The relative order of equivalent elements is preserved. All iterators remain valid and continue to point to the same elements. The number of comparisons is approximately $N \log N$, where N is the list's size.

bool operator==(const list&, const list&)
Tests two lists for equality.
(Described in Forward Container.)

bool operator<(const list&, const list&)
Lexicographical comparison.
(Described in Forward Container.)

16.1.3   slist

slist<T, Allocator>

An slist is a singly linked list, where each element is linked to the next element but not to the previous element. That is, an slist is a Sequence that supports forward (but not backward) traversal, as well as (amortized) constant time insertion and removal of elements. Singly linked lists are familiar from such programming languages as Common LISP, Scheme, and ML. In some languages, almost all data structures are represented as singly linked lists.

Like list, slist has the important property that insertion and splicing do not invalidate iterators to list elements. Even erase invalidates only iterators pointing to the elements that are erased. The ordering of iterators may be changed (that is, an slist<T>::iterator might have a different predecessor or successor after a list operation than it did before), but the iterators themselves will not be invalidated or made to point to different elements unless that invalidation or mutation is explicit.

The main difference between slist and list is that list's iterators are Bidirectional Iterators, while slist's iterators are Forward Iterators. This means that slist is less versatile than list. Frequently, though, the extra functionality of Bidirectional Iterators turns out to be unnecessary. You should use slist unless you need that extra functionality because singly linked lists are smaller and faster than doubly linked lists.

There is, however, an important caveat. Like every other Sequence, slist defines the member functions insert and erase. Using these member functions carelessly can result in disastrously slow programs. The problem is that insert's first argument is an iterator pos, and it inserts the new element(s) *before* pos, not after. That means that insert must find the iterator that precedes pos. This is a constant-time operation for list since it has Bidirectional Iterators, but for slist it involves traversing the list all the way from the beginning. In other words, insert and erase are slow operations anywhere but near the beginning of the slist.

The slist class provides member functions insert_after and erase_after, which are constant time operations. You should use them instead of insert and erase whenever possible. If you find that insert_after and erase_after aren't adequate for your needs and that you often need to use insert and erase instead, you should probably use list instead of slist.

Example

Construct an slist and insert several elements into it.

```
int main() {
  slist<int> L;
  L.push_front(0);
  L.push_front(1);
  L.insert_after(L.begin(), 2);
  copy(L.begin(), L.end(),
      ostream_iterator<int>(cout, " "));
  cout << endl;
}
// The output is 1 2 0
```

It's often convenient to be able to build a list one element at a time. The most obvious way to do that if you're using an slist is to use push_front. (There is no push_back member function; slist is a model of Front Insertion Sequence but not of Back Insertion Sequence.) This has the consequence, of course, that the elements will appear in the slist in the opposite of the order you added them.

If you want the elements to appear in the same order as you added them, you have two options. First, you can just use the member function reverse after you're through adding elements. Second, you can use a trick that's very common in LISP programs. You can maintain an iterator that points to the last element. This example shows how to do that.

```
int main() {
  slist<double> L;
  double x = 1;
  L.push_front(x);
  slist<double>::iterator back = L.begin();

  while (x < 1000000.)
    back = L.insert_after(back, x *= 2);
```

```
        copy(L.begin(), L.end(),
            ostream_iterator<double>(cout, "\n"));
    }
    // The output is the powers of 2 from 1 through 1048576.
```

Where Defined

The class slist was not part of the HP implementation, and is not part of the C++ standard, but it is a common extension. In the SGI implementation it is defined in the header <slist>.

Template Parameters

T   The slist's value type: the type of object stored in the slist.

Allocator The slist's allocator, used for all internal memory management.
           Default: allocator<T>

Model Of

Front Insertion Sequence (page 141).

Type Requirements

- T is a model of **Assignable**.
- Allocator is a model of **Allocator** whose value type is T.

Public Base Classes

None.

Members

Some of slist's members are not defined in the Front Insertion Sequence requirements but are specific to slist. These special members are flagged with the symbol ✳.

slist::value_type
The type of object, T, stored in the slist.
(Described in Container.)

slist::pointer
Pointer to T.
(Described in Container.)

slist::const_pointer
Pointer to const T.
(Described in Container.)

slist::reference
Reference to T.
(Described in Container.)

slist::const_reference
Reference to const T.
(Described in Container.)

slist::size_type
An unsigned integral type, usually size_t.
(Described in Container.)

slist::difference_type
A signed integral type, usually ptrdiff_t.
(Described in Container.)

slist::iterator
The slist's iterator type, a mutable Forward Iterator.
(Described in Container.)

slist::const_iterator
The slist's constant iterator type, a constant Forward Iterator.
(Described in Container.)

slist::begin()
Returns an iterator pointing to the beginning of the slist.
(Described in Container.)

slist::end()
Returns an iterator pointing to the end of the slist.
(Described in Container.)

slist::begin() const
Returns a const_iterator pointing to the beginning of the slist.
(Described in Container.)

slist::end() const
Returns a const_iterator pointing to the end of the slist.
(Described in Container.)

size_type slist::size() const
Returns the number of elements in the slist. Note that size's runtime complexity is required only to be $\mathcal{O}(N)$. You should not assume that it is $\mathcal{O}(1)$.
(Described in Container.)

size_type slist::max_size() const
Returns the slist's maximum possible size.
(Described in Container.)

bool slist::empty() const
Returns true if and only if the slist's size is zero.
(Described in Container.)

explicit slist::slist(const Allocator& A = Allocator())
Creates an empty slist using the specified allocator.
(Described in Sequence.)

explicit slist::slist(size_type n, const T& x = T(),
                    const Allocator& A = Allocator())
Creates an slist with n copies of x, using the specified allocator.
(Described in Sequence.)

slist::slist(const slist& l)
The copy constructor.
(Described in Container.)

```
template <class InputIterator>
slist::slist(InputIterator f, InputIterator l,
              const Allocator& A = Allocator())
```
Creates an slist with a copy of the range [f,l), using the specified allocator.
(Described in Sequence.)

`slist::~slist()`
The destructor.
(Described in Container.)

`slist& operator=(const slist&)`
The assignment operator.
(Described in Container.)

✳ `allocator_type slist::get_allocator() const`
Returns a copy of the allocator with which the slist was constructed.

`void slist::swap(slist&)`
Swaps the contents of two slists.
(Described in Container.)

`reference slist::front()`
Returns the first element.
(Described in Sequence.)

`const_reference slist::front() const`
Returns the first element.
(Described in Sequence.)

`void slist::push_front(const T& t)`
Inserts t at the beginning.
(Described in Front Insertion Sequence.)

`void slist::pop_front()`
Removes the first element.
(Described in Front Insertion Sequence.)

✳ `iterator previous(iterator pos)`
Returns pos's predecessor. The argument pos must be a valid iterator in *this, and the return value is an iterator prev such that ++prev == pos. Complexity: linear in the number of iterators that precede pos.

This member function expresses the essential difference between list and slist. It is linear time rather than constant time because slist provides Forward Iterators rather than Bidirectional Iterators. Member functions such as insert and erase are linear time because they must call previous.

✳ `const_iterator previous(const_iterator pos)`
Return pos's predecessor. The argument pos must be a valid iterator in *this, and the return value is an iterator prev such that ++prev == pos. Complexity: linear in the number of iterators that precede pos.

`iterator slist::insert(iterator pos, const T& t)`
Inserts x before pos. No iterators are invalidated.
(Described in Sequence.)

```
template <class InputIterator>
void slist::insert(iterator pos, InputIterator f, InputIterator l)
```
Inserts the range [f,l) before pos. No iterators are invalidated.
(Described in Sequence.)

    void slist::insert(iterator pos, size_type n, const T& x)
Inserts n copies of x before pos. No iterators are invalidated.
(Described in Sequence.)

    iterator slist::erase(iterator pos)
Deletes the element pointed to by pos. No iterators other than pos are invalidated.
(Described in Sequence.)

    iterator slist::erase(iterator first, iterator last)
Deletes the elements in the range [first, last). No iterators are invalidated, except for
iterators pointing to the deleted elements themselves.
(Described in Sequence.)

    void slist::clear()
Erases all of the slist's elements.
(Described in Sequence.)

    void slist::resize(size_type n, const T& t = T())
Changes the slist's size to n.
(Described in Sequence.)

✳ **template <class InputIterator>**
    void slist::assign(InputIterator first, InputIterator last)
Equivalent to erasing all of the elements in *this and replacing them with the elements
in the range [first, last).

✳ **void slist::assign(size_type n, const T& x)**
Equivalent to erasing all of the elements in *this and replacing them with n copies of x.

✳ **iterator slist::insert_after(iterator pos, const T& t)**
Inserts x after pos, which must be a dereferenceable iterator in *this. (That is, pos may
not be end().) The return value is an iterator that points to the new element. No iterators
are invalidated. Complexity: $\mathcal{O}(1)$.

✳ **template <class InputIterator>**
    void slist::insert_after(iterator pos, InputIterator f, InputIterator l)
Inserts elements from the range [f, l) into *this, inserting them immediately *following*
pos. No iterators are invalidated. Complexity: linear in last − first.

✳ **void slist::insert_after(iterator pos, size_type n, const T& x)**
Inserts n copies of x immediately *following* pos. No iterators are invalidated. Complexity:
linear in n.

✳ **iterator slist::erase_after(iterator pos)**
Erases the element pointed to by the iterator *following* pos. Complexity: constant time.

✳ **iterator slist::erase_after(iterator before_first, iterator last)**
Erases all of the elements in the range [before_first + 1, last). Complexity: linear in
the number of elements in that range.

✳ **void slist::splice(iterator pos, slist& x)**
Removes all of x's elements and inserts them before pos. The iterator pos must be a valid
iterator in *this, and x must be an slist that is distinct from *this. All iterators remain
valid, including iterators that point to elements of x. Complexity: linear in the number
of elements before pos.

✳ **void slist::splice(iterator pos, slist& x, iterator i)**
Moves the element that i points to from x to *this, inserting it before pos. (The two
lists x and *this are not necessarily distinct.) The iterator pos must be a valid iterator in

*this, and i must be a dereferenceable iterator in x. All iterators remain valid, including iterators that point to elements of x. If pos == i or pos == ++i, this function is a null operation. Complexity: proportional to $c_1(\text{pos} - \text{begin}()) + c_2(\text{i} - \text{x.begin}())$, where c_1 and c_2 are unknown constants.

* **void slist::splice(iterator pos, slist& x, iterator f, iterator l)**
Moves the elements in [f,l) from x to *this, inserting them immediately before pos. The iterator pos must be a valid iterator in *this, and [f,l) must be a valid range in x. The two lists x and *this are not necessarily distinct, but pos may not be an iterator in the range [f,l). All iterators remain valid, including iterators that point to elements of x. Complexity: proportional to $c_1(\text{pos} - \text{begin}()) + c_2(\text{f} - \text{x.begin}()) + c_3(\text{l} - \text{f})$, where c_1, c_2, and c_3 are unknown constants.

* **void slist::splice_after(iterator pos, iterator prev)**
Moves the element *following* prev to *this, inserting it immediately *after* pos. The iterator pos must be a dereferenceable iterator in *this, and prev must be a dereferenceable iterator either in *this or in some other slist. (Since pos and prev are required to be dereferenceable, neither iterator may be end().) Complexity: $\mathcal{O}(1)$.

* **void slist::splice_after(iterator pos,**
                          iterator before_first, iterator before_last)
Moves the range [before_first + 1, before_last + 1) to *this, inserting it immediately *after* pos. The iterator pos must be a dereferenceable iterator in *this, and before_first and before_last must be dereferenceable iterators either in *this or in some other slist. Complexity: $\mathcal{O}(1)$.

* **void slist::remove(const T& val)**
Removes all elements that compare equal to val. The relative order of elements that are not removed is unchanged, and iterators pointing to elements that are not removed remain valid. This function is $\mathcal{O}(N)$. It performs exactly size() comparisons for equality.

* **template <class Predicate>**
void slist::remove_if(Predicate p)
Removes all elements *i such that p(*i) is true. The relative order of elements that are not removed is unchanged, and iterators pointing to elements that are not removed remain valid. This function is $\mathcal{O}(N)$. It performs exactly size() applications of p.

* **void slist::unique()**
Removes all but the first element in every consecutive group of equal elements. The relative order of elements that are not removed is unchanged, and iterators pointing to elements that are not removed remain valid. This function is $\mathcal{O}(N)$. It performs exactly size() − 1 comparisons for equality.

* **template <class BinaryPredicate>**
void slist::unique(BinaryPredicate p)
Removes all but the first element in every consecutive group of equivalent elements, where two elements *i and *j are considered equivalent if p(*i, *j) is true. The relative order of elements that are not removed is unchanged, and iterators pointing to elements that are not removed remain valid. This function is $\mathcal{O}(N)$. It performs exactly size() − 1 comparisons for equality.

* **void slist::merge(slist& x)**
Merges two sorted slists, removing all of x's elements and inserting them into *this. Both *this and x must be sorted according to operator<, and the two lists must be distinct. The merge is stable. If an element from *this is equivalent to one from x, the element from *this will precede the one from x. All iterators pointing to elements in

*this and x remain valid. This function is $\mathcal{O}(N)$. It performs at most size()+x.size() − 1 comparisons.

* `template <class StrictWeakOrdering>`
  `void slist::merge(slist& x, StrictWeakOrdering Comp)`
  Merges two sorted slists, removing all of x's elements and inserting them into *this, where the ordering relation is defined by Comp. The comparison function Comp must be a Strict Weak Ordering whose argument type is T, and both *this and x must be sorted according to that ordering. The two lists x and *this must be distinct. The merge is stable. If an element from *this is equivalent to one from x, then the element from *this will precede the one from x. All iterators pointing to elements in *this and x remain valid. This function is $\mathcal{O}(N)$. It performs at most size() + x.size() − 1 applications of Comp.

* `void slist::reverse()`
  Reverses the order of elements in the list. All iterators remain valid and continue to point to the same elements. This member function is $\mathcal{O}(N)$.

* `void slist::sort()`
  Sorts *this according to operator<. The sort is stable. The relative order of equivalent elements is preserved. All iterators remain valid and continue to point to the same elements. The number of comparisons is approximately $N \log N$, where N is the slist's size.

* `template <class StrictWeakOrdering>`
  `void slist::sort(StrictWeakOrdering Comp)`
  Sorts *this according to the Strict Weak Ordering Comp. The sort is stable. The relative order of equivalent elements is preserved. All iterators remain valid and continue to point to the same elements. The number of comparisons is approximately $N \log N$, where N is the slist's size.

  `bool operator==(const slist&, const slist&)`
  Tests two slists for equality.
  (Described in Forward Container.)

  `bool operator<(const slist&, const slist&)`
  Lexicographical comparison.
  (Described in Forward Container.)

16.1.4 deque

`deque<T, Allocator>`

A deque[2] is very much like a vector (page 435). Like vector, it is a Sequence that supports random access to elements, constant-time insertion and removal of elements at the end, and linear-time insertion and removal of elements at the beginning or in the middle.

The main way in which deque differs from vector is that deque also supports constant-time insertion and removal of elements at the beginning of the sequence. Inserting an element at the beginning or end of a deque takes amortized constant

---

2. The name deque is pronounced "deck," and it stands for "double-ended queue." Knuth [Knu97] reports that the name was coined by E. J. Schweppe. See Section 2.2.1 of Knuth for further information.

time, and inserting an element in the middle is linear in n, where n is the minimum of the distance to the beginning of the deque and to the end.

Another difference is that deque does not have any member functions that are analogous to vector's capacity() and reserve(), and it does not provide any of the guarantees on iterator validity that are associated with those member functions. Instead, it guarantees that inserting elements at the beginning or end of a deque doesn't cause any of the deque's existing elements to be copied. There is no operation for a deque that is analogous to vector's reallocation.

Generally, insert (including push_front and push_back) invalidates all iterators that point into the deque, erase in the middle invalidates all iterators that point into the deque, and erase at the beginning or end (including pop_front and pop_back) invalidates an iterator only if it points to the erased element.

Typically, deque is implemented as a dynamic segmented array. A deque usually consists of a header that points to a set of nodes, where each node contains a fixed number of elements stored contiguously. New nodes can be added when the deque grows.

The internal details of deque are unimportant. What is important for you to recognize is that deque is a far more complicated data structure than vector. Incrementing a deque iterator can't just be a simple pointer increment; it must also include at least one comparison. So, while vector and deque both provide **Random Access Iterators**, you should expect any operation on a deque iterator to be much slower than the same operation on a vector iterator.

Unless you need a specific feature that only deque provides (such as constant time insertion at both the beginning and the end), you should use vector instead. Similarly, sorting a deque is almost never a good idea. It is faster to copy the deque's elements into a vector, sort the vector, and then copy the elements back into the deque.

Example

```
int main()
{
  deque<int> Q;
  Q.push_back(3);
  Q.push_front(1);
  Q.insert(Q.begin() + 1, 2);
  Q[2] = 0;
  copy(Q.begin(), Q.end(), ostream_iterator<int>(cout, " "));
}
```

The output is:

```
1 2 0
```

Where Defined

In the HP implementation, deque was defined in the header <deque.h>. According to the C++ standard, it is declared in the header <deque>.

Template Parameters

T   The deque's value type: the type of object stored in the deque.

Allocator   The deque's allocator, used for all internal memory management.
            Default: allocator<T>

Type Requirements

- T is a model of Assignable.
- Allocator is a model of Allocator whose value type is T.

Model Of

Random Access Container (page 135), Front Insertion Sequence (page 141), Back Insertion Sequence (page 143).

Members

One of deque's member functions is not defined in the Random Access Container, Front Insertion Sequence, and Back Insertion Sequence requirements but is specific to deque. This special member function is flagged with the symbol $*$.

deque::value_type
The type of object, T, stored in the deque.
(Described in Container.)

deque::pointer
Pointer to T.
(Described in Container.)

deque::const_pointer
Pointer to const T.
(Described in Container.)

deque::reference
Reference to T.
(Described in Container.)

deque::const_reference
Reference to const T.
(Described in Container.)

deque::size_type
An unsigned integral type, usually size_t.
(Described in Container.)

deque::difference_type
A signed integral type, usually ptrdiff_t.
(Described in Container.)

deque::iterator
The deque's iterator type, a mutable Random Access Iterator.
(Described in Container.)

deque::const_iterator
The deque's constant iterator type, a constant Random Access Iterator.
(Described in Container.)

deque::reverse_iterator
Iterator used to iterate backward through a deque, a mutable Random Access Iterator.
(Described in Reversible Container.)

deque::const_reverse_iterator
Iterator used to iterate backward through a deque, a constant Random Access Iterator.
(Described in Reversible Container.)

deque::begin()
Returns an iterator pointing to the beginning of the deque.
(Described in Container.)

deque::end()
Returns an iterator pointing to the end of the deque.
(Described in Container.)

deque::begin() const
Returns a const_iterator pointing to the beginning of the deque.
(Described in Container.)

deque::end() const
Returns a const_iterator pointing to the end of the deque.
(Described in Container.)

deque::rbegin()
Returns a reverse_iterator pointing to the beginning of the reversed deque.
(Described in Reversible Container.)

deque::rend()
Returns a reverse_iterator pointing to the end of the reversed deque.
(Described in Reversible Container.)

deque::rbegin() const
Returns a const_reverse_iterator pointing to the beginning of the reversed deque.
(Described in Reversible Container.)

deque::rend() const
Returns a const_reverse_iterator pointing to the end of the reversed deque.
(Described in Reversible Container.)

size_type deque::size() const
Returns the number of elements in the deque.
(Described in Container.)

size_type deque::max_size() const
Returns the deque's maximum possible size.
(Described in Container.)

bool deque::empty() const
Returns true if and only if the deque's size is zero.
(Described in Container.)

reference deque::operator[](size_type n)
Returns the nth element.
(Described in Random Access Container.)

```
const_reference deque::operator[](size_type n) const
```
Returns the nth element.
(Described in Random Access Container.)

```
explicit deque::deque(const Allocator& A = Allocator())
```
Creates an empty deque using the specified allocator.
(Described in Sequence.)

```
explicit deque::deque(size_type n, const T& x = T(),
                      const Allocator& A = Allocator())
```
Creates a deque with n copies of x, using the specified allocator.
(Described in Sequence.)

```
deque::deque(const deque& d)
```
The copy constructor.
(Described in Container.)

```
template <class InputIterator>
deque::deque(InputIterator f, InputIterator l,
             const Allocator& A = Allocator())
```
Creates a deque with a copy of the range [f,l), using the specified allocator.
(Described in Sequence.)

```
deque::~deque()
```
The destructor.
(Described in Container.)

```
deque& operator=(const deque&)
```
The assignment operator.
(Described in Container.)

❋ `allocator_type deque::get_allocator() const`
Returns a copy of the allocator with which the deque was constructed.

```
void deque::swap(deque&)
```
Swaps the contents of two deques.
(Described in Container.)

```
reference deque::front()
```
Returns the first element.
(Described in Sequence.)

```
const_reference deque::front() const
```
Returns the first element.
(Described in Sequence.)

```
reference deque::back()
```
Returns the last element.
(Described in Back Insertion Sequence.)

```
const_reference deque::back() const
```
Returns the last element.
(Described in Back Insertion Sequence.)

```
void deque::push_front(const T& t)
```
Inserts t at the beginning of the deque.
(Described in Front Insertion Sequence.)

```
void deque::pop_front()
```
Removes the first element.
(Described in Front Insertion Sequence.)

```
void deque::push_back(const T& t)
```
Appends t to the deque.
(Described in Back Insertion Sequence.)

```
void deque::pop_back()
```
Removes the last element.
(Described in Back Insertion Sequence.)

```
iterator deque::insert(iterator pos, const T& t)
```
Inserts x before pos.
(Described in Sequence.)

```
template <class InputIterator>
void deque::insert(iterator pos, InputIterator f, InputIterator l)
```
Inserts the range [f,l) before pos.
(Described in Sequence.)

```
void deque::insert(iterator pos, size_type n, const T& x)
```
Inserts n copies of x before pos.
(Described in Sequence.)

```
iterator deque::erase(iterator pos)
```
Deletes the element pointed to by pos.
(Described in Sequence.)

```
iterator deque::erase(iterator first, iterator last)
```
Deletes the elements in the range [first,last).
(Described in Sequence.)

```
void deque::clear()
```
Erases all of the deque's elements.
(Described in Sequence.)

```
void deque::resize(size_type n, const T& t = T())
```
Changes the deque's size to n.
(Described in Sequence.)

✳ ```
template <class InputIterator>
void deque::assign(InputIterator first, InputIterator last)
```
Equivalent to erasing all of the elements in *this and replacing them with the elements in the range [first,last).

✳ ```
void deque::assign(size_type n, const T& x)
```
Equivalent to erasing all of the elements in *this and replacing them with n copies of x.

```
bool operator==(const deque&, const deque&)
```
Tests two deques for equality.
(Described in Forward Container.)

```
bool operator<(const deque&, const deque&)
```
Lexicographical comparison.
(Described in Forward Container.)

16.2   Associative Containers

There are four Associative Container classes in the C++ standard: set, map, multiset, and multimap. All four of these classes are models of Sorted Associative Container.

The standard does not include any Hashed Associative Containers, but hash tables are a common extension. One early version of STL hash tables was written by Javier Barreiro and David Musser, and another was written by Bob Fraley. These versions were documented in "Hash Tables for the Standard Template Library" [BFM95].

At present, the most widely used version of STL hash tables is the one that is included in SGI's implementation of the STL. This chapter documents the four Sorted Associated Containers defined in the C++ standard as well as the four Hashed Associative Containers from the SGI STL.

16.2.1 set

```
set<Key, Compare, Allocator>
```

A set is a Sorted Associative Container that stores objects of type Key. It is a Simple Associative Container, meaning that its value type, as well as its key type, is Key. It is also a Unique Associative Container, meaning that no two elements are the same.

Since set is a Sorted Associative Container, its elements are always sorted in ascending order. The template parameter Compare defines the ordering relation.

The classes set and multiset are particularly well suited to the generic set algorithms (set_union, set_intersection, etc.) The reason for this is twofold. First, the set algorithms require their arguments to be sorted ranges, and the Sorted Associative Container requirements ensure that set and multiset always satisfy that constraint. Second, the output range of these algorithms is also always sorted, and inserting a sorted range into a set or multiset is a fast operation. The Sorted Associative Container requirements guarantee that inserting a range takes only linear time if the range is already sorted. The insert_iterator adaptor makes it especially convenient to insert the output of one of these algorithms into a set.

Like list (page 441), set has the important property that inserting a new element does not invalidate iterators that point to existing elements. Erasing an element from a set does not invalidate any iterators either, except, of course, for iterators that actually point to the element being erased.

Example

```
struct ltstr
{
  bool operator()(const char* s1, const char* s2) const
  {
    return strcmp(s1, s2) < 0;
  }
};

int main()
{
  const int N = 6;
  const char* a[N] = {"isomer", "ephemeral", "prosaic",
                      "nugatory", "artichoke", "serif"};
```

```
        const char* b[N] = {"flat", "this", "artichoke",
                            "frigate", "prosaic", "isomer"};

        set<const char*, ltstr> A(a, a + N);
        set<const char*, ltstr> B(b, b + N);
        set<const char*, ltstr> C;

        cout << "Set A: ";
        copy(A.begin(), A.end(), ostream_iterator<const char*>(cout, " "));
        cout << endl;
        cout << "Set B: ";
        copy(B.begin(), B.end(), ostream_iterator<const char*>(cout, " "));
        cout << endl;

        cout << "Union: ";
        set_union(A.begin(), A.end(), B.begin(), B.end(),
                  ostream_iterator<const char*>(cout, " "),
                  ltstr());
        cout << endl;

        cout << "Intersection: ";
        set_intersection(A.begin(), A.end(), B.begin(), B.end(),
                         ostream_iterator<const char*>(cout, " "),
                         ltstr());
        cout << endl;

        set_difference(A.begin(), A.end(), B.begin(), B.end(),
                       inserter(C, C.begin()),
                       ltstr());
        cout << "Set C (difference of A and B): ";
        copy(C.begin(), C.end(), ostream_iterator<const char*>(cout, " "));
        cout << endl;
    }
```

Where Defined

In the HP implementation, set was defined in the header <set.h>. According to the C++ standard, it is declared in the header <set>.

Template Parameters

Key   The set's key type and value type. This is also defined as set::key_type and as set::value_type.

Compare   The key comparison function, a Strict Weak Ordering (page 119) whose argument type is key_type. It returns true if its first argument is less than its second argument, and false otherwise. This is also defined as set::key_compare and set::value_compare.
           Default: less<Key>

Allocator The set's allocator, used for all internal memory management.
Default: allocator<Key>

Model Of

Sorted Associative Container (page 156), Simple Associative Container (page 153), Unique Associative Container (page 149).

Type Requirements

- Key is a model of Assignable.
- Compare is a model of Strict Weak Ordering.
- Compare's value type is Key.
- Allocator is a model of Allocator whose value type is Key.

Public Base Classes

None.

Members

One of set's member functions is not defined in the Sorted Associative Container, Simple Associative Container, and Unique Associative Container requirements but is specific to set. This special member function is flagged with the symbol ∗.

set::value_type
The type of object stored in the set. The value type is Key.
(Described in Container.)

set::key_type
The type of the key associated with an object of type value_type. The key type is Key.
(Described in Associative Container.)

set::key_compare
Function object (a Strict Weak Ordering) that compares two keys for ordering.
(Described in Sorted Associative Container.)

set::value_compare
Function object that compares two values for ordering. (Same type as key_compare.)
(Described in Sorted Associative Container.)

set::pointer
Pointer to Key.
(Described in Container.)

set::const_pointer
Pointer to const Key.
(Described in Container.)

set::reference
Reference to Key.
(Described in Container.)

`set::const_reference`
Reference to const Key.
(Described in Container.)

`set::size_type`
An unsigned integral type, usually size_t.
(Described in Container.)

`set::difference_type`
A signed integral type, usually ptrdiff_t.
(Described in Container.)

`set::iterator`
The set's iterator type, a constant Bidirectional Iterator. (The class set has no mutable
iterator type. Elements may be inserted into or removed from a set, but they may never
be modified in place.)
(Described in Container.)

`set::const_iterator`
The set's constant iterator type, also a constant Bidirectional Iterator. (Possibly the same
type as iterator.)
(Described in Container.)

`set::reverse_iterator`
Iterator used to iterate backward through a set, a constant Bidirectional Iterator.
(Described in Reversible Container.)

`set::const_reverse_iterator`
Iterator used to iterate backward through a set, also a constant Bidirectional Iterator.
(Described in Reversible Container.)

`iterator set::begin() const`
Returns an iterator pointing to the beginning of the set.
(Described in Container.)

`iterator set::end() const`
Returns an iterator pointing to the end of the set.
(Described in Container.)

`reverse_iterator set::rbegin() const`
Returns a reverse_iterator pointing to the beginning of the reversed set.
(Described in Reversible Container.)

`reverse_iterator set::rend() const`
Returns a reverse_iterator pointing to the end of the reversed set.
(Described in Reversible Container.)

`size_type set::size() const`
Returns the number of elements in the set.
(Described in Container.)

`size_type set::max_size() const`
Returns the set's maximum possible size.
(Described in Container.)

`bool set::empty() const`
Returns true if and only if the set's size is zero.
(Described in Container.)

```
key_compare set::key_comp() const
```
Returns the key_compare object used by the set.
(Described in Sorted Associative Container.)

```
value_compare set::value_comp() const
```
Returns the value_compare object used by the set.
(Described in Sorted Associative Container.)

```
explicit set::set(const key_compare& comp = key_compare(),
                  const Allocator& A = Allocator())
```
Creates an empty set using the specified key comparison function object and the specified allocator.
(Described in Sorted Associative Container.)

```
template <class InputIterator>
set::set(InputIterator f, InputIterator l,
         const key_compare& comp = key_compare(),
         const Allocator& A = Allocator())
```
Creates a set with a copy of the range [f,l), using the specified key comparison function object and the specified allocator.
(Described in Sorted Associative Container.)

```
set::set(const set&)
```
The copy constructor.
(Described in Container.)

```
set::~set()
```
The destructor.
(Described in Container.)

```
set& set::operator=(const set&)
```
The assignment operator.
(Described in Container.)

* ```
  allocator_type set::get_allocator() const
  ```
  Returns a copy of the allocator with which the set was constructed.

```
void set::swap(set&)
```
Swaps the contents of two sets.
(Described in Container.)

```
pair<iterator, bool>
set::insert(const value_type& x)
```
Inserts x into the set. The second part of the return value is true if x was actually inserted and false if it was not inserted because it was already present.
(Described in Unique Associative Container.)

```
iterator set::insert(iterator pos, const value_type& x)
```
Inserts x into the set using pos as a hint as to where it will be inserted.
(Described in Sorted Associative Container.)

```
template <class InputIterator>
void set::insert(InputIterator f, InputIterator l)
```
Inserts the range [f,l) into the set.
(Described in Unique Associative Container.)

```
void set::erase(iterator pos)
```
Erases the element that pos points to.
(Described in Associative Container.)
```

```
size_type set::erase(const key_type& k)
```
Erases the element (if any) whose key is k. Return value is the number of elements erased—either zero or one.
(Described in Associative Container.)

```
void set::erase(iterator f, iterator 1)
```
Erases all elements in the range [f,1).
(Described in Associative Container.)

```
iterator set::find(const key_type& k) const
```
Finds the element whose key is k.
(Described in Associative Container.)

```
size_type set::count(const key_type& k) const
```
Returns the number of elements whose keys are k. The return value is either zero or one.
(Described in Associative Container.)

```
iterator set::lower_bound(const key_type& k) const
```
Finds the first element whose key is not less than k.
(Described in Sorted Associative Container.)

```
iterator set::upper_bound(const key_type& k) const
```
Finds the first element whose key is greater than k.
(Described in Sorted Associative Container.)

```
pair<iterator, iterator> set::equal_range(const key_type& k) const
```
Finds a range containing all elements whose keys are equivalent to k.
(Described in Sorted Associative Container.)

```
bool operator==(const set&, const set&)
```
Tests two sets for equality.
(Described in Forward Container.)

```
bool operator<(const set&, const set&)
```
Lexicographical comparison.
(Described in Forward Container.)

16.2.2 map

```
map<Key, T, Compare, Allocator>
```

A map is a Sorted Associative Container that associates objects of type Key with objects of type T. It is a Pair Associative Container, meaning that its value type is pair<const Key, T>. It is also a Unique Associative Container, meaning that no two elements have the same key.

The containers map and set are very similar. The main difference is that set is a Simple Associative Container (its value type is the same as its key type) while map is a Pair Associative Container (its value type is its key type plus some other associated piece of data.) One consequence of this difference is that set does not distinguish between iterator and const_iterator, but map does.

Like list (page 441), map has the important property that inserting a new element does not invalidate iterators that point to existing elements. Erasing an element from a map does not invalidate any iterators either, except, of course, for iterators that point to the element that is being erased.

Example

Because map associates objects of one type with objects of another, you can use a map as an associative array.

```cpp
struct ltstr
{
  bool operator()(const char* s1, const char* s2) const
  {
    return strcmp(s1, s2) < 0;
  }
};

int main()
{
  map<const char*, int, ltstr> days;

  days["january"] = 31;
  days["february"] = 28;
  days["march"] = 31;
  days["april"] = 30;
  days["may"] = 31;
  days["june"] = 30;
  days["july"] = 31;
  days["august"] = 31;
  days["september"] = 30;
  days["october"] = 31;
  days["november"] = 30;
  days["december"] = 31;

  cout << "june -> " << days["june"] << endl;
  map<const char*, int, ltstr>::iterator cur  = days.find("june");
  map<const char*, int, ltstr>::iterator prev = cur;
  map<const char*, int, ltstr>::iterator next = cur;
  ++next;
  --prev;
  cout << "Previous (in alphabetical order) is "
       << (*prev).first << endl;
  cout << "Next (in alphabetical order) is "
       << (*next).first << endl;
}
```

When you're using a map as an associative array, it's natural to index elements with operator[] because it looks so much like ordinary array indexing. It's important to remember that operator[] is just shorthand. There's nothing you can do with operator[] that you can't do with find and insert. In fact, the reverse is true: operator[] doesn't give you a way of finding out whether you're changing a preexisting value or inserting a new one, but find does.

```cpp
int main() {
  map<string, int> M;
```

```
    M.insert(make_pair("A", 17))
    M.insert(make_pair("B", 74));

    if (M.find("Z") == M.end())
      cout << "Not found: Z" << endl;

                    // Insert a new element into the map.
    pair<map<string, int>::iterator, bool> p = M.insert(make_pair("C", 4));
    assert(p.second);

                    // Try to insert a new element.  It doesn't
                    // get inserted because the map already has
                    // an element whose key is B.
    p = M.insert(make_pair("B", 3));
    assert(!p.second);

                    // Change the value associated with B.
    cout << "Value associated with B: " << p.first->second << endl;
    p.first->second = 7;
    cout << "Value associated with B: " << p.first->second << endl;
  }
```

Where Defined

In the HP implementation, map was defined in the header <map.h>. According to the C++ standard, it is declared in the header <map>.

Template Parameters

Key	The map's key type. This is also defined as map::key_type.
T	The map's mapped type. This is also defined as map::mapped_type.
Compare	The key comparison function, a Strict Weak Ordering (page 119) whose argument type is key_type. It returns true if its first argument is less than its second argument and false otherwise. This is also defined as the nested type map::key_compare. **Default**: less<Key>
Allocator	The map's allocator, used for all internal memory management. **Default**: allocator<pair<const Key, T> >

Model Of

Sorted Associative Container (page 156), Pair Associative Container (page 155), and Unique Associative Container (page 149).

Type Requirements

- Key is a model of Assignable.
- T is a model of Assignable.

- Compare is a model of **Strict Weak Ordering**.
- Compare's value type is Key.
- Allocator is a model of **Allocator** whose value type is the same as the map's value type.

Public Base Classes

None.

Members

Some of map's member functions are not defined in the Sorted Associative Container, Pair Associative Container, and Unique Associative Container requirements but is specific to map. These special member functions are flagged with the symbol ∗.

`map::key_type`
The map's key type, Key.
(Described in **Associative Container**.)

`map::mapped_type`
The type of object associated with a key. The mapped type is T.
(Described in **Pair Associative Container**.)

`map::value_type`
The type of object stored in the map. The value type is `pair<const Key, T>`.
(Described in **Pair Associative Container**.)

`map::key_compare`
Function object (a **Strict Weak Ordering**) that compares two keys for ordering.
(Described in **Sorted Associative Container**.)

`map::value_compare`
Function object that compares two values for ordering. (Equivalent to extracting the values' keys and then comparing the keys.)
(Described in **Sorted Associative Container**.)

`map::pointer`
Pointer to `map::value_type`.
(Described in **Container**.)

`map::const_pointer`
Pointer to const `map::value_type`.
(Described in **Container**.)

`map::reference`
Reference to `map::value_type`.
(Described in **Container**.)

`map::const_reference`
Reference to const `map::value_type`.
(Described in **Container**.)

`map::size_type`
An unsigned integral type, usually `size_t`.
(Described in **Container**.)

`map::difference_type`
A signed integral type, usually `ptrdiff_t`.
(Described in Container.)

`map::iterator`
The map's iterator type, a Bidirectional Iterator. Note that `map::iterator` isn't a mutable
iterator, since `map::value_type` is not Assignable. (If `i` is of type `map::iterator`, you
can't write `*i = x`.) It isn't a fully constant iterator, either, because it can be used to
modify the object that it points to. You can write `i->second = x`.
(Described in Container.)

`map::const_iterator`
The map's constant iterator type, a constant Bidirectional Iterator.
(Described in Container.)

`map::reverse_iterator`
Iterator used to iterate backward through a map.
(Described in Reversible Container.)

`map::const_reverse_iterator`
Constant iterator used to iterate backward through a map.
(Described in Reversible Container.)

`map::begin()`
Returns an `iterator` pointing to the beginning of the map.
(Described in Container.)

`map::end()`
Returns an `iterator` pointing to the end of the map.
(Described in Container.)

`map::begin() const`
Returns a `const_iterator` pointing to the beginning of the map.
(Described in Container.)

`map::end() const`
Returns a `const_iterator` pointing to the end of the map.
(Described in Container.)

`map::rbegin()`
Returns a `reverse_iterator` pointing to the beginning of the reversed map.
(Described in Reversible Container.)

`map::rend()`
Returns a `reverse_iterator` pointing to the end of the reversed map.
(Described in Reversible Container.)

`map::rbegin() const`
Returns a `const_reverse_iterator` pointing to the beginning of the reversed map.
(Described in Reversible Container.)

`map::rend() const`
Returns a `const_reverse_iterator` pointing to the end of the reversed map.
(Described in Reversible Container.)

`size_type map::size() const`
Returns the number of elements in the map.
(Described in Container.)

```
size_type map::max_size() const
```
Returns the map's maximum possible size.
(Described in Container.)

```
bool map::empty() const
```
Returns true if and only if the map's size is zero.
(Described in Container.)

```
key_compare map::key_comp() const
```
Returns the key_compare object used by the map.
(Described in Sorted Associative Container.)

```
value_compare map::value_comp() const
```
Returns the value_compare object used by the map.
(Described in Sorted Associative Container.)

```
explicit map::map(const key_compare& comp = key_compare(),
                  const Allocator& A = Allocator())
```
Creates an empty map using the specified key comparison function object and the specified allocator.
(Described in Sorted Associative Container.)

```
template <class InputIterator>
map::map(InputIterator f, InputIterator l,
         const key_compare& comp = key_compare(),
         const Allocator& A = Allocator())
```
Creates a map with a copy of the range [f,1), using the specified key comparison function object and the specified allocator.
(Described in Sorted Associative Container.)

```
map::map(const map&)
```
The copy constructor.
(Described in Container.)

```
map::~map()
```
The destructor.
(Described in Container.)

```
map& map::operator=(const map&)
```
The assignment operator.
(Described in Container.)

✳ `allocator_type map::get_allocator() const`
Returns a copy of the allocator with which the map was constructed.

```
void map::swap(map&)
```
Swaps the contents of two maps.
(Described in Container.)

```
pair<iterator, bool> map::insert(const value_type& x)
```
Inserts x into the map. The second part of the return value is true if x was inserted and false if it was not inserted because it was already present.
(Described in Unique Associative Container.)

```
iterator map::insert(iterator pos, const value_type& x)
```
Inserts x into the map, using pos as a hint as to where it will be inserted.
(Described in Sorted Associative Container.)

```
template <class InputIterator>
void map::insert(InputIterator f, InputIterator l)
```
Inserts the range [f,l) into the map.
(Described in Unique Associative Container.)

```
void map::erase(iterator pos)
```
Erases the element that pos points to.
(Described in Associative Container.)

```
size_type map::erase(const key_type& k)
```
Erases the element (if any) whose key is k. The return value is the number of elements erased—either zero or one.
(Described in Associative Container.)

```
void map::erase(iterator f, iterator l)
```
Erases all elements in the range [f,l).
(Described in Associative Container.)

```
iterator map::find(const key_type& k)
```
Finds the element whose key is k.
(Described in Associative Container.)

```
const_iterator map::find(const key_type& k) const
```
Finds the element whose key is k.
(Described in Associative Container.)

```
size_type map::count(const key_type& k) const
```
Returns the number of elements whose keys are k. The return value is either zero or one.
(Described in Associative Container.)

```
iterator map::lower_bound(const key_type& k)
```
Finds the first element whose key is not less than k.
(Described in Sorted Associative Container.)

```
const_iterator map::lower_bound(const key_type& k) const
```
Finds the first element whose key is not less than k.
(Described in Sorted Associative Container.)

```
iterator map::upper_bound(const key_type& k)
```
Finds the first element whose key is greater than k.
(Described in Sorted Associative Container.)

```
const_iterator map::upper_bound(const key_type& k) const
```
Finds the first element whose key is greater than k.
(Described in Sorted Associative Container.)

```
pair<iterator, iterator> map::equal_range(const key_type& k)
```
Finds a range containing all elements whose keys are equivalent to k.
(Described in Sorted Associative Container.)

```
pair<const_iterator, const_iterator> map::equal_range(const key_type& k)
```
Finds a range containing all elements whose keys are equal to k.
(Described in Sorted Associative Container.)

✳ `mapped_type& map::operator[](const key_type&)`
Since map is a Unique Associative Container, a map contains at most one element whose key is k. This member function returns a reference to the object that is associated with the key k. If the map does not already contain such an object, operator[] inserts the default object mapped_type(). (Note that the return type is mapped_type&, not value_type&.

That is, operator[] doesn't return a reference to one of the map's elements but rather a reference to part of an element.)

You might wonder why there is no const version of operator[]. It isn't an oversight. The question is what m[k] is supposed to do when m doesn't contain any element whose key is k. Since operator[] inserts a new element under those circumstances, it couldn't have been defined as const.

Strictly speaking, operator[] is redundant. It is nothing more than an abbreviation. The expression m[k] is equivalent to

```
m.insert(value_type(k, mapped_type())).first->second
```

bool operator==(const map&, const map&)
Tests two maps for equality.
(Described in Forward Container.)

bool operator<(const map&, const map&)
Lexicographical comparison.
(Described in Forward Container.)

16.2.3 multiset

multiset<Key, Compare, Allocator>

A multiset is a Sorted Associative Container that stores objects of type Key. It is a Simple Associative Container, meaning that its value type, as well as its key type, is Key. It is also a Multiple Associative Container, meaning that it may contain two or more identical elements. (This is the only way in which set and multiset differ.)

Since multiset is a Sorted Associative Container, its elements are always sorted in ascending order. The template parameter Compare defines the ordering relation.

The classes set and multiset are particularly well suited to the generic set algorithms (set_union, set_intersection, etc.) The reason for this is twofold. First, the set algorithms require their arguments to be sorted ranges, and the Sorted Associative Container requirements ensure that set and multiset always satisfy that constraint. Second, the output range of these algorithms is also always sorted, and inserting a sorted range into a set or multiset is a fast operation. The Sorted Associative Container requirements guarantee that inserting a range takes only linear time if the range is already sorted. The insert_iterator adaptor makes it especially convenient to insert the output of one of these algorithms into a multiset.

Like list (page 441), multiset has the important property that inserting a new element does not invalidate iterators that point to existing elements. Erasing an element from a multiset does not invalidate any iterators either, except, of course, for iterators that point to the element that is being erased.

Examples

```
int main()
{
  const int N = 10;
  int a[N] = {4, 1, 1, 1, 1, 1, 0, 5, 1, 0};
  int b[N] = {4, 4, 2, 4, 2, 4, 0, 1, 5, 5};
```

```
    multiset<int> A(a, a + N);
    multiset<int> B(b, b + N);
    multiset<int> C;

    cout << "Set A: ";
    copy(A.begin(), A.end(), ostream_iterator<int>(cout, " "));
    cout << endl;
    cout << "Set B: ";
    copy(B.begin(), B.end(), ostream_iterator<int>(cout, " "));
    cout << endl;

    cout << "Union: ";
    set_union(A.begin(), A.end(), B.begin(), B.end(),
            ostream_iterator<int>(cout, " "));
    cout << endl;

    cout << "Intersection: ";
    set_intersection(A.begin(), A.end(), B.begin(), B.end(),
                    ostream_iterator<int>(cout, " "));
    cout << endl;

    set_difference(A.begin(), A.end(), B.begin(), B.end(),
                inserter(C, C.begin()));
    cout << "Set C (difference of A and B): ";
    copy(C.begin(), C.end(), ostream_iterator<int>(cout, " "));
    cout << endl;
}
```

Where Defined

In the HP implementation, multiset was defined in the header <multiset.h>. According to the C++ standard, it is declared in the header <set>.

Template Parameters

Key   The multiset's key type and value type. This is also defined as the nested
           types multiset::key_type and multiset::value_type.

Compare   The key comparison function, a **Strict Weak Ordering** (page 119) whose
           argument type is key_type. It returns true if its first argument is less
           than its second argument and false otherwise. This is also defined as the
           nested types multiset::key_compare and multiset::value_compare.
           Default: less<Key>

Allocator The multiset's allocator, used for all internal memory management.
           Default: allocator<Key>

Model Of

Sorted Associative Container (page 156), Simple Associative Container (page 153), Multiple Associative Container (page 152).

Type Requirements

- Key is a model of Assignable.
- Compare is a model of Strict Weak Ordering.
- Compare's value type is Key.
- Allocator is a model of Allocator whose value type is Key.

Public Base Classes

None.

Members

One of multiset's members is not defined in the Sorted Associative Container, Simple Associative Container, and Multiple Associative Container requirements but is specific to multiset. This special member function is flagged with the symbol ∗.

multiset::value_type
The type of object stored in the multiset. The value type is Key.
(Described in Container.)

multiset::key_type
The type of the key associated with an object of type value_type. The key type is Key.
(Described in Associative Container.)

multiset::key_compare
Function object (a Strict Weak Ordering) that compares two keys for ordering.
(Described in Sorted Associative Container.)

multiset::value_compare
Function object that compares two values for ordering. (The same type as key_compare.)
(Described in Sorted Associative Container.)

multiset::pointer
Pointer to Key.
(Described in Container.)

multiset::const_pointer
Pointer to const Key.
(Described in Container.)

multiset::reference
Reference to Key.
(Described in Container.)

multiset::const_reference
Reference to const Key.
(Described in Container.)

`multiset::size_type`
An unsigned integral type, usually `size_t`.
(Described in Container.)

`multiset::difference_type`
A signed integral type, usually `ptrdiff_t`.
(Described in Container.)

`multiset::iterator`
The `multiset`'s iterator type, a constant Bidirectional Iterator. (The class `multiset` has no mutable iterator type. Elements may be inserted into or removed from a `multiset`, but they may never be modified in place.)
(Described in Container.)

`multiset::const_iterator`
The `multiset`'s constant iterator type, also a constant Bidirectional Iterator. Possibly the same type as `iterator`.
(Described in Container.)

`multiset::reverse_iterator`
Iterator used to iterate backward through a `multiset`, a constant Bidirectional Iterator.
(Described in Reversible Container.)

`multiset::const_reverse_iterator`
Iterator used to iterate backward through a `multiset`, also a constant Bidirectional Iterator.
(Described in Reversible Container.)

`iterator multiset::begin() const`
Returns an `iterator` pointing to the beginning of the `multiset`.
(Described in Container.)

`iterator multiset::end() const`
Returns an `iterator` pointing to the end of the `multiset`.
(Described in Container.)

`reverse_iterator multiset::rbegin() const`
Returns a `reverse_iterator` pointing to the beginning of the reversed `multiset`.
(Described in Reversible Container.)

`reverse_iterator multiset::rend() const`
Returns a `reverse_iterator` pointing to the end of the reversed `multiset`.
(Described in Reversible Container.)

`size_type multiset::size() const`
Returns the number of elements in the `multiset`.
(Described in Container.)

`size_type multiset::max_size() const`
Returns the `multiset`'s maximum possible size.
(Described in Container.)

`bool multiset::empty() const`
Returns `true` if and only if the `multiset`'s size is zero.
(Described in Container.)

`key_compare multiset::key_comp() const`
Returns the `key_compare` object used by the `multiset`.
(Described in Sorted Associative Container.)

`value_compare multiset::value_comp() const`
Returns the `value_compare` object used by the `multiset`.
(Described in Sorted Associative Container.)

`explicit multiset::multiset(const key_compare& comp = key_compare(),`
                       `const Allocator& A = Allocator())`
Creates an empty `multiset` using the specified key comparison function object and the specified allocator.
(Described in Sorted Associative Container.)

`template <class InputIterator>`
`multiset::multiset(InputIterator f, InputIterator l,`
               `const key_compare& comp = key_compare(),`
               `const Allocator& A = Allocator())`
Creates a `multiset` with a copy of the range [f,l), using the specified key comparison function object and the specified allocator.
(Described in Sorted Associative Container.)

`multiset::multiset(const multiset&)`
The copy constructor.
(Described in Container.)

`multiset::~multiset()`
The destructor.
(Described in Container.)

`multiset& multiset::operator=(const multiset&)`
The assignment operator.
(Described in Container.)

✳ `allocator_type multiset::get_allocator() const`
Returns a copy of the allocator with which the `multiset` was constructed.

`void multiset::swap(multiset&)`
Swaps the contents of two `multiset`s.
(Described in Container.)

`iterator multiset::insert(const value_type& x)`
Inserts x into the `multiset`.
(Described in Multiple Associative Container.)

`iterator multiset::insert(iterator pos, const value_type& x)`
Inserts x into the `multiset` using pos as a hint as to where it will be inserted.
(Described in Sorted Associative Container.)

`template <class InputIterator>`
`void multiset::insert(InputIterator f, InputIterator l)`
Inserts the range [f,l) into the `multiset`.
(Described in Multiple Associative Container.)

`void multiset::erase(iterator pos)`
Erases the element that pos points to.
(Described in Associative Container.)

`size_type multiset::erase(const key_type& k)`
Erases all elements whose keys are k. Return value is the number of elements erased.
(Described in Associative Container.)

```
void multiset::erase(iterator f, iterator l)
```
Erases all elements in the range [f,l).
(Described in Associative Container.)

```
iterator multiset::find(const key_type& k) const
```
Finds an element whose key is k.
(Described in Associative Container.)

```
size_type multiset::count(const key_type& k) const
```
Returns the number of elements whose keys are k.
(Described in Associative Container.)

```
iterator multiset::lower_bound(const key_type& k) const
```
Finds the first element whose key is not less than k.
(Described in Sorted Associative Container.)

```
iterator multiset::upper_bound(const key_type& k) const
```
Finds the first element whose key is greater than k.
(Described in Sorted Associative Container.)

```
pair<iterator, iterator> multiset::equal_range(const key_type& k) const
```
Finds a range containing all elements whose keys are equivalent to k.
(Described in Sorted Associative Container.)

```
bool operator==(const multiset&, const multiset&)
```
Tests two multisets for equality.
(Described in Forward Container.)

```
bool operator<(const multiset&, const multiset&)
```
Lexicographical comparison.
(Described in Forward Container.)

16.2.4 multimap

```
multimap<Key, T, Compare, Allocator>
```

A multimap is a Sorted Associative Container that associates objects of type Key
with objects of type T. It is a Pair Associative Container, meaning that its value type
is pair<const Key, T>. It is also a Multiple Associative Container, meaning that it
may contain two or more identical elements. (This is the only way in which map and
multimap differ.) That is, the multimap class doesn't map a value of type Key to *an*
object of type T, but rather to *one or more* objects of type T.

Since multimap is a Sorted Associative Container, its elements are always sorted
in ascending order. The template parameter Compare defines the ordering relation.

Like list (page 441), multimap has the important property that inserting a new
element does not invalidate iterators that point to existing elements. Erasing an element from a multimap does not invalidate any iterators either, except, of course, for
iterators that point to the element that is being erased.

Example

```
struct ltstr
{
  bool operator()(const char* s1, const char* s2) const {
```

```
          return strcmp(s1, s2) < 0;
      }
  };

  int main()
  {
    multimap<const char*, int, ltstr> m;

    m.insert(make_pair("a", 1));
    m.insert(make_pair("c", 2));
    m.insert(make_pair("b", 3));
    m.insert(make_pair("b", 4));
    m.insert(make_pair("a", 5));
    m.insert(make_pair("b", 6));

    cout << "Number of elements with key a: " << m.count("a") << endl;
    cout << "Number of elements with key b: " << m.count("b") << endl;
    cout << "Number of elements with key c: " << m.count("c") << endl;

    cout << "Elements in m: " << endl;
    for (multimap<const char*, int, ltstr>::iterator it = m.begin();
         it != m.end();
         ++it)
      cout << "  [" << (*it).first << ", " << (*it).second << "]" << endl;
  }
```

Where Defined

In the HP implementation, `multimap` was defined in the header `<multimap.h>`. According to the C++ standard, it is declared in the header `<map>`.

Template Parameters

Key   The `multimap`'s key type. Also defined as `multimap::key_type`.

T   The `multimap`'s mapped type. Also defined as `multimap::mapped_type`.

Compare   The key comparison function, a Strict Weak Ordering (page 119) whose argument type is `key_type`. It returns `true` if its first argument is less than its second argument and `false` otherwise. This is also defined as the nested type `multimap::key_compare`.
          Default: `less<Key>`.

Allocator The `multimap`'s allocator, used for all internal memory management.
          Default: `allocator<pair<const Key, T> >`

Model Of

Sorted Associative Container (page 156), Pair Associative Container (page 155), Multiple Associative Container (page 152).

Type Requirements

- Key is a model of Assignable.
- T is a model of Assignable.
- Compare is a model of Strict Weak Ordering.
- Compare's value type is Key.
- Allocator is a model of Allocator.
- Allocator's value type is the same as the multimap's value type.

Public Base Classes

None.

Members

One of multimap's member functions is not defined in the Sorted Associative Container, Pair Associative Container, and Multiple Associative Container requirements but is specific to multimap. This special member function is flagged with the symbol ✳.

multimap::key_type
The multimap's key type, Key.
(Described in Associative Container.)

multimap::mapped_type
The type of object associated with a key. The mapped type is T.
(Described in Pair Associative Container.)

multimap::value_type
The type of object stored in the multimap. The value type is pair<const Key, T>.
(Described in Pair Associative Container.)

multimap::key_compare
Function object (a Strict Weak Ordering) that compares two keys for ordering.
(Described in Sorted Associative Container.)

multimap::value_compare
Function object that compares two values for ordering. (Equivalent to extracting the values' keys and then comparing the keys.)
(Described in Sorted Associative Container.)

multimap::pointer
Pointer to multimap::value_type.
(Described in Container.)

multimap::const_pointer
Pointer to const multimap::value_type.
(Described in Container.)

multimap::reference
Reference to multimap::value_type.
(Described in Container.)

`multimap::const_reference`
Reference to const `multimap::value_type`.
(Described in Container.)

`multimap::size_type`
An unsigned integral type, usually `size_t`.
(Described in Container.)

`multimap::difference_type`
A signed integral type, usually `ptrdiff_t`.
(Described in Container.)

`multimap::iterator`
The `multimap`'s iterator type, a Bidirectional Iterator. Note that `multimap::iterator` isn't a mutable iterator, since `multimap::value_type` is not Assignable. (If `i` is of type `multimap::iterator`, you can't write `*i = x`.) It isn't a fully constant iterator, either, because it can be used to modify the object that it points to. You can write `i->second = x`. (Described in Container.)

`multimap::const_iterator`
The `multimap`'s constant iterator type, a constant Bidirectional Iterator.
(Described in Container.)

`multimap::reverse_iterator`
Iterator used to iterate backward through a `multimap`.
(Described in Reversible Container.)

`multimap::const_reverse_iterator`
Constant iterator used to iterate backward through a `multimap`.
(Described in Reversible Container.)

`multimap::begin()`
Returns an `iterator` pointing to the beginning of the `multimap`.
(Described in Container.)

`multimap::end()`
Returns an `iterator` pointing to the end of the `multimap`.
(Described in Container.)

`multimap::begin() const`
Returns a `const_iterator` pointing to the beginning of the `multimap`.
(Described in Container.)

`multimap::end() const`
Returns a `const_iterator` pointing to the end of the `multimap`.
(Described in Container.)

`multimap::rbegin()`
Returns a `reverse_iterator` pointing to the beginning of the reversed `multimap`.
(Described in Reversible Container.)

`multimap::rend()`
Returns a `reverse_iterator` pointing to the end of the reversed `multimap`.
(Described in Reversible Container.)

`multimap::rbegin() const`
Returns a `const_reverse_iterator` pointing to the beginning of the reversed `multimap`.
(Described in Reversible Container.)

`multimap::rend() const`
Returns a `const_reverse_iterator` pointing to the end of the reversed `multimap`.
(Described in Reversible Container.)

`size_type multimap::size() const`
Returns the number of elements in the `multimap`.
(Described in Container.)

`size_type multimap::max_size() const`
Returns the `multimap`'s maximum possible size.
(Described in Container.)

`bool multimap::empty() const`
Returns `true` if and only if the `multimap`'s size is zero.
(Described in Container.)

`key_compare multimap::key_comp() const`
Returns the `key_compare` object used by the `multimap`.
(Described in Sorted Associative Container.)

`value_compare multimap::value_comp() const`
Returns the `value_compare` object used by the `multimap`.
(Described in Sorted Associative Container.)

`explicit multimap::multimap(const key_compare& comp = key_compare(),`
`                            const Allocator& A = Allocator())`
Creates an empty `multimap` using the specified key comparison function object and the
specified allocator.
(Described in Sorted Associative Container.)

`template <class InputIterator>`
`multimap::multimap(InputIterator f, InputIterator l,`
`                   const key_compare& comp = key_compare(),`
`                   const Allocator& A = Allocator())`
Creates a `multimap` with a copy of the range [f,l), using the specified key comparison
function object and the specified allocator.
(Described in Sorted Associative Container.)

`multimap::multimap(const multimap&)`
The copy constructor.
(Described in Container.)

`multimap::~multimap()`
The destructor.
(Described in Container.)

`multimap& multimap::operator=(const multimap&)`
The assignment operator.
(Described in Container.)

✳ `allocator_type multimap::get_allocator() const`
Returns a copy of the allocator with which the `multimap` was constructed.

`void multimap::swap(multimap&)`
Swaps the contents of two `multimap`s.
(Described in Container.)

`iterator multimap::insert(const value_type& x)`
Inserts x into the `multimap`.
(Described in Unique Associative Container.)

```
iterator multimap::insert(iterator pos, const value_type& x)
```
Inserts x into the multimap using pos as a hint as to where it will be inserted.
(Described in Sorted Associative Container.)

```
template <class InputIterator>
void multimap::insert(InputIterator f, InputIterator l)
```
Inserts the range [f,l) into the multimap.
(Described in Multiple Associative Container.)

```
void multimap::erase(iterator pos)
```
Erases the element that pos points to.
(Described in Associative Container.)

```
size_type multimap::erase(const key_type& k)
```
Erases all elements whose keys are k. Return value is the number of elements erased.
(Described in Associative Container.)

```
void multimap::erase(iterator f, iterator l)
```
Erases all elements in the range [f,l).
(Described in Associative Container.)

```
iterator multimap::find(const key_type& k)
```
Finds an element whose key is k.
(Described in Associative Container.)

```
const_iterator multimap::find(const key_type& k) const
```
Finds an element whose key is k.
(Described in Associative Container.)

```
size_type multimap::count(const key_type& k) const
```
Returns the number of elements whose keys are k.
(Described in Associative Container.)

```
iterator multimap::lower_bound(const key_type& k)
```
Finds the first element whose key is not less than k.
(Described in Sorted Associative Container.)

```
const_iterator multimap::lower_bound(const key_type& k) const
```
Finds the first element whose key is not less than k.
(Described in Sorted Associative Container.)

```
iterator multimap::upper_bound(const key_type& k)
```
Finds the first element whose key is greater than k.
(Described in Sorted Associative Container.)

```
const_iterator multimap::upper_bound(const key_type& k) const
```
Finds the first element whose key is greater than k.
(Described in Sorted Associative Container.)

```
pair<iterator, iterator> multimap::equal_range(const key_type& k)
```
Finds a range containing all elements whose keys are equivalent to k.
(Described in Sorted Associative Container.)

```
pair<const_iterator, const_iterator>
multimap::equal_range(const key_type& k) const
```
Finds a range containing all elements whose keys are equivalent to k.
(Described in Sorted Associative Container.)

```
bool operator==(const multimap&, const multimap&)
```
Tests two multimaps for equality.
(Described in Forward Container.)

```
bool operator<(const multimap&, const multimap&)
```
Lexicographical comparison.
(Described in Forward Container.)

16.2.5 hash_set

hash_set<Key, HashFun, EqualKey, Allocator>

A hash_set is a Hashed Associative Container that stores objects of type Key. It is a
Simple Associative Container, meaning that its value type, as well as its key type, is
Key. It is also a Unique Associative Container, meaning that no two elements compare
equal using the Binary Predicate EqualKey.

The hash_set class is useful in applications where it is important to be able to
search for an element quickly. If it is important for the elements to be in a particular
order, however, then set (page 461) is more appropriate.

Example

```
struct eqstr
{
  bool operator()(const char* s1, const char* s2) const
  {
    return strcmp(s1, s2) == 0;
  }
};

void lookup(const hash_set<const char*, hash<const char*>, eqstr>& Set,
            const char* word)
{
  hash_set<const char*, hash<const char*>, eqstr>::const_iterator it
    = Set.find(word);
  cout << "  " << word << ": "
       << (it != Set.end() ? "present" : "not present")
       << endl;
}

int main()
{
  hash_set<const char*, hash<const char*>, eqstr> Set;
  Set.insert("kiwi");
  Set.insert("plum");
  Set.insert("apple");
  Set.insert("mango");
  Set.insert("apricot");
  Set.insert("banana");

  lookup(Set, "mango");
  lookup(Set, "apple");
  lookup(Set, "durian");
```

```
    // The output is:
    //   mango: present
    //   apple: present
    //   durian: not present
}
```

Where Defined

The hash_set class was not present in the original HP implementation, nor is it present in the C++ standard. In the SGI implementation, it is defined in the header <hash_set>.

Template Parameters

Key   The hash_set's key type and value type. This is also defined as the nested types hash_set::key_type and hash_set::value_type.

HashFun   The Hash Function used by the hash_set. This is also defined as the nested type hash_set::hasher.
           Default: hash<Key>

EqualKey   The hash_set's key equality function: a Binary Predicate used to determine whether two keys are the same. This is also defined as the nested type hash_set::key_equal.
           Default: equal_to<Key>

Allocator The hash_set's allocator, used for all internal memory management.
           Default: allocator<Key>

Model Of

Hashed Associative Container (page 161), Simple Associative Container (page 153), Unique Associative Container (page 149).

Type Requirements

- Key is a model of Assignable.
- HashFun is a model of Hash Function.
- HashFun's value type is Key.
- EqualKey is a model of BinaryPredicate.
- EqualKey is an equivalence relation.
- EqualKey's value type is Key.
- Allocator is a model of Allocator whose value type is Key.

Public Base Classes

None.

Members

One of `hash_set`'s member functions is not defined in the Hashed Associative Container, Simple Associative Container, and Unique Associative Container requirements but is specific to `hash_set`. This special member function is flagged with the symbol ✳.

`hash_set::value_type`
The type of object stored in the `hash_set`. The value type is Key.
(Described in Container.)

`hash_set::key_type`
The type of the key associated with an object of type `value_type`. The key type is Key.
(Described in Associative Container.)

`hash_set::hasher`
The `hash_set`'s Hash Function.
(Described in Hashed Associative Container.)

`hash_set::key_equal`
A Binary Predicate that compares keys for equality.
(Described in Hashed Associative Container.)

`hash_set::pointer`
Pointer to Key.
(Described in Container.)

`hash_set::const_pointer`
Pointer to const Key.
(Described in Container.)

`hash_set::reference`
Reference to Key.
(Described in Container.)

`hash_set::const_reference`
Reference to const Key.
(Described in Container.)

`hash_set::size_type`
An unsigned integral type, usually `size_t`.
(Described in Container.)

`hash_set::difference_type`
A signed integral type, usually `ptrdiff_t`.
(Described in Container.)

`hash_set::iterator`
The `hash_set`'s iterator type, a constant Forward Iterator. (The class `hash_set` has no mutable iterator type.)
(Described in Container.)

`hash_set::const_iterator`
The `hash_set`'s constant iterator type, also a constant Forward Iterator. (Possibly the same type as `iterator`.)
(Described in Container.)

`iterator hash_set::begin() const`
Returns an `iterator` pointing to the beginning of the `hash_set`.
(Described in Container.)

`iterator hash_set::end() const`
Returns an `iterator` pointing to the end of the `hash_set`.
(Described in Container.)

`size_type hash_set::size() const`
Returns the number of elements in the `hash_set`.
(Described in Container.)

`size_type hash_set::max_size() const`
Returns the `hash_set`'s maximum possible size.
(Described in Container.)

`bool hash_set::empty() const`
Returns `true` if and only if the `hash_set`'s size is zero.
(Described in Container.)

`size_type hash_set::bucket_count() const`
Returns the number of buckets in the hash table.
(Described in Hashed Associative Container.)

`void hash_set::resize(size_type n)`
Increases the bucket count to at least n.
(Described in Hashed Associative Container.)

`hasher hash_funct() const`
Returns the `hasher` object used by the `hash_set`.
(Described in Hashed Associative Container.)

`key_equal key_eq() const`
Returns the `key_equal` object used by the `hash_set`.
(Described in Hashed Associative Container.)

```
explicit hash_set::hash_set(size_type n = 0,
                    const hasher& h = hasher(),
                    const key_equal& k = key_equal(),
                    const Allocator& A = Allocator())
```
Creates an empty `hash_set` with at least n buckets, using the specified hash function, key equality function, and allocator.
(Described in Hashed Associative Container.)

```
template <class InputIterator>
hash_set::hash_set(InputIterator f, InputIterator l,
                size_type n = 0,
                const hasher& h = hasher(),
                const key_equal& k = key_equal(),
                const Allocator& A = Allocator())
```
Creates a `hash_set` with a copy of the range [f, l) and a bucket count of at least n, using the specified hash function, key equality function, and allocator.
(Described in Hashed Associative Container.)

`hash_set::hash_set(const hash_set&)`
The copy constructor.
(Described in Container.)

`hash_set::~hash_set()`
The destructor.
(Described in Container.)

`hash_set& hash_set::operator=(const hash_set&)`
The assignment operator.
(Described in Container.)

✳ `allocator_type hash_set::get_allocator() const`
Returns a copy of the allocator with which the hash_set was constructed.

`void hash_set::swap(hash_set&)`
Swaps the contents of two hash_set objects.
(Described in Container.)

`pair<iterator, bool> hash_set::insert(const value_type& x)`
Inserts x into the hash_set. The second part of the return value is true if x was inserted and false if it was not inserted because it was already present.
(Described in Unique Associative Container.)

`template <class InputIterator>`
`void hash_set::insert(InputIterator f, InputIterator l)`
Inserts the range [f,l) into the hash_set.
(Described in Unique Associative Container.)

`void hash_set::erase(iterator pos)`
Erases the element that pos points to.
(Described in Associative Container.)

`size_type hash_set::erase(const key_type& k)`
Erases the element (if any) whose key is k. The return value is the number of elements erased—either zero or one.
(Described in Associative Container.)

`void hash_set::erase(iterator f, iterator l)`
Erases all elements in the range [f,l).
(Described in Associative Container.)

`iterator hash_set::find(const key_type& k) const`
Finds the element whose key is k.
(Described in Associative Container.)

`size_type hash_set::count(const key_type& k) const`
Returns the number of elements whose keys are k. The return value is either zero or one.
(Described in Associative Container.)

`pair<iterator, iterator> hash_set::equal_range(const key_type& k) const`
Finds a range containing all elements whose keys are equal to k.
(Described in Associative Container.)

`bool operator==(const hash_set&, const hash_set&)`
Tests two hash_set objects for equality.
(Described in Forward Container.)

16.2.6 hash_map

`hash_map<Key, T, HashFun, EqualKey, Allocator>`

A hash_map is a Hashed Associative Container that associates objects of type Key with objects of type T. It is a Pair Associative Container, meaning that its value type is pair<const Key, T>. It is also a Unique Associative Container, meaning that no two elements have keys that compare equal using EqualKey.

Looking up an element in a hash_map by its key is efficient, so hash_map is useful for "dictionaries," or associative arrays, where an object of type Key is associated with an object of type T but where the order of elements is irrelevant. If it is important for the elements to be arranged in some particular order, however, map (page 466) is more appropriate.

Example

```
struct eqstr
{
  bool operator()(const char* s1, const char* s2) const
  {
    return strcmp(s1, s2) == 0;
  }
};

int main()
{
  hash_map<const char*, int, hash<const char*>, eqstr> days;

  days["january"] = 31;
  days["february"] = 28;
  days["march"] = 31;
  days["april"] = 30;
  days["may"] = 31;
  days["june"] = 30;
  days["july"] = 31;
  days["august"] = 31;
  days["september"] = 30;
  days["october"] = 31;
  days["november"] = 30;
  days["december"] = 31;

  cout << "september -> " << days["september"] << endl;
  cout << "april     -> " << days["april"] << endl;
  cout << "june      -> " << days["june"] << endl;
  cout << "november  -> " << days["november"] << endl;
}
```

Where Defined

The hash_map class was not present in the original HP implementation, nor is it present in the C++ standard. In the SGI implementation, it is defined in the header <hash_map>.

Template Parameters

Key   The hash_map's key type. Also defined as hash_map::key_type.

T   The hash_map's mapped type. Also defined as hash_map::mapped_type.

HashFun   The Hash Function used by the hash_map. This is also defined as the
            nested type hash_map::hasher.
            Default: hash<Key>

EqualKey   The hash_map's key equality function: a **Binary Predicate** used to deter-
            mine whether two keys are the same. This is also defined as the nested
            type hash_map::key_equal.
            Default: equal_to<Key>

Allocator   The hash_map's allocator, used for all internal memory management.
            Default: allocator<pair<const Key, T> >

Model Of

Hashed Associative Container (page 161), Pair Associative Container (page 155),
Unique Associative Container (page 149).

Type Requirements

- Key is a model of **Assignable**.
- T is a model of **Assignable**.
- HashFun is a model of **Hash Function**.
- HashFun's value type is Key.
- EqualKey is a model of **BinaryPredicate**.
- EqualKey is an equivalence relation.
- EqualKey's value type is Key.
- Allocator is a model of **Allocator**.
- Allocator's value type is the same as the hash_map's value type.

Public Base Classes

None.

Members

Some of hash_map's member functions are not defined in the Hashed Associative Container, Pair Associative Container, and Unique Associative Container requirements
but are specific to hash_map. These special member functions are flagged with the
symbol ✷.

hash_map::key_type
The hash_map's key type, Key.
(Described in Associative Container.)

`hash_map::mapped_type`
The type of object associated with a key. The mapped type is T.
(Described in Pair Associative Container.)

`hash_map::value_type`
The type of object stored in the hash_map. The value type is `pair<const Key, T>`.
(Described in Pair Associative Container.)

`hash_map::hasher`
The hash_map's Hash Function.
(Described in Hashed Associative Container.)

`hash_map::key_equal`
A Binary Predicate that compares keys for equality.
(Described in Hashed Associative Container.)

`hash_map::pointer`
Pointer to `hash_map::value_type`.
(Described in Container.)

`hash_map::const_pointer`
Pointer to const `hash_map::value_type`.
(Described in Container.)

`hash_map::reference`
Reference to `hash_map::value_type`.
(Described in Container.)

`hash_map::const_reference`
Reference to const `hash_map::value_type`.
(Described in Container.)

`hash_map::size_type`
An unsigned integral type, usually `size_t`.
(Described in Container.)

`hash_map::difference_type`
A signed integral type, usually `ptrdiff_t`.
(Described in Container.)

`hash_map::iterator`
The hash_map's iterator type, a Forward Iterator. Note that `hash_map::iterator` isn't
a mutable iterator, since `hash_map::value_type` isn't Assignable. (If i is an iterator of
type `hash_map::iterator`, you can't write `*i = x`.) It isn't a fully constant iterator, either,
because it can be used to modify the object that it points to. You can write `i->second = x`.
(Described in Container.)

`hash_map::const_iterator`
The hash_map's constant iterator type, a constant Forward Iterator.
(Described in Container.)

`iterator hash_map::begin()`
Returns an `iterator` pointing to the beginning of the hash_map.
(Described in Container.)

`iterator hash_map::end()`
Returns an `iterator` pointing to the end of the hash_map.
(Described in Container.)

`const_iterator hash_map::begin() const`
Returns a `const_iterator` pointing to the beginning of the `hash_map`.
(Described in Container.)

`const_iterator hash_map::end() const`
Returns a `const_iterator` pointing to the end of the `hash_map`.
(Described in Container.)

`size_type hash_map::size() const`
Returns the number of elements in the `hash_map`.
(Described in Container.)

`size_type hash_map::max_size() const`
Returns the `hash_map`'s maximum possible size.
(Described in Container.)

`bool hash_map::empty() const`
Returns `true` if and only if the `hash_map`'s size is zero.
(Described in Container.)

`size_type hash_map::bucket_count() const`
Returns the number of buckets in the hash table.
(Described in Hashed Associative Container.)

`void hash_map::resize(size_type n)`
Increases the bucket count to at least n.
(Described in Hashed Associative Container.)

`hasher hash_funct() const`
Returns the hasher object used by the `hash_map`.
(Described in Hashed Associative Container.)

`key_equal key_eq() const`
Returns the key_equal object used by the `hash_map`.
(Described in Hashed Associative Container.)

```
explicit hash_map::hash_map(size_type n = 0,
                    const hasher& h = hasher(),
                    const key_equal& k = key_equal(),
                    const Allocator& A = Allocator())
```
Creates an empty `hash_map` with at least n buckets, using the specified hash function, key equality function, and allocator.
(Described in Hashed Associative Container.)

```
template <class InputIterator>
hash_map::hash_map(InputIterator f, InputIterator l,
                    size_type n = 0,
                    const hasher& h = hasher(),
                    const key_equal& k = key_equal(),
                    const Allocator& A = Allocator())
```
Creates a `hash_map` with a copy of the range [f, l) and a bucket count of at least n, using the specified hash function, key equality function, and allocator.
(Described in Hashed Associative Container.)

`hash_map::hash_map(const hash_map&)`
The copy constructor.
(Described in Container.)

`hash_map::~hash_map()`
The destructor.
(Described in Container.)

`hash_map& hash_map::operator=(const hash_map&)`
The assignment operator.
(Described in Container.)

✳ `allocator_type hash_map::get_allocator() const`
Returns a copy of the allocator with which the hash_map was constructed.

`void hash_map::swap(hash_map&)`
Swaps the contents of two hash_map objects.
(Described in Container.)

`pair<iterator, bool> hash_map::insert(const value_type& x)`
Inserts x into the hash_map. The second part of the return value is true if x was inserted and false if it was not inserted because it was already present.
(Described in Unique Associative Container.)

`template <class InputIterator>`
`void hash_map::insert(InputIterator f, InputIterator l)`
Inserts the range [f,l) into the hash_map.
(Described in Unique Associative Container.)

`void hash_map::erase(iterator pos)`
Erases the element that pos points to.
(Described in Associative Container.)

`size_type hash_map::erase(const key_type& k)`
Erases the element (if any) whose key is k. Return value is the number of elements erased—either zero or one.
(Described in Associative Container.)

`void hash_map::erase(iterator f, iterator l)`
Erases all elements in the range [f,l).
(Described in Associative Container.)

`iterator hash_map::find(const key_type& k)`
Finds the element whose key is k.
(Described in Associative Container.)

`const_iterator hash_map::find(const key_type& k) const`
Finds the element whose key is k.
(Described in Associative Container.)

`size_type hash_map::count(const key_type& k) const`
Returns the number of elements whose keys are k. The return value is either zero or one.
(Described in Associative Container.)

`pair<iterator, iterator> hash_map::equal_range(const key_type& k)`
Finds a range containing all elements whose keys are equal to k.
(Described in Associative Container.)

`pair<const_iterator, const_iterator>`
`hash_map::equal_range(const key_type& k) const`
Finds a range containing all elements whose keys are equal to k.
(Described in Associative Container.)

* `mapped_type& hash_map::operator[](const key_type&)`

Since hash_map is a Unique Associative Container, a hash_map contains at most one element whose key is k. This member function returns a reference to the object that is associated with the key k. If the hash_map does not already contain such an object, operator[] inserts the default object mapped_type(). (Note that the return type is mapped_type&, not value_type&. That is, operator[] doesn't return a reference to one of the hash_map's elements but rather a reference to part of an element.)

There is no const version because operator[] has the potential to insert a new element into a hash_map.

Strictly speaking, operator[] is redundant. It is nothing more than an abbreviation. The expression m[k] is equivalent to

```
    m.insert(value_type(k, mapped_type())).first->second
```

`bool operator==(const hash_map&, const hash_map&)`
Tests two hash_map objects for equality.
(Described in Forward Container.)

16.2.7 hash_multiset

hash_multiset<Key, HashFun, EqualKey, Allocator>

A hash_multiset is a Hashed Associative Container that stores objects of type Key. It is a Simple Associative Container, meaning that its value type, as well as its key type, is Key. It is also a Multiple Associative Container, meaning that it may contain two or more identical elements. (This is the only way in which hash_set and hash_multiset differ.)

The hash_multiset class is useful in applications where it is important to be able to search for an element quickly. If it is important for the elements to be in a particular order, however, multiset (page 473) is more appropriate.

Example

```
struct eqstr
{
  bool operator()(const char* s1, const char* s2) const
  {
    return strcmp(s1, s2) == 0;
  }
};

typedef hash_multiset<const char*, hash<const char*>, eqstr>
        Hash_Multiset;

void lookup(const Hash_Multiset& Set, const char* word)
{
  int n_found = Set.count(word);
  cout << "  " << word << ": "
       << n_found << " "
       << (n_found == 1 ? "instance" : "instances")
       << endl;
}
```

```
int main()
{
  Hash_Multiset Set;

  Set.insert("mango");
  Set.insert("kiwi");
  Set.insert("apple");
  Set.insert("pear");
  Set.insert("kiwi");
  Set.insert("mango");
  Set.insert("pear")
  Set.insert("mango");
  Set.insert("apricot");
  Set.insert("banana");
  Set.insert("mango");

  lookup(Set, "mango");
  lookup(Set, "apple");
  lookup(Set, "durian");

  // The output is:
  //   mango: 4 instances
  //   apple: 1 instance
  //   durian: 0 instances
}
```

Where Defined

The hash_multiset class was not present in the original HP implementation, nor is it present in the C++ standard. In the SGI implementation it is defined in the header <hash_set>.

Template Parameters

Key   The hash_multiset's key type and value type. Also defined as the nested types hash_multiset::key_type and hash_multiset::value_type.

HashFun   The Hash Function used by the hash_multiset. This is also defined as the nested type hash_multiset::hasher.
            Default: hash<Key>

EqualKey   The hash_multiset's key equality function: a Binary Predicate that determines whether two keys are the same. This is also defined as the nested type hash_multiset::key_equal.
            Default: equal_to<Key>

Allocator   The hash_multiset's allocator, used for all internal memory management.
            Default: allocator<Key>

Model Of

Hashed Associative Container (page 161), Simple Associative Container (page 153), Multiple Associative Container (page 152).

Type Requirements

- Key is a model of Assignable.
- HashFun is a model of Hash Function.
- HashFun's value type is Key.
- EqualKey is a model of BinaryPredicate.
- EqualKey is an equivalence relation.
- EqualKey's value type is Key.
- Allocator is a model of Allocator whose value type is Key.

Public Base Classes

None.

Members

One of hash_multiset's member functions is not defined in the Hashed Associative Container, Simple Associative Container, and Multiple Associative Container requirements but is specific to hash_multiset. This special member function is flagged with the symbol ✶.

hash_multiset::value_type
The type of object stored in the hash_multiset. The value type is Key.
(Described in Container.)

hash_multiset::key_type
The type of the key associated with an object of type value_type. The key type is Key.
(Described in Associative Container.)

hash_multiset::hasher
The hash_multiset's Hash Function.
(Described in Hashed Associative Container.)

hash_multiset::key_equal
A Binary Predicate that compares keys for equality.
(Described in Hashed Associative Container.)

hash_multiset::pointer
Pointer to Key.
(Described in Container.)

hash_multiset::const_pointer
Pointer to const Key.
(Described in Container.)

hash_multiset::reference
Reference to Key.
(Described in Container.)

`hash_multiset::const_reference`
Reference to const Key.
(Described in Container.)

`hash_multiset::size_type`
An unsigned integral type, usually `size_t`.
(Described in Container.)

`hash_multiset::difference_type`
A signed integral type, usually `ptrdiff_t`.
(Described in Container.)

`hash_multiset::iterator`
The `hash_multiset`'s iterator type, a constant Forward Iterator. (There is no mutable
iterator type.)
(Described in Container.)

`hash_multiset::const_iterator`
The `hash_multiset`'s constant iterator type, also a constant Forward Iterator. (Possibly
the same type as `iterator`.)
(Described in Container.)

`iterator hash_multiset::begin() const`
Returns an `iterator` pointing to the beginning of the `hash_multiset`.
(Described in Container.)

`iterator hash_multiset::end() const`
Returns an `iterator` pointing to the end of the `hash_multiset`.
(Described in Container.)

`size_type hash_multiset::size() const`
Returns the number of elements in the `hash_multiset`.
(Described in Container.)

`size_type hash_multiset::max_size() const`
Returns the `hash_multiset`'s maximum possible size.
(Described in Container.)

`bool hash_multiset::empty() const`
Returns `true` if and only if the `hash_multiset`'s size is zero.
(Described in Container.)

`size_type hash_multiset::bucket_count() const`
Returns the number of buckets in the hash table.
(Described in Hashed Associative Container.)

`void hash_multiset::resize(size_type n)`
Increases the bucket count to at least n.
(Described in Hashed Associative Container.)

`hasher hash_funct() const`
Returns the hasher object used by the `hash_multiset`.
(Described in Hashed Associative Container.)

`key_equal key_eq() const`
Returns the key_equal object used by the `hash_multiset`.
(Described in Hashed Associative Container.)

```
explicit hash_multiset::hash_multiset(size_type n = 0,
                                      const hasher& h = hasher(),
                                      const key_equal& k = key_equal(),
                                      const Allocator& A = Allocator())
```
Creates an empty hash_multiset with at least n buckets, using the specified hash function, key equality function, and allocator.
(Described in Hashed Associative Container.)

```
template <class InputIterator>
hash_multiset::hash_multiset(InputIterator f, InputIterator l,
                            size_type n = 0,
                            const hasher& h = hasher(),
                            const key_equal& k = key_equal(),
                            const Allocator& A = Allocator())
```
Creates a hash_multiset with a copy of the range [f,l) and a bucket count of at least n, using the specified hash function, key equality function, and allocator.
(Described in Hashed Associative Container.)

```
hash_multiset::hash_multiset(const hash_multiset&)
```
The copy constructor.
(Described in Container.)

```
hash_multiset::~hash_multiset()
```
The destructor.
(Described in Container.)

```
hash_multiset& hash_multiset::operator=(const hash_multiset&)
```
The assignment operator.
(Described in Container.)

❊ `allocator_type hash_multiset::get_allocator() const`
Returns a copy of the allocator with which the hash_multiset was constructed.

```
void hash_multiset::swap(hash_multiset&)
```
Swaps the contents of two hash_multiset objects.
(Described in Container.)

```
iterator hash_multiset::insert(const value_type& x)
```
Inserts x into the hash_multiset.
(Described in Multiple Associative Container.)

```
template <class InputIterator>
void hash_multiset::insert(InputIterator f, InputIterator l)
```
Inserts the range [f,l) into the hash_multiset.
(Described in Multiple Associative Container.)

```
void hash_multiset::erase(iterator pos)
```
Erases the element that pos points to.
(Described in Associative Container.)

```
size_type hash_multiset::erase(const key_type& k)
```
Erases all elements whose keys are k. Return value is the number of elements erased.
(Described in Associative Container.)

```
void hash_multiset::erase(iterator f, iterator l)
```
Erases all elements in the range [f,l).
(Described in Associative Container.)

iterator hash_multiset::find(const key_type& k) const
Finds an element whose key is k.
(Described in Associative Container.)

size_type hash_multiset::count(const key_type& k) const
Returns the number of elements whose keys are k.
(Described in Associative Container.)

pair<iterator, iterator>
hash_multiset::equal_range(const key_type& k) const
Finds a range containing all elements whose keys are equal to k.
(Described in Associative Container.)

bool operator==(const hash_multiset&, const hash_multiset&)
Tests two hash_multiset objects for equality.
(Described in Forward Container.)

16.2.8 hash_multimap

hash_multimap<Key, T, HashFun, EqualKey, Allocator>

A hash_multimap is a Hashed Associative Container that associates objects of type
Key with objects of type T. It is a Pair Associative Container, meaning that its value
type is pair<const Key, T>. It is also a Multiple Associative Container, meaning that
it may contain two or more identical elements. (This is the only way in which hash_map
and hash_multimap differ.) That is, the hash_multimap class doesn't map a value of
type Key to *an* object of type T but rather to *one or more* objects of type T.

Looking up an element in a hash_multimap by its key is a fast operation, so
hash_multimap is useful for "dictionaries," or associative arrays, where an object
of type Key is associated with objects of type T but where the order of elements is
irrelevant. If it is important for the elements to be arranged in some particular order,
however, multimap (page 478) is more appropriate.

Example

```
struct eqstr
{
  bool operator()(const char* s1, const char* s2) const
  {
    return strcmp(s1, s2) == 0;
  }
};

typedef hash_multimap<const char*, int, hash<const char*>, eqstr>
        map_type;

void lookup(const map_type& Map, const char* str)
{
  cout << "   " << str << ": ";
  pair<map_type::const_iterator, map_type::const_iterator> p
    = Map.equal_range(str);
```

```
    for (map_type::const_iterator i = p.first; i != p.second; ++i)
      cout << (*i).second << " ";
    cout << endl;
  }

  int main()
  {
    map_type M;
    M.insert(map_type::value_type("H", 1));
    M.insert(map_type::value_type("H", 2));
    M.insert(map_type::value_type("C", 12));
    M.insert(map_type::value_type("C", 13));
    M.insert(map_type::value_type("O", 16));
    M.insert(map_type::value_type("O", 17));
    M.insert(map_type::value_type("O", 18));
    M.insert(map_type::value_type("I", 127));

    lookup(M, "I");
    lookup(M, "O");
    lookup(M, "Rn");

    // The output is:
    //   I: 127
    //   O: 16 18 17
    //   Rn:
  }
```

Where Defined

The hash_multimap class was not present in the original HP implementation, nor is it present in the C++ standard. In the SGI implementation it is defined in the header <hash_map>.

Template Parameters

Key   The hash_multimap's key type. This is also defined as the nested type hash_multimap::key_type.

T   The hash_multimap's mapped type. This is also defined as the nested type hash_multimap::mapped_type.

HashFun   The Hash Function used by the hash_multimap. This is also defined as the nested type hash_multimap::hasher.
            Default: hash<Key>

EqualKey   The hash_multimap's key equality function, a Binary Predicate used to determine whether two keys are the same. This is also defined as the nested type hash_multimap::key_equal.
            Default: equal_to<Key>

Allocator   The hash_multimap's allocator, used for all internal memory management.
            Default: allocator<pair<const Key, T> >

Model Of

Hashed Associative Container (page 161), Pair Associative Container (page 155), Multiple Associative Container (page 152).

Type Requirements

- Key is a model of Assignable.
- T is a model of Assignable.
- HashFun is a model of Hash Function.
- HashFun's value type is Key.
- EqualKey is a model of BinaryPredicate.
- EqualKey is an equivalence relation.
- EqualKey's value type is Key.
- Allocator is a model of Allocator.
- Allocator's value type is the same as the `hash_multimap`'s value type.

Public Base Classes

None.

Members

One of `hash_multimap`'s member functions is not defined in the Hashed Associative Container, Pair Associative Container, and Multiple Associative Container requirements but is specific to `hash_multimap`. This special member function is flagged with the symbol ✳.

`hash_multimap::key_type`
The `hash_multimap`'s key type, Key.
(Described in Associative Container.)

`hash_multimap::mapped_type`
The type of object associated with a key. The mapped type is T.
(Described in Pair Associative Container.)

`hash_multimap::value_type`
The type of object stored in the `hash_multimap`. The value type is pair<const Key, T>.
(Described in Pair Associative Container.)

`hash_multimap::hasher`
The `hash_multimap`'s Hash Function.
(Described in Hashed Associative Container.)

`hash_multimap::key_equal`
A Binary Predicate that compares keys for equality.
(Described in Hashed Associative Container.)

`hash_multimap::pointer`
Pointer to `hash_multimap::value_type`.
(Described in Container.)

hash_multimap::const_pointer
Pointer to const hash_multimap::value_type.
(Described in Container.)

hash_multimap::reference
Reference to hash_multimap::value_type.
(Described in Container.)

hash_multimap::const_reference
Reference to const hash_multimap::value_type.
(Described in Container.)

hash_multimap::size_type
An unsigned integral type, usually size_t.
(Described in Container.)

hash_multimap::difference_type
A signed integral type, usually ptrdiff_t.
(Described in Container.)

hash_multimap::iterator
The hash_multimap's iterator type, a Forward Iterator. Note that this isn't a mutable
iterator type, since hash_multimap::value_type isn't Assignable. (If i is an iterator of
type hash_multimap::iterator, you can't write *i = x.) It isn't a fully constant iterator
type, either, because it can be used to modify the object that it points to. You can write
i->second = x.
(Described in Container.)

hash_multimap::const_iterator
The hash_multimap's constant iterator type, a constant Forward Iterator.
(Described in Container.)

iterator hash_multimap::begin()
Returns an iterator pointing to the beginning of the hash_multimap.
(Described in Container.)

iterator hash_multimap::end()
Returns an iterator pointing to the end of the hash_multimap.
(Described in Container.)

const_iterator hash_multimap::begin() const
Returns a const_iterator pointing to the beginning of the hash_multimap.
(Described in Container.)

const_iterator hash_multimap::end() const
Returns a const_iterator pointing to the end of the hash_multimap.
(Described in Container.)

size_type hash_multimap::size() const
Returns the number of elements in the hash_multimap.
(Described in Container.)

size_type hash_multimap::max_size() const
Returns the hash_multimap's maximum possible size.
(Described in Container.)

bool hash_multimap::empty() const
Returns true if and only if the hash_multimap's size is zero.
(Described in Container.)

`size_type hash_multimap::bucket_count() const`
Returns the number of buckets in the hash table.
(Described in Hashed Associative Container.)

`void hash_multimap::resize(size_type n)`
Increases the bucket count to at least n.
(Described in Hashed Associative Container.)

`hasher hash_funct() const`
Returns the `hasher` object used by the `hash_multimap`.
(Described in Hashed Associative Container.)

`key_equal key_eq() const`
Returns the `key_equal` object used by the `hash_multimap`.
(Described in Hashed Associative Container.)

`explicit hash_multimap::hash_multimap(size_type n = 0,`
`                          const hasher& h = hasher(),`
`                          const key_equal& k = key_equal(),`
`                          const Allocator& A = Allocator())`
Creates an empty `hash_multimap` with at least n buckets, using the specified hash function, key equality function, and allocator.
(Described in Hashed Associative Container.)

`template <class InputIterator>`
`hash_multimap::hash_multimap(InputIterator f, InputIterator l,`
`                          size_type n = 0,`
`                          const hasher& h = hasher(),`
`                          const key_equal& k = key_equal(),`
`                          const Allocator& A = Allocator())`
Creates a `hash_multimap` with a copy of the range [f,l) and a bucket count of at least n, using the specified hash function, key equality function, and allocator.
(Described in Hashed Associative Container.)

`hash_multimap::hash_multimap(const hash_multimap&)`
The copy constructor.
(Described in Container.)

`hash_multimap::~hash_multimap()`
The destructor.
(Described in Container.)

`hash_multimap& hash_multimap::operator=(const hash_multimap&)`
The assignment operator.
(Described in Container.)

✳ `allocator_type hash_multiset::get_allocator() const`
Returns a copy of the allocator with which the `hash_multiset` was constructed.

`void hash_multimap::swap(hash_multimap&)`
Swaps the contents of two `hash_multimap` objects.
(Described in Container.)

`iterator hash_multimap::insert(const value_type& x)`
Inserts x into the `hash_multimap`.
(Described in Multiple Associative Container.)

```
template <class InputIterator>
void hash_multimap::insert(InputIterator f, InputIterator l)
```
Inserts the range [f,l) into the hash_multimap.
(Described in Multiple Associative Container.)

```
void hash_multimap::erase(iterator pos)
```
Erases the element that pos points to.
(Described in Associative Container.)

```
size_type hash_multimap::erase(const key_type& k)
```
Erases all elements whose keys are k. Return value is the number of elements erased.
(Described in Associative Container.)

```
void hash_multimap::erase(iterator f, iterator l)
```
Erases all elements in the range [f,l).
(Described in Associative Container.)

```
iterator hash_multimap::find(const key_type& k)
```
Finds an element whose key is k.
(Described in Associative Container.)

```
const_iterator hash_multimap::find(const key_type& k) const
```
Finds an element whose key is k.
(Described in Associative Container.)

```
size_type hash_multimap::count(const key_type& k) const
```
Returns the number of elements whose keys are k.
(Described in Associative Container.)

```
pair<iterator, iterator> hash_multimap::equal_range(const key_type& k)
```
Finds a range containing all elements whose keys are equal to k.
(Described in Associative Container.)

```
pair<const_iterator, const_iterator>
hash_multimap::equal_range(const key_type& k) const
```
Finds a range containing all elements whose keys are equal to k.
(Described in Associative Container.)

```
bool operator==(const hash_multimap&, const hash_multimap&)
```
Tests two hash_multimap objects for equality.
(Described in Forward Container.)

16.3   Container Adaptors

The classes stack, queue, and priority_queue, are not containers but rather are classes that provide a limited subset of container operations. For example, stack allows you to insert, remove, or examine the one element at the top of the stack. These classes are *adaptors* because they are implemented in terms of underlying container.

Stacks, queues, and priority queues are familiar data structures, but one aspect of these container adaptors' interface might seem unfamiliar. All three of these classes have a member function pop, which removes the top element, and that member function has no return value. You might wonder why pop() doesn't return the value that it removes.

If `pop` did return that element, it would have to return it by value rather than by reference. (Since the element is being removed, there wouldn't be anything left to refer to.) Return by value, however, would be inefficient because it involves at least one redundant copy constructor call. Since it is impossible for `pop()` to return a value both efficiently and correctly, it is more sensible for it to return no value at all. You can call a separate member function if you want to inspect the top element.

16.3.1 `stack`

`stack<T, Sequence>`

A `stack` is an adaptor that provides a restricted subset of Container functionality. It provides insertion, removal, and inspection of the element at the top of the `stack`. It is a "last in first out" (LIFO) data structure. The element at the top of a `stack` is the one that was most recently added.

There is no way to access any of a `stack`'s elements except for the top element; `stack` does not allow iteration through its elements. This restriction is the only reason that `stack` exists, since any Front Insertion Sequence or Back Insertion Sequence can already be used as a stack. In the case of `vector`, for example, the stack operations are the member functions `back`, `push_back`, and `pop_back`. The only reason to use the container adaptor `stack`, instead of directly using a Sequence, is to make it clear that you are performing stack operations only.

Since `stack` is a container *adaptor*, it is implemented on top of some underlying container type. By default that underlying type is `deque`, but a different type may be selected explicitly.

Stacks are a standard data structure and are discussed in all algorithm books. See, for example, Section 2.2.1 of Knuth [Knu97].

Example

```
int main() {
  stack<int> S;
  S.push(8);
  S.push(7);
  S.push(4);
  assert(S.size() == 3);

  assert(S.top() == 4);
  S.pop();

  assert(S.top() == 7);
  S.pop();

  assert(S.top() == 8);
  S.pop();

  assert(S.empty());
}
```

Where Defined

In the HP implementation, stack was defined in the header <stack.h>. According to the C++ standard, it is declared in the header <stack>.

Template Parameters

T   The type of object stored in the stack.

Sequence   The type of the underlying container used to implement the stack.
           Default: deque<T>

Model Of

Assignable (page 83), Default Constructible (page 84). Additionally, it is a model of Equality Comparable (page 85) if and only if T is Equality Comparable, and a model of LessThan Comparable (page 86) if and only if T is LessThan Comparable.

Type Requirements

- T is a model of Assignable.
- Sequence is a model of Back Insertion Sequence.
- Sequence's value type is T.
- If operator== is used, then T is a model of Equality Comparable.
- If operator< is used, then T is a model of LessThan Comparable.

Public Base Classes

None.

Members

Some of stack's member functions are not defined in the Assignable, Default Constructible, Equality Comparable, or LessThan Comparable requirements but are specific to stack. These special members are flagged with the symbol ✶.

✶ **stack::value_type**
  The type of object stored in the stack. It is the same type as T and Sequence::value_type.

✶ **stack::size_type**
  An unsigned integral type. Equivalent to Sequence::size_type.

  stack::stack()
  The default constructor.
  (Described in Default Constructible.)

✶ **stack::stack(const Sequence& S)**
  Constructs a new stack that contains the same elements as S. This constructor initializes the stack's underlying Sequence object with S.

`stack::stack(const stack&)`
The copy constructor.
(Described in Assignable.)

`stack::~stack()`
The destructor. Destroys all of the `stack`'s elements.

`stack& stack::operator=(const stack&)`
The assignment operator.
(Described in Assignable.)

✳ `size_type stack::size() const`
Returns the number of elements contained in the `stack`.

✳ `bool stack::empty() const`
Returns `true` if and only if the `stack` contains no elements. `S.empty()` is equivalent to `S.size() == 0`.

✳ `value_type& stack::top()`
Returns a mutable reference to the element at the top of the `stack`. Precondition: `empty()` is false.

✳ `const value_type& stack::top() const`
Returns a `const` reference to the element at the top of the `stack`. Precondition: `empty()` is false.

✳ `void stack::push(const value_type& x)`
Inserts x at the top of the `stack`. Postconditions: `size()` will be incremented by 1, and `top()` will be a copy of x.

✳ `void stack::pop()`
Removes the element at the top of the `stack`. Precondition: `empty()` is `false`. Postcondition: `size()` will be decremented by 1.

`bool operator==(const stack&, const stack&)`
Equality operator. Two stacks are equal if they contain the same number of elements and if they are equal element-by-element.

`bool operator<(const stack&, const stack&)`
Lexicographical (element-by-element) comparison.

16.3.2 queue

`queue<T, Sequence>`

A queue is an adaptor that provides a restricted subset of Container functionality. It is a "first in first out" (FIFO) data structure. That is, elements are added to the back of the queue and may be removed from the front; `Q.front()` is the element that was added to the queue least recently.

There is no way to access any of a queue's elements except for the ones at the front and the back; queue has no iterators. This restriction is the only reason that queue exists, since any container that is both a Front Insertion Sequence and a Back Insertion Sequence can already be used as a queue. For example, deque and `list` have member functions front, back, push_front, push_back, pop_front, and pop_back. The only reason to use the container adaptor queue, rather than the container deque, is to make it clear that you are performing queue operations only and no other operations.

Since `queue` is a container adaptor, it is implemented on top of some underlying container type. By default, that underlying type is `deque`, but a different type may be selected explicitly.

Queues are a standard data structure and are discussed in all algorithm books. See, for example, Section 2.2.1 of Knuth [Knu97].

Example

```
int main() {
    queue<int> Q;
    Q.push(8);
    Q.push(7);
    Q.push(6);
    Q.push(2);

    assert(Q.size() == 4);
    assert(Q.back() == 2);

    assert(Q.front() == 8);
    Q.pop();

    assert(Q.front() == 7);
    Q.pop();

    assert(Q.front() == 6);
    Q.pop();

    assert(Q.front() == 2);
    Q.pop();

    assert(Q.empty());
}
```

Where Defined

In the HP implementation, `queue` was defined in the header `<stack.h>`. According to the C++ standard, it is declared in the header `<queue>`.

Template Parameters

T   The type of object stored in the `queue`.

Sequence   The type of the underlying container used to implement the `queue`.
             Default: `deque<T>`

Model Of

Assignable (page 83), Default Constructible (page 84). Additionally, it is a model of Equality Comparable (page 85) if and only if T is Equality Comparable, and it is a model of LessThan Comparable (page 86) if and only if T is LessThan Comparable.

Type Requirements

- T is a model of Assignable.
- Sequence is a model of Front Insertion Sequence.
- Sequence is a model of Back Insertion Sequence.
- Sequence's value type is T.
- If operator== is used, then T is a model of Equality Comparable.
- If operator< is used, then T is a model of LessThan Comparable.

Public Base Classes

None.

Members

Some of queue's member functions are not defined in the Assignable, Default Constructible, Equality Comparable, or LessThan Comparable requirements but are specific to queue. These special members are flagged with the symbol ∗.

∗ **queue::value_type**
The type of object stored in the queue. It is the same type as T and Sequence::value_type.

∗ **queue::size_type**
An unsigned integral type. Equivalent to Sequence::size_type.

queue::queue()
The default constructor.
(Described in Default Constructible.)

∗ **queue::queue(const Sequence& S)**
Constructs a new queue that contains the same elements as S. This constructor initializes the queue's underlying Sequence object with S.

queue::queue(const queue&)
The copy constructor.
(Described in Assignable.)

queue::~queue()
The destructor. Destroys all of the queue's elements.

queue& queue::operator=(const queue&)
The assignment operator.
(Described in Assignable.)

∗ **size_type queue::size() const**
Number of elements contained in the queue.

∗ **bool queue::empty() const**
Returns true if and only if the queue contains no elements. Q.empty() is equivalent to Q.size() == 0.

∗ **value_type& queue::front()**
Returns a mutable reference to the element at the front of the queue, that is, the element least recently inserted. Precondition: empty() is false.

✳ **`const value_type& queue::front() const`**
Returns a `const` reference to the element at the front of the `queue`, that is, the element least recently inserted. Precondition: `empty()` is `false`.

✳ **`value_type& queue::back()`**
Returns a mutable reference to the element at the back of the `queue`, that is, the element most recently inserted. Precondition: `empty()` is `false`.

✳ **`const value_type& queue::back() const`**
Returns a `const` reference to the element at the back of the `queue`, that is, the element most recently inserted. Precondition: `empty()` is `false`.

✳ **`void queue::push(const queue::value_type& x)`**
Adds x at the back of the `queue`. Postconditions: `size()` will be incremented by 1, and `back()` will be a copy of x.

✳ **`void queue::pop()`**
Removes the element at the front of the `queue`. Precondition: `empty()` is `false`. Postcondition: `size()` will be decremented by 1.

`bool operator==(const queue&, const queue&)`
Equality operator. Two `queues` are equal if they contain the same number of elements and if they are equal element-by-element.

`bool operator<(const queue&, const queue&)`
Lexicographical (element-by-element) comparison.

16.3.3 `priority_queue`

`priority_queue<T, Sequence, Compare>`

A `priority_queue` is an adaptor that provides a restricted subset of **Container** functionality. It provides insertion of elements, and inspection and removal of the top element. There is no mechanism for modifying any of the `priority_queue`'s elements, or for iterating through them.

A `priority_queue` is organized such that the top element is always the largest, where the function object **Compare** defines the ordering. This is the reason that `priority_queue` does not provide individual access to its elements. The fact that the largest element is the top is a class invariant.

Since `priority_queue` is a container *adaptor*, it is implemented on top of some underlying container type. By default that underlying type is `vector`, but a different type may be selected explicitly.

Priority queues are a standard data structure and can be implemented in many different ways. The class `priority_queue` is typically implemented as a heap, where the heap condition is maintained using the algorithms `make_heap`, `push_heap`, and `pop_heap`. Priority queues are discussed in all algorithm books; see, for example, Section 5.2.3 of Knuth [Knu98b].

Example

```
int main() {
  priority_queue<int> Q;
  Q.push(1);
```

```
    Q.push(4);
    Q.push(2);
    Q.push(8);
    Q.push(5);
    Q.push(7);

    assert(Q.size() == 6);
    while (!Q.empty()) {
      cout << Q.top() << " ";
      Q.pop();
    }
    cout << endl;
    // The output is 8 7 5 4 2 1.
  }
```

In the preceding example, the top of the priority_queue was always the largest element. Since the ordering can be given by a function object, it's just as easy to create a priority_queue where the top is always the smallest element.

```
int main() {
  priority_queue<int, vector<int>, greater<int> > Q;
  Q.push(1);
  Q.push(4);
  Q.push(2);
  Q.push(8);
  Q.push(5);
  Q.push(7);

  assert(Q.size() == 6);
  while (!Q.empty()) {
    cout << Q.top() << " ";
    Q.pop();
  }
  cout << endl;
  // The output is 1 2 4 5 7 8.
}
```

Where Defined

In the HP implementation, priority_queue was defined in the header <stack.h>. According to the C++ standard, it is declared in the header <queue>.

Template Parameters

T   The type of object stored in the priority_queue.

Sequence   The underlying container type used to implement the priority_queue.
             Default: vector<T>

Compare   The comparison function used to test whether one element is smaller than another element.
Default: less<T>

Model Of

Assignable (page 83), Default Constructible (page 84).

Type Requirements

- T is a model of Assignable.
- Sequence is a model of Sequence.
- Sequence is a model of Random Access Container.
- Sequence's value type is T.
- Compare is a model of Strict Weak Ordering.
- Compare's value type is T.

Public Base Classes

None.

Members

Some of priority_queue's members aren't defined in the Assignable and Default Constructible requirements but are specific to priority_queue. These special members are flagged with the symbol ✳.

✳ **priority_queue::value_type**
The type of object stored in the priority_queue. This is the same type as T and as Sequence::value_type.

✳ **priority_queue::size_type**
An unsigned integral type. Equivalent to Sequence::size_type.

explicit priority_queue::priority_queue(const Compare& c = Compare())
Creates an empty priority_queue, using c as the comparison object. (The default constructor uses Compare() as the comparison object.)
(Described in Default Constructible.)

✳ **template <class InputIterator>**
priority_queue::priority_queue(InputIterator f, InputIterator l,
                                const Compare& c = Compare())
Creates a priority_queue initialized to contain the elements in the range [f, l) and using c as the comparison function.

✳ **priority_queue::priority_queue(const Compare& c, const Sequence& S)**
Creates a priority_queue containing the same elements as S and using c as the comparison function. This constructor initializes the priority_queue's underlying Sequence object using S and then reorders the elements in that underlying Sequence object so that they satisfy the priority_queue invariant.
(Described in Default Constructible.)

* `template <class InputIterator>`
  `priority_queue::priority_queue(InputIterator f, InputIterator l,`
  `                              const Compare& c,`
  `                              const Sequence& S)`

  Create a `priority_queue` initialized to contain the elements in the range [f, l) as well as those in S. This constructor initializes the `priority_queue`'s underlying Sequence object using S, adds the elements in [f, l), and then reorders its elements appropriately.

  `priority_queue::~priority_queue()`
  The destructor. Destroys all of the `priority_queue`'s elements.

  `priority_queue&`
  `priority_queue::operator=(const priority_queue&)`
  The assignment operator.
  (Described in Assignable.)

* `size_type priority_queue::size() const`
  Number of elements contained in the `priority_queue`.

* `bool priority_queue::empty() const`
  Returns true if and only if the `priority_queue` contains no elements. `Q.empty()` is equivalent to `Q.size() == 0`.

* `const value_type& priority_queue::top() const`
  Returns a const reference to the element at the top of the `priority_queue`. The element at the top is guaranteed to be the largest element, as determined by the comparison function Comp. That is, for every other element x in the `priority_queue`, `Comp(Q.top(), x)` is false. Precondition: `!empty()`.

* `void priority_queue::push(const value_type& x)`
  Inserts x into the `priority_queue`. Postcondition: `size()` will be incremented by 1. Note that, in general, x will not become the top element. It will become the top only if it happens to be larger than any of the elements already in the `priority_queue`.

* `void priority_queue::pop()`
  Removes the element at the top of the `priority_queue`, that is, the largest element in the `priority_queue`. Precondition: `!empty()`. Postcondition: `size()` will be decremented by 1.

Appendix A

Portability and Standardization

The C++ language is currently in a state of transition.

In the early days of the language, when the only C++ implementation in existence was AT&T's Cfront compiler, the definitive reference manual was the first edition of Bjarne Stroustrup's book *The C++ Programming Language* [Str86]. Later, when C++ compilers from other vendors became available, Margaret Ellis and Stroustrup's *Annotated C++ Reference Manual* [ES90], known to C++ aficionados as the ARM, became the *de facto* standard.

C++ is now on the verge of becoming an international standard (the Final Draft International Standard was approved on November 14, 1997), and the language definition is now controlled by a joint committee of the International Standards Organization (ISO) and the American National Standards Institute (ANSI). The language has changed during the standardization process. The differences between the C++ standard [ISO98] and the ARM are at least as dramatic as the differences between the "ANSI C" standard and the first edition of *The C Programming Language* [KR78]. Many new language features have been added to C++, and many others have been clarified.

All of these bureaucratic details might seem irrelevant to ordinary programmers, but the result is that portability between different C++ implementations isn't automatic. At present, no existing compiler implements the entire C++ standard. Likewise, very few compilers are restricted only to features from the ARM. Almost all C++ compilers implement a language that lies somewhere in between the C++ of the ARM and standard C++.

The status of the STL is similar. The original STL was defined in a technical report written by Alexander Stepanov and Meng Lee [SL95]. Now, however, the STL is part of the standard C++ library. The C++ standardization committee made changes in the definition of the STL, just as it made changes in the definition of the core C++ language.

A further complication is that even though the original demonstration "HP implementation" of the STL was written by the same people who designed the library's formal specification, the implementation did not follow the formal definition. There was no way that it could have. The STL definition called for language features that, at

515

the time it was written, weren't yet available. The HP implementation was a compromise between the formal design of the library and the limitations of 1994 compiler technology.

As of 1998, no existing STL implementation conforms fully either to the original Stepanov-Lee definition or to the definition in the C++ standard. One reason for this is that, technically, the standard is still a draft, and until very recently it was still subject to change. Trying to track a changing standard would be like the race between Alice and the Red Queen: "All the running you can do, to keep in the same place." Most library implementors have chosen to be cautious about making changes until the C++ standard officially becomes final.

A second problem is that, even today, no single C++ compiler supports every language feature used by the STL. (Compiler vendors also have to be cautious!) If a particular language feature is unavailable, some library features either have to be left out or have to be provided through nonstandard workarounds. These limitations and workarounds are often, unfortunately, documented poorly or not at all.

Most parts of the STL are completely stable in that they aren't affected by compiler limitations and that they haven't been changed by the standardization committee. You can count on those parts to be the same in every implementation. Other parts, however, are much less stable. Sometimes the variation between different implementations is important.

Fortunately, most of this confusion appears only at the margins. None of the changes to the STL and none of the implementation difficulties affect the core design of the library. The basic principles of generic programming and the bulk of STL code are valid no matter which compiler and which library implementation you use. Most of the variations are concentrated in a few problem areas.

This appendix describes the portability issues that you have to be aware of. It includes components that are defined differently in different implementations, places where compiler limitations have made it impossible to implement the library as it is formally defined, components whose definition has changed, and language changes that affect the use of the STL.

A.1   Language Changes

A.1.1   The Template Compilation Model

Ever since templates were first added to C++, separate compilation of templates has been part of the language definition. The intention has always been that function templates and class templates could be used just as ordinary functions and classes are. That is, you can declare an ordinary function in one source file and use it in a different source file. You can compile the two files independently of each other, provided that you link the two object files together.

The ARM mandates separate compilation of templates, and although some of the details have changed, so does the C++ standard. Version 3.0 of the AT&T Cfront compiler included a limited form of separate compilation of templates, and many other compilers also have a limited form of separate compilation.

Unfortunately, no two versions of separate compilation are quite the same. Some involve special #pragma declarations in source code, some require that names of source files follow a special naming convention, and many compilers don't have separate compilation of templates at all.

Your compiler may have a scheme that permits some sort of separate compilation, but if you use it, you may have trouble porting your code to other compilers. It will probably be several years before every compiler supports separate compilation as defined in the C++ standard.

At present, the only portable solution is to follow the rule that a function template's *definition*, not just its prototype, must be visible before the function is used. In practice, this means that function templates and class templates must be defined in header (*.h) files and that to use a template you include the appropriate header. This is the reason that all existing STL implementations consist mostly—or even entirely—of header files.

A.1.2   Default Template Parameters

Just as functions in C++ can have default parameters, so can class templates. If you declare a class template as

```
template <class A, class B = A>
class X {
   ...
};
```

then you may omit the second template parameter whenever you instantiate X. The second template parameter takes on the default value A whenever it is omitted. The type X<int> is thus the same as the type X<int, int>.

All of the STL container classes use default template parameters. For example, vector has two template parameters, where the first is the type of object stored in the vector and the second, an "allocator," parameterizes the vector's memory allocation strategy. This second template parameter is a default template parameter, since most of the time, when you use a vector, you have no reason to use a non-standard allocation strategy.

At present, not all C++ compilers support default template parameters fully. Some compilers restrict default template parameters (for example, some allow a default value only if it doesn't depend on the other template parameters), and some don't allow default template parameters at all. Since the STL relies heavily on default template parameters, it can't be implemented on those compilers precisely as designed.

When a compiler is missing this language feature, there are fundamentally two ways to implement a class that is supposed to have a default template parameter: either require that users always supply the parameter or remove the parameter altogether. Again using the example of a vector, the first method would require that you always write vector<int, allocator<int> > even if you just want to use the default allocator. The second method would allow you to write simply vector<int>, but there would be no way to use an alternative allocator. Neither of these compromises is entirely satisfactory.

The original HP STL, written at a time when no compilers supported default template parameters, used the second option. Both options have been used in subsequent STL implementations.

A.1.3   Member Templates

When templates were first added to the C++ language, only two things could be templates: global classes and global functions. That is, template declarations could not occur within class scope. This meant that member functions could not be function templates.

This restriction turned out to be unnecessary, and the standard now permits nonvirtual member functions[1] to be function templates. Member function templates are called the same way ordinary function templates are. The compiler deduces the template parameters from the arguments that the function is called with, and it automatically creates the appropriate instance of the member function.

A class's constructor is a member function, so, like other member functions, it may be a template. This turns out to be one of the most important uses for member templates. The utility class pair, for example, has a "generalized copy constructor"

```
template <class T1, class T2> template <class U1, class U2>
pair<T1, T2>::pair(const pair<U1, U2>&);
```

that allows a pair<T1, T2> to be constructed from any pair<U1, U2>, provided that U1 is convertible to T1 and U2 to T2. (This syntax looks odd, but it is correct. The keyword template has to appear twice because there are two template parameter lists: one for the pair template itself and one for its member template constructor.)

The STL container classes use member templates heavily. Again, one of the main uses is in constructors. You can construct a container from a range of iterators, and member templates allow that range to consist of any type that is a model of Input Iterator. You can, for example, create a vector V that contains the same elements as a list L by writing:

```
vector<T> V(L.begin(), L.end());
```

This is valid as long as L's value type is convertible to T. Similarly, containers' insert member functions, which also take a range of iterators, use member templates.

This functionality is unavailable on compilers that do not yet support member templates. If your compiler doesn't support member templates, it is impossible to write the fully general constructor that allows a vector to be created from a range of Input Iterators. All that is possible is to overload vector's constructor for a few selected iterator types—presumably the ones that your library implementor expects to be the most useful. If your compiler doesn't support member templates, you will need to find out which types those are. Typically you should at least be able to construct a container from a range of pointers and from a range of the container's own iterators.

The member template constructor in pair is partly a matter of convenience. For example, the standard container map is an Associative Container whose elements are

---

1. For technical reasons described in *The Design and Evolution of C++* [Str94], virtual member functions still cannot be templates.

of type pair<const Key, Data>. Like every other Associative Container, map has a member function that lets you insert a single element into the container. You write

```
M.insert(p)
```

where p is an object of the same type as M's elements—that is, where p is an object of type pair<const Key, Data>. The question is how to construct that object p.

Using the member template constructor, you can insert an element into a map without writing out pair's constructor in full. You can write:

```
M.insert(make_pair(k, d))
```

This creates an object of type pair<Key, Data>, converts that object to the type pair<const Key, Data>, and inserts it into the map. Without the member template constructor, there is no such conversion. On a compiler that lacks support for member templates, you must instead use a less convenient form:

```
M.insert(pair<const Key, Data>(k, d))
```

A.1.4 Partial Specialization

For as long as templates have been part of the C++ language, it has been possible to specialize a class template. If you have a class X<T>, but for some reason, the general definition of X doesn't apply to some particular type, you can give X a different definition for that type. You might, for example, be able to implement X<int> more efficiently than the general version. The class X<int> can be completely unrelated to the general X<T>, and it can have a completely different set of member functions.

Specialization of class templates has now been extended to *partial specialization*. As in the following example, you can give a template a different definition for an entire category of types, not just for a single type.

```
template <class T> class X
{
  // Most general version.
};

template <class T> class X<T*>
{
  // Version for general pointers.
};

template <> class X<void*>
{
  // Version for one specific pointer type.
}
```

Full specialization did not always use the same syntax as partial specialization. This is one of the changes that was made during the standardization process. If you are using a compiler that conforms to the C++ standard, you must write

```
template <> class X<void*>
```

as shown above, but if you are using an older compiler then you must instead write

```
class X<void*>
```

without using the `template` keyword. There is no way, other than using preprocessor macros, to write a full specialization that is legal under both the old rules and the new rules.

Partial specialization is often a useful optimization. For example, you can sometimes write a special version of a class that's optimized specifically for pointers. Additionally, partial specialization enables some programming techniques that are otherwise completely impossible. The STL relies on those techniques.

First, for reasons of storage efficiency, the STL includes a specialized version of the `vector` container class: `vector<bool>`. This may not appear at first to be an example of partial specialization, but it is: Like all STL sequences, `vector` has *two* template parameters: the value type and the allocator. The `vector<bool>` class is a partial specialization because it gives the first template parameter a specific type while leaving the allocator completely general. On compilers that do not support partial specialization, STL implementations typically declare a class `bit_vector` instead. The `bit_vector` class is only a temporary workaround. It is not part of the C++ standard, and it will probably disappear once partial specialization is universally available.

More importantly, one of the STL's fundamental building blocks relies crucially on partial specialization: `iterator_traits`.

The `iterator_traits` class, described in Section 3.1, is the basic mechanism for accessing information about iterators' associated types. For any iterator type `I`,

        iterator_traits<I>::value_type
is `I`'s value type and
        iterator_traits<I>::difference_type
is `I`'s difference type. This necessarily relies on partial specialization because we can't define `iterator_traits` the same way for pointers as we do for those iterators that are declared as classes.

You can use `iterator_traits` in your own programs. It is also used in other parts of the STL itself.

- The iterator adaptor `reverse_iterator` takes a single template parameter, `Iter`, a Bidirectional Iterator. This adaptor uses the `iterator_traits` mechanism, so that `reverse_iterator<Iter>` has the same difference type and value type as `Iter` itself.

- The algorithms `distance` (page 181), `count` (page 214), and `count_if` (page 216) all operate on ranges of input iterators. Each of these algorithms returns a value of type `typename iterator_traits<InputIter>::difference_type`.

The original HP STL did not rely on partial specialization and did not have the `iterator_traits` class. It instead provided a clumsier mechanism for accessing iterators' type information, one that involved three query functions `distance_type`, `value_type`, and `iterator_category`. Those three functions are no longer part of the C++ standard. Most STL implementations still support them, but they are deprecated and will eventually be removed.

If your compiler doesn't support partial specialization, you won't be able to use `iterator_traits` in its full generality. You might instead have to use the older mechanism from the HP STL, and you might have to use the older versions of `count`, `count_if`, and `reverse_iterator`.

"Partial Specialization" of Functions

The C++ standard includes one other feature that is very much like partial specialization: partial ordering of function templates.

Template functions, like other functions, may be overloaded. This raises the possibility of calling a function in such a way that more than one version is an exact match. Suppose, for example, that you have declared

```
template <class T> void f(T)
```

and

```
template <class U> void f(U*)
```

Which version do you get when you write `f((int*) 0)`? That call could match the first version (if `T` is `int*`) or the second version (if `U` is `int`).

When templates were first introduced, a function call of that sort was illegal because there was more than one exact match. The new rule relaxes that restriction. Whenever a function call could match one of several overloaded function templates, the compiler will choose the one that is more specialized. In this case, for example, the second version of `f` is more specialized than the first. The first matches any type, but the second only matches pointers.

The STL uses partial ordering of functions in only one place. It contains a `swap` function (page 237) that exchanges the contents of any two variables, and it also defines a more specialized version of `swap` for each of its container classes. If you write `swap(v1, v2)`, where both `v1` and `v2` are vectors, then you will be calling the function

```
template <class T, class Allocator>
void swap(vector<T, Allocator>&, vector<T, Allocator>&)
```

rather than the more general function

```
template <class T> void swap(T&, T&)
```

This is important because the general version of `swap` must work by assignment, and assigning one vector to another is a slow operation. (It has to copy all of the vector's arguments.) The specialized version works directly with `vector`'s internal representation and is quite fast.

On compilers that do not support partial ordering of function templates, the STL does not define the specialized versions of `swap`. This doesn't affect what code you can write—you can still use `swap` to exchange two vectors—but it does mean that some programs will run much more slowly than they ought to.

A.1.5 New Keywords

The C++ language now has more than a dozen keywords that it didn't have when the ARM was first published. Two are especially important for the STL and for programs that use templates: `explicit` and `typename`.

The Keyword `explicit`

The purpose of `explicit` is to suppress certain kinds of automatic type conversions. Ordinarily, if a class X has a constructor that takes a single argument of type T, the C++ compiler will automatically use that constructor to convert values of type T to type X. So, for example, if you have a function f that takes an argument of type X and if t is of type T, you can write f(t) instead of having to write out the conversion by hand.

Sometimes this is what you want. Other times, this automatic conversion could lead to very unexpected results. If f expects its argument to be a `vector<string>`, for example, do you really want to be able to write f(3)? After all, `vector<string>(3)` is a perfectly reasonable constructor call.

Declaring a single-argument constructor as `explicit` suppresses this automatic conversion. You can still use the constructor, but you must write it explicitly. The C++ standard declares most containers' single-argument constructors to be explicit.

Since the whole purpose of `explicit` is to suppress something that would otherwise happen automatically, this does mean that some programs that used to be valid under the old rules will cease to be valid with a standard-conforming compiler and library. You can't write f(3) to call a function whose argument type is `vector<string>`. If your intent really was to pass a newly constructed vector of three empty strings, you will have to write that explicitly: f(vector<string>(3)). The same applies to variable declarations. Instead of

```
    vector<string> v = 3;
```
you must write
```
    vector<string> v(3);
```
or
```
    vector<string> v = vector<string>(3);
```

The Keyword `typename`

The `explicit` keyword affects only a few rather obscure constructs. It forbids some things that were probably never a good idea in the first place. By contrast, `typename` appears in many contexts that are very fundamental to generic programming in C++. If you ever write any nontrivial C++ program that uses templates, you will have to understand how to use `typename`.

The basic issue is technical, but not terribly complicated. When the compiler sees some expression that involves a template parameter, should it treat that expression as if it refers to a type or should it treat it as if it refers to something else (such as a member function or a member variable)?

For example, in the function
```
template <class X> void f(X) {
   X::T(x);
}
```
should the compiler interpret T as a type, in which case X::T is a constructor call—it constructs an anonymous temporary object and then throws it away—or should the

compiler interpret T as a static member function or a static member variable? And similarly, in the function

```
template <class X> void g(X) {
  X::T t;
}
```

should the compiler interpret T as a type, in which case the function is using T's default constructor to create an object t, or should the compiler interpret T as a static member function or member variable, in which case X::T t is a syntax error?

The latter case is particularly troublesome. Once g has been instantiated, the compiler can tell whether X::T is a class, a member function, a member variable, or something else. But it would be unfortunate if there was no way to check a template for syntactic correctness without instantiating it. If that were the case, separate compilation of templates would be hopeless.

The C++ language was designed so that it is possible to check the syntax of a template. Accordingly, C++ has a very simple rule for deciding whether to interpret a name like X::T as a type. If a name might refer either to a type or to something else, then *the compiler always assumes, unless you explicitly tell it otherwise, that the name does not refer to a type.*

The typename keyword is the way to tell the compiler that it should interpret a particular name as a type. The correct way to write the function g is:

```
template <class X> void g(X) {
  typename X::T t;
}
```

By prefixing X::T with the keyword typename, you are telling the compiler that it should interpret X::T as a type. Note that you must use typename every time you refer to that type. That is, you must write:

```
template <class X> void g1(X) {
  typename X::T t;
  typename X::T* pt;
}
```

The second typename is just as obligatory as the first.

The basic rule is that you must use typename whenever the compiler wouldn't be able to tell that something was a type without it. That is, you must use it for a name that:

1. Is a *qualified name*—that is, one that's nested within some other type.

2. *Depends on* a template parameter—that is, it varies depending on the template arguments with which the template is instantiated.

For example, in the function g, X::T is a qualified name (it's qualified by X::) that depends on the template parameter X. Similarly, an expression like Y<X>::T is also a qualified name that depends on the template parameter X.

What does this mean for writing programs that use the STL? Well, the first thing it means is that, whether you're writing new STL components yourself or using existing ones that other people have defined, you'll have to use typename a lot—even when you're doing something that seems perfectly innocent, like writing a template function that operates on a vector<T> and that has to refer to that vector's iterators. For example:

```
template <class T>
void f(vector<T>& v) {
  typename vector<T>::iterator i = v.begin();
  ...
}
```

Odd as it may seem, typename really is required here. To you, as a human, it's obvious that vector<T>::iterator must always refer to vector's nested iterator type, but to the compiler it's just another qualified name that depends on a template parameter T. Unless you explicitly tell the compiler that vector<T>::iterator is the name of a type, it has no way of knowing that.

This applies to iterator_traits as well. We saw (in Section 3.1.5) that we had to use typename when we were defining the iterator_traits class; similarly, we almost always have to use typename whenever we use iterator_traits. The count algorithm (page 214), for example, has this signature:

```
template <class InputIterator, class EqualityComparable>
typename iterator_traits<InputIterator>::difference_type
count(InputIterator first, InputIterator last,
      const EqualityComparable& value)
```

Needless to say, typename presents a portability problem. Some compilers (ones that conform to the C++ standard) require it, but others (ones that were written before the typename keyword was added to the language) forbid it. As of 1998, both kinds of compilers are still common.

The only way to write a program that you can use both with a compiler that requires typename and with a compiler that forbids typename is by playing tricks with the preprocessor. You could, for example, define a macro TYPENAME that expands to typename on some compilers and to nothing on others.

The typename keyword is a technical detail that was introduced for a specific technical purpose. Unfortunately, it is not a detail that you can ignore. The one piece of good news is that, if you make a mistake with typename, the compiler will always tell you so by giving you an error message. Leaving out a typename by mistake won't turn a working program that does one thing into a working program that does something different.

A.2   Library Changes

A.2.1   Allocators

As described in Section 9.4, STL containers are all parameterized by their memory allocation scheme. This facility is sometimes useful, but historically it has been one of the least stable parts of the STL. Four different allocator designs have been in common use: allocators from the HP STL, allocators from the SGI STL, and two different allocator designs from different versions of the draft C++ standard.

Portability is an issue for two further reasons. First, the C++ standard grants library implementors a good deal of latitude in how containers use allocators. Second, many STL implementations don't actually provide any of those four designs. The HP version of allocators cannot be implemented without a somewhat obscure language feature called "template template parameters,"[2] and neither of the draft standard versions is implementable without member templates. If your compiler doesn't support member templates, you can't use the version of allocators described in the C++ standard. At best, you can use some sort of vendor-specific compromise version.

If you are concerned about portability, the safest course is not to use allocators at all; you can use the default allocator. The allocator is always a default template parameter, so you should never have to mention the default by name. If you do have to write your own allocator, you should read your documentation carefully and find out which allocator design your library implementation uses. In particular, if your compiler doesn't support member templates, you should make sure that you understand the necessary workarounds and restrictions. You should also expect to make some changes whenever you use a different compiler or library.

The most visibly innovative aspect of allocators as defined in the C++ standard is allocator *instances*. The member functions allocate and deallocate are associated with specific allocator objects. If you allocate memory through an allocator object a, you must deallocate it through an allocator that is equal to a. Different allocators might, for example, refer to different memory pools.

It isn't enough for an allocator to be part of a container's type. Each container object must contain a specific allocator instance. Even if two container objects have the same type, they do not necessarily allocate memory the same way.

It doesn't make any sense to change a container's allocator after the container has been constructed, but there must be some way to control which allocator instance the container uses. If a container is parameterized in terms of allocators, then all of the container's constructors must take an allocator parameter.

All of the STL containers defined in the C++ standard (vector, list, deque, set, map, multiset, and multimap) define their constructors this way. Every one of these containers' constructors has a parameter of type Allocator. In every case this parameter is the last one in the constructor, and in every case it has a default value of Allocator(). You can thus avoid allocator instances by not mentioning them. So, for example, writing

```
vector<int> V(100, 0);
```
is equivalent to writing:
```
vector<int, allocator<int> > V(100, 0, allocator<int>());
```

A.2.2 Container Adaptors

The STL defines three container adaptors: stack, queue, and priority_queue. They aren't Containers. By design, they don't provide the entire Container interface but only a restricted subset of that interface. A container adaptor is just a "wrapper" for

---

2. That feature is mentioned nowhere else in this book because it is not used by any other part of the STL. See Section C.13.3 of *The C++ Programming Language* [Str97].

some underlying container, and that underlying container is a template parameter. The precise form of the parameterization, however, has changed.

In the original HP STL, the stack adaptor took a single template parameter, the type of the stack's underlying representation. If you wanted to create a stack of ints using a deque as the underlying representation, you would declare the type as:

```
stack<deque<int> >
```

This was unambiguous, but confusing. It looks too much as if the values in the stack are deques, not ints. Furthermore, it forces you to declare something explicitly, the underlying representation, that ought to be only an implementation detail.

This has been changed in the C++ standard, and stack now takes two template parameters. The first is the type of object stored in the stack, and the second is the stack's underlying representation. The underlying representation is, of course, a default template parameter. For stack, it defaults to deque. A stack of ints thus has the much simpler type stack<int>.

This change presents two portability issues. First, most—but not all—STL implementations have changed the container adaptors to conform to the C++ standard. Depending on which library implementation you have, you may have to use the older version of the container adaptors. Second, if you are using a compiler that does not support default template parameters, you can't use container adaptors precisely as specified in the C++ standard. You should read your documentation to find out which workaround your library implementor has used. One common workaround is requiring that you provide both template parameters. You might, for example, have to declare a stack of ints as

```
stack<int, deque<int> >
```

A.2.3 Minor Library Changes

During the standardization process, the STL's interface was changed and extended in several minor ways.

New Algorithms

The C++ standard includes three algorithms that weren't defined in the original HP STL: find_first_of, which is similar to the C library function strpbrk; find_end, which is similar to the STL algorithm search; and search_n.

The standard also contains the three generic algorithms, uninitialized_copy, uninitialized_fill, and uninitialized_fill_n, and the two temporary memory allocation functions, get_temporary_buffer and return_temporary_buffer, all of which were present but undocumented in the HP implementation. These specialized functions are mainly useful if you are writing your own container or adaptive algorithm.

Changes to the Iterator Interface

The C++ standard has made one minor addition to iterators as they were defined in the original HP STL. All iterators (except for Output Iterators, where it would make no sense) now define an `operator->` member function. As you would expect from pointers, `i->m` means the same thing that `(*i).m` does.

This is especially convenient for `map` and `multimap`, since the elements of those containers are pairs. If `i` is an iterator whose value type is `pair<const T, X>`, you can write `i->first` or `i->second`, just as if `i` were a pointer.

Changes to the Sequence Interface

All `Sequences` now contain three new member functions that were not present in the original HP STL: `resize`, which erases or appends elements at the end in order to bring the `Sequence` to a prescribed size; `assign`, which is a sort of generalized assignment operation; and `clear`, which is shorthand for `erase(begin(), end())`. Additionally, the return type of the `erase` member function has been changed. In the HP STL, its return type was `void`, but the C++ standard has changed its return type to `iterator`. The return value from `erase` is an iterator that points immediately past the element or elements that were erased.

The `multiplies` Function Object

Finally, the HP implementation contained a function object `times`, which computed the product of its two arguments. In the C++ standard the name has been changed to `multiplies`.

Unfortunately, there is no good way for an implementation to provide both the old name and the new one. The name was changed because `times` conflicted with a name from one of the UNIX header files, so keeping both names would defeat the whole purpose of the change. If you are porting code between an older STL implementation and a newer one, you may have to be careful about the name of this function object.

A.3 Naming and Packaging

What's in a name? That which we call a rose
By any other word would smell as sweet.

Naming issues may be trivial, but they are the most visible way in which the STL of the C++ standard differs from the original HP STL. In the original STL, for example, this is a complete and correct program (albeit not a very interesting one):

```
#include <vector.h>

int main() {
  vector<int> v;
}
```

According to the standard, there are two reasons why it is not a valid program:

1. The C++ language now has a *namespace* system, and according to the standard, `vector` is defined, not in the global namespace, but within the namespace `std`.

Or, to put it differently, the C++ standard doesn't have a class called vector. Instead, it has a class called std::vector.

2. According to the standard the class std::vector is declared, not in the header <vector.h>, but in the header <vector>.

There are several ways that we can modify this program so that it adheres to all of the rules of the C++ standard. One is

```
#include <vector>

int main() {
    std::vector<int> v;
}
```

and another is

```
#include <vector>

int main() {
    using std::vector;
    vector<int> v;
}
```

In the first version we are explicitly referring to std::vector by its full name. In the second, the line
     using std::vector;
(which is called a *using declaration*) means that the compiler should treat the name vector as an abbreviation for std::vector. (There's also a third method. Instead of the using declaration you could write the *using directive*
     using namespace std;
which would import all of the names from the std namespace. Using this method is discouraged.)

With one small exception, all of the components in the standard C++ library are defined in namespace std. Whenever you use a container, an algorithm, or any other name from the standard library, you must either explicitly qualify it with std:: or import it with a using declaration.

The exception to this rule is the set of templates that define the operators !=, >, <=, and >= in terms of the operators == and <. They are declared not in the namespace std itself but in a nested namespace called std::rel_ops.

Header names are slightly more complicated. The standard renamed all of the headers from the HP STL. All of the new header names, like <vector>, have no .h extension. However, there is no simple one-to-one correspondence between the old names and the new. It is a reorganization as much as it is a renaming. Even the header <vector> is an example of that. In the HP STL, the template vector<> was declared in the header <vector.h>, and the class bit_vector, the equivalent of the specialization vector<bool>, was declared in <bvector.h>. The header <vector> contains both the template and the specialization.

Table A.1: Correspondence between Header Names in the C++ Standard and in the HP STL.

Standard Header	Corresponding HP STL Header(s)	
`<algorithm>`	`<algo.h>`	(most)
`<deque>`	`<deque.h>`	(all)
`<functional>`	`<function.h>`	(most)
`<iterator>`	`<iterator.h>`	(all)
`<list>`	`<list.h>`	(all)
`<memory>`	`<defalloc.h>`	(all)
	`<tempbuf.h>`	(all)
	`<iterator.h>`	(part)
	`<algo.h>`	(part)
`<numeric>`	`<algo.h>`	(part)
`<queue>`	`<stack.h>`	(part)
`<utility>`	`<pair.h>`	(all)
	`<function.h>`	(part)
`<stack>`	`<stack.h>`	(part)
`<vector>`	`<vector.h>`	(all)
	`<bvector.h>`	(all)
`<map>`	`<map.h>`	(all)
	`<multimap.h>`	(all)
`<set>`	`<set.h>`	(all)
	`<multiset.h>`	(all)

Table A.1 is a rough guide to the correspondence between the old-style headers and the standard headers. For more detailed information, you should consult Part IV of this book. The documentation of each function and class specifies which standard header and which old-style header declares it.

The fact that the standard header names are completely different from the old-style names turns out to be an aid to portability, not a hindrance. It gives implementors a hook that they can use for backward compatibility.

The standard doesn't mention old-style names like `<algo.h>` and `<list.h>`. Library implementors aren't required to provide such headers, but neither are they forbidden to do so. Implementors can—and many do—provide headers that have old-style names and that declare their contents in the global namespace rather than in the namespace `std`. Typically, in that case, the header `<vector>` would contain the actual implementation

```
namespace std {
  template <class T, class Allocator>
  class vector {
    ...
  };
}
```

and the header <vector.h> would just consist of two lines:

```
#include <vector>
using std::vector;
```

This scheme is not mandated anywhere in the C++ standard, but it is permitted, and it is reasonably common. Historically, one of the motivations for renaming the STL headers was to make this scheme possible. It allows you to make a gradual transition to new-style header names and to explicit use of namespaces.

Bibliography

[Amm97]   Leen Ammeraal. *STL for C++ Programmers*. John Wiley, Chichester, UK, 1997.

[Aus97]   Matthew H. Austern. The SGI Standard Template Library. *Dr. Dobb's Journal*, 22(8):18–27, Aug 1997.

[BFM95]   Javier Barreiro, Robert Fraley, and David R. Musser. Hash tables for the Standard Template Library. Technical Report X3J16/94-0218 and WG21/N0605, International Standards Organization, Feb 1995.

[Boo94]   Grady Booch. *Object-Oriented Analysis and Design with Applications*. Benjamin Cummings, Redwood City, CA, Second edition, 1994.

[Bre98]   Ulrich Breymann. *Designing Components with the C++ STL: A New Approach to Programming*. Addison Wesley Longman, Harlow, UK, 1998.

[CLR90]   Thomas H. Cormen, Charles E. Leiserson, and Ronald L. Rivest. *Introduction to Algorithms*. MIT Press, Cambridge, MA, 1990.

[Dur64]   Richard Durstenfeld. Algorithm 235, random permutation. *Communications of the ACM*, 7(7):420, Jul 1964.

[ES90]   Margaret A. Ellis and Bjarne Stroustrup. *The Annotated C++ Reference Manual*. Addison–Wesley, Reading, MA, 1990.

[FMR62]   C. T. Fan, Mervin E. Muller, and Ivan Rezucha. Development of sampling plans by using sequential (item by item) selection techniques and digital computers. *Journal of the American Statistical Association*, 57:387–402, 1962.

[GHG93]   John V. Guttag, James J. Horning, S. J. Garland, K. D. Jones, A. Modet, and J. M. Wing. *Larch: Languages and Tools for Formal Specification*. Springer-Verlag, New York, NY, 1993.

[GS96]   Graham Glass and Brett Schuchert. *The STL Primer*. Prentice-Hall, Englewood Cliffs, NJ, 1996.

[Hoa62]   C. A. R. Hoare. Quicksort. *Computer Journal*, 5(1):10–15, 1962.

[ISO98]   International Organization for Standardization (ISO), 1 rue de Varembé, Case postale 56, CH-1211 Genève 20, Switzerland. *ISO/IEC Final Draft International Standard 14882: Programming Language C++*, 1998.

[KM92]   Deepak Kapur and David R. Musser. Tecton: A framework for specifying and verifying generic system components. Computer Science Technical Report 92-20, Rensselaer Polytechnic Institute, Jul 1992. Available via http://www.cs.rpi.edu/~musser/Tecton.

[KM97]   Andrew Koenig and Barbara Moo. *Ruminations on C++: A Decade of Programming Insight and Experience.* Addison–Wesley, Reading, MA, 1997.

[KMS82]   Deepak Kapur, David R. Musser, and Alexander A. Stepanov. Tecton: A language for manipulating generic objects. In J. Staunstrup, editor, *Program Specification: Proceedings of Workshop, Aarhus, Denmark*, volume 134 of *Lecture Notes in Computer Science.* Springer-Verlag, Berlin, 1982.

[KMS88]   Aaron Kershenbaum, David R. Musser, and Alexander A. Stepanov. Higher-order imperative programming. Computer Science Technical Report 88-10, Renssalaer Polytechnic Institute, Apr 1988. Available via http://www.cs.rpi.edu/~musser/genprog.html.

[Knu97]   Donald E. Knuth. *Fundamental Algorithms*, volume I of *The Art of Computer Programming.* Addison–Wesley, Reading, MA, Third edition, 1997.

[Knu98a]   Donald E. Knuth. *Seminumerical Algorithms*, volume II of *The Art of Computer Programming.* Addison–Wesley, Reading, MA, Third edition, 1998.

[Knu98b]   Donald E. Knuth. *Sorting and Searching*, volume III of *The Art of Computer Programming.* Addison–Wesley, Reading, MA, Second edition, 1998.

[Koe89]   Andrew Koenig. *C Traps and Pitfalls.* Addison–Wesley, Reading, MA, 1989.

[KR78]   Brian W. Kernighan and Dennis M. Ritchie. *The C Programming Language.* Prentice-Hall, Englewood Cliffs, NJ, 1978.

[Lip91]   Stanley B. Lippman. *C++ Primer.* Addison–Wesley, Reading, MA, Second edition, 1991.

[LL98]   Stanley B. Lippman and Josée Lajoie. *C++ Primer.* Addison–Wesley, Reading, MA, Third edition, 1998.

[Mey97]   Bertrand Meyer. *Object-Oriented Software Construction.* Prentice-Hall, New York, Second edition, 1997.

[MO63]   Lincoln E. Moses and Robert V. Oakford. *Tables of Random Permutations.* Stanford University Press, Stanford, CA, 1963.

[MS89a]   David R. Musser and Alexander A. Stepanov. *The Ada Generic Library: Linear List Processing Packages.* Springer-Verlag, New York, NY, 1989.

[MS89b]   David R. Musser and Alexander A. Stepanov. Generic programming. In P. Gianni, editor, *Symbolic and Algebraic Computation: International Symposium ISSAC 1988*, volume 358 of *Lecture Notes in Computer Science*, pages 13–25. Springer-Verlag, Berlin, 1989.

[MS96]   David R. Musser and Atul Saini. *STL Tutorial and Reference Guide: C++ Programming with the Standard Template Library*. Addison-Wesley, Reading, MA, 1996.

[Mus97]   David R. Musser. Introspective sorting and selection algorithms. *Software Practice and Experience*, 27(8):983–993, 1997.

[Nel95]   Mark Nelson. *C++ Programer's Guide to the Standard Template Library*. IDG Books Worldwide, Foster City, CA, 1995.

[Rob98]   Robert Robson. *Using the STL*. Springer-Verlag, New York, 1998.

[Sin69]   Richard C. Singleton. Algorithm 347, an efficient algorithm for sorting with minimal storage. *Communications of the ACM*, 12:185–187, Mar 1969.

[SL95]   Alexander Stepanov and Meng Lee. The Standard Template Library. Technical Report HPL-95-11 (R.1), Hewlett-Packard Laboratories, Nov 1995. Available by anonymous FTP from butler.hpl.hp.com.

[Str86]   Bjarne Stroustrup. *The C++ Programming Language*. Addison-Wesley, Reading, MA, 1986.

[Str94]   Bjarne Stroustrup. *The Design and Evolution of C++*. Addison-Wesley, Reading, MA, 1994.

[Str97]   Bjarne Stroustrup. *The C++ Programming Language*. Addison-Wesley, Reading, MA, Third edition, 1997.

[Vil94]   Michael J. Vilot. An introduction to the Standard Template Library. *C++ Report*, 6(8):22–29, Oct 1994.

[Wil64]   J. W. J. Williams. Algorithm 232, heapsort. *Communications of the ACM*, 7:347–348, 1964.

Index

References to concepts are indicated by sans serif text. References to classes and other C++ names are indicated by typewriter text.

References to concepts are indicated by sans serif text. References to classes and other C++ names are indicated by typewriter text.

References to concepts are indicated by sans serif text. References to classes and other C++ names are indicated by typewriter text.

References to concepts are indicated by sans serif text. References to classes and other C++ names are indicated by typewriter text.

References to concepts are indicated by sans serif text. References to classes and other C++ names are indicated by typewriter text.

References to concepts are indicated by sans serif text. References to classes and other C++ names are indicated by typewriter text.

References to concepts are indicated by sans serif text. References to classes and other C++ names are indicated by typewriter text.

References to concepts are indicated by sans serif text. References to classes and other C++ names are indicated by typewriter text.

References to concepts are indicated by sans serif text. References to classes and other C++ names are indicated by typewriter text.

References to concepts are indicated by sans serif text. References to classes and other C++ names are indicated by typewriter text.

References to concepts are indicated by sans serif text. References to classes and other C++ names are indicated by typewriter text.

References to concepts are indicated by sans serif text. References to classes and other C++ names are indicated by typewriter text.

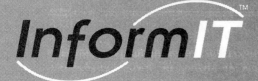
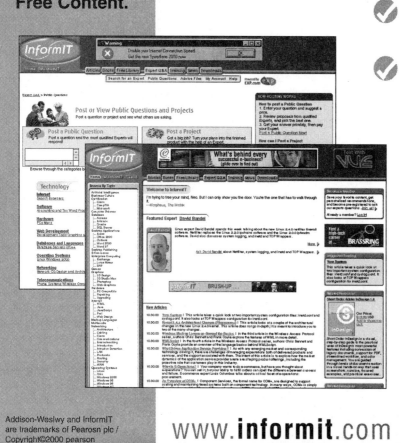

Register Your Book

at www.aw.com/cseng/register

You may be eligible to receive:

- Advance notice of forthcoming editions of the book
- Related book recommendations
- Chapter excerpts and supplements of forthcoming titles
- Information about special contests and promotions throughout the year
- Notices and reminders about author appearances, tradeshows, and online chats with special guests

Contact us

If you are interested in writing a book or reviewing manuscripts prior to publication, please write to us at:

Editorial Department
Addison-Wesley Professional
75 Arlington Street, Suite 300
Boston, MA 02116 USA
Email: AWPro@aw.com

Addison-Wesley

Visit us on the Web: http://www.aw.com/cseng

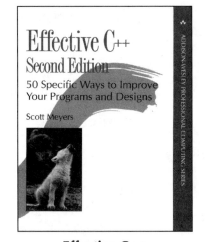